The New Orleans Cabildo

The New Orleans Cabildo

COLONIAL LOUISIANA'S FIRST

CITY GOVERNMENT

1769–1803

Gilbert C. Din and
John E. Harkins

John E. Harkins
8-6-'96

Louisiana State University Press

Baton Rouge and London

Copyright © 1996 by Louisiana State University Press

ALL RIGHTS RESERVED

Manufactured in the United States of America

First printing

05 04 03 02 01 00 99 98 97 96   5 4 3 2 1

Designer: Barbara Werden
Typeface: Garmond #3
Typesetter: Impressions Book and Journal Services, Inc.
Printer and binder: Thomson-Shore, Inc.

Library of Congress Cataloging-in-Publication Data

Din, Gilbert C.
    The New Orleans Cabildo : colonial Louisiana's first city
government, 1769–1803 / Gilbert C. Din and John E. Harkins.
        p.   cm.
    Includes bibliographical references (p.   ) and index.
    ISBN 0-8071-2042-1 (alk. paper)
    1. New Orleans (La.)—Politics and government.   2. New Orleans
(La.). Cabildo.   3. Municipal government—Louisiana—New Orleans—
History—18th century.   I. Harkins, John E., 1938–   . II. Title.
F379.N557D56 1996
976.3'3503—dc20   95-45715
                                                                       CIP

Dedicated to the memory of a loving, steadfast, and
idealistic young man
WILLIAM MICHAEL HARKINS II
(September 13, 1973–April 29, 1995)

Contents

Illustrations

Figures and Tables

Preface

INSTITUTIONAL history in colonial Louisiana has been a neglected field. Few historians have attempted to write studies in this important area. For example, in-depth examinations of law, government, and the military have generally not been produced. Consequently, much of Louisiana's colonial history remains either totally unexamined or only cursorily studied. Perhaps nowhere is this more true than in the investigation of city government in New Orleans, particularly the Spanish Cabildo.

In the 1960s, Louisiana State University graduate student and later professor Jo Ann Carrigan became aware of the Cabildo's neglect when she conducted research for her doctoral dissertation on yellow fever in New Orleans. She learned that the standard histories of Louisiana were riddled with errors and misinterpretations about the institution. In the winter of 1967–1968, she encouraged graduate student John E. Harkins to undertake an M.A. thesis on the regulatory functions of the New Orleans Cabildo, using Works Progress Administration translations of Spanish documents. Soon Carrigan left LSU for the University of Nebraska and Harkins returned home to Memphis to teach high school. He completed his thesis at LSU in 1971 under the direction of John Preston Moore, an authority on the cabildos of Spanish South America.

In the meantime, Ronald R. Morazán, a fellow graduate student at

LSU who had helped Harkins with translations of documents not available in English, became interested in the New Orleans Cabildo. In 1972 he completed his Ph.D. dissertation of translations of and commentaries on documents from the Cabildo's last four years of governance. His dissertation was the first detailed examination of the institution, although it covered only the final years.

By then Harkins was enrolled in the Ph.D. program in history at Memphis State University. His major professor, William R. Gillaspie, persuaded him to expand his M.A. study on the Cabildo into a doctoral dissertation. It resulted in a longer work with a broader use of sources, in which Harkins scrutinized the numerous Cabildo functions. In 1976, upon completion of his dissertation, "The Neglected Phase of Louisiana's Colonial History: The New Orleans Cabildo, 1769–1803," he sought to get it published.

When Harkins submitted the manuscript to interested academic presses for publication, however, the weakness of basing his study on WPA translations of uneven quality became apparent. Reviewers for the presses suggested that he examine other sources, including many available only in Spanish and in foreign repositories. By then, Harkins was working as an archivist and developing interests in other fields of history. He was not at leisure to pursue the research recommended. As time passed, it seemed increasingly unlikely that his study would be published.

In the mid-1980s, he contacted me and suggested that I finish the work, making the revisions necessary for publication. Aware of the importance of the Cabildo and the paucity of good information about it, I agreed. While continuing my work on two other book projects, I collected materials to incorporate in the new Cabildo study.

Only in 1991, with the projects completed, was I able to begin the revision. I immediately saw that Harkins' study needed a more solid foundation than the WPA English translation of the Cabildo minutes. I went back to the Spanish Actas del Cabildo and converted the text and notes to conform with the original minutes. Having worked in the Spanish archives, I examined my notes and microfilm to see what I had on the Cabildo. I made several research trips and pored through additional documentation from the Spanish archives. I investigated the literature on cabildos published since Harkins had finished his dissertation. I wanted to provide a broader perspective of New Orleans and the Cabildo and expand the thoroughness of the study.

In my revision, I restructured the entire manuscript, omitting sections that did not immediately concern the Cabildo. I added chapters on Spanish New Orleans and the Cabildo's relations with Africans and slavery. I changed some of Harkins' conclusions and introduced interpretations based on my study of Spanish Louisiana. The result, it is hoped, is a work that more thoroughly examines the Cabildo, its membership, its relations with other officials and agencies, and its role in resolving municipal problems.

A study of the Very Illustrious New Orleans Cabildo, to use its formal title, in Spanish Borderlands history has long been needed. Other regions of the borderlands, particularly Texas, New Mexico, and California, have long led the way in cabildo studies. These works, however, reveal that their towns and governments differed enormously from New Orleans because only the latter municipality could genuinely be called a city. Moreover, the Spaniards imposed the Cabildo on a French population after a rebellion, replacing a council that had evolved into an independent provincial governing force. Among other differences, New Orleans had a larger population, greater economic activity, and access by water to Spanish and foreign markets. By contrast, towns in the Southwest Borderlands of the same time were smaller in population and predominantly hispanic, had weaker economies, and were far removed from the markets that might stimulate their economic development. In other words, these towns lacked the financial and human resources and the communications to attempt the many activities that New Orleans engaged in. Their smaller importance can be seen in their cabildos that had fewer officials with lesser responsibilities. New Orleans, consequently, stands out uniquely among the urban centers of both the Southeast and Southwest Borderlands.

Another problem that has long plagued the New Orleans Cabildo has been its depiction in the published literature. Many historians have viewed the institution unfavorably, primarily because these historians relied on the readily available published accounts of French and American travelers to colonial New Orleans, whose often biased remarks have all too frequently been accepted as accurate. Moreover, they visited the city in the late Spanish period when the Cabildo's influence had declined and two venal and poorly qualified governors held office. Based on these descriptions, historians inaccurately concluded that the stories about the Cabildo and Spanish rule were true for the entire period. They also failed to use documents that would have provided a more accurate view of the institution.

The first men to write significant books about Louisiana's colonial past were François-Xavier Martin, Charles Gayarré, and Alcée Fortier. Martin's history, first published in 1827, used some local documents, but he only sketched the colonial period. Gayarré, a descendant of a Spanish colonial civil servant, provided the most information in his four-volume history. Fortier, a professor of Romance languages at Tulane University, filled his history with French Creole attitudes and biases. All their discussions of the Cabildo, however, were woefully inadequate.

In the twentieth century, Louisiana historians did not greatly expand the descriptions of the Cabildo. Some of them, Henry C. Rightor, Stanley C. Arthur, Henry Chambers, and Edwin Davis, for example, uncritically followed the traditional interpretation. In fact, these later works perhaps had more flaws because they were inspired by the Creole mythology of the late nineteenth century, of which Fortier and Grace King were leading exponents. This mythology held that Spain had had little influence on Louisiana and that the Cabildo had not administered New Orleans effectively. It portrayed Spanish government as intolerant, cruel, and corrupt. According to the mythology, French Creoles had survived Iberian domination by not learning Spanish or being changed in any appreciable way. It also asserted that French law and custom had in many ways continued. Fortier would even have readers believe that the Spaniards had left only a few place names to commemorate their forty-year ownership of Louisiana.

The documentary evidence, however, disputed these views. Although some scattered documentation survived in Louisiana in judicial, notarial, and land records, the Actas del Cabildo, and scattered personal papers that fortuitously escaped destruction, the preponderance of the Spanish documents had left Louisiana, going first to Pensacola and later to Havana and Seville. Alone among nineteenth-century historians, Gayarré had employed copies of documents from Spain to write a richer and less biased state history, but it earned him the condemnation of French filiopietists.

Nevertheless, the Spanish documentation has slowly been revealing a different story of eighteenth-century Louisiana.

Works contradicting the traditional histories and Creole mythology first emerged outside the state in the 1920s. Ph.D. and M.A. students of Herbert Eugene Bolton at the University of California led the way. Before long a handful of graduate students at other universities, including LSU and Tulane, joined them. Their studies generally disagreed with the state histories and cast doubt on the Creole mythology so favored by Fortier and King. Unfortunately, within Louisiana, the mythology abetted by uncorrected state histories has not yet completely fallen out of favor.

The present work attempts to go beyond the distortions of earlier histories and to depict the first genuine city government of New Orleans accurately. Harkins and I trust that we have succeeded in correctly examining the New Orleans Cabildo and its role in the history of Louisiana and the Spanish Borderlands.

—GILBERT C. DIN

Abbreviations

AGI	Archivo General de Indias, Seville
PC	Papeles Procedentes de la Isla de Cuba
SD	Audiencia de Santo Domingo
AGS	Archivo General de Simancas, near Valladolid
AHN	Archivo Histórico Nacional, Madrid
Est.	Sección de Estado
GM	Guerra Moderna
exped.	*expediente* (a file of documents)
leg.	*legajo* (a bundle of documents)
LH	*Louisiana History*
LHQ	*Louisiana Historical Quarterly*
SMV	Lawrence Kinnaird, ed. *Spain in the Mississippi Valley, 1765–1794.* Three parts

The New Orleans Cabildo

ONE

Spanish New Orleans

T HE New Orleans the Spaniards saw on their arrival in 1766 was very different from the city they left nearly forty years later. Although it is an exaggeration to claim that they found "a town of hovels and left it a city of palaces,"[1] the *villa* changed significantly in extent, population, and importance by the end of the Spanish period.

New Orleans was nearly a half century old when the Spaniards first arrived in French Louisiana. During those five decades, however, little had been done to improve living conditions in the town. In 1718 Jean-Baptiste

1. Herbert Asbury, *The French Quarter: An Informal History of the New Orleans Underworld* (New York, 1936), 59. This chapter is meant only as an introduction to the city where the Cabildo governed, and it does not attempt to portray every aspect of the city's life in the Spanish period. Additional information on Spanish New Orleans can be found in subsequent chapters. See also Minter Wood, "Life in New Orleans in the Spanish Period," *LHQ,* XXII (1939), 642–709.

As French Creoles were becoming a minority group in New Orleans in the late nineteenth century, writers engaged in myth-making about them. Although the myth that emerged was largely anti-Spanish, it put forth the belief that the New Orleans that was rebuilt after the fires of 1788 and 1794 was graceful, solidly constructed, and Spanish in design and architecture. In reality, however, aside from some government and church buildings and the homes of the more affluent residents, the rest of New Orleans consisted of little better than shacks. The myth-making is discussed in Joseph Tregle, Jr., "Creoles and Americans," in *Creole New Orleans: Race and Americanization,* ed. Arnold R. Hirsch and Joseph Logsdon (Baton Rouge, 1992), 180–84.

Le Moyne, Sieur de Bienville, founder of New Orleans, had selected a site thirty leagues up the Mississippi River on its left bank, near where it forms a crescent. He purposely placed it adjacent to an Indian portage, where Audubon Park is today, that led to Lake Pontchartrain several miles away. Some French settlers were already established on Bayou St. John in 1718. Three years later engineer Adrien de Pauger formally laid out a new settlement at the city's present location. He gave it the shape of a large square, from which it derives its local name, Vieux Carré ("Old Square").[2]

The location was a morass that flooded yearly and filled with alligators and snakes. As Claude Joseph Dubreuil, who built the first levee on the Mississippi, described it: "The establishment of New Orleans in the beginning was awful, the river when it was high spreading over the whole ground, and in all the houses there were two feet of water, which caused general and mortal diseases."[3] By 1729 New Orleanians had built a levee that helped to protect them from spring floods, but it was only a slight improvement on the Mississippi's natural bank. At least until the 1790s, when Governor Francisco Luis Héctor, Barón de Carondelet, undertook work to prevent recurring inundations, floodwaters occasionally invaded the city.

Most of the housing throughout New Orleans' colonial era was crude and built on the ground. More substantial buildings were gradually erected through the eighteenth century, but the majority of the city's residents continued to live in one-story dwellings that resembled huts. Many buildings of this kind were still in use in 1803.[4]

In the 1760s, much of the Vieux Carré was still unimproved. Only the first four streets from the river had structures on them. Theoretically, eleven streets ran in straight lines, roughly paralleling the river, while another six intersected them at right angles, giving the city sixty-six blocks. In reality, however, only the streets and blocks closest to the river and having structures on them were laid out; the rest of the town was

2. Stanley Clisby Arthur, *Old New Orleans,* ed. Susan Cole Dore (1936; rpr. Gretna, La., 1990), 15–16.

3. Alcée Fortier, *A History of Louisiana,* ed. Jo Ann Carrigan (2 vols.; 2nd ed.; Baton Rouge, 1966–72), I, 103.

4. Berquin-Duvallon, *Travels in Louisiana and the Floridas in the Year 1802,* trans. John Davis (New York, 1806), 22–24.

undeveloped. The best buildings were made of brick, but they were few and costly. A less expensive and more widely used building style was brick between posts called *colombage*. The better housing consisted of one floor with galleries on the outside around them and raised eight feet above the ground to fend off floodwaters. The area beneath the house at ground level served as a cellar. It was impossible to have underground rooms because of the high water table.[5]

The French writer Berquin-Duvallon noted in the late Spanish period that the city's principal buildings, which included the more expensive dwellings, were situated near the river but that in the rear and suburbs shanties predominated. He estimated that the city covered about three hundred acres, not all of which was built up even then. The greater part of the houses were wooden one-story structures, roofed with shingles, all made of highly flammable cypress.[6]

While New Orleans was expanding within its walls, there was also sizable population growth outside the walls. Three suburbs had grown up before 1800, Santa María, San Carlos, and Bayou St. John. The first two

5. Captain Philip Pittman, *The Present State of the European Settlements on the Mississippi* (1770; rpr. Gainesville, Fla., 1973), 1–2, 11. Pittman overestimated the city's population, which he gave as seven thousand. He calculated that houses numbered seven to eight hundred whereas under five hundred was more accurate. Grace King, in *New Orleans: The Place and the People* (New York, 1907), 138, claims that secret dungeons and torture instruments were discovered at the site of the former Spanish jail during excavation in the nineteenth century. This assertion forgets that the rooms could not have been below the surface of the ground and surely iron torture instruments would have rotted away. It appears that King sought to "spice up" her account of the Spanish era to make the French Creoles appear more virtuous. See Tregle, "Creoles and Americans," 180–83. Archaeologists today believe that the "dungeon" was in reality a privy.

6. Berquin-Duvallon, *Travels in Louisiana*, 22–23. Paul Alliot, "Historical and Political Reflections on Louisiana," in *Louisiana Under the Rule of Spain, France, and the United States, 1785–1807*, ed. James Alexander Robertson (2 vols.; 1910–11; rpr. Freeport, N.Y., 1969), I, 65–67, also comments on the many poor houses in New Orleans. Robertson, ed., *Louisiana Under the Rule*, I, 167, translates a portion of Berquin-Duvallon's original work, *Vue de la colonie espagnol du Mississippi, ou des provinces de Louisiane et Floride occidentale* (1803; 2nd ed.; Paris, 1804). Matthew Phelps, in *Memoirs and Adventures of Captain Matthew Phelps* (Vermont, 1802), 33, states that New Orleans had one thousand houses in 1783. Francis Baily, in *Journal of a Tour in Unsettled Parts of North America in 1796 and 1797*, ed. Jack D. L. Holmes (Carbondale, Ill., 1969), 175, gives the same number of houses more than a decade later. And Victor Collot, who was in the city in 1796, states, in *A Journey in North America*, trans. J. Christian Bay (Florence, 1924), 95, that it had a population of ten thousand, six thousand of whom were white.

were at the upper and lower ends of the city and the third behind the city's rear walls. Santa María, where many wealthy planters and merchants resided, was a center of illicit trade. In 1796 the governor widened and deepened Carondelet Canal, which increased boat traffic between the city and Lake Pontchartrain. The Spaniards preferred using the route through Lakes Pontchartrain and Borgne to communicate with Mobile and Pensacola. City residents already used the lakefront for picnics, swimming, and fishing. A basin in the rear of the city, near Charity Hospital, permitted several small boats to anchor there.[7]

Herbert Asbury provides a description of New Orleans about 1803 that is reasonably accurate:

> From Levee [Decatur] Street the town was 600 yards in depth, although the houses beyond Dauphine Street in that direction were few in number. The settled area extended along the river front for about 1,200 yards. The stockade enclosed most of the town, with forts at the four corners, and the present Rampart Street was a line of palisaded fortifications, while what is now Canal Street . . . was a moat filled with water, ending in a military gate on the Tchoupitoulas Road, near the levee. All the public buildings, of which the Cabildo [casa capitular], the Arsenal, and the French Market remain today substantially as they were then, faced the [Plaza de Armas], which was no more than a grass plot, barren of trees and shrubbery.[8]

One of the buildings in New Orleans constructed twice during the Spanish era was the casa capitular,[9] which housed the city government, the Cabildo. In December, 1769, Governor Alejandro O'Reilly made arrange-

7. Alliot, "Historical and Political Reflections," I, 65–67; John G. Clark, New Orleans, 1718–1812: An Economic History (Baton Rouge, 1970), 253; [Casa-Calvo] to Vidal, New Orleans, January 20, 1801, AGI, PC, leg. 72. Berquin-Duvallon, in Travels in Louisiana, 33, gives the population of the two suburbs of San Carlos and San Luis as 1,048, but he omits the free blacks of San Carlos.

8. Asbury, French Quarter, 70.

9 To avoid confusion, casa capitular is used here to denote the building where the Cabildo, i.e., city government, met. This is at variance with common usage today in New Orleans, where cabildo refers to the building. But usage here is akin to eighteenth-century Spanish usage.

ments for construction of the first *casa capitular*. Its location was at the same place it occupies today, alongside St. Louis Cathedral. The building completed in August, 1770, however, was smaller. It measured sixty-two French feet long by twenty-four feet wide and had two principal rooms, the *sala capitular*, where the officials met, and a waiting room for persons seeking justice. Between them was a small connecting corridor and behind it a smaller room to store the archives. In the 1770s and 1780s, the building was illuminated for celebrations such as the king's birthday, the birth of royal children, and victories in the war against Great Britain.[10]

A fire in 1788 destroyed the first *casa capitular* and, for several years, city officials met in the Government House (Casa del Gobierno) and later in a rented house. Not until January, 1795, did the Cabildo consider reconstructing its *casa capitular*. At that time Andrés Almonester y Roxas, who was the senior *regidor* (councilman) and *alférez real* in the municipal government, offered to build it with his own money if the city would reimburse him when it could afford to do so. He promised to construct it along the same lines as the cathedral and presbytery he had built earlier. Work began under his proposal, with Gilberto Guillemard as the building's architect and the Cabildo making erratic payments. Almonester died before the structure was completed, and his widow, Luisa de La Ronde, soon asked to be released from her husband's contract. The council agreed, construction continued, and the Cabildo occupied the finished building on May 10, 1799. The city paid Almonester's widow 32,348 pesos for construction of the building. The council held its meetings in the new *casa capitular* until the last one took place on November 18, 1803.[11] Twelve days later the Spanish era in Louisiana ended.

In the 1760s, a mixture of whites (French, Canadians, Creoles, Germans, Swiss, and a few other Europeans), blacks, and mulattoes (both slaves and free men of color) gave the city a population of approximately

10. Samuel Wilson, Jr., and Leonard V. Huber, *The Cabildo on Jackson Square* (Gretna, La., 1970), 13–16. The word *cabildo* in their title refers to the building, not the city government. The word *cabildo* will be capitalized only when referring to the New Orleans city government.

11. *Ibid.*, 15–35, 37–39; Actas del Cabildo, Libro V, Tomo I, 101–102, November 18, 1803, Works Progress Administration typescript in Spanish on microfilm. Subsequent citations will be by *libro* in Roman numerals, followed by *tomo* if appropriate in parentheses, page number(s), and date.

3,000.[12] Nearly twenty years later, the city had increased by two-thirds. A 1785 census shows 4,980 inhabitants for New Orleans.[13] Growth then leveled off. Two censuses of 1788 and 1791 failed to register a significant increase inasmuch as the city's population remained about 5,000. Perhaps the 1788 fire in New Orleans halted growth, causing some white inhabitants and many slaves to depart.[14]

After 1791, the Spaniards failed to make a comprehensive population count of New Orleans or Louisiana. A census of 1805, after the Spanish period ended, places the city's inhabitants at 3,551 whites, 1,556 free blacks, and 3,105 slaves, for a total of 8,212.[15] This figure was probably low by

12. Marc de Villiers du Terrage, *Les dernières années de la Louisiane française* (Paris, 1903), 231. New Orleans' population was almost one-fourth of the colony's total, excluding Native Americans. A census of 1769 ordered by O'Reilly listed 3,190 persons living in the city, in 468 houses. Whites numbered 1,803, black and mulatto slaves 1,127, free people of color 99, and Indian slaves 61 (Charles Gayarré, *History of Louisiana* [4 vols.; 3rd ed.; New York, 1885], II, 355; the "Census of Louisiana," September 2, 1771, *SMV,* Pt. I, 196, employs 1769 figures for New Orleans). The colony's total population, using the figures for 1769 and 1771, was only 11,344. A census for New Orleans of 1771 shows 3,190 inhabitants, of whom 2,003 were white (AGI, PC, leg. 2357).

13. Gayarré, *History of Louisiana,* III, 170–71. Two censuses of New Orleans in 1777 and 1778 vary slightly. In the first, the city's population is 1,736 whites, 315 free blacks, and 1,151 slaves, for a total of 3,202. The second reveals 1,552 whites, 353 free men of color, and 1,155 slaves, for a total population of 3,060. A New Orleans census for 1777, in AGI, PC, leg. 191, shows the presence of 1,330 whites and 1,479 blacks, slave and free, for a total of 2,809 inhabitants. See also Brian E. Coutts, "Martín Navarro: Treasurer, Contador, Intendant, 1766–1788: Politics and Trade in Spanish Louisiana" (Ph.D. dissertation, Louisiana State University, 1981), 144–45.

14. A 1788 census reveals 2,370 whites, 820 free blacks, and 2,131 slaves, for a total of 5,321 in the city. The biggest increase was in slaves, who were coming in rapidly in the 1780s. In 1791, the city had 2,386 whites, 862 free blacks, and 1,789 slaves, or 5,037 in all (Kimberly S. Hanger, "Personas de varias clases y colores: Free People of Color in Spanish Louisiana" [Ph.D. dissertation, University of Florida, 1991], 41).

Caroline Maude Burson, *The Stewardship of Don Esteban Miró* (New Orleans, 1940), 280, provides different figures for the 1791 New Orleans census: 2,065 whites, 1,462 free coloreds, 381 militia, and 1,589 slaves, for a total of 5,497 inhabitants. The census also reported occupations. Reflecting the city's commercial involvement, Burson lists 86 merchants, traders, or dealers; 48 cabaret keepers; 32 carpenters; 29 persons tied to commercial or shipping interests; 6 surgeons and 3 physicians; 3 painters; 1 singer; and 3 violinists (*ibid.,* 282). Either the census or Burson failed to include army officers, government officials, and employees who lived in the city. They were numerous.

15. Hanger, "Personas de varias clases," 41.

several thousand because censuses undercounted inhabitants, and visitors to the city reported larger numbers.[16]

By 1803 New Orleans' white population had become far more heterogeneous than it was forty years earlier. By then the French, both Creoles and Europeans, constituted only half the city's white population. In addition, a substantial number of Spaniards, Spanish Americans (Cubans and Mexicans mainly, although there were some from other areas, too), Acadians, Anglo-Americans, British subjects, refugees from France and Haiti, and no doubt a few more from yet other countries also resided in New Orleans. The city's population had taken on a cosmopolitan character, which later became a celebrated New Orleans tradition.[17]

Most modern writers have underestimated the number of Spaniards in colonial New Orleans. Although the Spanish population was small in the early years, consisting mainly of administrators and soldiers, it began growing in 1779, when approximately two thousand Canary Islanders started to arrive in the colony. Substantial numbers of Isleños, as they called themselves, remained in the city because they were not suited to agricultural work. Over the years, many more Isleños from the settlements

16. Four French writers give population figures that are larger. Berquin-Duvallon (in *Travels in Louisiana*, 33) lists the city's population in 1802 as 10,000, with whites numbering 4,000, free people of color 2,000 to 3,000, and the rest slaves; François Marie Perrin du Lac (in *Travels Through the Two Louisianas, and Among the Savage Nations of the Missouri; Also in the United States, Along the Ohio and Adjacent Provinces, in 1801, 1802, and 1803 . . .* [London, 1807], 89), who was in Louisiana in 1802, places the city's inhabitants at twelve thousand; Claude Cesar Robin (in *Voyage to Louisiana by C. C. Robin, 1803–1805*, ed. and trans. Stuart O. Landry, Jr. [New Orleans, 1966], 36), says it was ten to twelve thousand; and Alliot (in "Historical and Political Reflections," I, 71), states that in 1802 it was twelve thousand. Daniel Clark, the U.S. consul in New Orleans and a longtime resident, claims the population was 8,056, of whom 3,948 were white, 1,335 free people of color, and 2,773 slaves (Arthur Preston Whitaker, *The Mississippi Question, 1795–1803: A Study in Trade, Politics, and Diplomacy* [1934; rpr. Gloucester, Mass., 1962], 277n). Clark seems to have been using unrevised figures from the Spanish era.

We are of the opinion that ten to twelve thousand is reasonably accurate for the number of the city's residents at the end of the Spanish period. In addition, the surrounding area outside the city contained several thousand more inhabitants.

17. For the arrival of Acadians and Canary Islanders in Louisiana, see Carl A. Brasseaux, *The Founding of New Acadia: The Beginnings of Acadian Life in Louisiana, 1765–1803* (Baton Rouge, 1987), and *"Scattered to the Wind": Dispersal and Wanderings of the Acadians, 1755–1809* (Lafayette, La., 1991); and Gilbert C. Din, *The Canary Islanders of Louisiana* (Baton Rouge, 1988).

drifted back to New Orleans, where life was less arduous. By the end of the Spanish period, they alone numbered several hundred.[18] But the Spanish-speaking population was larger, at least by twice as many, and that was without counting the soldiers. Besides the Canary Islanders, there were Catalan merchants and their families, who made up a large part of the business community in the late Spanish period (governors' letters frequently referred to ships belonging to Catalans); Spanish army officers and their families and enlisted men who retired or were discharged in the city; and immigrants who entered from various parts of Spain and the empire. Cabildo records show that the city employed a number of them.[19]

Spanish influence was also greater than most people today realize. The French writer C. C. Robin, in his often-quoted *Voyage to Louisiana,* was wrong about the small impact that Spain had in Louisiana. He wrote: "The Spanish language was so little used and the French so generally adopted, that the majority of Frenchmen born in the colony during the Spanish rule did not need to learn this foreign tongue. I saw there Frenchmen who had lived since infancy under Spanish governors, related or married to them even, who did not understand a word of Spanish, an interesting observation I think as it shows how well the Spaniards took the measure of French character and how they respected, according to the letter of the treaty, our most sacred possessions, our laws and customs."[20]

Robin was obviously writing for an ethnocentric French public. He seemed unwilling to grasp that Spanish law prevailed and French custom was permitted only as long as it did not clash with Spanish jurisprudence. Governor Alejandro O'Reilly in 1769 insisted on putting Spanish law into

18. Din, *Canary Islanders,* 25, 29, 39, 61. Jerah Johnson's statement in "Colonial New Orleans: A Fragment of the Eighteenth-Century French Ethos," in *Creole New Orleans: Race and Americanization,* ed. Arnold R. Hirsch and Joseph Logsdon (Baton Rouge, 1992), 46, that the Spanish presence in the city "was minimal, limited largely to administrative personnel, who constituted an essentially military presence," is false. It ignores many Spaniards who settled in the city.

19. Din, *Canary Islanders,* 29, 44, 71, 72, 83; Robin, *Voyage to Louisiana,* 36–37. José Montero de Pedro, in *Españoles en Nueva Orleans y Luisiana* (Madrid, 1979), 130–31, based on Larry Bartlett's article in a publication called *Dixie* of July 31, 1977, thinks that Spanish-speaking Filipinos were present in the Spanish era. Filipinos were in Louisiana in the nineteenth century, but their presence in the colonial period is speculative.

20. Robin, *Voyage to Louisiana,* 95–96.

practice, and legal documents, which Robin obviously did not consult, do not show that French law survived.

The long-held idea that French Creoles, including the Creole wives of Spanish army officers and their children, did not learn Spanish is blatantly untrue. One has only to look at the sons of Francisco Bouligny and Pedro Piernas, who became army officers. Even the children of Gilbert Antoine de St. Maxent, a Frenchman married to a French Creole, learned it, as he himself did. All his daughters married Spaniards. Many French Creoles in the Fixed Louisiana Infantry Regiment became proficient in Spanish. To cite several examples, Captain Antonio de St. Maxent and particularly his brother Francisco Maximiliano de St. Maxent, who stayed in the army after 1803 and rose to the rank of brigadier general by 1815; Colonel Carlos de Grand-Pré; Lieutenant Colonel Jacobo Dubreuil; Lieutenant Colonel Gilberto Guillemard; Captain Gilberto Andry; Captain Zenon Trudeau; Lieutenant Colonel Carlos de Vilemont; Captain Ignacio Delinó de Chalmette; and Lieutenant Carlos de Reggio. Grand-Pré, Dubreuil, Andry, Vilemont, Reggio, and the younger St. Maxent, among others, remained in Spanish service after 1803. Rising in rank in the army depended on a good knowledge of Spanish, including the ability to write it, and those who did not learn were passed over (*postergados*) in promotion. The Spanish presence in New Orleans clearly had a greater impact than most historians have acknowledged.[21]

In addition, shopkeepers, merchants, and others, including prostitutes, who catered to Spanish soldiers and sailors, acquired at least a functional use of Spanish. Slaves owned by Spaniards learned it, too. Berquin-Duvallon admitted in the early nineteenth century that the use of Spanish and English in the city was fairly universal. Finally, it should be kept in mind, to quote John S. Kendall, "that some of the first newspapers established in New Orleans were Spanish." The first Spanish-language paper, *El Misisipí*, a semiweekly, appeared in 1808, which meant that a significant

21. Much of the information on French Creoles who learned Spanish is scattered through the Papeles de Cuba. Among the historians who repeat the falsehood that they did not learn the language is Edwin Adams Davis, *Louisiana: A Narrative History* (3rd ed.; Baton Rouge, 1971), 141. On the passing over of young French Creole officers who did not learn Spanish well, see for example, Carondelet to Las Casas, No. 80, New Orleans, April 26, 1792, AGI, PC, leg. 1441.

Spanish-reading population was still present, if not increasing. A second Spanish-language newspaper, *El Mensajero,* started in 1810.[22]

Edwin Davis estimates that in 1803 half of the city's white population was French Creole and 25 percent was Spanish, with the rest being Americans, British, Germans, and others. Therefore, if the white inhabitants numbered five thousand, more than twelve hundred were Spaniards, a not inconsequential number and reasonably accurate.[23] Again this figure does not include Spanish soldiers and sailors, whose numbers probably often added another thousand native Spanish-speakers to the city's multitude in the 1790s.

Another group not counted in the censuses were the Native Americans. They were the remnants of tribes who once inhabited lower Louisiana, and they resided near the city throughout the eighteenth century. They hawked their game, firewood, baskets, mats, plants, and herbs on the levee or through the city streets, and the men worked occasionally as day laborers and dock workers. By their knowledge of foods such as corn, beans, and other indigenous plants, native women influenced Louisiana cuisine. The Native Americans also participated during Carnival, wearing their distinctive colorful costumes.[24]

Laws regulating Indian behavior were similar to those governing slaves. Among them, natives could not carry firearms, trade without permission, or consume alcohol, but enforcement was lax. A French visitor, Paul Alliot, claims that in the early nineteenth century several hundred Indians lived in huts on vacant lands outside New Orleans. In 1769 Governor O'Reilly outlawed Indian slavery, which the French had permitted. But in reality it meant only no further enslavement of Indians because those who were already slaves usually remained in bondage.[25]

22. Berquin-Duvallon, *Travels in Louisiana,* 48–49; John S. Kendall, "The Foreign Language Press of New Orleans," *LHQ,* XII (1929), 363. See also the works by Raymond R. MacCurdy, "A Tentative Bibliography of the Spanish-Language Press in Louisiana, 1808–1871," *Americas,* X (1953–54), 307–29; and *A History and Bibliography of Spanish-Language Newspapers and Magazines in Louisiana, 1808–1949* (Albuquerque, 1951).

23. Davis, *Louisiana,* 143.

24. Daniel H. Usner, Jr., "American Indians in Colonial New Orleans," in *Powhatan's Mantle: Indians in the Colonial Southeast,* ed. Peter H. Wood, Gregory A. Waselkov, and M. Thomas Hatley (Lincoln, Nebr., 1989), 104–27.

25. Alliot, "Historical and Political Reflections," I, 81–82; Stephen Webre, "The Problem of Indian Slavery in Spanish Louisiana, 1769–1803," *LH,* XXV (1984), 117–35.

Most whites in the city probably did not think about the natives, who were a marginalized and dispossessed people. They were often seen outside the city gates drunk. Typical of the white attitude toward them, the French visitor Robin noted in 1799 a group of "upwards of fifty Indians of both sexes, chiefly intoxicated, singing, drinking, rolling in the dirt, and . . . exhibiting a scene very disgustful."[26]

In addition to those living near the city, throughout the eighteenth century Indian chiefs from upper and lower Louisiana and West Florida journeyed to New Orleans to visit the governor, the "white father," who represented the distant king. They came from numerous tribes and were often accompanied by warriors, women, and children. While in the city they expected to be entertained with food, alcohol, and gifts and to be given medals, which increased their prestige within the tribe. When the governor negotiated a treaty with a tribe, he often put on a spectacle that entertained the natives and much of the town. For example, when Big and Little Osage chiefs visited in 1794, Governor Carondelet ordered the soldiers in the garrison to parade and the artillerymen to fire salvos. It was important for the governors to impress upon the natives that whites were more numerous and stronger than the handfuls found at distant outposts or in the wilderness. At times, Indians provided dances, music, and gifts for the governor. But so many came to New Orleans that governors repeatedly instructed post commandants not to let Indians go there unless it was absolutely necessary.[27]

As Daniel H. Usner, Jr., has noted: "Perhaps the most fascinating Indian contribution to New Orleans social life was the ball game called *toli* by the Choctaws and *raquettes* by the French, the city's most popular spectator sport until the arrival of baseball. Before United States acquisition of New Orleans, contests [were] Sunday afternoon events [held] behind the city gates. Spectators assembled on the 'Communes de la Ville,' also called Congo Plains, where players carrying short sticks in both hands tossed the small buckskin ball between two goalposts sometimes placed a half-mile apart."[28] Indian teams even competed against white teams.

26. Robin, *Voyage to Louisiana*, 162.

27. Gilbert C. Din and A. P. Nasatir, *The Imperial Osages: Spanish-Indian Relations in the Mississippi Valley* (Norman, Okla., 1983), 260; King, *New Orleans*, 139–40.

28. Usner, "American Indians in Colonial New Orleans," 120.

African Americans made up a substantial part of New Orleans' colonial population. For them the city under the Spaniards offered at least limited opportunities not available under the French. Some slaves managed to gain their freedom during the Spanish era. The practice of *coartación,* or purchase of freedom, began soon after O'Reilly replaced the French Code Noir with Spanish slave laws. Black slaves worked for themselves in New Orleans on Sundays and holidays. Some of them garnered enough funds to purchase their freedom. Each decade of Spanish rule saw growth in the number of free people of color in the city. In time, purchase by other blacks to emancipate slaves became more common than self-purchase. No figure is available for the number of free people of color in New Orleans at the end of 1803, but the census for 1805 lists them as 1,819.[29] Because Spanish slave laws continued in effect for several years after 1803, the free black population kept growing.[30]

Slaves in Louisiana generally had Sunday for themselves, and many of those living in the vicinity went to New Orleans to sell the products of their labor, work to earn money, purchase necessities at stores that eagerly sought their business, and generally enjoy themselves. Slave-operated open-air markets were present in the French era, having been preceded by an Indian market located about a mile outside the city along the Bayou St. John road. With increased economic activity and a larger population, markets flourished under the Spaniards. Congo Market at the rear of the city was principally for slaves and was used by a smaller number of free blacks. The Cabildo never sought to regulate it. About fifteen years after the American takeover, Benjamin Latrobe was astonished to see several hundred unsupervised blacks dancing in Congo Square. By then this custom was about three-quarters of a century old.[31]

29. Kimberly S. Hanger, "Avenues to Freedom Open to New Orleans' Black Population, 1769–1779," *LH,* XXXI (1990), 237–64; "Personas de varias clases," 41. Freedom also came to some slaves for good service and to some mistresses and children of white men.

30. See H. E. Sterkx, *The Free Negro in Antebellum Louisiana* (Cranbury, N.J., 1972).

31. Jerah Johnson, "New Orleans's Congo Square: An Urban Setting for Early Afro-American Culture Formation," *LH,* XXXII (1991), 117–39; Robert A. Sauder, "The Origin and Spread of the Public Market System in New Orleans," *LH,* XXII (1981), 281–97; Benjamin Henry Latrobe, *Impressions Respecting New Orleans: Diary and Sketches, 1818–1820,* ed. Samuel Wilson, Jr. (New York, 1951), 46–49. Although Governors Miró and Carondelet decreed Sunday as a day of rest in their *bandos de buen gobierno* of 1786 and 1792, it applied to slaves only when they

Blacks, who arrived in New Orleans without skills, usually acquired some if they remained in the city. Besides working at tasks that did not require special competence, they became carpenters, tailors, cobblers, barbers, coachmen, and household servants. A few free people of color even operated taverns.[32]

Often overlooked is the fact that throughout the colonial era New Orleans was a military town. Soldiers resided in New Orleans to protect the colony, not just the city. For many years it was believed that any invading force would come up from the river's mouth. Only after the United States became independent and its population in the West expanded greatly was there fear of invasion from upriver. This threat caused the Spaniards to strengthen Natchez and erect new forts at New Madrid, Nogales (Vicksburg), and San Fernando de las Barrancas (Memphis). Governor Carondelet also rebuilt New Orleans' fortifications, including putting up a new stockade around the Vieux Carré, and increased the number of troops in the city. But within a few years the city's defenses began to decay, and by 1803 they were no longer impressive.[33]

Soldiers and sailors, among others, were the uncounted inhabitants in the city. Spain posted one infantry battalion in Louisiana from 1769 to about 1783, two to the late 1780s, and three to the end of the Spanish era. Each battalion had about six hundred men at full strength. In 1777 the Fixed Louisiana Infantry Battalion became the Fixed Louisiana Infantry

---

worked for their masters and not for themselves. Shops were open on Sunday except during religious services (for the *bandos,* see Gayarré, *History of Louisiana,* III, 178–79, 312–13). Beginning in the French era, slaves usually received Sundays off, except at harvest, when they were paid for those days, to obtain their own food and clothing, which many but not all owners no longer chose to provide.

32. Hanger, "Personas de varias clases," 110–52; Jack D. L. Holmes, "Spanish Regulation of Taverns and the Liquor Trade in the Mississippi Valley," in *The Spanish in the Mississippi Valley, 1762–1804,* ed. John Francis McDermott (Urbana, Ill., 1974), 152; Donald E. Everett, "Free People of Color in Colonial Louisiana," *LH,* VII (1966), 36. Free women of color, particularly mulattoes and quadroons, often entered into a relationship with white men called *plaçage,* which was usually a long-term relationship. After it ended, many of the women operated boarding establishments for well-to-do white bachelors.

33. Barón de Carondelet, "Extracto que manifiesta en compendio . . ." (New Orleans), November 24, 1794, AHN, Est., leg. 3899; published as "Carondelet on the Defense of Louisiana, 1794," *American Historical Review,* II (1897), 474–505; and in Robertson, ed., *Louisiana Under the Rule,* I, 293–345.

Regiment when the crown authorized the creation of a second battalion for the unit. Its formation, however, did not begin until 1783. In addition, the 1790s saw the presence in New Orleans of military units from Havana and Mexico. As many as five hundred troops were stationed in the city and nearby in that decade. These soldiers, their officers, and Spanish civilian employees spent large sums of money in New Orleans and contributed mightily to the city's commercial life.[34]

For military personnel as well as for many of the city's inhabitants, Spain's participation in the American revolutionary war against Great Britain was perhaps the most exciting time in the Spanish era in Louisiana. Upon learning of Spain's declaration of war, Governor Bernardo de Gálvez worked to amass supplies, foodstuffs, and men to attack the British forts in West Florida. Gathering his troops, militia, and volunteers, he first led his soldiers up the Mississippi on August 27, 1779. His victories at Manchac and Baton Rouge gave him possession of Natchez as well, and he took a large number of prisoners down to New Orleans by October. He kept them in the city until he sent them to Mexico early the next year.

The captain general of Cuba sent army units to Louisiana to protect the province during the war, but Gálvez refused to surrender military initiative, and he wanted to seize Mobile and Pensacola from the British. Because he had only a modest number of soldiers, he moved to attack less stoutly defended Mobile first, his expedition embarking in January, 1780. By March he had forced the British garrison at Fort Charlotte to surrender. But his effort to seize more heavily fortified Pensacola with an invasion fleet from Cuba later that year failed when an October hurricane scattered his ships. Some of the battered vessels found their way to New Orleans, where they remained until the second invasion fleet against the British stronghold sailed the following spring. Meantime, a substantial number of soldiers and sailors crowded the town, causing its nightlife and taverns to burgeon.[35]

34. Gilbert C. Din, *Francisco Bouligny: A Bourbon Soldier in Spanish Louisiana* (Baton Rouge, 1993), 40–41, 130–31, 141, 192.

35. John Walton Caughey, *Bernardo de Gálvez in Louisiana, 1776–1783* (1934; rpr. Gretna, La., 1972), 149–214; Albert W. Haarmann, "The Spanish Conquest of British West Florida, 1779–1781," *Florida Historical Quarterly*, XXXIX (1960), 107–34; Actas del Cabildo, II, 47, January 19, 1781. See also Gálvez' campaign diaries, "Diary that I, Dn. Bernardo de Gálvez,

A transient and heterogeneous population in the city was present not only during the war. New Orleans experienced a steady influx of outsiders who helped to give it a shady character and an exotic air. Many military personnel and visitors from the posts and elsewhere frequented its bustling taverns and houses of ill repute. Their single status in a town already known for its wicked ways no doubt contributed to the desire to carouse. Vicar General Cirilo de Barcelona, who arrived in New Orleans in 1772, noted concubinage even among the French Capuchin priests.[36]

While conducting the investigation of the ringleaders responsible for the French Creole rebellion of 1768 and before he decided on the form of government for Louisiana, Governor O'Reilly imposed new regulations on the city's drinking establishments. By a proclamation of October 8, 1769,[37] he allowed twelve taverns, six billiard halls, and one *limonadier* (lemonade seller) to dispense alcoholic drinks. The license fee for tavern keepers was originally forty pesos, but it dropped to a more reasonable thirteen pesos in 1771. In December, 1775, the Cabildo permitted twenty-four taverns to operate. They continued to vary in number over the years. The high point came in 1789 when perhaps ninety-four flourished in the city. O'Reilly's regulation prohibited criminals, vagabonds, and prostitutes from frequenting these establishments, and it forbade the use of swear words and blasphemy. These prohibitions were usually honored more in the breach than in practice.[38]

Brigadier of the Royal Army and Governor of the Province of Louisiana, and charged by His Majesty with the Expedition against Pensacola and Mobile, formed of the events that occur in it," Mobile, March 18, 1780, AGS, GM, leg. 6912; and *Diario de las operaciones contra la plaza de Panzacola, 1781* (2nd ed.; Madrid, 1959).

36. Coutts, "Martín Navarro," 107–108; Cirilo de Barcelona to the king, New Orleans, April 20, 1774, AGI, SD, leg. 2586. Barcelona even accused the French Capuchins of permitting prostitution of their female black servants (Coutts, "Martín Navarro," 107).

37. Florence M. Jumonville, in "Frenchmen at Heart: New Orleans Printers and Their Imprints, 1764–1803," *LH,* XXXII (1991), 305, gives the date September 21, 1769, for O'Reilly's proclamation, but Holmes, in "Spanish Regulation of Taverns," 151, employs October 8, 1769. Perhaps the different dates result from when the proclamation was first issued and when it was printed.

38. Holmes, "Spanish Regulation of Taverns," 153, 156; Holmes, ed., "O'Reilly's Regulations on Booze, Boarding Houses, and Billiards," *LH,* VI (1965), 295. The figure of ninety-four taverns in 1789 is based on the number of individuals who paid license fees. There were probably fewer taverns.

O'Reilly placed other restrictions on the establishments and limited the libations each could sell. Taverns sold wine and the hard beverages, brandy and rum. O'Reilly ordered them to close at 8 P.M., but through the years, hours fluctuated. According to Berquin-Duvallon, it was possible to pay the night watch to look the other way and, allegedly, the police earned a fair amount for doing so. Many establishments sold adulterated wines and to slaves, both of which practices were prohibited.[39]

Each billiard hall was permitted only one table, barred players under age sixteen, and cautioned patrons to observe the rules of the game carefully. Businesses had to close on feast days and Sundays during mass. They could serve "bottled liquors, like syrup," lemonade, beer, and cider. The *limonadier*'s cafe could sell "all kinds of lemonade, liquors, fruit brandies . . . syrups, liqueurs, sugared almonds, coffee beans, powder and in beverages, as well as chocolate." The cafe could allow club games such as chess, checkers, and piquets but not gambling or prohibited diversions. It had to close on feast days and Sundays and by 10 P.M. on other days.[40]

Although O'Reilly had sought to regulate drinking parlors, some of them were beyond regulation. Berquin-Duvallon described them in the late Spanish era: "The city abounds with tippling houses. At every cross street of the town and suburbs, one sees those places of riot and intoxication crowded day and night." No doubt not every tavern had the same clientele, but in the bawdy bistros located outside the city gates, all colors mingled: white, red, black, free and slave. These dens of iniquity reeked of tobacco smoke and cheap liquor. Besides imbibing, denizens commonly gambled and patronized available prostitutes. Slaves and even fugitive slaves exchanged stolen items for alcohol, tobacco, and gunpowder. Dancing, too, went on in many of the taverns.[41]

39. Holmes, "Spanish Regulation of Taverns," 158, 159. Governor Gayoso, in his *bando de buen gobierno* of 1798, ordered taverns and billiard halls to close at sundown (the hour of retreat) (Richard E. Chandler, "Life in New Orleans in 1798," *Revue de Louisiane/Louisiana Review,* VI [1978], 181).

40. Holmes, ed., "O'Reilly's Regulations," 298–99, 300.

41. Berquin-Duvallon, *Travels in Louisiana,* 53–55, quotation on p. 53; Louis Narcisse Baudry des Lozières, *Second Voyage a la Louisiane, faisant suite au premier de l'auteur de 1794 a 1798* (2 vols.; Paris, 1803), I, 314. The night watchmen (*serenos*), who have been called the police, began working in 1794. Tavern keepers outside the city gates did not have to pay them off because they stayed within the city. Because taverns caused families to suffer, Baudry des Lozières believed men should do their drinking at home (*ibid.,* 316).

Asbury has a colorful description of the drinking establishments: "There was a great increase in the number of low taverns, gambling-halls, coffee-houses, bagnios, and especially resorts of the type called *cabarets,* which combined groceries, dram-shops, gambling dens, and houses of prostitution under one roof. Perhaps the most celebrated of these places was the Maison Coquet, situated on Royal Street in the heart of New Orleans, which advertised by posters at the street corners with, as was stated on the placards, 'The express permission of the Honorable Civil Governor of the City.'"[42] The reference was to Nicolás María Vidal, who was New Orleans' only civil governor in the Spanish era. Regular governors held both military and civil appointments.

For the genteel teetotaling public, New Orleans had other establishments, cafes that served only coffee, tea, and chocolate to its sober clientele. One of them was the Cafe de Aguila, located at the corner of St. Ann and Chartres streets.[43]

New Orleans had numerous and severe problems, many of which attracted the attention and comment of travelers. Visitors often remarked that the streets were dusty and potholed in the dry season and mired in mud during the rainy season. Sanitation to many residents consisted of throwing refuse out the nearest window into the street to putrefy.[44] That mentality extended to dead animals that undoubtedly befouled the air as they decomposed. Berquin-Duvallon summed up the condition of the streets: "During the greater part of the year, they are a common sewer; a sink of nastiness, dirt, and corruption."[45] Although the Cabildo made efforts to clean up the streets, particularly in the late 1790s, it did nothing to encourage residents to change the ways they discarded refuse.

The levee just above the Plaza de Armas was a public walkway. Ships that brought foreign cargo tied up to the levee opposite the plaza because the Customs House was nearby. The levee was about eight feet wide at the top. Ships in the "harbor" were visible from the levee, but only the masts of the nearest vessels could be seen from street level. John Pintard

42. Asbury, *French Quarter,* 69.

43. Nathaniel Cortlandt Curtis, *New Orleans: Its Old Houses, Shops and Public Buildings* (Philadelphia, 1933), 76.

44. *Ibid.,* 52–53.

45. Berquin-Duvallon, *Travels in Louisiana,* 24.

in 1801 painted a disagreeable picture of the walkway, where "all sorts & conditions of people" flocked. He complained about the noise caused by "drunken labourers & sailors." In the evening, the mariners came ashore to cook their suppers, making numerous fires. Because it was the only recreational area within the city, numerous people gravitated toward it. Pintard added, "Almost naked Indians—Negroes & Mulattoes are patrolling this walk [the levee] & jostling against the ladies whose delicacy must often be offended at such disgusting sights." The Creole ladies, however, accustomed to the experience, refrained from revulsion, as later did Pintard, whose "repugnance . . . diminished by becoming more familiar with what at first was very singular & shocking."[46]

Francis Baily, who was in New Orleans in June, 1797, was more pleased with the levee promenade. He described it as "a handsome raised gravel walk, planted with orange-trees; and in the summer-time served for a mall, and in an evening was always a fashionable resort for the beaux and belles of the place."[47]

Businesses in New Orleans were open seven days a week, which often shocked puritanical visitors. The shops closed on Sunday only during religious services. Many of the Sabbath customers and vendors were slaves, who flocked in from nearby plantations.[48]

The pursuit of pleasure in New Orleans was not confined to males and the riffraff. The well-to-do enjoyed festive occasions, too. The social season began in November, after the last harvest and when many planters and their families moved to the city for the winter, and continued until spring with balls that often lasted until the next day. The partying even went on during the winter of 1780–1781, when the Spaniards were preparing to attack British-held Pensacola.[49] Festivities increased around holy days, such as All Saints Day, Christmas, New Year's, and Epiphany or Twelfth Night, and culminated in the last few days before Lent, called Carnival.[50]

46. John Pintard, "New Orleans, 1801: An Account by John Pintard," ed. David Lee Sterling, *LHQ*, XXXIV (1951), 231.

47. Baily, *Journal of a Tour*, 164–65.

48. Actas del Cabildo, I, 67–68, January 10, 1772; Clark, *New Orleans*, 253.

49. Navarro to Bernardo de Gálvez, New Orleans, March 4, 1781, AGI, PC, leg. 83.

50. Coutts, "Martín Navarro," 108. Along this same line, Robin wrote: "Winter is the gay season, balls are frequent. Indeed, in a place so bare of the means of education, and where the

White public balls were held twice weekly, once for adults and once for children.[51] Individuals of all colors, adults and children, dressed up in costumes and mingled on the streets in impromptu mummery. Public mask balls were held intermittently between Twelfth Night and the Tuesday before Ash Wednesday, or Mardi Gras. Carnival then was as much for children as for adults, and many costumed youngsters reveled through the city streets. Mardi Gras parades did not appear in New Orleans until after the American era began.[52]

In addition to amusement, other activities went on in the city. Education was in most instances a private matter. Except in limited cases, it did not go far beyond the primary level. Several private schools and tutors were present in New Orleans but knowledge about them is scarce. More is known about the public school the Spanish government began in 1772. Its director, Andrés López de Armesto, and three teachers operated it as a free institution. Although instruction was supposed to be in Spanish as part of a program to increase the language's use and hispanicize the colony, the teachers often taught the lessons in French. The school's enrollment never exceeded 150. López de Armesto devoted less than full time to his post. He was so engaged in other jobs, among them as government secretary beginning in 1780, that he neglected to begin a library the government wished to create. The 3,183 books earmarked for its use remained in crates for years before they vanished, possibly falling into private hands. Although a July, 1800, document still called López de Armesto director, by then and perhaps for some time he had had nothing to do with the school. Father Uvaldo Delgado, who began teaching in the school in the 1780s, was running it by 1789, and Fernando Ibáñez was the only other teacher.[53]

---

privileges of religion are so curtailed, there is an abundance of amusement" (quoted in King, *New Orleans*, 168–69).

51. Berquin-Duvallon, *Travels in Louisiana*, 26; James Pitot, *Observations on the Colony of Louisiana from 1796 to 1802*, trans. and intro. Henry C. Pitot (Baton Rouge, 1979), 32. Davis (in *Louisiana*, 150) says the public balls for whites were held on Sunday and Thursday evenings. Berquin-Duvallon described the public hall used in 1802 as plain, resembling a barracks (*Travels in Louisiana*, 26).

52. King, *New Orleans*, 391, 393.

53. David K. Bjork, ed. and trans., "Documents Related to the Establishment of Schools in Louisiana, 1771," *Mississippi Valley Historical Review*, XI (1925), 561–69; Abraham P. Nasatir,

The city's private schools were also generally small. In 1788 all eight of them enrolled only about four hundred students. Probably more private schools opened in the 1790s, with the arrival of refugees from Saint Domingue and an increase in the city's Anglo-American population.[54]

A military school to train cadets who sought to become officers in the Fixed Louisiana Infantry Regiment closed in 1789 for lack of a teacher. By order of the captain general, it reopened in 1791 or 1792 and continued functioning until the Spanish era ended. Not every cadet could become an officer in the regiment so it never had more than thirty or forty students at one time. Its instruction went beyond the *primeras letras* (elementary education) of the other schools and was in Spanish. Many of its cadets were French Creoles and the sons of Spanish army officers and government employees.[55]

The Ursuline Convent school that began in the French era catered exclusively to girls, although private tutors also probably instructed some girls. Approximately seventy schoolgirls boarded at the convent and a hundred more from the city attended classes during the week.[56]

---

ed., "Government Employees and Salaries in Spanish Louisiana," *LHQ*, XXIX (1946), 926, 936; Davis, *Louisiana,* 153; Henry P. Dart, ed., "Public Education in New Orleans in 1800," *LHQ*, XI (1928), 247; Ernest R. Liljegren, "Frontier Education in Spanish Louisiana," *Missouri Historical Review,* XXXV (1940–41), 347–50; Carondelet to Las Casas, New Orleans, July 5, 1794, AGI, PC, leg. 1443A; see enclosures in Carondelet to Las Casas, No. 155 reserved, February 6, 1796, AGI, PC, leg. 1447; *asiento* of López de Armesto, AGI, PC, leg. 538A. The three teachers who helped to set up the Spanish school were Francisco de la Colina y Escudero, Manuel Díaz de Lara, and Pedro de Aragón y Villegas. Burson, in *Stewardship.* 265, says that Manuel Díaz de Lara was the Spanish school's director in the 1780s and perhaps earlier, and there were only twenty-three students in 1788. When the school building was destroyed in the fire that year, Almonester furnished a house rent-free for the school. López de Armesto's given names were Manuel Andrés, but he generally used only Andrés.

54. Burson, *Stewardship.* 264. See Dart, ed., "Public Education in New Orleans in 1800," 240–52, which deals with the arrival in New Orleans of Luis Francisco Lefort, who petitioned for the right to teach school. He was referred to Andrés López de Armesto, director of the Royal Schools, who examined and certified him as qualified to teach. He seems to have regained his old post.

55. Davis, *Louisiana,* 152–53; Din, *Francisco Bouligny.* 181–82. The cadet school should not be confused with the civilian Spanish school as Johnson does in "Colonial New Orleans," 49–50.

56. Davis, *Louisiana,* 153. There are many works on the Ursuline nuns in Louisiana. One of the more recent and based on primary sources is Karen Greene, "The Ursuline Mission in Colonial Louisiana" (M.A. thesis, Louisiana State University, 1982).

New Orleans' first newspaper, *Le Moniteur de la Louisiane,* appeared in 1794. Louis Duclot was the printer of the four-page weekly. It published virtually no local news but contained foreign news and agricultural and trade information. It also published government decrees and advertisements.[57]

Although bookstores appear not to have existed in colonial New Orleans, residents who wanted books probably could acquire them with relative ease. Jean Baptiste Prevost, who died in 1769, owned a library of more than three hundred books. Even more impressive was the library of Governor General Manuel Gayoso de Lemos, who died in 1799. He left a personal collection of 411 volumes in 165 titles in Spanish, English, French, Portuguese, and Latin, which has often been ignored by Louisiana writers. Although he no doubt brought some of these works with him to Louisiana in 1789, he must have acquired others after his arrival.[58]

Personal libraries of three and four hundred volumes sound small when compared to collections today, but they should be compared to college libraries then. Harvard College Library, the largest in the United States at the time, contained about four thousand books, and the library at the College of William and Mary had three thousand.[59]

Probably more than the coastal North American cities, colonial New Orleans society emphasized class distinctions. As early as the 1720s, an embryonic class structure was already developing. In the beginning, top government officials, military officers, and missionaries placed themselves in a class above the rest. Immediately below them were the educated professionals such as lawyers, merchants, notaries, registrars, secretaries, and storekeepers. At the bottom of white society were the illiterate com-

57. Wood, "Life in New Orleans," 685–86; Jack D. L. Holmes, ed., "Louisiana in 1795, the Earliest Extant Issue of the *Moniteur de la Louisiane*," *LH,* VII (1966), 133–51.

58. E. D. Price, "Inventory of the Estate of Sieur Jean Baptiste Prevost, July 13, 1769," *LHQ,* IX (1926), 411–57; Irving Leonard, "A Frontier Library, 1799," *Hispanic American Historical Review,* XXIII (1943), 21–51. Another Spanish army officer, Francisco Bouligny, had a private book collection of 48 titles and 146 volumes (Gilbert C. Din, "The Death and Succession of Francisco Bouligny," *LH,* XXII [1981], 314–15). See also Roger Philip McCutcheon, "Books and Booksellers in New Orleans, 1730–1830," *LHQ,* XX (1937), 606–18, and "Libraries in New Orleans, 1771–1831," *LHQ,* XX (1937), 152–58.

59. Beverly McAnear, "College Founding in the American Colonies, 1745–1775," in *Essays on American Colonial History,* ed. Paul Goodman (2nd ed.; New York, 1972), 467.

moners. Wealth did not matter greatly in the early days because no one had much of it.[60]

But as prosperity grew, the upper classes—persons of noble birth and titles, planters, merchants, professionals, and the educated—increasingly pulled themselves away from the masses, the poor, uneducated, and common whites. Clothing helped to distinguish class, and the well-to-do loved displaying their apparel. The more affluent and positioned males enjoyed wearing their army, navy, or militia uniforms. Militia officers sported their military attire at all times and did not confine their use to official duty. Many civilian Spanish government officials also wore special uniforms. Even the uniforms of army sergeants gave them status among white commoners.[61]

François Marie Perrin du Lac, a visitor in New Orleans in the late Spanish period, noted about Creoles and uniforms: "Nothing pleases them so much as the military uniform, which they wear at thirteen or fourteen. The government employs them in the militia, or in the regiments of Louisiana."[62] Of course, Perrin du Lac was writing about the well-to-do Creole youth who were cadets. Normally, the sons of army officers became cadets at sixteen, but sometimes they entered earlier.

An example of the love of uniforms can be seen in the case of Evan Jones in 1799. A Spanish subject resident in Louisiana for many years, militia captain, and former commandant at Lafourche de Chetimachas,

60. Marcel Giraud, *A History of French Louisiana,* Vol. II, *Years of Transition, 1715–1717,* trans. Brian Pearce (Baton Rouge, 1993), 124–26.

61. New Orleanians shared their affection for clothing with other colonials. See, for example, Amy Turner Bushnell, *The King's Coffer: Proprietors of the Spanish Florida Treasury, 1565–1702* (Gainesville, Fla., 1981), 26–27; and David J. Weber, *The Spanish Frontier in North America* (New Haven, 1992), 314–15. The Spanish documentation in the AGI, PC, contains many records on army and militia uniforms. Jack D. L. Holmes, ed., in *Honor and Fidelity: The Louisiana Infantry Regiment and the Louisiana Militia Companies, 1766–1821* (Birmingham, Ala., 1965), 13–78, describes the different uniforms with their colors and styles. Army officers seem to have worn their uniforms at all times. This was true of Francisco Bouligny, regimental commandant from 1791 to 1800. He had no civilian clothes when he died in 1800 and an inventory was made of his possessions (Din, "Death and Succession of Francisco Bouligny," 307–15). Spanish military records in AGI, PC, show that there were able sergeants who were denied advancement to officer status because their wives were judged "indecent." This spared the officers' wives from having to deal with them.

62. Perrin du Lac, *Travels,* 90.

Jones appeared in uniform with his appointment as U.S. consul before Colonel Francisco Bouligny, when the latter was the acting military governor. Bouligny was astonished to see Jones still wearing his militia uniform, and he recommended that Jones not be recognized as consul because he had accepted the appointment while still a Spanish subject and a militia officer. The captain general in Havana agreed, although Jones functioned as consul in an unofficial capacity for many months.[63]

More than the other Spanish governors, Gálvez and Carondelet catered to the whims of the class-conscious Creoles by creating special militia units for them. Many of them detested serving in units with commoners. The wealthier residents often received militia posts as officers. Carondelet's reorganization of the militia in 1792 created many posts for them to fill. Another factor that attracted civilians to the militia was enjoyment of the *fuero,* or judicial privilege. A person possessing the *fuero,* and even his family and servants, could be tried only by a special military court, which presumably would rule more favorably than a civil one.[64]

The wearing of uniforms to denote status extended to the more highly regarded professions in the city, including medicine. Clothes distinguished gentlemen, and the dress of doctors was distinct. John Duffy describes them: "A well-dressed physician wore a powdered wig, a highly colored coat, short breeches, stockings, buckled shoes, and a three-cornered hat; a resplendent vest, lace cravat and ruffles, and a gold-headed cane usually completed the attire." By the early nineteenth century, the medical community dressed more somberly in black and gray, although older physicians continued to cling to ruffles, frills, and knee breeches.[65]

The *alcaldes ordinarios,* who were Cabildo magistrates, were expected to appear in public dressed appropriately and carrying a wand symbolizing royal justice. Equally conscious of their status, the Cabildo *regidores* wanted

63. Bouligny to Captain General Someruelos, reserved, New Orleans, August 8, 1799, AGI, PC, leg. 1550.

64. Marqués de Sonora (José de Gálvez) to the Conde de Gálvez (Bernardo de Gálvez), Aranjuez, May 20, 1786, AGI, PC, leg. 1375; Holmes, ed., *Honor and Fidelity,* 23–32, 47–57, 76, 77.

65. John Duffy, ed., *The Rudoph Matas History of Medicine in Louisiana* (2 vols.; Baton Rouge, 1958–62), I, 170–71; see also W. J. Bishop, "Notes on the History of Medical Costume," *Annals of Medical History,* n.s., VI (1934), 193–218.

uniforms to distinguish themselves. In the summer of 1798, the newly enlarged city council asked that its members be accorded military honors, rank, and uniforms. Many of them were already militia officers, and two were army officers. The annual commissioners wrote the request and forwarded it through the proper channels to the king, who never responded.[66]

New Orleanians have long been noted for their devotion to entertainment. During the Spanish period, amusements became elaborate and diverse. Plays were performed in New Orleans at least as early as the 1780s, but nothing else is known about them except that they were amateur productions. Not until October 4, 1792, did the first theater open and offer diversion to a paying public. Two brothers from France, Jean-Marie and Louis-Alexander Henry, operated it. Their theater on St. Peter Street between Royal and Bourbon streets was small, having twelve boxes, an amphitheater, a pit, and a gallery. There was also balcony seating for free people of color. The Spaniards called it El Teatro de la Comedia and El Coliseo, but it had several other names. By the mid-1790s, it had a mulatta singer and used quadroon actresses. The theater, however, had financial problems almost from the start, and they continued throughout the Spanish era. The first opera was performed in New Orleans in 1796.[67]

Not all the patrons of the theater were well-behaved, and the management had to post regulations for the conduct of the audience: "No one will be allowed to throw or pretend to throw oranges or anything else, be it in the theatre or in any other part of the hall, nor, in a word, shall anyone be allowed to start quarrels with his neighbor or with anyone; nor shall anyone insult anybody or come to blows or speak ill of another in

66. The Code O'Reilly (in Benjamin Franklin French, ed., *Historical Memoirs of Louisiana, from the First Settlement of the Colony to the Departure of Governor O'Reilly in 1770: With Historical and Biographical Notes* [5 vols.; New York, 1853], V, 254–88 [hereafter cited as Code O'Reilly], 259); Burson, *Stewardship,* 209; Davis, *Louisiana,* 133; Actas del Cabildo, IV, (2), 131, June 1, 1798. The Code O'Reilly consists of two documents, the first called "Ordinances and Instructions of Alexander O'Reilly," which was designed for the New Orleans Cabildo, and the second, "Instructions as to the Manner of Instituting Suits, Civil and Criminal, and Pronouncing Judgments in General, in Conformity to the laws of the Nueva Recopilación de Castilla, and the Recopilación de Indias," which was for the courts of the *alcaldes ordinarios.*

67. Grace King, *Creole Families of New Orleans* (1921; rpr. Baton Rouge, 1971), 377; René J. Le Gardeur, Jr., *The First New Orleans Theatre, 1792–1803* (New Orleans, 1963); Davis, *Louisiana,* 154. *Comedia* in Spanish means drama, not comedy.

order to stir up trouble." Contemporary western American audiences were also often rowdy and disrespectful to the actors. Governors in New Orleans sometimes issued instructions on the operation of the theater. Perhaps in response to complaints, in 1795 Carondelet ordered plays to begin at 5:30 P.M., the audience to behave well, and actors not to repeat their lines.[68]

Musicians were no doubt present from an early time in New Orleans, but perhaps the only full-size orchestra or band present in the Spanish era belonged to the army. Spanish military musicians were in New Orleans during the American revolutionary war. An orchestra in 1789, probably composed of military musicians, helped to celebrate the accession of Carlos IV to the Spanish throne. It also performed in parades and at other public functions. Possibly the regimental military band occasionally entertained the city inhabitants on Sundays or holidays in the Plaza de Armas. Civilian musicians worked in smaller bands and orchestras that played at public and private balls. In addition, individual guitar players and fiddlers strolled through crowds on the streets, playing their instruments. Harpists, too, occasionally performed on the street.[69]

A local custom that excited the Creole public was the charivari. It often took place at marriages of widows or prominent persons. Perhaps there were other reasons for having them. Charivari consisted of hazing the newlyweds, and sometimes the participants became rowdy. In October, 1803, Judge Advocate Nicolás María Vidal informed the post commandant of Pointe Coupee not to permit the charivari for any reason. A recent charivari there had committed numerous excesses. Vidal's injunction might have been applicable to New Orleans as well. Because his prohibition came late in the Spanish era, the practice did not stop for long, if indeed at all.[70]

68. Lura Robinson, *It's an Old New Orleans Custom* (New York, 1948), 41; Richard C. Wade, *The Urban Frontier: The Rise of Western Cities, 1790–1830* (Cambridge, Mass., 1959), 145; Carondelet instructions, May 12, 1795, AGI, PC, leg. 30.

69. Gilbert C. Din, "Domingo de Assereto: An Adventurer in Carondelet's Louisiana," *LH*, XXXIV (1993), 84. On October 1, 1783, Governor Miró complained to acting captain general José de Ezpeleta about not having enough musicians in the regiment because many had left with the troops withdrawn to Cuba. He asked for clarinetists, trumpeters, and a *maestro* (director) (Miró to Ezpeleta, New Orleans, October 1, 1783, AGI, PC, leg. 1377).

70. Wood, "Life in New Orleans," 693; Asbury, *French Quarter*, 116; Vidal to Casa-Calvo, New Orleans, October 8, (1803), AGI, PC, leg. 73. John Lee Williams, in *A View of West Florida*

Occasionally, auctions held in the street broke the monotony in the city. The Cabildo announced its auctions in "all the accustomed places," which possibly were "bulletin boards" located at the church, *casa capitular,* riverfront, main government buildings, and important street intersections. The Cabildo auctions were conducted outside the *casa capitular.* As one writer described them: "The beating of drums at all crossings informed the citizens that an auction was about to take place."[71] Possibly public auctions took place inside the *casa capitular* after it was rebuilt, or so Pintard, who was in New Orleans in 1801, claimed.[72]

Because of isolation and ignorance, colonial New Orleanians suffered from boredom. They no doubt enjoyed the occasions when the city held wartime victory parades or peacetime military processions and Cabildo pageantry. But beyond these events, many city inhabitants also relished the days when extraordinary happenings took place.

No ceremonial event in New Orleans in the Spanish period compared to those held in 1789 to commemorate the death of King Carlos III and the accession to the throne of his son, Carlos IV. The Cabildo was at the center of these activities and spent generously on them. Upon hearing of the king's death the previous December, the council met on April 4 and 17, 1789, to plan events. It decreed six months of mourning, sent a letter of condolence to the royal family, and published the news of the king's demise. It ordered a solemn high mass with military honors. The council requested Governor Esteban Miró to invite all military officers, govern-

---

(1827; Gainesville, Fla., 1976), 79, wrote about the charivari: "Sherrivarees are parties of idle people, who dress themselves in masquerade, whenever a widow or widower are married. They often parade about, and play buffoon tricks, for two or three days; haunting the residence of the married pair, and disturbing the whole city with their riots, until they can be bought off with money or liquor."

71. Robinson, *Old New Orleans Custom,* 64–65. Robinson also states: "When [the auctioneers] arrived at the scene, a small piece of candle was lighted, the signal for bidding to begin on the first article offered. The person making the final bid before the wisk fell became the owner." This is probably too dramatic to have been practiced. At some Cabildo auctions, no one bid and, at others, bids were too low to be accepted.

72. Pintard, "New Orleans, 1801," 227. Pintard wrote: "On the ground floor of the town House the public Auctions are held—This is an exclusive privilege for which the present occupant paid it is said $12,000" (*ibid.*). The Cabildo minutes, however, do not mention that it permitted auctions in its building or that it received 12,000 pesos for doing so. Pintard was probably wrong.

ment officials, and distinguished citizens to participate in the accompanying procession and religious service. The councillors delayed celebrating the accession of Carlos IV until they completed the mourning ceremonies for Carlos III.[73]

On April 22, the funeral procession, with participants dressed in mourning, marched from Government House to the chapel of Charity Hospital. The chapel was used because a fire the year before had destroyed the St. Louis Church. A mace bearer preceded the dignitaries announcing the king's passing. With the royal banner in the vanguard, the mourners entered the chapel for the singing of the *Te Deum*. A sepulchral urn, scepter, and crown represented the dead king. Decorations included a five-tiered funeral bier, a brightly festooned canopy, royal insignias and medals, and sixty royal coats of arms. The rest of the chapel was draped in mourning, with numerous candles and torches providing illumination.

Fray Antonio de Sedella, acting vicar general, delivered the eulogy. He praised the virtues of the deceased king and his paternal affection for his subjects. At intervals, the artillery and infantry corps in the Plaza de Armas punctuated the services by discharging their ordnance in salutes to the dead monarch. Upon completion of the ceremony, the somber assembly returned to Government House, where it dispersed.[74]

On May 4, the city temporarily suspended mourning to celebrate the accession to the throne of Carlos IV. At 4 P.M., the participants, who included the Cabildo officials, governor, army officers, government employees, and distinguished citizens, assembled at Government House. Escorted by infantry soldiers and mounted dragoons, they proceeded to the home of Alférez Real Carlos de Reggio, custodian of the royal banner. His house and yard were decorated for the occasion, and the party stopped to enjoy refreshments and exchange pleasantries.[75]

73. Actas del Cabildo, III, (2), 52–54, April 4, 1789, III, (2), 54–56, April 17, 1789.

74. *Ibid.*, III, (2), 56–59, April 24, 1789; Burson, *Stewardship*, 258–59. The Cabildo ordered a description of the rites to be recorded, sealed, and preserved forever as a testimony of the city's loyalty and affection for its late sovereign. In compliance with the royal order, the Cabildo noted that the funeral expenses amounted to 1,216 pesos, 5 reales, which the city treasury paid. It forwarded an account of the ceremonies and expenses to the crown (Actas del Cabildo, III, [2], 56–59, April 24, 1789; Burson, *Stewardship*, 258–59).

75. Actas del Cabildo, IV, (2), 59–61, May 8, 1789.

The dignitaries then continued to the chapel of Charity Hospital, where Father Sedella, the clergy, and the choir received them. Sedella blessed the royal banner that Reggio brought and led the assembled group in singing the *Te Deum*. The celebrants then returned to Government House, where Reggio waved the royal banner from the balcony and proclaimed the name and titles of the new king. He repeated his proclamation in the Plaza de Armas and at the church to the accompaniment of artillery salvos and outcries of merriment from the masses throughout the city.[76]

Afterward, the royal banner and portraits of the new king and queen were exhibited from the front gallery of Government House. They were ensconced under a canopy and a pavilion of bright red damask and protected by an honor guard of grenadiers. Three nights of citywide celebration followed the May 4 ceremonies. The festivities included a general illumination of the city, orchestra music from the balcony of Government House, the performance of two plays, and a reception by Governor Miró. The governor furnished "abundant and delicious refreshments" to his guests at his personal expense.[77]

Although New Orleans never again witnessed the pageantry that marked these ceremonies, it did have more expensive festivities. In 1798 members of the ousted French royal family, the dukes of Orleans, Montpensier, and Beaujolais, descended on New Orleans, having come downriver from the United States. The three brothers stayed in the city for thirty-three days during which time Governor Gayoso and other notable citizens entertained them lavishly. Gayoso opened his house to them and took them on an excursion by boat down Carondelet Canal and Bayou St. John to Lake Pontchartrain. The princes also visited other residents who

76. *Ibid.*

77. *Ibid.*; Burson, *Stewardship*, 221–22. The Cabildo minutes record a city expenditure of 201 pesos, 7 reales for this celebration. But the amount disagrees with the *mayordomo's* records for 1789, which put the expenses at 1,380 pesos. If the *mayordomo's* figures are accurate, it was a substantial sum for a city that had suffered a catastrophic fire only one year before and had become more dependent on royal largess than ever before. Possibly the spending was an attempt to curry royal favor and thus an act of self-interest. Mayordomo de Propios Matías de Alpuente used his own funds to help pay the expenses. He loaned the city interest-free money to carry out the celebrations (Actas del Cabildo, IV, [2], 59–61, May 8, 1789, III, [2], 193–94, March 23, 1792; Henry P. Dart, ed., "Account of the Credit and Debit of the Funds of the City of New Orleans for the year 1789," trans. Laura L. Porteous, *LHQ,* XIX [1936], 594).

honored them with dinners, dances, and merriment. The Fixed Louisiana Infantry Regiment gave them a dinner that had 360 guests and a dance probably attended by more townspeople. No doubt all the regular army and militia officers and their wives appeared. The marathon event lasted all night and into the next morning, continuing for fifteen hours. Philippe de Marigny also entertained the brothers at his house and lent them money.[78]

A smaller event that attracted fewer people but was an omen of things to come occurred on February 5, 1800. Upon learning of the death of George Washington, Evan Jones and William Hullings, leaders in the American community in New Orleans, requested permission to have a procession from their houses and a service on the levee. An American naval ship on the river would fire several cannons to commemorate the event. The acting governor, the Marqués de Casa-Calvo (Sebastián Calvo de la Puerta y O'Farrill), consented. Although no description of the ceremony has survived, it was probably held and attracted the attention of both the Americans and the curious.[79]

An important day in the life of Andrés Almonester y Roxas and New Orleans occurred on September 8, 1796. He had accumulated a tidy fortune and was easily one of the richest men in New Orleans. Among the posts he then held were those of *alférez real* on the Cabildo and colonel of the New Orleans militia. Although he had constructed at his own expense several buildings for the city's use, among them Charity Hospital, St. Lazarus Hospital for lepers, St. Louis Cathedral, and the adjoining presbytery, he was not well liked. That, however, did not trouble the elderly Spaniard, who was determined to put on a show for the town's inhabitants. In 1796 the king honored Almonester for his many civic accomplishments by making him a knight in the Order of Carlos III. The investiture took

78. King, *New Orleans,* 151–52; Din, *Francisco Bouligny,* 211–12. Gayoso claims to have spent 4,300 pesos to entertain the princes. For his description of their stay, see Gayoso to the Prince of the Peace, New Orleans, February 24, two letters of March 1, April 18, 1798, all in AHN, leg. 3900, exped. 4.

79. Nicolás María Vidal to the Marqués de Casa-Calvo, New Orleans, February 3, 1800, and [Casa-Calvo] to Vidal, New Orleans, February 4, 1800, both in AGI, PC, leg. 71A. In his letter, Vidal stated that the right to approve such an event belonged to him as civil governor. Because arms were to be used, however, Casa-Calvo said authority was his as military governor, and he cited Art. 6, Trat. 6, Tít. 2 of the Royal Ordinances.

place at the cathedral, after which he returned home dressed in a great robe. There he held a reception for more than three hundred well-wishers, no doubt the cream of New Orleans society. As part of the celebration, that same evening of September 8, a balloon was inflated at the Plaza de Armas and rose above the city. Perhaps it was the first time New Orleans had witnessed such a spectacle. This was followed by a display of fireworks. By ten o'clock, the celebration was over, but it assuredly had created an impression among those who witnessed the event.[80]

During both the French and Spanish eras, Roman Catholicism enjoyed a monopoly in religion in New Orleans. Religious celebrations were common both in the city's only church and in the streets. During the Spanish period, they seemed to grow, particularly after Bishop Luis Peñalver y Cárdenas arrived. Soon after his coming in 1795, he deplored the lack of religious observance on the part of many of the city's inhabitants. A celebration common in Catholic countries was Corpus Christi, held on the Thursday after Trinity Sunday in June. New Orleans under Bishop Peñalver observed the day with a procession through the streets. Francis Baily, who was there in 1797, described what he saw from his Protestant vantage point a bit removed from the "rabble":

> A few soldiers went first to clear the way [for the gentlemen]; next to these followed the ecclesiastical multitude, consisting of priests of different kinds and in different habits, carrying tapers, crosses, and all the instruments of idolatrous superstition, and conveying the host, which was carried on a kind of bier dressed round with flowers and trinkets. . . . After this came the bishop, walking in solemn state under a canopy supported by half a dozen priests, and scattering his *fruitless* blessings around on a gaping multitude. Close to the bishop followed the Baron de Carondelet, the governor of the province, together with his suite; and at the close of these a party of horse and foot to preserve order, and to keep off the rabble which followed behind.[81]

80. Henry Renshaw, "Jackson Square," *LHQ*, II (1919), 38–39. A reason for public dislike of Almonester arose from his raising the rent for his apartments after the 1788 fire, but it did not prevent the elite from attending this event. Many people seemed to ignore that Almonester spent much of his money for the benefit of the city's inhabitants.

81. Baily, *Journal of a Tour*, 174; Bishop Luis [Peñalver], to Eugenio Llaguno y Amirola,

Protestant writers then seemed habitually obliged to describe Catholic rituals as superstition.

Also differing from ordinary days in colonial New Orleans were the occasions when public executions occurred. They served a functional purpose because they showed the populace by example that crime did not pay and punishment could be dreadful. Public executions were not unusual in colonial New Orleans. They had been grim affairs in the French era. One of the largest turnouts in Spanish New Orleans was for the execution of the renegade slave bandit Juan San Malo and three of his lieutenants. They were hanged in the Plaza de Armas on June 19, 1784, for murdering whites and blacks. Two Anglo-Americans, William Jones and Alexander Greydon, who counterfeited currency in Natchez, suffered the same fate at 6 P.M. on August 15, 1783. To cite one final example, two of the participants in the abortive slave conspiracy in Pointe Coupee of 1795 were also hanged in New Orleans. Probably less public, however, were military executions, usually for murder, which were carried out in the barracks area of the city. Often it was by a firing squad, although the penalty for more heinous crimes was hanging.[82] Stocks were also present in the Plaza de Armas, where lower-class delinquents were subjected to public humiliation in two-hour stretches for minor offenses.

But besides occasions of merriment, celebration, and drama, disasters plagued the Spanish era in New Orleans. At least three major hurricanes and several minor ones occurred during Spain's rule. The first severe hurricane struck on August 18, 1779. Scarcely a house escaped damage, and nearly all the boats on the river sank. The hurricane caused Lake Pontchartrain to swell and Bayou St. John to experience a tidal surge.[83]

New Orleans, November 1, 1795, Biblioteca Nacional [Madrid], Colección de varios documentos para la historia de Florida y tierras adjuntas, II.

82. Burson, *Stewardship*, 195; Carondelet to Las Casas, No. 690, June 16, 1795, AGI, PC, leg. 1443B; Juan José Andreu Ocariz, *Movimientos rebeldes de los esclaros negros durante el dominio español en Luisiana* (Zaragoza, Spain, 1977), 160–61. For military punishment, see Appendix VII in Derek Noel Kerr, "Petty Felony, Slave Defiance and Frontier Villainy: Crime and Criminal Justice in Spanish Louisiana, 1770–1803" (Ph.D. dissertation, Tulane University, 1983). Although the information in the appendix is incomplete, it provides a good idea of military crimes committed in Louisiana during the Spanish period.

83. Martín Navarro to José de Gálvez, No. 1, September 30, 1779, AGI, PC, leg. 633. This hurricane hit as Governor Gálvez was preparing to lead an assault on British troops in West Florida. It delayed him for several days (Caughey, *Bernardo de Gálvez*, 149–53).

The following year at almost the same time, another hurricane battered the city. The winds began about 11:30 A.M. on August 24 and continued until 3 A.M. the next day, blowing with varied intensity. The storm damaged or destroyed virtually all the structures in New Orleans and the smaller ships on the river. At least ten persons died, and perhaps more perished in the countryside. The city lost its flour supply, the tobacco stored in warehouses, and goods and supplies belonging to merchants. Among other buildings, the military barracks, Royal Hospital, warehouses, and Charity Hospital sustained heavy damage. The government estimated losses in the city at six hundred thousand pesos, a substantial sum for that age.[84]

On August 18 and 19, 1793, a third hurricane slammed into lower Louisiana, bringing more death and destruction. It inflicted serious damage along the river as far north as Baton Rouge. At least twenty-two persons died. Although New Orleans was not as seriously affected as in 1779 and 1780, shipping on the Mississippi, crops, and Fort San Felipe de Placaminas above Balize all sustained heavy damage.[85]

Only a year later, on August 10 and 21, 1794, two smaller hurricanes hit Louisiana, causing less harm than the earlier storms. The first inflicted injury to shipping on the Mississippi, pummeled crops, and soaked the lower province. Before Louisiana recovered, the next hurricane struck with stronger winds and greater rain and flooding.[86] All these storms forced

84. Navarro to José de Gálvez, No. 22, August 29, 1780, AGI, SD, leg. 2586. The hurricane inflicted an estimated 105,596 pesos in damage to houses in New Orleans and 18,549 pesos to housing on plantations near New Orleans (see undated statements in AGI, PC, leg. 113).

85. Carondelet to Las Casas, New Orleans, August 31, 1793, AGI, PC, leg. 1442. In his letter of August 27, 1793, Carondelet told Las Casas that the hurricane of August 18 had sunk four royal galleys and twenty-nine other ships in the river (AGI, PC, leg. 1444). See also two other letters of Carondelet to Las Casas, August 30, 1793, AGI, PC, leg. 1442, for the damage caused by this hurricane.

86. Carondelet to Las Casas, No. 579, New Orleans, August 31, 1794, AGI, PC, leg. 1443A; Din, Canary Islanders, 41. Governor Carondelet did not write about the August 21 hurricane, but no doubt New Orleans again experienced some damage and perhaps even flooding. On August 20, 1794, Carondelet asked for three thousand pesos in assistance to repair the damage done by the August 10 hurricane. On December 25, 1794, Diego de Gardoqui approved the request, and the treasury in New Orleans made the money available in June, 1795 (Francisco Rendón to Carondelet, New Orleans, June 1, 1795, AGI, PC, leg. 31).

the Cabildo to spend scarce funds to repair the damage caused to city property.

The two fires of 1788 and 1794, however, proved to be even more devastating. The first, on March 21, burned 856 buildings or nearly 80 percent of the city. It destroyed businesses, the church and presbytery, the *casa capitular,* the jail, armory, and numerous houses. It spared, however, the Customs House, tobacco warehouses, Government House, Royal Hospital and Charity Hospital, Ursuline Convent, and artillery and customs warehouses. Governor Miró estimated the loss at 2,595,561 pesos. He set up army tents for the homeless and sent ships for food, clothing, and other needed goods. Many homeless people left the city, moving into the countryside temporarily or permanently.[87] Reconstruction went on rapidly after the fire, and by 1791 the governor could boast that much of the city had been rebuilt, except for several major buildings.

A setback, however, occurred on December 8, 1794, when another fire consumed 212 buildings, but at a greater cost than in 1788 because the losses in buildings and contents were higher. They included warehouses, government structures, barracks, stores, and dwellings. Three lives were lost when a military warehouse containing gunpowder exploded killing two soldiers and a carter; theirs were the only deaths. Exacerbating the harm caused by the flames, however, was looting that went on throughout the city. Volunteers used the six municipal fire engines (pumps) to help fight the fire, but they were hindered by low water in the river and wells because it was winter. Governor Carondelet estimated that a third of the city, meaning area not buildings, was destroyed. It again necessitated rebuilding and calling in master craftsmen to provide skills that few people in New Orleans possessed. The artisans who came were exempted from the restriction of not working on Sundays and religious holidays. Carondelet believed that the new buildings should be made of brick, or at least have tile roofs. He also sought special help, lower taxes, loans, and new Cabildo regulations on construction. The regulations were probably not

87. Miró to José de Ezpeleta, New Orleans, April 1 and 13, 1788, AGI, PC, leg. 1394; Coutts, "Martín Navarro," 81; Curtis, *New Orleans,* 70–72. John Pintard says that the 1788 fire reduced New Orleans to 200 homes and that 856 had been burned, which meant that the city had had approximately 1,056 buildings (Pintard, "New Orleans, 1801," 224 and note).

responsible, but the city experienced no further major catastrophe during the remainder of the Spanish period.[88]

Storms and fires attacked primarily property, but diseases snuffed out the lives of New Orleanians. The city was not exempt from their ravages, and the illnesses were little understood in the late eighteenth century. The public possessed some knowledge about smallpox, but the only known method to fight it was isolating the afflicted. Beginning in the 1780s, however, inoculation was also used to contain the disease.[89] Only as the Spanish era in Louisiana ended did a better way to fight the dreaded scourge appear. About 1802 an expedition to vaccinate persons with cowpox went to the Spanish colonies to introduce its use there. Persons in New Orleans had heard of the procedure, but no one knew how to administer it and the cowpox serum was unavailable in Louisiana.

The New Orleans medical community and public knew even less about yellow fever that claimed hundreds of lives in 1796. Among the victims was Governor Carondelet's brother, who was a monk. The Cabildo displayed its ignorance of this malady by paying it almost no attention. Isolation to combat the yellow scourge did not work. The disease claimed more Protestant than Catholic lives, many of them craftsmen who had recently arrived to build or rebuild the city. They generally came from colder climates and were perhaps unaccustomed to mosquito netting that the city residents used. The locals employed the netting to prevent being bitten by the pesky insects and not to fight the disease, whose cause was then unknown. Home remedies to prevent the contagion included the use of garlic, camphor, hartshorn, and vinegar. So many people fled the city in fear, at least temporarily, that it took on a deserted appearance.[90]

88. Carondelet to Las Casas, New Orleans, December 23 and 28, 1794, AGI, PC, leg. 1443A; Gayoso to Carondelet, Natchez, December 25, 1794, AGI, PC, leg. 30; Jack D. L. Holmes, "The 1794 New Orleans Fire: A Case Study of Spanish *Noblesse Oblige,*" *Louisiana Studies,* XV (1976), 21–43.

89. Inoculation was giving healthy individuals the smallpox virus, which usually produced a mild case of the illness and thereafter rendered the persons immune to the disease. See Chapter Ten for more information.

90. Jo Ann Carrigan, "The Pestilence of 1796—New Orleans' First Officially Recorded Yellow Fever Epidemic," *McNeese Review,* XIII (1962), 27–36; Jack D. L. Holmes, "The New Orleans Yellow Fever Epidemic as Seen by the Baron de Pontalba," *Alabama Journal of Medical Sciences,* II (1965), 205–15; King, *New Orleans,* 106. Berquin-Duvallon describes mosquito netting

Despite these afflictions, the importance of New Orleans grew in the Spanish era as more people settled in the Mississippi Valley and economic activity multiplied. By 1803 the city differed vastly from what it had been in 1762. In the early nineteenth century, New Orleans no longer resembled a frontier outpost, searching for identity and isolated from the main channels of trade. Goods now poured in from the United States, England, Spain, France, Mexico, Cuba, and the West Indies. Foodstuffs available in the city varied from basics such as flour, rice, corn, and vegetables to gourmet foods and exotic delicacies. Alcoholic beverages were available, from cheap drinks such as *tafia* and *aguardiente* for the masses, to fine liqueurs, brandy, and choice wines for affluent and cultivated palates. In addition, clothing ranged from sturdy work clothes for simple farmers and slaves to silks, satins, and other expensive cloth for the grandes dames of New Orleans society.[91]

Industry in the city grew markedly in the late Spanish era. Among the enterprises in and around New Orleans were sawmills, distilleries, cordage factories, cotton mills, sugar refineries, and a small rice mill. Ships were sometimes built in New Orleans. The biggest employer in the city outside the government was the harbor, which required numerous stevedores, dock workers, and carters. Many men found work in the boats that carried goods up the Mississippi or on ships that plied the Gulf, the Caribbean, and the Atlantic. Construction in the city employed numerous workers to rebuild after every major disaster as well as to add new facilities. Because many of the city laborers were unskilled, foreign craftsmen often came to perform specialized tasks and teach the locals, mostly through on-the-job training or as apprentices.[92]

Locals also obtained jobs as tailors, cobblers, hairdressers, servants, ven-

as "a veil of linen or muslin . . . which forms a continuous curtain around the bed" (*Vue de la Colonie,* 107).

91. Coutts, "Martín Navarro," 404; Clark, *New Orleans,* 250–51. According to Intendant Navarro in the 1780s, merchants were marking up linens, cottons, and other cloths 40 percent; liqueurs and foodstuffs 60 percent; and high-quality fusils and gunpowder 100 percent. As an example of the imported foodstuffs, in the 1790s Berte Grima, a New Orleans merchant, sent his friend François Valle II in Ste. Genevieve anchovies imported from Europe (Carl J. Ekberg, *Colonial Ste. Genevieve: An Adventure on the Mississippi Frontier* [Gerald, Mo., 1985], 172–73).

92. Clark, *New Orleans,* 269–70.

dors, coachmen, clerks, and in many other occupations. Nevertheless, many of these people in lowly and ill-paid jobs lived miserably. Their crudely built houses in the rear of the city reflected their lowly status. Life in New Orleans was not easy for the lower classes of any color.[93]

As New Orleans struggled to overcome adversity and improve during the Spanish period, American towns on the western frontier, the trans-Appalachian region of the United States, also began growing and experiencing similar problems. Because Americans hungered for western lands and the population of the United States was both large and near, their frontier settlements grew faster than New Orleans had in its first years. Common to all of them, including New Orleans, was a need for economic development. Commerce was the impetus that pushed these western towns to grow and develop. The fur and Indian trade, outfitting settlers moving west, and supplying goods to the army or newly settled farmers were the economic ingredients that expedited urban growth. Other factors, however, were also important. The presence of a navigable stream to ease communications and the development of industry were significant, too. Among the towns that were founded and grew during the Spanish presence in the Mississippi Valley were Pittsburgh, Lexington, Cincinnati, and Louisville. But their important growth came in the nineteenth century after Spain had left the Mississippi Valley.[94]

New Orleans also grew rapidly in the American era, outpacing the western towns founded in the late eighteenth century. For decades, New Orleans remained the only significant city in the deep South. Despite its location in a troublesome site, its presence at the base of the Mississippi Valley made it the natural emporium for a vast hinterland upriver. The growth that New Orleans experienced in the nineteenth century was set in the Spanish period in Louisiana.

93. *Ibid.,* 268. Clark states that the lower classes did not live well. He gives the example of Juan Percetto, a guard at the city prison, who earned 150 pesos yearly, or 12½ pesos monthly. Clark calculated that in 1797 food cost 31 percent of his income and the next year 40 percent. He asks if the remaining 60 percent allowed Percetto enough to pay for clothing, drink, and shelter, and, if he had a family, how did they live? Clark believes that New Orleans had "an economy of scarcity" (*ibid.,* 268–69).

94. Wade, *Urban Frontier,* 7–71; Ray Allen Billington, *Westward Expansion: A History of the American Frontier* (4th ed.; New York, 1974), 239–57.

New Orleans residents who lived through the Spanish era and under the Cabildo's governance must have noticed the major changes that had occurred by 1803. It had grown from a village of three thousand to a city of at least ten thousand and it was ready for further expansion. Louisiana was then quickly developing a plantation economy, and the region's prosperity was burgeoning. Most noticeably, the colony's trade had steadily developed, particularly from the 1780s, and the city's merchants were busier than ever. Cotton and sugarcane became profitable crops in Louisiana in the 1790s, and planters toiled vigorously to increase their production. A discordant note, however, emerged from planters who accused the merchants, who provided credit to many of them, of regulating the prices of the agricultural commodities that they purchased.[95] That practice permitted the merchants, who were the middlemen, to earn more than the planters. Capital formation rested more in the hands of the business community than those of the agriculturalists.

The many economic developments deeply affected municipal government. Residents increasingly expected the city to provide services that would improve the quality of life and protect their property. The Cabildo, consequently, could not ignore problems that vexed the inhabitants such as floods, crime, health, fire hazards, sanitation, streets, drainage, and still more. Starting early in the Spanish era, the Cabildo slowly began to address these matters. Problem solving, however, did not go smoothly because the city sometimes lacked the means to improve conditions, and major disasters exacerbated them.

Nevertheless, city officials learned with time and tried within the framework of their experience, the laws under which they functioned, their fiscal capabilities, and their immediate and distant superior authorities to make life in New Orleans more secure and enjoyable for the inhabitants. The chapters that follow will show how Cabildo officials responded to the demands placed on them and their success or failure in doing so.

95. Clark, *New Orleans*, 269–70; Robertson, ed., *Louisiana Under the Rule*, I, 69; John G. Clark, "The Role of the City Government in the Economic Development of New Orleans: Cabildo and City Council, 1783–1812," in *The Spanish in the Mississippi Valley, 1762–1804*, ed. John Francis McDermott (Urbana, Ill., 1974), 139–40.

TWO

Background to the New Orleans Cabildo

T HE French were the first Europeans to begin settlement in the Mississippi Valley, a region they named Louisiana. From Canada, where they had established themselves in the early seventeenth century, Frenchmen pushed westward along the waterways into the interior, claiming new lands. They soon entered into a rivalry with the English, who also explored westward from their colonies on the North American Atlantic coast.[1]

French interest in midcontinental North America began in earnest when René Robert Cavelier, Sieur de La Salle, attempted to colonize the mouth of the Mississippi River in 1685. France aspired to block English expansion west of the Allegheny Mountains, exploit the precious metals believed to exist in the Mississippi Valley, and trade with the Spaniards and Indians. La Salle, who had explored the mighty Mississippi River in 1682, failed in his colonization attempt when his naval expedition missed the river's mouth and ended in Texas.[2]

Soon, however, other Frenchmen continued his efforts and established

1. On the French in Canada, see two works by W. J. Eccles, *France in America* (New York, 1972), and *The Canadian Frontier, 1534–1760* (New York, 1969).
2. See Henri Folmer, *Franco-Spanish Rivalry in North America, 1524–1763* (Glendale, Calif., 1953), and Robert S. Weddle, *Wilderness Manhunt: The Spanish Search for La Salle* (Austin, 1973).

themselves in Mobile in 1699, before Jean-Baptiste Le Moyne, Sieur de Bienville, founded New Orleans in 1718. That settlement boosted French colonization in lower Louisiana; Frenchmen had begun occupying the Illinois country two decades earlier. But the War of the Spanish Succession, the schemes of Antoine Crozat and John Law, hostile Indians, the large amounts of capital needed, and nature—tremendous distances, harsh terrain, and the lack of adequate harbors and ready wealth—all combined to frustrate French efforts at colonization and development. With the loss of Canada in the Seven Years' War, France willingly ceded Louisiana (the "Isle of Orleans" on which New Orleans rested and the west bank of the Mississippi) to Spain as compensation for inducing the Iberian nation to enter the war as its ally and losing Florida. The belligerent parties signed the preliminary peace treaty at Fountainbleau on November 3, 1762, and ratified the definitive treaty in Paris on February 10, 1763.[3]

As a paternal gesture to his former subjects, Louis XV asked Spain to leave undisturbed in Louisiana, as far as practical, French offices, employment, traditions, legal practices, and land titles. This stipulation, however, was not included in the treaty, and Spain only tacitly agreed not to make immediate changes. It placed the colony under the ministry of state, not the ministry of the Indies. When in September, 1764, the Louisiana inhabitants learned of the province's cession to Spain, which the French government had kept secret, many of the distinguished and influential residents petitioned the king to rescind the act. He, however, had no desire to retain the costly and unproductive colony. But Spain's delay in taking possession kept alive in Louisiana the hope that the transfer might not occur.[4]

3. Eccles, *France in America,* 158–70, 216–17; Herbert Eugene Bolton and Thomas Maitland Marshall, *The Colonization of North America, 1492–1783* (New York, 1920), 96–101; Arthur S. Aiton, "The Diplomacy of the Louisiana Cession," *American Historical Review,* XXXVI (1931), 701–20. The role of Florida in the 1763 treaty is discussed in Robert L. Gold, *Borderland Empires in Transition: The Triple-Nation Transfer of Florida* (Carbondale, Ill., 1969). Marcel Giraud's study *Histoire de la Louisiane française* (5 vols.; Paris, 1953–87), which goes to 1731, is being published in English by Louisiana State University Press. Volumes I, II, and V have already appeared.

4. Eccles, *France in America,* 228–29; Gayarré, *History of Louisiana,* II, 109–12, 126–27, 158; John Preston Moore, *Revolt in Louisiana: The Spanish Occupation, 1766–1770* (Baton Rouge, 1976), 43. Vicente Rodríguez Casado, "O'Reilly en la Luisiana," *Revista de Indias,* II (1943), 117, states that the petition of Louisiana inhabitants to the Superior Council contained 536 signatures.

Following the humiliation Spain received in the Seven Years' War with the British capture of Havana and Manila and the cession of Florida to regain Havana, Spaniards vowed that it would not happen again. Moreover, the entry of the British into the Gulf of Mexico required more fortifications and manpower in Cuba and Mexico. These crucial matters took precedence over occupying Louisiana. In addition, the Spanish court knew literally nothing about the colony and it sought information. Much of its early knowledge came from memoirs written by Jean Pierre Gerald de Vilemont, a French army officer who had spent several years in Louisiana and who was then in Paris. The new Spanish secretary of state, the Marqués de Grimaldi, while ambassador in France had become acquainted with Vilemont and invited him to Madrid in 1764.[5]

Meanwhile, the Spanish government searched for a governor for Louisiana. In January, 1764, it relieved the respected scientist Antonio de Ulloa of his post as superintendent of the Huancavelica mercury mine in Peru. Orders later in the year authorized his departure for Havana, where he was to wait pending further instructions. By February 3, 1765, Ulloa was in Cuba, and in June he learned of his appointment as the first Spanish governor of Louisiana. The government ordered him to wait there for a ship bringing officials, soldiers, and supplies from Spain before proceeding to New Orleans. The ship La Liebre was only then being prepared in El Ferrol. It sailed for Havana in September, arriving two months later. After changing to two smaller vessels, El Volante and El Rey de Prusia, on January 17, 1766, Governor Ulloa, the officials, and the troops proceeded to New Orleans.[6]

When the Spaniards arrived in New Orleans on March 5, 1766, they received a cold and formal reception from the locals. French soldiers, whom the Spaniards had expected to enter their army, refused because

5. Vilemont's memoirs concerning French troops, commerce, religion, and conditions in Louisiana are in AHN, Est., leg. 3882, exped. 12. Vilemont is discussed in Din, *Francisco Bouligny*, 46–48.

6. Moore, *Revolt in Louisiana*, 8–20. See also Arthur Preston Whitaker, "Antonio de Ulloa," *Hispanic American Historical Review*, XV (1935), 155–94. Ulloa's July 10, 1765, letter to the Superior Council of New Orleans communicating news of his appointment is in AGI, SD, leg. 2543, and is translated in Gayarré, *History of Louisiana*, II, 130. Documents on Ulloa's appointment and instructions are in AGI, SD, leg. 2542.

they had been in uniform for too long and were anxious to return home. Ulloa's unwise reduction of pay for Spanish soldiers to match French army wages further discouraged them from joining. Because he had only ninety Spanish soldiers, Ulloa postponed taking formal possession of the colony. Nevertheless, Spain, in the course of the next two years, furnished the funding that paid for Louisiana's administration and, through acting French governor Charles Philippe Aubry, Ulloa in fact administered the colony. Moreover, at Balize and at several new army posts on the Mississippi, the Spaniards raised their flag and showed that they were in charge of the colony.[7] To overcome the shortage of soldiers, Ulloa requested additional troops. The Spanish government responded by slowly sending officers and men in small batches to Havana, where they would form the Fixed Louisiana Infantry Battalion before proceeding to New Orleans.[8]

Ulloa faced difficult issues during his thirty months as governor. The unpleasant reception he received on arriving had disillusioned him. His efforts to redeem the inflated paper money then in circulation had been unappreciated. Moreover, many of the later French accusations against his conduct were spurious and had little to do with real issues. Ulloa's problems in the colony centered on his jurisdictional conflict with the French Superior Council, which represented a privileged group of residents, mainly planters and merchants, who enjoyed economic control of the province. France had exercised little dominion over commerce, permitting these individuals to trade much as they pleased. During Ulloa's governorship, however, they saw power slipping from their grasp because he spurned them. He considered the Superior Council as nothing more than a civil judicial tribunal with no authority in administration. He preferred to deal with French royal officials.[9]

7. Moore, *Revolt in Louisiana,* 42–59, 60–83; J. H. Schlarman, *From Quebec to New Orleans* (Belleville, Ill., 1929), 411. An important reason why Ulloa declined to take formal possession and left Aubry seemingly in charge was that he would lose the French soldiers, who had no desire to serve the Spaniards. Gayarré, in *History of Louisiana,* II, 167, states: "It was further understood that, considering that the French troops refused to obey the Spanish governor, Aubry would remain the apparent and nominal chief of the colony, but would govern according to the dictates of Ulloa."

8. Gilbert C. Din, "Protecting the '*Barreda*': Spain's Defenses in Louisiana, 1763–1779," *LH,* XIX (1978), 184–92.

9. Moore, *Revolt in Louisiana,* 105–107; Gayarré, *History of Louisiana,* II, 181–83, 212. On

The Superior Council, which in the French administrative system was a court, was founded on a permanent basis in 1715. Louisiana's governor and the king's lieutenants were honorific nonvoting members, whereas its working members consisted of the *commissaire-ordonnateur* (commissary), who was the first judge, the attorney general, the chief notary, the councillors, and a *huissier* (bailiff). When in 1731 the Company of the Indies retroceded Louisiana to the king, the administrative Conseil de Régie was abolished and the Superior Council assumed its duties, thus acquiring administrative and legislative roles. In addition, the post of attorney general gained more power over the years in large measure because of two long-term officeholders, François Fleuriau and Jean-Baptiste Raguet. When Nicolas Chauvin de Lafrénière became attorney general in 1763, his charismatic personality catapulted him into the front ranks of leadership in the Superior Council and in the colony.[10]

A clash between the new Spanish governor and the Superior Council was inevitable because Ulloa regarded it as an obstruction to carrying out his duties. He saw its supporters as opportunists who had manipulated the upheavals generated by the Seven Years' War to augment their authority. He refused to countenance any claim by the council that exceeded the powers he believed it should have; to have done otherwise would have diminished his own authority. In January, 1767, Ulloa recommended dissolving the council, citing that the councillors, with the possible exception of Lafrénière, had no training in law and were remiss in attending meetings. Ulloa's reports of opposition to his administration prompted the

---

page 132, Gayarré writes about Ulloa's clash with the Superior Council: "Nothing can be more unforgiving than the wounded pride and self-love of petty functionaries; and there is no doubt but that the cavalier and unconciliating manner in which the members of the Council thought they were treated by Ulloa, was one of the causes of subsequent events." The causes, however, were deeper than this.

10. Jerry A. Micelle, "From Law Court to Local Government: Metamorphosis of the Superior Council of French Louisiana," *LH,* IX (1968), 103–107; Carl A. Brasseaux, *Denis-Nicolas Foucault and the New Orleans Rebellion of 1768* (Ruston, La., 1987), 58–61. See also James D. Hardy, Jr., "The Superior Council in Colonial Louisiana," in *Frenchmen and French Ways in the Mississippi Valley,* ed. John Francis McDermott (Urbana, Ill., 1969), 87–101; Henry P. Dart, "Courts and Law in Colonial Louisiana," *LHQ,* IV (1921), 255–70; and Donald Lemieux, "The Office of Commissaire Ordonnateur in French Louisiana, 1731–1763" (Ph.D. dissertation, Louisiana State University, 1972).

Spanish government to reconsider its initial decision to leave French institutions unchanged. The Marqués de Grimaldi instructed Ulloa on March 22, 1767, to abolish the Superior Council as soon as he completed the transfer of authority.[11]

That same year Ulloa assumed functions that the Superior Council had previously exercised, and by early 1768 he was openly disputing its judicial role. The crown also revised its earlier instructions and ordered the governor to dismiss the Superior Council forthwith. He was to establish a judicial tribunal consisting of an *asesor* (legal adviser), a Spanish *escribano* (scribe or clerk), and a French clerk. The governor would be the chief judge with authority to impose sentences on all persons, Spaniards and non-Spaniards alike. When Ulloa received the instructions, however, he believed that the small tribunal would not work. Instead, he created a larger assembly composed of three Spaniards (Juan José de Loyola, Esteban Gayarré, and José Melchor de Acosta) and four Frenchmen (Francisco María de Reggio, Francisco Olivier de Vezin, Auguste[?] de La Chaise, and [?] Dreux). Contrary to his orders, Ulloa left the Superior Council intact. Sensing that he would soon abolish it, the council resented the intrusive new tribunal. As the latter became involved in dispensing justice, opposition to Spanish rule and to Ulloa's presence mounted.[12]

Public opinion within Louisiana's French and Creole community, however, was not uniform. The lack of a French-appointed governor created what Carl Brasseaux has called a "crisis of authority." The last appointed governor and commissary was Jean-Jacques Blaise d'Abbadie, who died in February, 1765. He was succeeded by Aubry, the senior ranking military officer, as the acting governor and by Denis-Nicolas Foucault as the acting

11. Caughey, *Bernardo de Gálvez,* 31; Gayarré, *History of Louisiana,* II, 262, III, 2; Ulloa to Bucareli, No. 37, New Orleans, August 28, 1767, *SMV,* Pt. I, 32, refers to an order from Grimaldi of May 27, 1767; see also Moore, *Revolt in Louisiana,* 52–53.

12. Bucareli to Ulloa, Havana, June 7, 1768, AGI, PC, leg. 1054; Gayarré, *History of Louisiana,* II, 224–25. A Superior Council letter to the French king, dated November 12, 1768, is in AHN, Est., leg. 3883, exped. 2. Bucareli appointed José Fernández to be the clerk for the Spaniards and the departments of war and the treasury. He went to New Orleans on the ship *La Hermosa Limeña.* Because fees from Spanish legal cases would be small (there were few Spaniards in Louisiana), the government furnished his transportation and house rent, in addition to his yearly salary of six hundred pesos (Ulloa to Bucareli, No. 52, New Orleans, July 20, 1768, *SMV,* Pt. I, 57).

commissary. Inasmuch as Aubry represented the French crown that had ceded Louisiana to Spain, Frenchmen and Creoles hostile to that position viewed him with disdain (an attitude that still has not dissipated in Louisiana). Nevertheless, there were planters, army officers, and other men of substance who bowed before the king's wishes and offered their services to the new monarch and his representatives.[13]

Meanwhile, the Superior Council represented the men who would lose the most with its abolition. They included merchants and planters, who engaged in smuggling, and debtors. They led the opposition against Aubry, who intended to carry out the government's wishes. Chief among them were the Superior Council's attorney general Lafrénière and probably the commissary Foucault, an ex-officio member of the council. Both men enjoyed position and influence.[14] Many of the leaders in opposition to Spanish rule were related to Lafrénière by kinship or marriage, a similarity that characterized the support that caudillos in Spanish America received after independence.[15]

13. Among the residents who took the Spanish side were Jean Trudeau, Laussel, Barthelmy Daniel de Macarty, Hypolite Amelot, Grand-Pré, Philippe Rocheblave, François Fleuriau, Vilard, Molino, Lassias, Gilbert Antoine de St. Maxent, Roche, Chevalier Bellevue, Pierre François Olivier de Vezin, Francisco María de Reggio, Honorato de la Chaisse, and Dreux. Many of them were or had been French army officers. Gayarré, who lists them (in *History of Louisiana,* II, 183), uses only their last names, which leaves identification for some incomplete. Vicente Rodríguez Casado, in *Primeros años de la dominación española* (Madrid, 1942), 161–63, makes it clear that Ulloa wanted to avoid bloodshed. The rebels later used the lack of victims in the coup as a point in their favor. But the decision not to resist, and thus to avoid bloodshed, rested with the legitimate authorities. The rebels probably would have used force had they encountered resistance.

14. Rebels included Balthasar Masan (a retired infantry captain, wealthy planter, and knight of Saint Louis), Pierre Marquis (a Swiss army captain in French service), Jean Baptiste Noyan (a retired infantry captain), Bienville Noyan (a naval lieutenant and nephew of the colony's founder), Julien Jerome Doucet (a distinguished lawyer), Jean and Joseph Milhet, Pierre Caresse, Joseph Petit, Pierre Poupet (the last five all prominent merchants), Pierre Hardy de Boisblanc (a former member of the Superior Council and prominent planter), and Joseph Villere (commandant of the German Coast) (Gayarré, *History of Louisiana,* II, 187). Brasseaux, in *Denis-Nicolas Foucault,* uses French documents to support his contention that Foucault was not a leader in the rebellion. But Foucault's intimate involvement in the revolt was such that other writers, Moore and Rodríguez Casado in particular, have insisted that he was.

15. Brasseaux, *Denis-Nicolas Foucault,* 60–61; Gayarré, *History of Louisiana,* II, 234; Donald E. Worcester and Wendell G. Schaeffer, *The Growth and Culture of Latin America* (New York, 1956), 611. It is possible that some individuals in Louisiana tried to play both sides to gain an

In 1768 the pace of events quickened as the Spanish government pre-pared to assume full direction of the colony. On March 23, the crown canceled the earlier decree of May 6, 1766, that permitted Louisiana to trade with the New World French colonies and French ships to come to New Orleans if they had a passport from the Spanish minister of state. It now restricted the province's commerce to specified Spanish ports and to Spanish ships (Louisiana vessels would be regarded as Spanish). News of this decree generated greater discontent in May, when merchants and planters learned of it; earlier trade regulations and a curb on smuggling had already displeased them.

The summer of 1768 was especially critical as economic conditions worsened. Despite assurances to the contrary, Captain General Antonio María de Bucareli of Cuba sent only part of the royal subsidy to Louisiana, which was already desperately short of specie. Discontent in the colony increased. The disgruntled knew that soldiers were assembling in Havana for duty in Louisiana and that they would have to act quickly if they were to forestall total Spanish control. When, in October, Ulloa published the decree of the previous March manifesting his intention to enforce Spain's restrictive mercantilist laws, they realized the moment to oust the Span-iards had come.[16]

Using the powers accorded by precedence, the conspirators in the Su-perior Council voted on October 29 to expel the governor from the prov-ince. They also employed propaganda to sway public opinion to their side and distorted facts about Spanish intentions. The Superior Council por-trayed itself as the province's guardian against tyrannical Spanish laws. It was especially important to secure support from the French, Acadian, and German farmers because they could give the rebel leadership the man-power needed to overwhelm the loyalist soldiers garrisoned in New Or-leans.[17]

---

advantage. See Ameda Ruth King, "Social and Economic Life in Spanish Louisiana, 1763–1783" (Ph.D. dissertation, University of Illinois, 1931); and Helen Wall, "The Transfer of Louisiana from France to Spain" (M.A. thesis, Louisiana State University, 1960).

16. Moore, *Revolt in Louisiana*, 131–32; Rodríguez Casado, *Primeros años*, 125–26. The March 23, 1768, decree, "Regulation of Louisiana Commerce," is published in *SMV*, Pt. I, 45–50. For 1766, 1767, and 1768, the Spanish government set aside 600,000 pesos for Ulloa's use in Louisiana, but only 319,060 were actually received in New Orleans.

17. Rodríguez Casado, *Primeros años*, 131–36; Moore, *Revolt in Louisiana*, 151–58.

The Superior Council ordered the expulsion of all Spaniards except for the treasury officials, Juan José de Loyola, Martín Navarro, and Esteban Gayarré. The conspirators held them hostage to redeem the bonds and paper money Spanish officials had placed in circulation. The rebels next tried to legitimize their actions by offering command to Aubry, but he refused it. The council wrote several proclamations, aimed at sympathetic ears in France, to win support for their deeds. The conspirators, however, committed a major error in not sending representatives immediately to France to explain their side of the events and to implore the crown to resume control of the colony. By the time their delegates arrived, the Spanish government and Aubry had already notified the French king of the revolt. Louis XV never considered reclaiming Louisiana because it had always been a huge financial liability.[18]

Acting with unaccustomed vigor in April, 1769, Carlos III appointed Lieutenant General Alejandro O'Reilly to proceed immediately to Havana, where he would take charge of the forces to subdue the Louisiana rebels. O'Reilly, a tough-minded Irish-born soldier, had served in the Spanish army since his teens, except for authorized leaves to study the Austrian and French military systems. He had participated in numerous European military campaigns. Following the Seven Years' War, he reorganized the Cuban and Puerto Rican army and militia units. He was then the army's inspector general. The crown expected him to act expeditiously in implementing royal orders in Louisiana. He left Spain from Cádiz in late April and on June 24 reached Havana, where he assumed command of a two-thousand-man force Captain General Bucareli had prepared for him. By July 6, he was prepared to sail for New Orleans.[19]

News of the Spanish convoy's imminent arrival reached New Orleans by late July. It produced consternation among the rebel leaders because

18. There are several studies of the 1768 Louisiana revolt. The most complete are Gayarré, *History of Louisiana*, II, 186–228; Rodríguez Casado, *Primeros años*, 137–72; and Moore, *Revolt in Louisiana*, 143–64. The three rebel delegates sent to France represented the Superior Council, the planters, and the merchants.

19. Rodríguez Casado, "O'Reilly en la Louisiana," 115–38; Bibiano Torres Ramírez, *Alejandro O'Reilly en las Indias* (Seville, 1969), discusses O'Reilly in Cuba, Puerto Rico, and Louisiana. A genealogical examination of O'Reilly is in Eric Beerman, "Un bosquejo biográfico y genealógico del General Alejandro O'Reilly," *Hidalguía: La revista de genealogía, nobleza y armas,* XXIV (1981), 225–44.

the revolt had not gone well. France had rejected their effort to become its vassals again; the English declined to help them; attempts at creating a republic and a bank had both foundered; economic conditions, which precipitated the revolt, had worsened; and in the midst of incompetent administration came news of the powerful Spanish expedition to recover the colony. Few residents had the stomach to fight against overwhelming odds, and, in any case, their self-appointed rulers had disillusioned them. In the face of superior opposition and lack of support (Aubry's forces had increased in strength), the rebel leaders concluded that it was better to temporize, plead innocence, and ask for clemency. Three of them, Lafrénière, Pierre Marquis, and Joseph Milhet, met O'Reilly after his ships entered the Mississippi River at Balize. The general informed them of his determination to use force if needed to regain the colony. But he remained noncommittal about punishment for the rebels and said he would sort out the facts before reaching any decisions.[20]

The Spanish fleet arrived at New Orleans on August 17, and O'Reilly spent the day in preparation for the ceremonies scheduled for the next day. In the late afternoon of August 18, amid thundering cannons and great pageantry, his soldiers disembarked in the square before the New Orleans church, the Place d'Armes, which for the Spanish era became the Plaza de Armas. Aubry, who had earlier conferred with O'Reilly about the wishes of their respective monarchs, formally surrendered the colony to Spain. As the Spanish flag went up, O'Reilly's sentinels assumed posts throughout the city. After a *Te Deum* in the church attended by the leading authorities, the ceremonies ended and the soldiers retired to their barracks.

---

20. Moore, *Revolt in Louisiana,* 165–84; Gayarré, *History of Louisiana,* II, 272–84. See Din, *Francisco Bouligny,* 31–39, for the activities of O'Reilly's adjutant when the expedition first arrived in Louisiana. That the Superior Council governed well in its last years, as pro-French writers have argued, is not supported by the evidence. O'Reilly wrote in 1769: "For many years past there has been the greatest disorder in the administration of justice in this province. It has become nothing but partiality and mere formality. Even when suits between parties have been adjudicated by the council, the decisions have not been carried out" (O'Reilly to Julián de Arriaga, New Orleans, October 17, 1769, *SMV,* Pt. I, 99). Documents in the Rosemonde E. and Emile Kuntz Collection, Howard-Tilton Library, Tulane University, support O'Reilly's charge. Some writers have compared the French Creole revolt in Louisiana to the American Revolution in North America, claiming that it was for freedom. But the analogy is not accurate because independence was not the rebels' first choice.

The Spaniards had effectively taken control of New Orleans and Louisiana.[21]

With the ceremonies completed, O'Reilly quickly sought out information about the revolt and its fomenters. On August 20, he and Aubry discussed the rebel leadership. The Frenchman identified twelve individuals, who were arrested the next day. O'Reilly issued a general pardon to the rest of the inhabitants and invited them to take an oath of loyalty to the Spanish king. The rebel leaders were then tried according to Spanish law. Two months were spent in taking testimony and gathering evidence. Both Spanish and French witnesses gave depositions about events in 1768.

The Spanish prosecutor Félix del Rey, who had accompanied O'Reilly from Havana, presented the government's case. The principal charges against the accused were treason, sedition, writing inflammatory documents, and leading hostile troops, all aimed at expelling Spanish authority. Del Rey argued that Ulloa's governorship had been sufficiently recognized to permit Spanish financing of the colony's administration, issuing Spanish passports, and building and repairing military forts (Ulloa had administered the important areas of treasury, commerce, and war).

The defense of the accused rested on their contention, first, that the colony had never been formally transferred to Spain and, second, that they were subject to French, not Spanish, law because Spanish law had never been instituted. Several of the accused denied the charges against them, but both French and Spanish witnesses implicated them.[22]

O'Reilly received the recommendations from the government prosecutor del Rey on October 20. Four days later he handed down the sentences with the advice given him by Judge Advocate (*auditor de guerra*) Manuel José de Urrutia. Lafrénière, Marquis, Jean Baptiste de Noyan, Pierre Caresse, Milhet, and Joseph Villere (who had already died in prison) were

21. The most detailed description of O'Reilly taking charge is in Gayarré, *History of Louisiana,* II, 295–99; Bouligny's description is in the Kuntz Collection. See also David Ker Texada, "The Administration of Alejandro O'Reilly as Governor of Louisiana, 1769–1770" (Ph.D. dissertation, Louisiana State University, 1968), and Hans W. Baade, "Marriage Contracts in French and Spanish Louisiana: A Study in 'Notarial Jurisprudence,'" *Tulane Law Review,* LIII (1979), 32–36.

22. Discussions of the trials are in Gayarré, *History of Louisiana,* II, 300–338; David Ker Texada, *Alejandro O'Reilly and the New Orleans Rebels* (Lafayette, La., 1970), 36–63; and Rodríguez Casado, *Primeros años,* 328–43.

condemned to death. Others sentenced were Joseph Petit, life imprisonment; Baltasar Mason and Julien Jerome Doucet, ten years imprisonment; Jean Milhet, Pierre Poupet, and Pierre Hardy de Boisblanc, six years imprisonment. O'Reilly banished them from Louisiana forever. The guilty also had their property confiscated except for the dowries of their wives.[23]

Punishment was swiftly carried out. A firing squad executed the condemned in the courtyard of the military barracks the next day. O'Reilly sent the other six prisoners to Havana's Morro Castle for confinement, where they served only a year and a half before being pardoned, with the stipulation that they not return to Louisiana. He also deported the commissary Foucault, who claimed his right as a French official to be tried by a French court. In France, he was arrested, confined in the Bastille for eighteen months, and then released (which coincided with the release of the other prisoners). The general also exiled more than twenty other individuals, most of them for engaging in contraband. He pardoned Denis Braud, the royal printer, who had published the Superior Council's decree expelling Ulloa, inasmuch as he was following the orders of his superiors.[24]

Besides putting down the 1768 rebellion and punishing its leaders, the Spanish crown had charged O'Reilly with choosing the form of government for Louisiana. The general soon began creating the institutions present in other Spanish colonies. He formally abolished the Superior Council, which in reality had ceased to function on his arrival. In the area of municipal government, from the outset he intended to establish a cabildo in New Orleans. The first entry in the book of minutes of the Cabildo (Actas del Cabildo) occurred on August 18, 1769, the day after his arrival in New Orleans, and it contains a description of O'Reilly's assumption of power as the governor and captain general of Louisiana. Scribes (*escribanos*) Francisco Xavier Rodríguez and José Fernández, who accompanied O'Reilly, made the entries because the Cabildo did not then exist. By late September, Joseph Ducros became the first Cabildo official to be mentioned in Spanish documents, serving as *regidor perpetuo* (perpetual councilman) and

23. Gayarré, *History of Louisiana*, II, 336–54; Texada, *Alejandro O'Reilly*, 58–63.

24. Gayarré, *History of Louisiana*, II, 313, 341–43; O'Reilly to Arriaga, No. 3, October 17, 1769, *SMV*, Pt. I, 96–99, 103. Coutts, in "Martín Navarro," 46n, identifies the place of execution as today being a parking lot near the French Market. A plaque located nearby commemorates the event.

depositario general (court custodian) and exercising the judicial functions of his office. Only on October 17 did O'Reilly inform Minister of the Indies Julián de Arriaga of his decision to establish the Spanish legal system and a cabildo for Louisiana.[25]

For several months, no local government had existed in Louisiana. To proceed with creating one, O'Reilly appointed del Rey and Urrutia, lawyers who had been involved in the recent trials, to draw up an abstract of Spanish laws to familiarize the inhabitants with them and another of regulations to govern the municipal council. Acting efficiently, they quickly composed the two documents, which were published in Spanish and French on November 25. Together they received the name "Code O'Reilly." The code acknowledged the extinction of the Superior Council and the creation of the New Orleans Cabildo. Soon after its promulgation, local government again existed in the city, but in a different form because the French superior council and the Spanish cabildo were not similar institutions.[26]

25. Actas del Cabildo, I, 1–2, August 18, 1769. See also Texada, "Alejandro O'Reilly," 130–31; David Knuth Bjork, "The Establishment of Spanish Rule in the Province of Louisiana, 1762–1770" (Ph.D. dissertation, University of California, Berkeley, 1923); Baade, "Marriage Contracts," 50. José Fernández del Campo, whom Bucareli had appointed as clerk of the court of Spaniards, war, and treasury in Louisiana, which the crown established in 1768, worked in New Orleans before the revolt and after the Spanish takeover. But it seems that he did not remain long in Louisiana (Ulloa to Bucareli, No. 52, New Orleans, July 20, 1768, *SMV,* Pt. I, 57; Laura L. Porteous, ed. and trans., "Index to the Spanish Judicial Records of Louisiana," *LHQ,* IV [1922], 147–48).

Cabildo minutes use the word *ayuntamiento* to denote the meetings of the officials and the word *cabildo* for the institution. Both terms were employed in the late eighteenth century. *Cabildo* is often treated as a colonial term for city government in Spanish America while *ayuntamiento* is more common for the national period and is still in use today.

26. O'Reilly formally abolished the Superior Council in the preface to the first of his two November 25, 1769, proclamations, "Ordinances and Instructions of Alexander O'Reilly, November 25, 1769." The second decree is "Instructions as to the manner of instituting suits, civil and criminal, and pronouncing judgments in general, in conformity to laws of the Nueva Recopilación de Castilla, and the Recopilación de las Indias, . . . November 25, 1769," both in French, ed., *Historical Memoirs,* V, 254–88; and in "Establishment of the New Orleans Cabildo," *SMV,* Pt. I, 107–25, which contains the first proclamation. Although the first document states that the French Superior Council was being abolished for its role in the 1768 rebellion, the Spanish crown had ordered its suppression earlier. On February 12, 1770, O'Reilly published additional measures for Spanish rule in Louisiana. They included ordinances for governing the medical establishment, land ordinances, and instructions to post commandants. See the appropriate chapters below for discussions of these measures.

The cabildo, the venerable institution O'Reilly introduced in Louisiana, had had a long history in Spain. Although cities in the Iberian Peninsula date back to the *civitas* of the Roman Empire and even earlier to the Greeks and Carthaginians, there was no continuity in the method of governing from Roman to medieval towns. As cities became more widespread in the Middle Ages, kings endowed them with special charters, giving them a distinct status during the Reconquest against the Moorish invaders of the peninsula. The taxes they paid, the troops they furnished, and the lands they held for Christianity made the towns valuable allies of the Iberian monarchies. Towns also constituted the most important element in the parliaments of the late Middle Ages. The Castilian monarchy, however, began in the fourteenth century to limit their power. In the next century as the Reconquest drew to a close and inspired by absolutism, the Catholic Kings Isabel and Fernando further curbed the strength of rival institutions. Royally appointed *corregidores* sat on municipal councils and soon came to dominate them. The vending of municipal posts that began in the fifteenth century also weakened the councils' strength and independence. Although the crown transferred the cabildo, along with other institutions, to the New World upon the discovery of America, it was patently in decline.[27]

The New World, however, revived the institution. One of the first tasks the Spaniards carried out in the lands they conquered was the establishment of local government. It went on at the same time that royal officials took charge of the new lands. The conquistadores, who seldom retained

27. Richard M. Morse, in "A Prolegomenon to Latin American Urban History," *Hispanic American Historical Review*, LII (1972), 364, points out that Spanish writers such as Eduardo de Hinojosa y Naveros, Claudio Sánchez Albornoz, and others have long argued that there was no institutional continuity between Roman and medieval towns (see, for example, Hinojosa, *Estudios sobre la historia del derecho español* [Madrid, 1903]; Rafael Altamira y Crevea, *Historia de España y de la civilización española* [4 vols.; Barcelona, 1909], II, 60, 64; Manuel Dánvila y Collado, *El poder civil en España* [6 vols.; Madrid, 1885–86], I, 172; Lois K. Dyer, "History of the Cabildo of Mexico City, 1524–1534," *LHQ*, IV [1923], 395–415). But see also John Preston Moore, *The Cabildo in Peru Under the Hapsburgs: A Study in the Origins and Powers of the Town Council of Peru, 1530–1700* (Durham, N.C., 1954), 4–34; C. H. Haring, *The Spanish Empire in America* (New York, 1947), 147–48; William Wheatley Pierson, "Some Reflections on the Cabildo as an Institution," *Hispanic American Historical Review*, V (1925), 575–78; Bailey W. Diffie, *Latin-American Civilization, Colonial Period* (Harrisburg, Pa., 1945), 611; Rafael Altamira, *A History of Spain* (Princeton, N.J., 1949), 311–13.

administrative power after defeating the natives, saw whatever legal authority they possessed arising from the municipal governments they created. Before long the nucleus of Creole strength in colonial government (that of the descendants of the conquistadores) rested in the cabildos. This was in opposition to the highest colonial officials, who were invariably Spanish-born and represented royal interests. The most dynamic era of the cabildos was the first three-quarters of the sixteenth century, after which the crown, intent on centralizing its power, reduced municipal authority to mundane affairs.[28]

Perhaps it was the loss of their military and colonizing functions that diminished the power and prestige of the cabildos in the late sixteenth century. The lack of adequate income and the sale of municipal offices that grew enormously in the seventeenth century sapped the cabildos' ability to govern vigorously. As John H. Parry has written about the sale of city offices, they "undoubtedly contributed to the apathy and incompetence in many of the towns of the Indies." The oligarchy that bought the offices did little to foster good government. In the eighteenth century, the introduction of the office of the intendancy, which exercised wide powers in many areas, further eroded authority, particularly in those cabildos located in cities possessing high-ranking colonial officials.[29]

But this was not uniformly the case. Cabildos in some quarters declined before the introduction of the intendancy, and in others the new office ushered in a resurgency in cabildo activity. It is difficult to generalize about the institution because it differed greatly throughout the Spanish

28. Helen M. Bailey and Abraham P. Nasatir, *Latin America: The Development of Its Civilization* (Englewood Cliffs, N.J., 1960), 96; Charles Gibson, *Spain in America* (New York, 1966), 148–49; Pierson, "Some Reflections," 578–79; F. A. Kirkpatrick, "Municipal Administration in the Spanish Dominions in America," *Transactions of the Royal Historical Society,* 3rd ser., IX (1915), 96–99.

29. Haring, *Spanish Empire in America,* 158; Pierson, "Some Reflections," 587–88; John Preston Moore, *The Cabildo in Peru Under the Bourbons: A Study in the Decline and Resurgence of Local Government in the Audiencia of Lima, 1700–1824* (Durham, N.C., 1966), 244; John Lynch, *Spanish Colonial Administration, 1782–1810: The Intendant System in the Viceroyalty of the Rio de La Plata* (London, 1958), 203–204. See also Lillian Estelle Fisher, *The Intendant System in Spanish America* (Berkeley, 1929); John H. Parry, *The Sale of Public Office in the Spanish Indies Under the Hapsburgs* (Berkeley, 1953); Arthur S. Aiton, "Spanish Colonial Reorganization Under the Family Compact," *Hispanic American Historical Review,* XII (1932), 269–80.

American colonies, sometimes "from period to period and from town to town."[30]

The same was true in the eighteenth-century Spanish Borderlands in North America (the southern fringe of the present United States), where cabildos in Santa Fe, San Antonio, Los Angeles, and San José, for example, were dissimilar. Only San Antonio's cabildo acted independently because military officers controlled the others. But even had a general municipal code existed—which the Spanish crown never issued—local conditions would probably have caused town governments to vary widely throughout the empire. In the late eighteenth century, cabildos declined in some areas of the Spanish Empire and were revitalized in other regions. As Hubert Herring has written about the quality of municipal government in Spanish America: "At their occasional best the *cabildos* were public spirited and honest; at their frequent worst they looted city treasuries and preyed on citizens. Municipal government was seldom more than an indifferent success and reminds us of certain unhappy chapters in the history of New York, Chicago, and San Francisco."[31]

O'Reilly's regulation of November 25, 1769, which the crown confirmed, constitutes the only evidence of a charter for the New Orleans Cabildo. In addition, the Spanish king granted the city special taxing privileges to increase its income and ability to act. These privileges, usu-

30. Lynch, *Spanish Colonial Administration,* 202.

31. John Fisher, "The Intendant System and the Cabildos of Peru, 1784–1810," *Hispanic American Historical Review,* XLIX (1969), 430–53; John Lynch, "Intendants and Cabildos in the Viceroyalty of the Rio de la Plata, 1782–1810," *Hispanic American Historical Review,* XXXV (1955), 337–38; Hubert Herring, *A History of Latin America from Its Beginnings to the Present* (3rd ed.; New York, 1968), 158. For cabildos in the borderlands, see Mattie Austin Hatcher, "The Municipal Government of San Fernando de Bexar, 1730–1800," *Southwestern Historical Quarterly,* VIII (1905), 227–352; Gilbert R. Cruz, *Let There Be Towns: Spanish Municipal Origins in the American Southwest, 1610–1810* (College Station, Tex., 1988); Marc Simmons, *Spanish Government in New Mexico* (Albuquerque, 1968); Florian F. Guest, "Municipal Institutions in Spanish California, 1769–1821" (Ph.D. dissertation, University of California, Los Angeles, 1961). The cities in the Southwest Borderlands, San Antonio, Laredo, Santa Fe, Los Angeles, and San José, all had weakly developed economies and small populations, and therefore these cities and their governments were dissimilar to that of New Orleans. In his concluding chapter, "Spanish Municipalities in North American History," Cruz continues to focus exclusively on the Southwest of what is now the United States because he seems unaware that New Orleans had a Spanish cabildo. See also Weber, *Spanish Frontier,* 322–25.

ally special decrees, reflected the liberal Bourbon reforms then being carried out by Carlos III.

In selecting the *regidores* (councillors) for the Cabildo, O'Reilly chose five of them from among the planters who had sided with Spain in the 1768 rebellion. He believed that government properly belonged to persons of substance who were rooted in the colony, a sentiment later Spanish governors shared. Propertied individuals would govern in the best interests of Louisiana society. French planters remained strongly represented on the Cabildo to the end. Although Spaniards early served on other posts in the Cabildo, mainly as *alcaldes ordinarios* (judges), the first one to become a *regidor* did so only in 1790. O'Reilly gave the sixth *regidor* seat to Denis Braud, who also became the printer for the Spaniards (see Tables 2 and 3, in the following chapter).

In carrying out their duties, the councilmen of the Cabildo generally followed the guidelines laid down in the Code O'Reilly and the Laws of the Indies. Whenever they erred, they obligingly rescinded their ruling. On the occasions when they disregarded a royal decree or the Laws of the Indies, which occurred more often, they justified their actions to the crown. The king then either reprimanded the council for exceeding its authority or enabled it to institute a change.[32]

But in addition to the mistakes that accidentally happened, the New Orleans Cabildo had its faults. The members showed that the council was a human institution replete with human frailties. The people who served on it reflected this in their class attitude and their occasional abuse of authority by taking advantage of situations that came to their attention first.[33]

Another factor that contributed to wrongdoing by the Cabildo was the lack of clear definition in the limits of municipal authority in Spanish America. The New Orleans Cabildo, consequently, often functioned uncertain of its power. This was equally true for the many colonial officials who labored in a system of overlapping jurisdictions. Furthermore, over the course of two hundred years, Spanish American colonial law had be-

32. O'Reilly to Arriaga, No. 16, New Orleans, December 10, 1769, *SMV,* Pt. I, 132–35.
33. Examples of Cabildo members using their offices to their advantage include trying to secure harsher slave laws, borrowing Cabildo endowment money, and overpaying themselves for slaves lost. These issues will be addressed in the chapters that follow.

come ambiguous, conflicting, and obsolete. The crown attempted to correct that condition when it issued the *Recopilación de leyes de los reynos de las Indias* in 1680 and in later revisions. Clarification, however, even in the eighteenth century, came only with an appeal to the crown, which served to emphasize the dependency of colonial government. Nevertheless, within the nebulous realm of ill-defined authority in which it operated, it was possible for the New Orleans Cabildo to exert a degree of power that never existed in the legal codes. Much of its strength, and that of other cabildos, lay more in what it could get by with than in what the law actually prescribed.[34]

34. Haring, *Spanish Empire in America*, 102, states about the *Recopilación* that "contradictions or inconsistencies abound." See also Jo Ann Carrigan, "Commentary," in Alcée Fortier, *A History of Louisiana*, Vol. II, 2nd ed. (Baton Rouge, 1972), 420–27.

THREE

Cabildo Officials and Employees

T HE New Orleans Cabildo or Spanish-style municipal government was a complex organization. The Code O'Reilly, the Laws of
the Indies, and specific royal orders and decrees issued over the
years governed its operations, but they provide an inadequate explanation
of how the Cabildo functioned. Therefore, to understand better how it
worked, the duties and responsibilities of the councillors, officials, and
employees who made up the Cabildo must be examined. According to the
Code O'Reilly, the Cabildo was to "assemble every Friday for the purpose
of deliberating on all that may concern the public welfare." On those
occasions, in conjunction with the governor and within the limits of Spanish law, the Cabildo was to execute and enforce the resolutions or actions
agreed upon. Under the law, the Cabildo's purview included police, taxation, market supervision, public works, health and building regulations,
distribution of lands, and organization of holiday festivities.[1] These numerous duties gave the officials of the city government many responsibilities.

The principal members of the Cabildo consisted of six *regidores perpetuos*
(twelve from 1797), two *alcaldes ordinarios,* a *mayordomo de propios,* a *síndico
procurador general,* and an *escribano.* In addition, the Cabildo had many lesser

---

1. Code O'Reilly, 255; Haring, *Spanish Empire in America,* 156.

TABLE 1

Structure of the Cabildo, According to Rank

Governor or his agent	President, *ex officio*

VOTING MEMBERS OF THE CABILDO
Alcaldes ordinarios

Alcalde de Primer Voto	Annually elected judges who were senior voting
Alcalde de Segundo Voto	members of the council

Regidores perpetuos, with collateral offices by order of rank
   Alférez Real–Royal Standard Bearer
   Alcalde Mayor Provincial–Chief Provincial Magistrate
   Alguacil Mayor–City Magistrate and Warden of the Royal Jail
   Depositario General–Custodian of Properties and Funds
   Receptor de Penas de Cámara–Receiver of Court Fines

Regidores perpetuos sencillos, without collateral offices. Only one present until 1797, when
   six new *regidores* were added, ranked according to seniority.

NONVOTING MEMBERS OF THE CABILDO

Síndico Procurador General and *mayordomo de propios*	Annually elected, both had executive functions
Escribano of the Cabildo	Permanent clerk of the council; also court recorder and registrar of mortgages
Lesser employees	Porters, public crier, public printer, *serenos,* appraisers, interpreters, inspector of weights and measures, jail employees, keeper of fire pumps, etc.
Lesser elective offices	*Alcaldes de Barrio* and syndics of the New Orleans district (*síndicos de distritos*)

officials and employees attached to it. It, however, lacked an American-style mayor or even the official called *alcalde mayor,* often found in many Spanish American municipal governments. The governor, who was the chief executive official in the colony, ex officio also held the post of Cabildo president (see Table 1). Even had an independent executive figure existed in the municipal government, the governor still would have overshadowed him.[2]

The nucleus of the Cabildo rested in its *regidores perpetuos*.[3] Five of the original *regidores* had collateral offices attached to them, which will be explained later. The sixth *regidor* had no collateral office and was called *regidor sencillo* (ordinary councilman). The office of *regidor perpetuo* was permanent, as its title suggests, inheritable, and salable.[4] O'Reilly appointed the first six *regidores* without charging them for their offices and assigned them a salary of one hundred pesos per year.[5] Transfers of the office after 1769, however, were handled differently.

The posts of *regidor* and *escribano* could be sold or assigned under conditions prescribed by law. Because they were salable and their value was expected to appreciate, purchasers paid three fees to the Royal Treasury when the offices were transferred. The first fee was a payment of one-half of the appraised value of the office. Subsequent transfers, however, required paying only one-third of the office's appraised value. In addition, the purchaser or assignee paid the *media anata* (one-half of the first year's salary) to the crown. The third fee consisted of 18 percent of the total cost to pay for transporting the funds to Madrid.[6]

2. The Code O'Reilly contains descriptions of many of the Cabildo offices. To examine how the New Orleans Cabildo differed from cabildos scattered across Spanish America, see Constantino Bayle, *Los cabildos seculares en la América española* (Madrid, 1952). Many offices present in other cabildos were not established in New Orleans.

3. The Spanish term *regidor* is generally used in this book because the English equivalents of commissioner, alderman, and magistrate do not adequately describe the office. In instances where the *regidores* and *alcaldes ordinarios* are treated together as voting members of the council, the terms councillors and councilmen are used interchangeably.

4. The office of *regidor* could not be mortgaged (Actas de Cabildo, III, [2], 10, March 14, 1788).

5. O'Reilly to Arriaga, No. 16, New Orleans, *SMV*, Pt. I, 132–33; Carrigan, "Commentary," 430–31. See the pay records of the *regidores* in AGI, PC, legs. 538B and 566. While the *Recopilación de leyes de los reynos de las Indias* (3 vols.; 1791; facsimile rpr., Madrid, 1942), states in libro II, título 10, ley iiii [*sic*], that the *regidor-alférez real* was to have double the salary of the other *regidores*, the Code O'Reilly states that they were to receive the same amount, which they did.

6. Code O'Reilly, 257; Ronald R. Morazán, "Letters, Petitions, and Decrees of the Cabildo of New Orleans, 1800–1803" (2 vols.; Ph.D. dissertation, Louisiana State University, 1972), I, 155–56. Many historians of Louisiana, critical of the Spanish practice of selling offices, do not appear to understand that most of the purchase price for subsequent sales went to the person vacating the office.

For the transfer of an office to be valid, the assignor needed to live twenty days past the date of the assignment. Within seventy days of the assignment, the assignee had to present himself to the governor with notarized evidence of the assignment and proof that the assignee had survived the requisite twenty days. If the assignee failed to fulfill either of these conditions, the office was declared vacant and reverted to the king's demesne. Furthermore, assignments were not valid unless they were made in favor of men at least twenty-six years old and demonstrably capable of performing the duties of the office.[7]

Once the governor accepted the transfer, the assignee received his seat on the council. He then had five years from the date of his commission to obtain the king's confirmation of his office and present it to the governor. Failure to do so could deprive him of the office.[8]

Despite these instructions about salable offices in the Code O'Reilly, they were not comprehensive. They do not mention that these offices were inheritable, yet on four occasions sons succeeded to their deceased father's post of *regidor* (see Table 2). The heirs paid the usual transfer fees for the office.[9]

If a *regidor* died without an heir or assigning his office, as happened with Antonio Bienvenu in 1772, the office fell vacant and was sold at public auction for the benefit of the Royal Treasury. In the example of Bienvenu, Nicolas Forstall purchased the office of *regidor sencillo* for 800 pesos, plus the standard fees of 173 pesos, 4 reales.[10]

Forstall, who held the post of *regidor* longer than any other man in Spanish Louisiana, was absent from Cabildo meetings on lengthy occasions. In November, 1779, Governor Gálvez appointed him commandant at New Iberia. He served there and later at Opelousas until 1795 without ever renouncing his seat on the Cabildo. He attended meetings only when he happened to be in the city. He received an official appointment to his new post at Opelousas about 1785 but did not leave New Orleans immediately because he was then *alcalde ordinario*. A royal order of September

7. Code O'Reilly, 257.
8. *Ibid.,* 267.
9. The *asientos* (pay records) in AGI, PC, leg. 538B show that sons who inherited their fathers' posts paid the requisite fees.
10. Actas del Cabildo, I, 80–81, June 4, 1772.

TABLE 2

Listing of *Regidores Perpetuos*

Alférez Real	*Alcalde Mayor Provincial*
Francisco María de Reggio	Pedro Francisco Olivier
Appointed December 1, 1769	Appointed December 1, 1769
Died October 7, 1787	Died April 21, 1776
Left post to his son	Left post to his son
Carlos de Reggio	Carlos Honorato Olivier
January 18, 1788	September 6, 1776
Renounced post March 16, 1790	Sold post May 14, 1779
Andrés Almonester y Roxas	Santiago Beauregard
March 18, 1790	May 14, 1779
Died April 26, 1798	Died November, 1779
Left post to his brother-in-law	Post vacant to 1783
Pedro Denis de La Ronde	Luis Toutant Beauregard
June, 1798	May 16, 1783
	Died June 2, 1792
	Post vacant to 1798
	Pedro de La Roche
	February 16, 1798

Alguacil Mayor	*Depositario General*
Carlos Fleurian	Joseph Ducros
December 1, 1769	December 1, 1769
Renounced post to successor	Died July 28, 1786
Francisco Pascalis de la Barre	Left post to his son
December 19, 1777	Rudolfo José Ducros
	November 17, 1786

5, 1787, gave Forstall the right to name a *teniente* (lieutenant) to his seat on the council. He quit attending Cabildo meetings on June 20, 1787, but he did not appoint Carlos de La Chaise as his lieutenant until April 25, 1788, and La Chaise did not present his appointment until March 12, 1790. The council gave him the post the same day. Forstall reclaimed his seat on September 4, 1795.[11]

11. *Ibid.*, III, (1), 4, January 18, 1788, III, (1), 22–23, April 25, 1788, III, (2), 92–93, March 12, 1790, IV, (1), 54, September 4, 1795; [Bernardo de Gálvez] to Bouligny, New Orleans, November 6, 1779, AGI, PC, leg. 600. Forstall's pay record of January 2, 1802, is in AGI, PC, leg. 538B; his badly faded appointment as *regidor* is in AGI, PC, leg. 566.

TABLE 2

(Continued)

Receptor de Penas de Cámara	*Regidor Sencillo*

Dionicio (Denis) Braud
  December 1, 1769
  Abandoned office without resigning,
  April, 1773
  Post sold at auction
Daniel Fagot de La Garcinière
  February 25, 1774
  Sold office November, 1776
Cristobal Galpion
  November 29, 1776
  Sold office
Juan Arnoul
  April 3, 1778
  Died September 3, 1789
  No replacement made
	Antonio Bienvenu
	  December 1, 1769
	  Died December 6, 1771
	  Post sold at auction
	Nicolas Forstall
	  June 4, 1772
	  Frequently absent after November, 1778,
	  except in 1785, when he was *alcalde*
	  ordinario. Crown permitted him to
	  name a temporary replacement.
	Carlos de La Chaise
	  March 12, 1790
	Forstall resumed office on
	  September 4, 1795

Six New *Regidores Sencillos* Added to the New Orleans Cabildo in 1797		

Francisco Riaño
  September 22, 1797
	Luis Darby Danicant
	  September 22, 1797
	  Renounced post April 29,
	  1799
	Gabriel Fonvergne
	  November 22, 1799
		Jaime Jordá
		  September 22, 1797

Gilberto Andry
  September 22, 1797
  Renounced office
  December 17, 1800
Domingo Bouligny
  December 19, 1800
	Joseph Leblanc
	  September 22, 1797
		Juan de Castañedo
		  September 22, 1797

When in 1774 Governor Luis de Unzaga declared Denis Braud's office of *regidor* and *receptor de penas de cámara* (a collateral office) vacant because Braud had departed for France without permission, he followed the same procedure used two years earlier to fill Bienvenu's office. Regidores Reggio and Forstall appraised the office at 1,000 pesos and the public crier announced the forthcoming auction three times. Daniel Fagot de la Garcinière purchased it for 1,202 pesos, plus the standard fees.[12]

More frequently, however, *regidores* disposed of their offices by assigning them to a second party. In these cases, the *regidor* renounced his position in favor of the assignee, contingent upon the king's approval. If the king rejected the transfer, the vacating official's renunciation was automatically withdrawn. The transfer arrangement between the parties was a private matter. The sale price did not affect the office's theoretical value; the new appointee paid fees based on its appraised value.

In instances when a *regidor* was seriously ill and had no son to succeed him, he could renounce his post in favor of a third party to salvage part of his investment for his heirs. Because regulations prescribed that he live for twenty days following his renunciation, it was wise for him to name the assignee and the assignee's succession to the office in his will. This precaution proved unnecessary when de la Garcinière renounced his office in favor of Cristobal Glampion in 1776 because de la Garcinière lived twenty-three days past the date of assignment.[13] Such a bequest, however, appears to have been binding because Andrés Almonester y Roxas left the office of *regidor-alférez real* in 1798 to his brother-in-law, Pedro de La Ronde. Had Almonester not consigned the post to him, La Ronde would have had to buy it at public auction. It saved him two-thirds of the more than two thousand pesos of the post's appraised value.[14]

The office of *regidor* was respected and sought throughout the Spanish period. Its purchase price remained relatively high, even after the Cabildo

12. Porteous, ed. and trans., "Index," *LHQ,* X (1927), 293; Actas del Cabildo, I, 151, February 25, 1774; Caughey, *Bernardo de Gálvez,* 49. For additional information on Denis Braud, see Henry P. Dart, ed., "The Adventures of Denis Braud, First Printer of Louisiana, 1764–1773," trans. Laura L. Porteous, *LHQ,* XIV (1931), 349–84; and Jumonville, "Frenchmen at Heart," 282–85, 289, 291–98.

13. The details of Daniel Fagot de la Garcinière's transfer of the office of *regidor-receptor de penas de cámara* to Cristobal Glampion in 1776 are in the records of Governor Unzaga's court (Porteous, ed. and trans., "Index," *LHQ,* XI [1928], 506–508).

14. Morazán, "Letters," I, 137. Jack D. L. Holmes, in *Gayoso: The Life and Times of a Spanish Governor in the Mississippi Valley, 1789–1799* (Baton Rouge, 1965), 208, states that the transfer of office was made at public auction and cost La Ronde nearly $16,000. The office, however, was not sold at public auction and Holmes mistakenly used one too many zeros.

entered a period of political impotence. After the first sale of the office of *regidor* in 1772 for eight hundred pesos, plus the standard fees, the value of the post grew gradually until the late 1790s. In 1797 the six new seats on the council, all of them *regidores sencillos,* sold for slightly more than sixteen hundred pesos each, plus the standard fees. The following year the office of *regidor-alférez real,* which sold for twelve hundred pesos plus fees in 1791, was valued at more than two thousand pesos. In 1799, after Governor Manuel Gayoso de Lemos' death and the beginning of the Cabildo's battles with civil governor Vidal, the value of the office of *regidor* sank to one thousand pesos. The next year, however, it rebounded to sixteen hundred pesos.[15]

In 1794 the Cabildo requested that the crown create six new *regidor* seats because it was then having difficulty conducting city business. It frequently was unable to muster a quorum. Two of the seats had been vacant for several years and two of the remaining voting members were chronically ill and frequently absent from meetings. Because the council's nominal membership was eight plus the president, five votes were needed to decide an issue. Even without dissenting votes, conducting business was nearly impossible.[16]

Because of seemingly interminable problems, two *regidor* offices were empty for many years. The post of *regidor-receptor de penas de cámara* fell vacant in 1789 on the death of Juan Arnoul. The assignee, Cirilo Arnoul, became involved in litigation with the Royal Treasury, and a question arose as to whether he was old enough to assume the office. The legal problems dragged on for years. In 1800 the Cabildo petitioned the crown for permission to fill the office on a provisional basis, but the Spanish era ended without the matter being resolved. The vacancy in the office of *regidor-alcalde mayor provincial* occurred in June, 1792, on the death of Luis Toutant Beauregard. Because the heirs quarreled over the post, it was not filled until February, 1798.[17]

15. Morazán, "Letters," I, 122–23, II, 8–9. The *regidor* seats having collateral offices were valued more than those without them. The *regidores* with collateral offices, except for the *alférez real,* received fees for their judicial services.

16. Actas del Cabildo, III, (3), 134–35, April 25, 1794, III, (3), 185, December 16, 1794, III, (3), 198–99, January 16, 1795, IV, (3), 229, August 29, 1800.

17. Exped. (e), No. 104, AGI, PC, leg. 700; "Alphabetical and Chronological Digest of

Besides the problems of reduced membership and flagging attendance, the city and the province had grown sufficiently to warrant more *regidores*. Armed with these arguments, the councillors directed a petition through the governor requesting the king to establish six additional *regidor* seats. Two years later, a royal *cédula* approved the request. It instructed the governor to sell the seats at auction to the highest qualified bidders. In the event the public failed to bid, the governor could appoint six persons to serve provisionally.[18]

When the offices were offered at auction, no one bid on them. Six individuals, however, were willing to purchase them for their appraised value of 1,605 pesos, 6 reales, 6⅔ maravedís. With the standard fees, the total cost per seat was approximately 1,921 pesos. The new *regidores* were Francisco Riaño, Luis Darby Danycan, Jaime Jordá, Gilberto Andry, José Leblanc, and Juan de Castañedo. Regidor-Alférez Real Andrés Almonester, however, immediately objected to admitting three of them. He believed that Andry and Leblanc were ineligible because they were army officers on active duty. Their military obligation, he argued, might cause them to be absent and thus was incompatible with their duties as *regidores*. In addition, Almonester claimed that Castañedo was unsuitable because he was already the Cabildo's *mayordomo de propios* and his dual posts would open the door to possible graft. Manuel Serrano led the resistance to Almonester's objections. He was the *alcalde ordinario de primer voto,* a licensed attorney, and assessor to the intendancy. He cited many precedents for admitting the new members. The council accepted Serrano's advice and approved the appointments. Governor Gayoso did the same and issued the new *regidores* their temporary commissions.[19]

---

the Acts and Deliberations of the Cabildo, 1769–1803. A Record of the Spanish Government in New Orleans," in the introduction to the WPA English translation of the Actas del Cabildo on microfilm (hereafter cited as "Digest"), 17, 21.

18. Actas del Cabildo, III, (3), 206–208, February 20, 1795, IV, (2), 11–12, July 28, 1797.

19. *Ibid.,* IV, (2), 38–41, September 22, 1797; Morazán, "Letters," I, 119–23. Andrés Almonester y Roxas was a self-made man and a power in the community. He arrived in New Orleans at age forty-five as an *escribano* with O'Reilly. His post as court clerk allowed him to make shrewd real estate investments. He also rose in offices and in influence. In 1773 he purchased the post of notary public. He did well in his investments and, by the 1780s, was engaging in philanthropic work. In 1789 and 1790 he was elected *alcalde ordinario* of the Cabildo. In 1790 he bought the office of *regidor-alférez real,* the most prestigious seat on the

Despite overwhelming opposition, Almonester continued to object. At his insistence, the Cabildo forwarded all the minutes on this issue to the crown for review. Outraged by Almonester's objections to his eligibility, Castañedo also requested copies of the records of the debate. Because such a request often presupposed a complaint to a higher tribunal, Almonester countered by asking that a statement of Castañedo's fees as *mayordomo* be included in the representation to the king. Castañedo had been charging 5 percent on the monies he managed for the city; the law, however, permitted a fee of only 1.5 percent. The council approved both requests.[20]

The king and the Council of the Indies replied to Almonester's objections with a royal order on July 27, 1799, which arrived in New Orleans in April, 1800. The king declared that admitting military personnel to cabildo offices was clearly within the law. The royal order, however, failed to clarify Castañedo's ability to hold the posts of *mayordomo* and *regidor* concurrently, and he continued to enjoy both.[21]

Besides their duties as councilmen, five of the *regidores* held permanent collateral offices that were attached ex officio to their council seats. Four of the collateral offices, in descending order of precedence, were *alcalde mayor provincial, alguacil mayor, depositario general,* and *receptor de penas de cámara,* which were exclusively judicial in nature. They will be described in Chapter Five. The fifth collateral office, *alférez real* or royal standard-bearer, had primarily administrative functions.

---

council. He also became a militia colonel and the head of the New Orleans militia battalion. Almonester is best remembered for his philanthropic endeavors, paying for the reconstruction of buildings such as the church after the 1788 fire. His civic enterprises earned him membership in the Order of Carlos III, but not respect from the French Creole community. Many of its members saw him as an outsider and envied his wealth and influence. Almonester's power made him a strong voice in the Cabildo (Morazán, "Letters," I, 72–74; and Jack D. L. Holmes, "Andrés Almonester y Roxas: Saint or Scoundrel?" *Louisiana Studies,* VII [1968], 47–64).

20. Actas del Cabildo, IV, (2), 51–52, September 30, 1797. Almonester's actions are significant in that Louisiana historians have emphasized the governor's power to reject prospective purchases of Cabildo offices. There is no evidence that any governor exercised that power. In this case, however, a *regidor* protested admitting three candidates on questionable grounds and obtained a royal review before permanent confirmation was granted. Thus, by implication, it seems the *regidores* shared some of the governor's power to reject candidates.

21. *Ibid.,* IV, (3), 173, May 2, 1800; Morazán, "Letters," I, 122–25. Castañedo later asked the crown to unite his two offices into a single venal office. The crown refused (Morazán, "Letters," II, 145).

The *regidor-alférez real* was the highest-ranking and most prestigious of the *regidores* on the council. After the *alcaldes ordinarios,* he had the first voice in debate and first vote in balloting. The *alférez real* presided at the council's sessions when the governor, his lieutenant, and the two *alcaldes ordinarios* were all absent. He administered the oaths for officeholding in the province, which included newly arriving governors. Whenever the Cabildo received a royal communication, the *alférez real* kissed it and held it above his head as symbolic gestures of the Cabildo's homage and the king's superior authority. He then perused it before the scribe read it to the assembled council. On state occasions, the *alférez real* carried the royal banner, as his title of office suggests. He was also the first supernumerary to fill in for an absent *alcalde ordinario.* If the *alférez real* was absent, the next ranking *regidor,* the *alcalde mayor provincial,* assumed his duties.[22]

Besides the collateral tasks assigned to five *regidor* seats on the council, all the *regidores* shared in performing certain executive and liaison functions for the Cabildo. These duties consisted of serving in the two posts of *comisario anual* (annual commissioner) and *comisario mensual* (monthly commissioner). The first was elective and the *regidores* served in the second by turns, according to rank and seniority.[23]

On the first regular meeting of each year, the councillors elected two *regidores* to serve as *comisarios anuales.* Their duties included ensuring that all of the Cabildo agreements made were carried out fully and faithfully. They were responsible for the formal communications (*oficios*) exchanged between the council and the other colonial administrative organs, which included the governor, the intendant, the church, and the crown. The annual commissioners oversaw major public works projects such as levee repairs, the construction of public buildings, drainage, bridges, lighting, and contracts. They acted as the city's agents in making major purchases. They arranged official Cabildo festivities such as the welcoming of a new governor and public celebrations. Perhaps their most important routine

22. Code O'Reilly, 256–57; Peter Marzahl, "Creoles and Government: The Cabildo of Popayán," *Hispanic American Historical Review,* LIV (1974), 640; Morazán, "Letters," I, xxiv, 134; Actas del Cabildo, I, 271–72, March 12, 1779.

23. Morazán, "Letters," I, xxxiv, 135, II, 8–10.

duty was the periodic auditing of the accounts of Charity Hospital, the parish church, and the city treasury.[24]

Neither law nor custom prescribed the method for the emergency replacement of an absent annual commissioner. When Luis Toutant Beauregard died in 1792 and left the position of annual commissioner vacant, the council elected Regidor Carlos de La Chaise to replace him. On another occasion, when illness prevented Gabriel Fonvergne from fulfilling his duties as annual commissioner in 1800, acting civil governor Vidal replaced him with the ranking *regidor,* Pierre de La Ronde. Evidently, annual commissioners also could be replaced for failure to perform their duties. In 1802 Pierre de La Roche complained that his co-commissioner was frequently absent from the city attending to his sugar plantation. La Roche wanted him replaced because he was not carrying his share of the burden. The Cabildo minutes, however, do not reveal what action the council took in this matter.[25]

The post of monthly commissioner involved executive and liaison duties, but for shorter terms and more routine obligations. He was charged with the enforcement of municipal ordinances and regulations, especially food prices and market conditions. He advised the Cabildo in setting food prices. In cases of violations, he had the power to exact the appropriate fines. He collected market rents and fees and helped to supervise night patrols. His duties frequently caused him to work jointly with the *mayordomo de propios* and the *síndico procurador general.* Assisted by the Cabildo scribe and the town crier, he conducted the public auction of city contracts. As New Orleans grew, his obligations became increasingly numerous and burdensome. They prevented him from performing his duties conscientiously. In July, 1801, on the advice of Governor Manuel Juan de Salcedo, the council appointed two *regidores* to share the duties of the monthly commissioner.[26]

---

24. Actas del Cabildo, I, 241, January 16, 1778, IV, (1), 169, December 2, 1796; Morazán, "Letters," I, xxxiv, 135, II, 8–10.

25. Actas del Cabildo, III, (3), 6, June 22, 1792, IV, (3), 159, March 21, 1800, IV, (4), 200, April 23, 1802; Morazán, "Letters," II, 80.

26. Code O'Reilly, 257; Actas del Cabildo, IV, (2), 75, November 10, 1797, IV, (4), 118, July 24, 1801; Morazán, "Letters," I, xxxiv, 135.

Other than in their capacities as annual or monthly commissioners, the *regidores* rarely acted as individuals on behalf of the council. Those responsibilities fell to elected officers. On the first day of each year the councillors elected four major officers to serve on the council for that year. These offices included two *alcaldes ordinarios* (judges who tried non-*fuero* cases), a *síndico procurador general* (public advocate), and a *mayordomo de propios* (city treasurer or steward). These elective posts could be filled by a simple plurality of the Cabildo's voting members, the *regidores* and the two *alcaldes ordinarios* from the preceding year (see Table 3). For immediate reelection, however, the unanimous vote of the council was required. Otherwise, the officeholders were required to wait two years before they could be reelected. The same two-year waiting period applied to officeholders who were unanimously reelected after they had served their two successive years. This provision, however, was not always observed in the case of the *mayordomo de propios.*[27]

To qualify for election to a Cabildo office, a man had to be at least twenty-six years old and a Catholic who was not a recent convert. Officers of the *real hacienda* (Royal Treasury), persons indebted to the *real hacienda,* and the bondsmen of either were all ineligible. Finally, candidates had to be persons of proven ability and respected in the community.[28]

Besides these general criteria, there were additional qualifications for nominees for *alcalde ordinario.* Only able and informed men were considered. They were required to have a residence in the city and to live there during their tenure of office. All four *regidores* holding collateral judicial posts were ineligible to serve as *alcaldes ordinarios* unless they appointed deputies to perform their regular duties.[29]

The disqualification of Royal Treasury officers, however, at least to serve as *alcalde ordinario,* was honored mainly in the breach. Martín Navarro, Juan Ventura Morales, José de Orue, Joseph Foucher, and Manuel Serrano, all treasury officials, each served one or more terms as *alcalde ordinario.* These open violations of the Code O'Reilly continued until 1797, when the Cabildo elected Serrano as *alcalde ordinario de primer voto* against his

27. Code O'Reilly, 255. *Ordinary,* in "ordinary judges" (*alcaldes ordinarios*), means simply that their courts were not for persons possessing *fueros,* or legal privileges.
28. Code O'Reilly, 255–56.
29. *Ibid.*

TABLE 3

Listing of *Alcaldes Ordinarios*

Alcalde Ordinario de Primer Voto	*Alcalde Ordinario de Segundo Voto*
Elected January 1 of Each Year by the City Council	

1770	Luis de La Chaise	Luis Trudeau
1771	Pedro Chabert	Nicolas Forstall
1772	Hipólito Amelot	Francisco de Villier
1773	Pedro Duplessis	Francisco Doriocourt
1774	Nicolas Forstall	Pedro Chabert
1775	Guy (Guido) Dufossat	Santiago de La Chaise
1776	Pedro Desneville	Santiago Livaudais
1777	Nicolas Forstall	Francisco de Villiery
1778	Martín Navarro	Guy (Guido) Dufossat
1779	Pedro Piernas	Pedro Deverges
1780	Pedro Piernas	Pedro Deverges
1781	Jacinto Panis	Guy (Guido) Dufossat
1782	Jacinto Panis	Guy (Guido) Dufossat
1783	Francisco Le Breton	Juan Morales
1784	Francisco María de Reggio	Esteban Bore
1785	Nicolas Forstall	Renato Hucher de Kernion
1786	Joseph de Orue	Guy (Guido) Dufossat
1787	Pedro Chabert	Carlos de Reggio
1788	Joseph Foucher	Antonio Argote
1789	Joseph de Ortega	Andrés Almonester
1790	Joseph de Ortega	Andrés Almonester
1791	Juan Ventura Morales	Pedro Marigny
1792	Pedro Marigny	José López de la Peña
1793	Manuel Serrano	Nicolas D'Aunoy
1794	Manuel Serrano	Nicolas D'Aunoy
1795	Ignacio de Lovio	José Javier de Pontalba
1796	Manuel Pérez	Carlos de La Chaise
1797	Manuel Serrano	Pedro Marín de Argote
1798	Manuel Serrano (Pedro Denis de La Ronde replaced him September 22, 1798)	Pedro Marín de Argote
1799	Francisco de Riaño	Gabriel Fonvergne
1800	Manuel Pérez	Juan Bautista Poeyfarre
1801	Nicolas Forstall	Francisco Caiserguez
1802	Nicolas Forstall	Francisco Caiserguez
1803	Pablo Lanusse	Francisco Merieult

wish, but acting intendant Morales opposed the election and threatened to place the matter before the king. Serrano then changed his mind and asked the council for a temporary ruling to permit him to serve until the king decided his case. The Cabildo, in danger of being unable to muster a quorum and without the services of the seriously ill Alférez Real Almonester (to serve as *alcalde ordinario* if Serrano resigned), decided to enforce the election and called on Serrano to serve. The council sent the king a representation, justifying its action. The council also attacked Morales for his disrespect to the Cabildo and Serrano. It argued that there were ample precedents for electing treasury officials in spite of the Laws of the Indies. It further explained that pettiness had motivated Morales' complaint because the council had not reelected him *alcalde ordinario de primer voto* in 1797 after he became acting intendant. The councillors asked that Morales apologize to both Serrano and the Cabildo. The minutes do not reveal a royal response, but Serrano served as *alcalde ordinario* in 1797 and 1798.[30]

The Cabildo seems to have applied the prohibition against electing treasury officers only to intendants and acting intendants. Not only was Morales disqualified from reelection in 1797, but Serrano was suspended from his duties as *alcalde ordinario* in 1798 when he served as acting intendant. In this instance, a special Cabildo tribunal headed by Alcalde Mayor Provincial Pierre de La Roche decided that the two offices were incompatible. After suspending Serrano, the tribunal named Alférez Real La Ronde as *alcalde ordinario*.[31]

In the elections on January 1 of each year, the councillors were prohibited from voting for their immediate relatives, step-relations, or in-laws. The presiding officer, whether governor, lieutenant governor, or *alcalde ordinario,* was denied an active voice and vote in these elections as well as any other elections through the year. An exception to the rule, however, permitted the council president to vote to break ties. Once the elections were concluded, a porter informed the governor, who was usually absent on these occasions, of the results. If a councillor objected to any of the candidates, the governor could nullify the election of that officer. After

---

30. Actas del Cabildo, IV, (1), 177–80, January 9, 1797.
31. *Ibid.,* IV, (2), 158, September 22, 1798; Morazán, "Letters," I, 134.

the governor gave his confirmation, the Cabildo porters notified the newly elected members of the results. When summoned, the officers-elect went to the *casa capitular,* took their oaths of office, and assumed their seats on the council.[32]

There is no evidence that any of the governors ever interfered in the Cabildo's annual elections. In fact, the elections were often decided beforehand, and the election day balloting was a formality. Only occasionally were elections contested.[33]

The post of *alcalde ordinario* was a judicial office. The New Orleans Cabildo had two such *alcaldes ordinarios,* who were designated as *alcalde ordinario de primer voto* and *alcalde ordinario de segundo voto,* respectively. They were voting members of the council, and they outranked the *regidores* in authority and prestige. Their judicial responsibilities, however, made it impossible for them to serve as *comisario anual* or *comisario mensual.* In the absence of the governor and his lieutenant, the *alcalde ordinario de primer voto* presided over the Cabildo sessions. The *alcaldes ordinarios* were not salaried, and they collected set fees from the cases they heard in their respective courts.[34]

The other two elected officers of the Cabildo, the *síndico procurador general* and the *mayordomo de propios,* were nonvoting members of the council (see Table 4).[35] Nevertheless, their contributions to the city's administration were of vital importance. Their work is prominent throughout the Cabildo records. In most respects, both posts individually were more important to the city's administration than that of any single *regidor* or *alcalde ordinario.* A description of both offices will help define their duties and explain their roles on the Cabildo.

32. Code O'Reilly, 155–56. See "Digest," 24ff., for the tallies of the annual elections. Although there is no evidence that any governor blocked the election of candidates, Miró and Carondelet cast tie-breaking votes in the elections of 1788 and 1792 respectively (Actas del Cabildo, III, [2], 2, January 1, 1788, III, [2], 163–64, January 1, 1792).

33. Actas del Cabildo, II, 44–45, January 1, 1781, IV, (1), 177, 193, January 9, 1797.

34. Moore, *The Cabildo in Peru Under the Hapsburgs,* 99; Morazán, "Letters," I, xxix–xxxi, II, 6; Code O'Reilly, 259.

35. Actas del Cabildo, I, 64–65, January 1, 1772. Not all cities had a *mayordomo de propios.* In the larger Spanish American municipalities, there were three offices: *mayordomo de la ciudad, mayordomo diputado de propios,* and *tesorero.* Smaller cities, like New Orleans, combined the functions into one office (Bayle, *Los cabildos,* 267).

TABLE 4
Other Elected Officers of the Cabildo

Síndico Procurador General	*Mayordomo de Propios*
Elected January 1 of Each Year by the City Council	

1770	Luis Ranson	Juan Durel
1771	Santiago Beauregard	Juan Durel
1772	Juan Bautista Lacosta	Juan Duforeste
1773	Pedro Deverges	Juan Bautista Garvin
1774	Pedro Deverges	Juan Durel
1775	Santiago Livaudais	Juan Durel
1776	Guillermo Boisseau	Luis Boisdore
1777	Enrique Despres	Luis Boisdore
1778	Juan Lacosta	Luis Boisdore
1779	Manuel Andrés de Armesto	Luis Boisdore
1780	Manuel Andrés de Armesto	Luis Boisdore
1781	Antonio Joseph Azetier	Francisco Blache
1782	Antonio Joseph Azetier	Francisco Blache
1783	Francisco Bernardy	Francisco Blache
1784	Leonardo Mazange	Francisco Blache
1785	Francisco de Riaño	Francisco Blache
1786	Carlos de Reggio	Francisco Blache
1787	Francisco José Dorville	Pedro Bertonier
1788	Antonio Bienvenu (never attended, replaced by his brother Juan, called his "deputy")	Matías Alpuente
1789	Roberto Avant	Matías Alpuente
1790	Roberto Avant	Matías Alpuente
1791	Francisco de Riaño	Matías Alpuente
1792	Juan Bautista Poeyfarré	Miguel Roche y Girona
1793	Juan Bautista Sarpy	Juan de Castañedo
1794	Juan Bautista Sarpy	Juan de Castañedo
1795	Miguel Fortier	Juan de Castañedo
1796	Gabriel Fonvergne	Juan de Castañedo
1797	Beltran Gravier, died in June; Francisco Caiserguez elected on July 7, 1797	Juan de Castañedo
1798	Francisco Caiserguez	Juan de Castañedo
1799	Felix Arnaud (Juan Soulier first refused the office)	Juan de Castañedo
1800	Pedro Dulcido Barran	Juan de Castañedo
1801	Pablo Lanusse	Juan de Castañedo (Juan Bautista Labatut elected first; rejected when he wanted higher fees for the office)
1802	Pablo Lanusse	Juan de Castañedo
1803	Salomon Prevost	Juan de Castañedo

Síndico procurador general has often been mistakenly translated as "attorney general." Although he had certain judicial duties, this official bore no similarity to a public prosecutor, which the term *attorney general* denotes in English. He was not the chief law officer in the colony, and he did not advise the chief executive. Moreover, the office has usually been described solely in terms of the Code O'Reilly.[36]

The *síndico procurador general*'s main function was to protect the public's rights. He was to see that municipal ordinances were strictly observed and the public safeguarded. He was to seek through the courts debts and revenues owed to the city. He was to ensure that Cabildo officers discharged their duties faithfully and that the *depositario general* and the *receptor de penas de cámara* posted sureties for their activities.[37]

Thus the *síndico procurador general* was responsible for detecting and investigating anything that could be construed as a municipal problem. If the problem involved a breach of the laws, he was to take it to the courts, particularly when it concerned an infringement of municipal rights. In other instances, he was empowered to propose solutions to problems. In this capacity, he was the principal initiator of legislation or Cabildo action to assure the protection of the public interest. In cases when another Cabildo member proposed a course of action, the *síndico procurador general* investigated the problem, determined the proposal's legality, assessed its probable effectiveness, and gauged the public's reaction. In these diverse capacities, he was the intermediary between the inhabitants and the local government. As intermediary, he represented public opinion and functioned as the last remnant of direct citizen participation in municipal affairs (excepting the "notables" who participated in the *cabildos abiertos*), a holdover from the more democratic cabildo of an earlier era.[38]

Filling a vacancy in the office of *síndico procurador general* differed from

36. Morazán, "Letters," I, xxxi; Bjork, "Establishment of Spanish Rule," 159. Texada, in "Alejandro O'Reilly," 142, uses the analogy of the Roman tribune to describe the office. The office of *síndico procurador general* did not exist in all cabildos, and it was more common in Spanish America than in Spain. Bayle states that this official could not be a *letrado* (lawyer). See his discussion of the office in *Los cabildos*, 225–51.

37. Code O'Reilly, 265–66.

38. *Ibid.*, 255; Morazán, "Letters," I, xxxi–xxxii. *Cabildos abiertos* were not open to the public but only to "notables," *i.e.*, leading citizens.

filling the post of *alcalde ordinario*. No supernumerary was designated to replace him in case of death, disability, or prolonged absence. In 1788 Juan Bienvenu replaced his deceased brother. The council gave him the title of "assistant to the *síndico procurador general*." It was the only example of a substitute serving in this office.[39]

The office of *síndico procurador general* was potentially the most demanding and challenging position on the Cabildo because its responsibilities were broad and ill-defined. The men who held it were generally able and energetic. In addition to the myriad tasks under their purview, they were the Cabildo officials most likely to come into conflict with the governor or the intendant. These conflicts included controversies over the importation of slaves and the granting of land, particularly near the end of the Spanish era. Despite the demands of the office, the *síndico procurador general* was not paid for his time, trouble, and effort. The rewards of this post were purely honorific.[40]

The office of *mayordomo de propios* was less well defined than that of *síndico procurador general*. The Code O'Reilly devotes only two paragraphs to explaining its duties. It calls for the official to receive and manage municipal funds. He was to keep records of the monies received and the receipts issued. He was to maintain records of all the expenditures made on behalf of the city and to submit his accounts for audit when his year in office expired. He could not lend money to individuals under any circumstance, and the penalty for doing so was prohibition from holding any office.[41]

The Code O'Reilly's brief description of the *mayordomo de propios*'s duties, however, is misleading. He was in many ways the city's chief executive for conducting ordinary business. In this respect, he worked in close cooperation with the annual and monthly commissioners. Although he

39. Actas del Cabildo, III, (2), 17–20, April 4, 1788, III, (3), 87, December 11, 1789, III, (3), 132–33, April 4, 1794, IV, (1), 227, July 7, 1797, IV, (2), 128, May 18, 1798.

40. Code O'Reilly, 285–88. Burson, in *Stewardship*, 15, states that this official was salaried by the crown, but she does not cite her source. The table of fees in the Code O'Reilly does not assign him any compensation; possibly he was covered by the general category of lawyers. Budgets for government expenses also fail to list Cabildo costs beyond the salaries paid to *regidores* (see Nasatir, ed., "Government Employees and Salaries," 885–1040).

41. Code O'Reilly, 266.

lacked detailed instructions for carrying out the duties of his office, he was at the orders of the council in nearly everything that pertained to city finance. As New Orleans grew, its finances became larger and more complex, with additional areas of responsibilities. Most significantly, his office acquired authority over the lighting department and the night watchmen (*serenos*).[42]

Besides the permanent and elective members of the Cabildo, many other employees and lesser elected officials served the city government in various ways. In an administrative sense, the most conspicuous of these functionaries were the *escribanos,* especially the Cabildo *escribano,* and the Cabildo porters. Although not elected and voteless, the Cabildo *escribano* was easily the most important of the council's employees, and he might be considered an honorary officer. He was a notary public, and the terms *notario público* and *escribano* were synonymous in the Cabildo minutes. The office required a royal appointment and, as such, was permanent, inheritable, and venal. The conditions for the transfer of office were the same as those for *regidor*.[43]

The office of *escribano* was both demanding and prestigious. This was particularly true for Louisiana because qualified notaries fluent in both Spanish and French were few. A notarial candidate had to undergo a rigorous examination administered by the judge advocate (*auditor de guerra*). Once he passed it, the candidate paid the requisite fees, registered his rubric (signature with ending flourish), and took the oath of office before the Cabildo. Only then was he admitted to office.[44]

42. Actas del Cabildo, III, (3), 49, February 1, 1793; Morazán, "Letters," I, xxxii–xxxiii; Henry E. Chambers, *A History of Louisiana: Wilderness, Colony, Province, State, People* (3 vols.; Chicago, 1925), I, 300.

43. Code O'Reilly, 258, 267; Moore, *The Cabildo in Peru Under the Hapsburgs,* 68; Morazán, "Letters," I, 20; Porteous, ed. and trans., "Index," *LHQ,* XX (1937), 875–79; Actas del Cabildo, IV, (3), 31, May 17, 1799. Besides the Cabildo notary, there were three other types of *escribano* in the New World: royal or public notary, government notary, and notary for customs, mines, and dispatches. The office of *escribano* was permanent and salable. The officeholder was not elected for five years as some Louisiana historians have stated (Actas del Cabildo, III, [2], 5, February 18, 1788; Code O'Reilly, 267). All of Book V, Title VIII, of the Laws of the Indies is devoted to the duties and privileges of the *escribanos*. For a further analysis of the office in practice, see Janaro Artiles, "The Office of Escribano in Sixteenth Century Havana," *Hispanic American Historical Review,* XLIX (1969), 489–502.

44. Miró to José de Ezpeleta, New Orleans, September 23, 1784, "Dispatches of the Spanish

The notaries public of New Orleans were vital to the legal and economic life of the province. Every sale of slaves and real estate normally
had to be notarized and recorded to be valid; but because notaries were
present only in New Orleans, real estate in rural areas could be transferred
if it was done before two witnesses. Wills, loans of money, betrothals, and
other contracts were also usually executed before a notary public. The New
Orleans notaries had numerous contacts with the Cabildo. Two of them
were court recorders, the Cabildo *escribano* and the royal notary. Other
notaries acted as advocates for laymen before the courts; New Orleans had
few lawyers. Several of the notaries held commissions as *procuradores del
número,* which were additional royal appointments, giving them special
status before the courts. The governor's office and the intendancy employed still other notaries. The qualifications and duties of the *escribanos*
were sufficiently similar that in the absence of one, another could assume
his tasks. Moreover, *escribanos* tended to advance from one notarial position
to another that was more remunerative or prestigious.[45]

The Code O'Reilly described the duties of the Cabildo *escribano.* He
was to preserve the papers of the Cabildo and its proceedings; enter in one
log all the securities and deposits related to the depositary general and in
another log those related to the receiver of fines; record in a third book
guardians and their sureties and the royal patents and commissions; and
preserve the original documents in the Cabildo archives. A fourth book

---

Governors, 1766–1792" (7 vols.; Works Progress Administration), III, (Book XIV), 12; Actas
del Cabildo, II, 4–6, November 26, 1779, IV, (2), 11–12, July 28, 1797; Porteous, ed. and trans.,
"Index," *LHQ,* XX (1937), 875–79. A rubric or paraph was an individual's flourish to his
signature. It was sometimes used as an abbreviated signature.

45. Porteous, ed. and trans., "Index," VIII (1925), 183; Actas del Cabildo, II, 4–6, November
26, 1779, II, 167, April 11, 1783, IV, (4), 194–95, April 2, 1802, IV, (4), 217–18, June 11, 1802.
Hans Baade, in "The Formalities of Private Real Estate Transactions in Spanish America: A
Report of Some Recent Discoveries," *Louisiana Law Review,* XXXVIII (1978), 684–85n, lists
the first two *escribanos* as being Juan Garic and Andrés Almonester y Roxas; a third *escribano*
post for New Orleans was added after 1788. A *cédula* of June 21, 1780, set the number of posts
at two (AGI, PC, leg. 180A). Other persons who exercised Garic's office after he vacated it
were Leonardo Mazange, 1780–82; Fernando Rodríguez, 1782–87; and Pedro Pedesclaux, 1787
to the end of the Spanish era. Almonester's office went to Rafael Perdomo, 1783–90, who lost
it because of usury; Carlos Ximénez then exercised it, 1790–1803. The third *escribano* office
began with Luis Liotau in 1788; it then went to Francisco Broutin, 1790–99; and Narciso
Broutin to the end of the Spanish era.

recorded the Cabildo minutes. Documents were not to be removed from the archives. If judges needed a document, the *escribano* made a copy for them. The Cabildo and government *escribano* was to note at the foot of all documents and copies the fees he had received, under penalty of forfeiting them and incurring a fine. The same official was to enter in a separate book the mortgages upon all contracts and certify at the foot of each deed the mortgage charge under which the sale or obligation was made, according to the law so as to prevent abuses and frauds.[46]

O'Reilly appointed Juan Bautista Garic, former clerk of the Superior Council, to serve as the first Cabildo *escribano*. Garic's knowledge of Louisiana's laws and customs was an important factor in the transition from French to Spanish rule. After ten years, Garic was succeeded in turn by Leonardo Mazange, Fernando Rodríguez, and Pedro Pedesclaux. They recorded many volumes of documents as notaries public: Mazange, 7 volumes; Rodríguez, 14 volumes; and Pedesclaux, who served to 1816, 72 volumes. Ten notaries public in New Orleans between 1764 and 1803 left records in 231 bound volumes, consisting of 220,000 manuscript pages.[47]

The posts of notary public, particularly that of Cabildo *escribano,* were remunerative. As a consequence, their value was greater than that of *regidor*. In 1783 the office of Cabildo *escribano* was valued at three thousand pesos. By 1788 it had risen to four thousand pesos. Although this post did not change hands again in the Spanish regime, the office of royal notary rose to a value of forty-five hundred pesos in the 1790s. These positions were not salaried and enjoyed only the modest fees prescribed by law. Tips, bribes, and peculation probably added to the income of the notaries.[48]

As the population of Louisiana and New Orleans grew, the workload

46. Code O'Reilly, 266–67; Morazán, "Letters," I, 18–20.

47. Carrigan, "Commentary," 423; O'Reilly to Arriaga, Nos. 19 and 16, New Orleans, both December 10, 1769, *SMV,* Pt. I, 127–28 and 133 respectively; Sally Kittredge Reeves, "Spanish Colonial Records of the New Orleans Notarial Archives," Louisiana Library Association *Bulletin,* LV (1992–93), 7, 9. Garic began a notarial practice in New Orleans in 1739. He was a trained lawyer and a doctor of civil and canon law. Earlier he had been an advocate at the *parlement* of Toulouse (Baade, "Marriage Contracts," 13).

48. Porteous, ed. and trans., "Index," *LHQ,* XX (1937), 875–79; Actas del Cabildo, II, 167, April 11, 1783, III, (2), 10, March 14, 1788, III, (2), 110–12, August 20, 1790, III, (3), 172, October 24, 1794; Code O'Reilly, 287.

of the Cabildo *escribano* also swelled. By 1792 Pedro Pedesclaux had hired two clerks to assist him in his tasks. He personally paid for their services and used them as a justification for asking the council to grant him a salary. The Cabildo responded by rewarding its *escribano* a salary of two hundred pesos per year.[49]

The *escribano* was vital to the functioning of the Cabildo. In 1802 the council became paralyzed when it lost its scribe. Dr. Luis Carlos de Jaén, who arrived to conduct Miró's *residencia,* commandeered the services of Pedesclaux. When the council was unable to find a replacement, the members appealed the judge's act to the crown. In their complaint, they insisted that Jaén could have used any of six other *escribanos* residing in New Orleans.[50]

The Cabildo *escribano* held an anomalous position. He was a royal appointee with a permanent commission and, simultaneously, a Cabildo employee. Although he needed the council's permission to take office, once he received royal confirmation the Cabildo could not revoke his appointment. If he was found to be remiss in the performance of his duties, the council could fine him for each infraction. The only known example of Cabildo dissatisfaction with its *escribano* occurred in 1802, when it threatened to prosecute Pedesclaux for dereliction of duty.[51]

The post of porter was the only other regular Cabildo position. From its inception, the council employed two porters to perform numerous menial tasks necessary to its operations. The porters served as gatekeepers, custodians of the *casa capitular,* and messengers. They wore bright and colorful uniforms when they participated in the Cabildo's ceremonial activities. The first porter served as mace bearer on state occasions. In 1786 one of the porters received the chore of cleaning the public market and guarding it at night. The two porters also collected the city taxes on various foodstuffs sold within the city.[52]

49. Actas del Cabildo, III, (3), 16, August 11, 1792. The Code O'Reilly contains a schedule of rates for *escribanos.*
50. Actas del Cabildo, IV, (4), 214, May 21, 1802, IV, (4), 217–18, June 11, 1802, IV, (4), 219–20, June 18, 1802.
51. *Ibid.,* IV, (4), 214, May 21, 1802.
52. *Ibid.,* III, (1), 80, February 17, 1786, III, (1), 105, September 15, 1786, III, (1), 106, October 6, 1786, III, (2), 102, May 14, 1790, IV, (3), 47, July 5, 1799.

The porters were responsible to the Cabildo and were frequently hired and fired. On at least two occasions, they were recruited from the court bailiffs. O'Reilly initially set their salary at five pesos monthly, but by 1771 it was eight pesos. It rose to fifteen pesos by 1781 and to twenty pesos monthly by 1790. Porters earned additional money for extra duties such as carrying the councillors' chairs to and from the cathedral and making minor repairs to the *casa capitular*.[53]

The city employed other full- and part-time personnel in primarily administrative capacities. Among the more noteworthy employees were an inspector of weights and measures, a public printer, and a town crier. Lesser workers were caretakers for the Carondelet Canal, the drawbridge spanning Bayou St. John, and the leper hospital.

In its judicial role, the city employed bailiffs, assistants to the *alguacil mayor,* an overseer of convict labor, and a hangman. The court system also used licensed attorneys to advise the *alcaldes ordinarios* in legal matters. Because of the scarcity of attorneys, the Cabildo certified *procuradores del número* (local solicitors) to argue court cases. On a part-time basis, the Cabildo hired interpreters, appraisers, and surveyors, all primarily for judicial purposes.[54]

The council began electing two groups of judicial officers in the 1790s for less important matters. The *alcaldes de barrio* (ward commissioners) and *síndicos de distrito* (district syndics) were roughly the equivalent of justices of the peace. The *alcaldes de barrio* served in the city and its suburbs, and the *síndicos* worked in the district posts outside of New Orleans. Not as easy to categorize were the *serenos* who were salaried municipal employees with a variety of duties. Although they worked largely in law enforcement as night watchmen, they were under the lighting department, a division of the city treasury.[55]

53. *Ibid.,* I, 6, December 2, 1769, I, 39–40, January 11, 1771, I, 202–203, February 9, 1776, II, 55, May 18, 1781, III, (2), 102, May 14, 1790, III, (2), 35, December 7, 1792, III, (3), 205–206, February 20, 1795, IV, (3), 162, March 21, 1800, IV, (3), 165, April 4, 1800; "Miscellaneous Spanish and French Documents, 1789–1816" (hereafter cited as "Miscellaneous Documents"), trans. for the WPA by Joseph Albert Gutiérrez (4 vols.; N.p., n.d.), III, 3, (unnumbered), July 29, 1791; II, 50, No. 258, December 31, 1800, New Orleans Public Library.

54. The Actas del Cabildo are filled with numerous references to these employees.

55. Bayle, in *Los cabildos,* 173, states that the *alcalde de barrio* was a relatively new office. It was created in Spain in 1768 and in Mexico City in 1782. Therefore, New Orleans was not far behind in establishing it.

The Cabildo also employed persons and businesses on a contractual basis. They included contractors for maintaining the streets and gutters, building and repairing the levees, furnishing the city with meat, and collecting the city's refuse. In emergencies, such as levee breaks, the Cabildo commandeered the labor of free blacks, slaves, and convicts. In these instances, the city paid a small wage and furnished the laborers with food.[56]

The officials and employees described herein composed the structure of municipal government for New Orleans. These brief descriptions of authority, however, tell little about how the New Orleans Cabildo actually functioned. The Cabildo was a governor's council and an agency of local administration. Nearly all of its ordinances concerned the city and its immediate district. The governor possessed the power to limit the Cabildo's authority. He could disapprove a Cabildo resolution simply by withholding his signature from the minutes of the meeting or by a letter explaining his views to the council. Furthermore, the governor had the duty of announcing Cabildo measures to the public, and withholding an announcement was tantamount to a veto. Because of the tendency toward accommodation and consensus rule, that seldom happened until the late 1790s. When it did occur, the crown or other superior authority could still reverse the council. If the governor did not suspend a Cabildo resolution, it was binding until rejected by higher authority outside the province. Moreover, when resolutions did not clash with existing Spanish law, they were not necessarily submitted to higher authority. Even when they were sent to the crown, a decision might be long in arriving, and it might never come. This meant that there existed simultaneously broad legislative decentralization in a theoretically absolutist empire. It created a confusing and sometimes contradictory maze of laws and regulations. The difficulty of unraveling the operations of these regulations, especially in the late Spanish era in Louisiana, might have given substance to the accusations by contemporary foreign observers of excessive legalism and inefficiency.[57]

The regulations and ordinances formed by the New Orleans Cabildo

56. See the appropriate chapters for discussions of these topics.
57. Moore, *The Cabildo in Peru Under the Hapsburgs,* 67; Burson, *Stewardship,* 13–14; Actas del Cabildo, III, (1), 32–33, October 29, 1784, IV, (3), 197–98, July 18, 1800; Morazán, "Letters," I, xlvii, 165–66, 172, 185.

were unlike those of Anglo-American municipalities. They were framed within a tribunal proceeding and carried a force similar to that of a court precedent. Frequently, when a situation arose that called for a council decision in a specific matter related to the welfare of the province, the Cabildo ruled on the case in point and published rules to be observed in future situations. Examples of this occurred when the Cabildo licensed New Orleans' first pharmacist and when it appointed the city's first inspector of weights and measures. Often the council repeated the enactment of legislation to stimulate enforcement.[58]

Although helpful, descriptions and analogies of the Cabildo's activities are inadequate for a full understanding of the institution. The divergence between theory and practice, added to the fact that the Cabildo was an institution in a state of flux, render most generalizations misleading. In essence, the Cabildo was what it did. It was a collage of the services that it provided in the areas of administration and justice through its thirty-four-year history. Consequently, a detailed examination of its functions is required to analyze its operations and place them in the proper perspective.

The question of whether the Cabildo had legislative powers is one that has troubled Louisiana historians, and most of them usually have not credited the Cabildo with these powers. But a few have disagreed. Edwin Davis calls the Cabildo "a quasi-deliberative, -administrative, and -judicial body," and John Clark goes even farther by calling it "a quasi-legislature." Theoretically, the Cabildo was a council for the entire province because it was the only cabildo in Louisiana. Under Spanish law and subject to gubernatorial approval, its powers extended throughout the colony.[59]

But a close examination of the Cabildo's records reveals that it exercised very limited authority outside the city. The only areas where it tried to extend its power were in regulating the slave fund, which applied only to lower Louisiana, and in maintaining the levees above the city to Tchoupitoulas, which is only a short distance outside New Orleans and still within the city district. Governor Miró in 1787 instructed the Natchitoches com-

58. These two examples are discussed in Chapters Eight and Nine, respectively. Only New Orleans had pharmacists.

59. Davis, *Louisiana*, 137; Clark, *New Orleans*, 264; Actas del Cabildo, I, 27–28, July 6, 1770; Carrigan, "Commentary," 422; Holmes, *Gayoso*, 208; John Walton Caughey, "Louisiana Under Spain, 1762–1783" (Ph.D. dissertation, University of California, Berkeley, 1928), 39.

mandant that medical doctors who practiced in that community needed to be licensed in New Orleans, by which he meant the Cabildo, but there is little evidence that this practice was followed. It showed activity in this area only in 1778, when it brought suit against Dr. Francisco La Casa of Natchitoches for practicing medicine without a license, for which it fined him a modest five pesos. Generally, the Cabildo never attempted to act as an executive or legislative body for the entire province. Judges of the Cabildo, the *alcaldes ordinarios,* heard cases that originated throughout the province, and in civil matters, when appeals were made, two *regidores* sat with the *alcalde ordinario* who originally had heard the lawsuit. Thus only in these very limited cases was the Cabildo involved beyond the city.[60]

60. See the appropriate chapters for discussions of these topics.

FOUR

Relations with the Governor, the Intendant, and the Church

T HE cabildo was the basic unit of local self-government in Spanish colonial administration. As we have already seen, it consisted basically of a council supported by a variety of employees. In addition, the cabildo worked closely with other local government officials and agencies. Because Spanish law often failed to specify the duties of government officials and agencies, there frequently was overlapping jurisdiction between administrators and institutions. Though disorderly in appearance, this method served the Spanish crown well because it curbed the power of any individual or agency. This was particularly important in the American colonies, which were separated from Spain by both time and distance (see Figure 1).[1]

Inasmuch as it dealt with local matters, the New Orleans Cabildo ranked near the bottom of Spain's imperial administrative system. Officials superior to the Cabildo in descending order were the king, the first secretary of state, the minister of the Indies, the viceroy of New Spain when

---

1. Most historians of Spanish Louisiana have misunderstood the New Orleans Cabildo as an institution. Exceptions, however, include Carrigan's "Commentary," an excerpt of which was published as "Government in Spanish Louisiana," *Louisiana Studies*, XI (1972), 215–29; Morazán's introduction to "Letters," I, xix–lxi, an excerpt of which was published as "The Cabildo of Spanish New Orleans, 1769–1803: The Collapse of Local Government," *Louisiana Studies*, XII (1973), 591–605; and Texada, "Alejandro O'Reilly."

Bernardo de Gálvez held that post, the captain general of Cuba, and, to a limited extent, the governor and the intendant of Louisiana.[2]

As an agency of local government, the New Orleans Cabildo often reflected the interests and aspirations of Louisiana's Creole elite, particularly the planters. A number of the council members came from the well-to-do and prestigious families of lower Louisiana. Their seats as *regidores* on the council were permanent and hereditary, which further entrenched their power. The authority they enjoyed as councillors generally exceeded that normally allowed by the Laws of the Indies and royal decrees. But because the Cabildo in Louisiana lasted only thirty-four years, the power of hereditary *regidores* did not rival that of the Creole elites in other Spanish American cities, where cabildos had existed for one or two centuries and sometimes longer. With one exception, posts on the New Orleans city council belonged more to individuals than to family dynasties. The exception was the Ducros family, which owned the seat of *regidor-depositario general* throughout the Spanish era. Two persons, however, who almost equaled the Ducros family were Francisco Pascalis de la Barre with twenty-six years and Nicolas Forstall with thirty-one years.[3]

As both a colonial administrative agency responsible to the crown and a local institution representing local interests, the New Orleans Cabildo had dual and potentially conflicting loyalties. In reality, however, the Cabildo usually acted to reconcile imperial policies and local concerns. Its work as a liaison between the various components of colonial government was one of its most positive contributions to the administration of Spanish Louisiana.[4]

2. On Spanish colonial administration, see Duvon Clough Corbitt, "The Administrative System in the Floridas, 1781–1821," *Tequesta,* I (August, 1942), 41–62. The role of intendants in the colonies is ably discussed in Lynch, *Spanish Colonial Administration.* Because of the influence of José de Gálvez, Bernardo de Gálvez acquired the captaincy general of Louisiana and the Floridas almost as his personal possession. When he became viceroy of Mexico, he continued to exercise authority over these areas and the captaincy general of Cuba, which he acquired in 1784. After his death in November, 1786, the provinces returned to their original chain of command, with the captain general of Cuba as the immediate executive over the Louisiana governor.

3. Texada, "Alejandro O'Reilly," 166–67; Marzahl, "Creoles and Government," 638. See also Table 2.

4. Marzahl, in "Creoles and Government," 654–55, analyzes the dual functions of the cabildo of Popayán, Ecuador. His analysis is valid for the New Orleans Cabildo.

Besides the confusion originating from its dual loyalties, the Cabildo contained additional complexities and ambiguities that arose out of its composition and functions. The Cabildo exercised authority in two areas, administration and justice. The council as a body shared administrative duties while several of its members individually served as judges. But because of overlapping authority and the Spanish government's tradition of using administrators as judges, a clear impression of how the Cabildo operated is not immediately apparent.[5] Also disturbing to an understanding of the Cabildo were the occasional conflicts of administrative and judicial authority that erupted between the Cabildo and other local government agencies.

Besides the Cabildo, other important Spanish institutions at the local level included the office of governor, the Royal Treasury or intendancy, and, to a lesser degree, the church. The municipal council's dealings with these institutions varied greatly. Contact with them was official, semi-official, and unofficial, and relations ranged from cordial and cooperative to hostile and obstructive. It is difficult to generalize about these relationships because personalities and circumstances influenced them considerably.[6] Some observations, however, can be made that shed light on the persons and conditions.

The Cabildo's relations with the office of governor were more intimate and complex than with any other office or institution. To understand how the Cabildo functioned, it must be examined against the power of the governor's office. It should be kept in mind, too, that the Cabildo possessed more than a modicum of power in its relationship with the governor (see Table 5).[7]

The governor's military and civil authority in Louisiana has often been

5. Lynch, *Spanish Colonial Administration,* 203, remarks on how confusing it is to persons not familiar with the Spanish system to understand how administrators could also function as judges. Lynch writes: "According to the Spanish tradition of combining judicial and administrative functions in the same office, the *alcalde {mayor}* was both an administrator and a judicial officer of the first instance." Although the New Orleans Cabildo did not have the office of *alcalde mayor,* other *regidores* exercised judicial functions, as we shall see in Chapter Five.

6. Marzahl, "Creoles and Government," 649; Carrigan, "Commentary," 418.

7. Carrigan, "Commentary," 415; Texada, "Alejandro O'Reilly," 129, 133; Chambers, *History of Louisiana,* I, 203.

TABLE 5

Spanish Governors of Louisiana

Governor	Term
Antonio de Ulloa	March 5, 1766–October 29, 1768
Alejandro O'Reilly	August 18, 1769–December 1, 1769[a]
Luis de Unzaga y Amezaga	December 1, 1769–January 1, 1777
Bernardo de Gálvez	January 1, 1777–March 1, 1782[b]
Esteban Miró	March 1, 1782[c]–December 30, 1791
Francisco Luis Hector, Barón de Carondelet	December 30, 1791–August 5, 1797
Manuel Gayoso de Lemos	August 5, 1797–July 18, 1799
Acting military governor	
Colonel Francisco Bouligny	July 18, 1799–September 18, 1799
Marqués de Casa-Calvo	September 18, 1799–July 15, 1801
Acting civil governor	
Nicolás María Vidal	July 18, 1799–July 15, 1801
Manuel Juan de Salcedo	July 15, 1801–November 30, 1803

[a] O'Reilly remained in Louisiana as captain general with authority over the province outside New Orleans and its immediate district. Unzaga assumed authority over all Louisiana when O'Reilly departed about March 1, 1770.

[b] Gálvez was acting governor until August 20, 1779, when he became proprietary governor. From 1780 to early 1782, he was frequently absent and Lieutenant Colonel Pedro Piernas and Martín Navarro exercised the offices of acting military and civil governors respectively.

[c] Miró was acting military and civil governor until December 16, 1785, when he became proprietary governor.

described as virtually absolute, limited only by the crown. This was correct in theory. As the king's agent, the governor represented royal authority, controlled the military establishment because he was always an army officer,[8] and from 1788 to 1794 managed finances as the intendant. He had the power to veto Cabildo resolutions and bar prospective candidates from joining the council. The metropolis expected the governor to administer the colony for its benefit. Because advancement in his career was linked to pleasing his superiors, he naturally responded more to the dictates of imperial policy than to the needs of the colonials.

In reality, however, the governor's power was limited. The law required him to post a three-thousand-peso bond with the council as a guarantee

8. Antonio de Ulloa was, of course, a naval officer, but the Cabildo was not created until after he had left Louisiana.

against malfeasance in office. Upon leaving office, he was subject to a *residencia,* or judicial review of his administration conducted by a royally appointed official. Any inhabitant could then bring charges against him because his office no longer protected him. The knowledge that the governor would have to undergo a *residencia* served as a deterrent to arbitrary action.[9]

There were other checks against the governor's capricious use of power. Although the Cabildo was subordinate to the governor and its correspondence with the crown was normally channeled through his office, the council could communicate directly with the king when circumstances warranted. In addition, the council could send to the crown the records of a dispute with the governor's office. In these cases, the king could reverse the decision of the governor and reprimand him. The threat of an appeal by the Cabildo sometimes made the governor reconsider his conduct.[10]

Another recourse in the Cabildo's arsenal to protect its interests was the employment of *procuradores* (special agents or solicitors) to represent it at the higher tribunals. The Cabildo kept agents at court in Madrid on retainer from 1781 at least until 1800 and at the *audiencia* in Cuba after it was established there.[11]

9. Marzahl, "Creoles and Government," 652. He contends that the governor's theoretically absolute power was a charade and that all parties knew it. Of the three Louisiana governors who underwent a *residencia,* Unzaga's and Carondelet's were mere formalities, and Miró's was conducted after his death. José de Orue, of the accounting office, had accused Miró of irregularities. The *residencia* acquitted him of the charges (Actas del Cabildo, III, [1], 82–83, March 17, 1786, III, [2], 23, May 9, 1788; Fortier, *History of Louisiana,* II, 109, 118; Burson, *Stewardship,* 203, 285–89). Louisiana historians are incorrect when they state that Carondelet's *residencia* found him guilty of executing a slave without waiting for confirmation of the sentence from an appeals court. It was not part of the *residencia,* and he was fined three hundred pesos, not five hundred (see the expediente titled "Sobre la muerte de horca mandada ejectuar en un mulato," in AGI, SD, leg. 2531). Frederick B. Pike, in "The Municipality and the System of Checks and Balances in Spanish American Colonial Administration," *Americas,* XV (1958–59), 139–58, points out that Cabildo officials in sixteenth- and seventeenth-century Spanish America underwent *residencias.* There is no evidence that this occurred in New Orleans.

10. Texada, "Alejandro O'Reilly," 166–67; Marzahl, "Creoles and Government," 638; Actas del Cabildo, III, (1), 46, April 8, 1785, II, 82–89, November 9, 1781. As Thomas Jefferson expressed it, the council had a "right to represent and even remonstrate the Governor, in respect to the interior government of the province" (Thomas Jefferson, "Description of Louisiana," [Preliminary Report to Congress], *American State Papers, Miscellaneous Documents* [Washington, D.C., 1934], I, 353).

11. Actas del Cabildo, II, 73–74, September 14, 1781, III, (1), 140–41, March 23, 1787, IV,

Besides institutional checks on the governor's authority, unofficial controls also existed. For example, the planter elite within the colony exercised considerable influence in economic and social matters. If it felt its interests were threatened, it could close ranks and demonstrate its solidarity through the Cabildo.[12] Although the planters exclusively controlled the Cabildo as *regidores* only from 1773 to 1790, they were still strongly represented during the rest of its history. Their numerical strength on the Cabildo, however, weakened after 1797, when six new *regidor* seats were added, but they still made up approximately half of the councillors.

Although it might appear that the limitations on the governor's power implied ingrained conflict between him and the Cabildo, a closer examination fails to support this assumption. Moreover, rivalries between governors and Cabildo councils tell only part of the story. The governor was a member of the Cabildo, serving ex officio as its president. In addition, the Cabildo acted in an advisory capacity to the governor. Thus the governor and the Cabildo were in the paradoxical position of being simultaneously partners and rivals in governing the city.[13]

The contradictory relationship between the two, however, militated for accommodation, not conflict. Except for the last four years of Spanish rule

---

(3), 24, April 5, 1799, IV, (4), 1, September 19, 1800, IV, (5), 6–7, July 30, 1802, IV, (5), 23–25, October 2, 1802; Morazán, "Letters," II, 159, 161–68.

12. Marzahl, "Creoles and Government," 638; Texada, "Alejandro O'Reilly," 166–67; Carrigan, "Commentary," 422. John G. Clark, in "The Role of the City Government in the Economic Development of New Orleans: Cabildo and City Council, 1783–1812," in *The Spanish in the Mississippi Valley, 1762–1804,* ed. John Francis McDermott (Urbana, Ill., 1974), 139n, argues against Frederick Pike's assertions (in "The Municipality and the System of Checks and Balances," 139–58), that checks and balances gave the cabildo power despite its inferior position against royal officials such as the governor. Pike claims that intervention and overlapping authority permitted the cabildos to fight. Taking a contrary position, Clark states that checks and balances as in Anglo-Saxon institutions could work only if the agencies were coequals constitutionally, an argument that Pike does not employ. Clark is, of course, correct in stating that appeals to higher authority (*i.e.,* the crown) could decide against the cabildo.

13. Marzahl, "Creoles and Government," 652–53. Many Louisiana historians have persisted in comparing the New Orleans Cabildo to the Anglo-American colonial assemblies. In reality, the Cabildo was more analogous to the Anglo-American upper houses or governors' councils than to the assemblies. Because there was no representative provincial assembly in Spanish Louisiana, however, the Cabildo fulfilled some of the functions of both Anglo-American colonial bodies. When a lieutenant governor was available, he sometimes served as president of the Cabildo (Actas del Cabildo, III, [2], 188–91, March 20, 1792).

in Louisiana, cooperation and consensus rule characterized their relations. When sporadic disputes arose, they usually resulted from specific issues or personality clashes, not from a maneuvering for power. When the governor and the council resolved their differences, the spirit of accommodation resumed.[14]

Within the generally prevailing spirit of accommodation, differences existed in the relationship between the Cabildo and the various governors. Understanding these differences is important to grasp the fluctuations in the status and viability of the Cabildo. As Jo Ann Carrigan has observed, "The vigor or debility of the council undoubtedly varied from time to time depending on its working relationship with the individual in the governor's office, on the issues and crises of the time, and on the personalities and interests of the members."[15]

Much of the Cabildo's thirty-four-year history is inextricably woven into its relations with seven of Louisiana's governors.[16] The Ulloa and O'Reilly administrations do not apply here. The Cabildo did not exist in Ulloa's time. Although O'Reilly remained in Louisiana after he established the Cabildo on December 1, 1769, on that same day he installed Unzaga as governor for the government of New Orleans while he, O'Reilly, retained power over the rest of the province until he departed in March, 1770. Therefore, the Cabildo fell to Unzaga's jurisdiction.[17]

As governor, Unzaga assumed a conciliatory stance toward the Creoles. Economic reality forced him to close his eyes to smuggling caused by Spain's restrictive mercantilist laws which O'Reilly had imposed. In confining Louisiana's trade to Spain and Cuba, O'Reilly focused on the ideal

14. Morazán, "Letters," I, xliii–xliv; Robertson, ed., *Louisiana Under the Rule*, I, 176–77. Marzahl, in "Creoles and Government," 650–54, makes a similar observation regarding the Popayán cabildo.

15. Carrigan, "Commentary," 418.

16. Included as one of the seven governors is acting civil governor Nicolás María Vidal, who dealt with the Cabildo, and omitted is the acting military governor, the Marqués de Casa-Calvo, who did not. Biographical sketches of Louisiana's Spanish governors, excepting Vidal, are in Joseph G. Dawson III, ed., *The Louisiana Governors: From Iberville to Edwards* (Baton Rouge, 1990). An uncritical sketch of Vidal is in Jack D. L. Holmes, "Dramatis Personae in Spanish Louisiana," *Louisiana Studies*, VI (1967), 152–55. Holmes fails to mention any of Vidal's relations with the Cabildo.

17. O'Reilly to Arriaga, No. 16, New Orleans, December 10, 1769, *SMV*, Pt. I, 132.

of mercantilist theory while stubbornly ignoring reality. Perhaps because of his tolerant administration, Governor Unzaga had no major conflicts with the Cabildo. His marriage into the Creole elite also helped him win local support. His bride, Marie Elizabeth de St. Maxent, was the daughter of the wealthy pro-Spanish merchant Gilbert Antoine de St. Maxent.[18]

The next two governors, Bernardo de Gálvez and Esteban Miró, also married daughters of the Creole elite, but each of them had more than an occasional flare-up in their relations with the Cabildo. Gálvez, whose uncle José de Gálvez was the minister of the Indies, was proud, ambitious, and power-hungry. Ruffled at the council's growing spirit of independence, he reprimanded it several times. Perhaps influenced by his father-in-law, the same St. Maxent who was Unzaga's father-in-law, in 1778 Gálvez and the planters tried to use the Cabildo to scrap Spanish slave laws and reintroduce the French Code Noir. The scheme did not work because Gálvez had a falling-out with the Cabildo and the Spanish government was against it. By 1782 Gálvez lost interest in Louisiana affairs. It was about then that his father-in-law, made lieutenant governor to trade with the Indians, a potentially lucrative post, was accused of smuggling and suspended from office.[19]

18. Caughey, *Bernardo de Gálvez,* 43; James Julian Coleman, Jr., *Gilbert Antoine de St. Maxent: The Spanish-Frenchman of New Orleans* (New Orleans, 1968), 52, is a sympathetic biography. See also Ramón Ezquerra Abadía, "Un patricio colonial: Gilberto de Saint-Maxent, teniente gobernador de Luisiana," *Revista de Indias,* XI (1950), 97–170; and Eric Beerman, "The French Ancestors of Felicité de St. Maxent," *Revue Louisiane/Louisiana Review,* VI (1977), 69–75. For a sketch of Unzaga, see Light Townsend Cummins, "Luis de Unzaga y Amezaga, Colonial Governor, 1770–1777," in *The Louisiana Governors: From Iberville to Edwards,* ed. Joseph G. Dawson III (Baton Rouge, 1990), 52–56.

19. Caughey, *Bernardo de Gálvez,* 84; Coleman, *Gilbert Antoine de St. Maxent,* 52–53. Gálvez married Marie Felicité de St. Maxent and Miró wedded Céléste Elenore de Macarty, daughter of a New Orleans merchant and planter. Carrigan stresses the importance of these marriages between Spanish officials and Creole families for establishing the patterns of social, political, and economic influence in the colony ("Commentary," 346. See also Burson, *Stewardship,* 14; Marzahl, "Creoles and Government," 653–54; Actas del Cabildo, II, 147–49, December 13, 1782, and II, 158, January 31, 1783). Probably unknown to the Cabildo, however, was Gálvez' private letter to his uncle José de Gálvez, minister of the Indies, in which he accused it of ingratitude and promised to send more information about the unappreciative persons in the Cabildo. It seems to have been a contrived accusation, and Gálvez did not pursue it because he had no evidence. The war that began a few months later appears to have diverted his attention (Gilbert C. Din's unpublished paper "The Gálvez-Bouligny Affair Revisited" in his possession).

As the acting governor from 1782 to 1785 for the absent Gálvez, Miró encountered a Cabildo that was attempting to gain a sense of identity and direction. But its effort to widen its powers placed the Cabildo on a collision course with the governor, who took his duties seriously. Conflict on specific issues in the early 1780s, however, never impaired the ability of the governor and the Cabildo to cooperate in other areas. By 1784 relations between Miró and the council had become harmonious, and by 1788 they were so amicable that the councillors requested the king to create a separate captaincy general for Louisiana and West Florida, which had existed under Bernardo de Gálvez, with Miró at its head. Although the request was denied by the government, it revealed the spirit of accommodation that had developed. After the clash with the governor had passed, the Cabildo reached the apex of its prestige and effectiveness during the remainder of Miró's tenure.[20]

When Francisco Luis Héctor, Barón de Carondelet, became governor at the end of 1791, the relationship between the Cabildo and the governor took a new turn. His governorship faced threats of external invasion and internal disorder, particularly after the outbreak of the Haitian revolution in 1791 and war in Europe two years later. Outgoing Governor General Miró and the governor of Natchez, Manuel Gayoso de Lemos, briefed incoming Governor General Carondelet about the dangers and the need to improve defenses. The baron, an energetic man who was perhaps frightened by the reports of Miró and Gayoso, immediately began strengthening forts, restructuring the militia, and requesting reinforcements. He also sought to centralize his authority in the province. Occasionally, his brother-in-law, Captain General Luis de Las Casas of Cuba, helped him. Carondelet regarded a strong governorship as imperative to counter threats of foreign invasion, Jacobin conspiracies, and slave revolts. As an administrator, he cooperated with the Cabildo much of the time, but when the council dawdled, he seized the initiative. Overall, Carondelet's aggres-

20. Burson, *Stewardship,* 15, 188; Clark, *New Orleans,* 264; Miró to Domingo Cabello, New Orleans, July 15, 1789, in "Dispatches of the Spanish Governors of Louisiana, 1766–1792," IV (XVII), 66; Actas del Cabildo, III, (2), 48, January 23, 1789. The issue of a separate captaincy general for Louisiana is discussed in Juan José Andreu Ocariz, "Los intentos de separación de la capitanía general de Luisiana de la de Cuba," *Estudios* (Universidad de Zaragoza), No. 78 (1978), 397–431.

siveness did not alienate the councillors, and his effectiveness often made them yield to his leadership. Part of the reason for permitting Carondelet to have his way stemmed from two vacant *regidor* seats and the frequent absence of sick *regidores,* both of which weakened the Cabildo's ability to act independently.[21]

Manuel Gayoso's two-year governorship (1797–1799) proved less effective than Carondelet's because of his brief tenure and troubles with acting intendant Juan Ventura Morales. Although Gayoso's relationship with the Cabildo was cordial, by 1797 the council's authority had already declined significantly, mostly because of poor attendance. That same year, the number of *regidores* grew from five to eleven permanent members. The increase diminished solidarity among the members because the new *regidores* came from varied backgrounds. Loyalty to the Spanish regime, however, was a prime ingredient among the new members because they were either Spaniards or Frenchmen and Creoles who identified closely with the Spanish government.[22]

With Gayoso's premature death, Nicolás María Vidal, the colony's judge advocate (*auditor de guerra*) and lieutenant governor, became the acting civil governor (the acting military governorship fell first to Francisco Bouligny, then to the Marqués de Casa-Calvo). Under Vidal the spirit of accommodation and goodwill between the governor and council ended abruptly. In the turmoil that followed, Vidal had the advantage of a near

21. Ramón Ezquerra Abadía, "Un presupuesto americano; el del cabildo de Nueva Orleans al terminar la soberanía española," *Anuario de estudios americanos,* V (1948), 681; Burson, *Stewardship,* 15; René J. Le Gardeur, Jr., and Henry C. Pitot, "An Unpublished Memoir of Spanish Louisiana, 1796–1802," in *Frenchmen and French Ways in the Mississippi Valley,* ed. John Francis McDermott (Urbana, Ill., 1969), 77; Actas del Cabildo, III, (3), 139–40, May 16, 1794; Stanley C. Arthur's introduction to "Dispatches of the Spanish Governors of Louisiana: Messages of Francisco Luis Hector, El Baron de Carondelet," I (I), (n.p.).

Carondelet was criticized for his tendency to overreact when invasion threatened or an emergency arose (see Abraham P. Nasatir, ed., *Spanish War Vessels on the Mississippi, 1792–1796* [New Haven, 1968], 29; and Carl A. Brasseaux, "François-Louis Hector, Baron de Carondelet et Noyelles," in *The Louisiana Governors: From Iberville to Edwards,* ed. Joseph G. Dawson III [Baton Rouge, 1990], 64–69).

22. Robin, *Voyage to Louisiana,* 95; Le Gardeur and Pitot, "Unpublished Memoir," 77–78; Ezquerra Abadía, "Un presupuesto americano," 684; Morazán, "Letters," I, lviii. The reason for only five and then eleven *regidor* seats was that the *regidor-receptor de penas de cámara* died in 1789 and was not replaced.

monopoly on legal expertise and seven years of experience under Carondelet and Gayoso in dealing with the Cabildo. Moreover, he appears not to have been subject to the checks that applied to royally appointed governors. The only recourse available to the Cabildo in dealing with him was obstruction as it fought to preserve its prerogatives.[23]

The knowledge that Vidal's post was temporary pending the arrival of a new governor might have encouraged the councillors to fight him. Unfortunately, when Manuel Juan de Salcedo, a fifty-eight-year-old army colonel and former *teniente del rey* (military commandant) of Santa Cruz de Tenerife, appeared in mid-1801, relations worsened. Vidal's role as the governor's legal counsel no doubt contributed to the continuing bad feelings. Besides serious points of conflict such as smallpox immunization and the renewal of slave importations, the council and Salcedo bickered over protocol and minutiae. Although an inferior administrator, Salcedo usually obtained his way, and the Cabildo continued its obstructionist tactics and appeals to the crown.[24] The Spanish period in Louisiana ended on this dismal note with the governor dominant and the Cabildo subordinate.

The Cabildo's problems with Vidal and Salcedo might have stemmed from Vidal's knowledge that in much of Spanish America cabildos were relatively powerless and financially poor. Once in Louisiana, he asserted himself to gain whatever power he could and enhance his prestige. Success came on Gayoso's death, and it continued under Salcedo, whom Vidal apparently manipulated.[25]

The Cabildo's relationship with the intendancy was both meaningful and unclear. The connection was close because the intendancy included the Royal Treasury, and Louisiana, an impoverished colony, depended upon royal subsidies. Several factors muddled the Cabildo's relationship with the intendancy. The intendancy was a new department in the Spanish colonial system, and it underwent several important changes during its presence in Louisiana. Between 1788 and 1794, the governor was also the intendant. Later, acting intendant Morales blocked many Cabildo initia-

---

23. Morazán, "Letters," I, xliv; Marzahl, "Creoles and Government," 655; Actas del Cabildo," III, (2), 188–89, March 20, 1792.

24. Morazán, "Letters," I, li–lii.

25. Din, *Francisco Bouligny*, 188–91, 199–200; Lynch, *Spanish Colonial Administration*, 204–205.

tives. Overall, however, it is difficult to generalize about the Cabildo's dealings with the intendancy. Available information permits only sketching their relationship (see Table 6).[26]

The office of intendant, which was created in Louisiana in 1780, combined the two types of Spanish intendants of the eighteenth century, army intendant and provincial intendant. Louisiana's provincial budget went overwhelmingly to the military. Moreover, the army ran the province, and every governor from 1769 was an army officer. The governor's primary responsibility was defense and conservation of the province. Martín Navarro was the first man to hold the post of intendant, although a subordinate office had existed since 1766 under several treasury officials (Juan José de Loyola, Esteban Gayarré, and Navarro). As a conscientious public servant, Navarro was deeply interested in promoting economic growth, which would provide badly needed revenue to help offset the tremendous expense of retaining Louisiana. Accordingly, he periodically sent reports to Madrid on how best to foster development.[27]

Upon Navarro's retirement in 1788, the intendancy was united with the governor's office, where it remained until 1794. Francisco Rendón held the office between 1794 and 1796. Juan Ventura Morales and Manuel Serrano served as acting intendants from 1796 to 1799. Ramón de López y Ángulo then held the office until 1801, when Morales again became interim intendant to the end of the Spanish era.[28]

The tie between the Cabildo and the intendancy was primarily financial. In times of distress, the city treasury and the Royal Treasury loaned each other money, and the loans occasionally amounted to substantial sums. Treasury department officers also reviewed the audits of the city's treasury revenue, which the Cabildo annual commissioners carried out,

26. The only study thus far of the intendancy in Spanish Louisiana is Coutt's "Martín Navarro." For a general study of the office of the intendancy, see Gisela Morazzani de Pérez Enciso, *La intendencia en España y América* (Caracas, 1966).

27. See Coutts, "Martín Navarro," for his efforts to develop the colony. Among Navarro's reports is his "Political Reflections on the Actual State of Louisiana," in Robertson, ed., *Louisiana Under the Rule*, I, 237–61. Although dated 1785, the correct date is 1780.

28. Morazán, "Letters," I, 152–53. On the office of intendant, see Henry D. Dart, "Fisher's *The Intendant System in Spanish America*," *LHQ*, XIII (1930), 304, which reviews Lillian E. Fisher's book; and Lynch, *Spanish Colonial Administration*.

TABLE 6

Spanish Intendants of Louisiana

Intendant	Term
[Juan José de Loyola, Esteban Gayarré, Martin Navarro, and Governors Luis de Unzaga and Bernardo de Gálvez exercised functions of the office of intendant before it was created. Navarro became interim intendant in 1779.]	1766–1780
Martin Navarro	December 9, 1780[a]–May 10, 1788
Governor Esteban Miró[b]	May 10, 1788–December 30, 1791
Governor Carondelet	December 30, 1791–1794
Francisco Rendón	1794–1796
Juan Ventura Morales[c]	1796–1799
Ramón López y Angulo	1799–1801
Juan Ventura Morales	1801–November 30, 1803

[a] Navarro became proprietary intendant on this date.

[b] The offices of governor and intendant were united from 1788 to 1794, when Francisco Rendón, who was appointed intendant in 1793, arrived.

[c] Manuel Serrano, legal adviser to the intendancy, served briefly as intendant in the absence of Morales during this time.

and forwarded the audits to Havana's Junta Superior de Hacienda (Superior Treasury Junta) for a final review.[29]

The Cabildo's judicial ties to the intendancy were significant. Jurisdictional disputes occurred between the courts of the two institutions. The municipal courts and the Royal Treasury shared the fines for certain offenses, and the revenue from fines above the costs of operating the courts reverted to the Royal Treasury. The intendancy's *asesor* (assessor or legal adviser), who was a trained lawyer, frequently served as adviser to the Cabildo courts. At times, members of the intendant's staff were elected to the Cabildo post of *alcalde ordinario*.

Perhaps the most important tie between the Cabildo and the intendancy was as liaison in coordinating royal and municipal financial policies and assisting the inhabitants in a variety of ways. In August, 1780, after a devastating hurricane, Intendant Navarro furnished relief to needy individuals. Following the catastrophic New Orleans fires of 1788 and 1794,

29. Code O'Reilly, 257; Morazán, "Letters," I, xxxiii.

the intendancy and the Cabildo cooperated in helping afflicted citizens. The Cabildo also asked the crown for liberal commercial regulations and to withdraw the paper money from circulation. These requests went through the proper channels, and the intendancy's support aided in securing royal approval.[30]

The city treasury and the Royal Treasury also cooperated in the area of taxation. The intendancy collected customs duties for the port of New Orleans for the crown. In 1769 O'Reilly granted the municipal government the revenue generated from imported liquors. Thereafter the Cabildo and the intendancy worked together in collecting these duties, as they did when the flour tax was imposed near the end of the Spanish period.[31]

The Cabildo and the intendancy also converged in areas not immediately related to finances. When the land office was transferred from the governor to the intendant in 1799, the Cabildo opposed the strict policies of Intendant Morales. After he suspended the right of deposit in 1802, which had permitted American goods to pass through Spanish territory untaxed, the Cabildo intervened on behalf of the residents to get the intendant to exempt foodstuffs.[32]

The intendancy performed vital services for Spanish Louisiana because the government subsidized the colony with large sums, exceeding half a million pesos annually in Spain's final years. The Cabildo played an important role in directing some of the crown's fiscal operations for the benefit of the inhabitants.[33]

The Cabildo's connection with the Catholic church and its officials was smaller and less formal than with the governor or the intendancy. In cer-

30. On this topic, see Chapter Twelve.
31. O'Reilly to Arriaga, No. 16, New Orleans, December 10, 1769, *SMV*, Pt. I, 132–35.
32. Clark, *New Orleans,* 246.
33. Royal expenditures on Louisiana from 1766 to 1785 are in "Statement of Expenses of the Province of Louisiana," José de Orue, New Orleans, May 31, 1787, *SMV*, Pt. II, 209; and shipments of the subsidy from Veracruz to Havana and designated for Louisiana in the later years are in tables in John J. TePaske, "La política española en el Caribe durante los siglos XVII y XVIII," in *La influencia de España en el Caribe, la Florida y la Luisiana, 1500–1800,* ed. Antonio Acosta and Juan Marchena (Madrid, 1983), 80–82. Not all the funds, however, reached Louisiana. The events highlighting the relationship between the intendancy and Cabildo are treated in their diverse contexts throughout this book.

tain areas, such as Charity Hospital, cemeteries, and church buildings, Cabildo and church authority overlapped and disputes frequently resulted. Jurisdictional clashes also occurred between the Cabildo's courts and the ecclesiastical court of the vicar general.[34]

The church in Louisiana in the Spanish era initially fell under the jurisdiction of the bishop of Havana. In 1772 he sent Vicar General Cirilo de Barcelona and several Spanish Capuchin priests to New Orleans. Barcelona later became the auxiliary bishop of Louisiana and West Florida. In 1793 the region became an independent diocese, but the first bishop, Luis Peñalver y Cárdenas, did not arrive until 1795. The laxity of the inhabitants in fulfilling their spiritual obligations shocked him, and he labored to improve religious observances. In 1801 he was raised to the archbishopric of Guatemala and left Louisiana. The government failed to assign a new bishop, and two priests, Tomás Hassett and Francisco Pérez y Guerrero, filled that office provisionally in Spain's closing years in Louisiana.[35]

Church and secular authorities in New Orleans shared ceremonial ties. The clergy performed special services for state reasons such as thanksgiving for victory in battle, the birth or death of a royal family member, patron saints' days, and other occasions. The army also had chaplains assigned to its units. In turn, government officials, including Cabildo members, had specified religious duties. The law required them to attend mass together on feast days and to sit in the front of the church as an example to the public. When in 1796 both the New Orleans elite and the councillors were remiss in their religious obligations, Bishop Peñalver chastised them, as did Governor Salcedo in 1801.[36]

34. Roger Baudier, *The Catholic Church in Louisiana* (New Orleans, 1939), contains a good account of the church's activities in colonial Louisiana. For short descriptions of disputes between the church and the Cabildo, see Carrigan, "Commentary," 391–92, 400–403; and Burson, *Stewardship*, 218–22. See also Richard Greenleaf, "The Inquisition in Spanish Louisiana, 1762–1800," *New Mexico Historical Review*, L (1975), 45–72.

35. Morazán, "Letters," I, 103n, 106–107n; Luis Peñalver to José Antonio Caballero, New Orleans, July 30, 1799, AGI, SD, leg. 2589. The Spanish crown enjoyed the privilege of *real patronato*, or appointment of churchmen to high church offices. On Peñalver, see Holmes, "Dramatis Personae," 147–52; Gilbert C. Din, "The Irish Mission to West Florida," *LH*, XII (1971), 331–32.

36. Baudier, *Catholic Church*, 226; Morazán, "Letters," I, li; Robertson, ed., *Louisiana Under*

The Cabildo and the church also had contact in other areas. In 1776 the bishop of Cuba requested that the New Orleans Cabildo dispatch a delegate to a synod to be held in Havana in April, 1777. The councillors appointed Regidor Juan Bautista Fleurian to attend the assembly. There is no evidence that he ever formally reported to the Cabildo on the proceedings at the synod or that the city benefited in any appreciable way from his participation. The experience was not repeated.[37]

On another occasion, in 1784, during an ongoing quarrel between the Cabildo and the vicar general, Cirilo de Barcelona, Síndico Procurador General Leonardo Mazange accused the Capuchin priests of charging excessively for marriage and funeral fees at a time when the public was undergoing economic hardship. The council requested that Barcelona reduce church fees, and it sought a tariff of standard rates from the bishop of Havana. The councillors planned to use the tariff to ensure against future overcharging. Although the records do not reveal how this issue ended, it is known that by 1798 the church used a tariff for fees charged for religious services. Perhaps the tariff began many years earlier.[38]

After its creation in 1769, the Cabildo acquired the right to approve the appointment of the steward of the St. Louis Church. In 1778, it abandoned this prerogative, stipulating that the pastor might fill the office every two years. The steward, however, would continue to give a biannual accounting to two Cabildo *regidores*. Seven years later, the Cabildo surrendered its remaining prerogatives over the church when the governor began to exercise his rights as the church's royal vice-patron.[39]

---

the Rule, I, 357; Actas del Cabildo, IV, (1), 91–92, February 5, 1796, IV, (4), 117–18, July 24, 1801.

37. Actas del Cabildo, I, 213, November 29, 1776, I, 218, January 10, 1777, I, 222, February 21, 1777, I, 232, October 10, 1777. After returning from Cuba, Fleurian complained that the five hundred pesos he had been given had not covered his expenses. The Cabildo granted him a three-hundred-peso bonus. The sum given to Fleurian was very generous and probably an abuse of the Cabildo's power.

38. Actas del Cabildo, III, (1), 5, July 9, 1784. In 1798 Governor Gayoso inquired of Bishop Peñalver about burial expenses in Pointe Coupee, where Claudio Gerbois was priest. Peñalver supplied Gayoso with a list of fees that church officials charged, depending on what kind of funeral was wanted. The schedule applied to all of Louisiana (Bishop Luis of Louisiana to Gayoso, New Orleans, August 14, 1798, with enclosures, AGI, PC, leg. 50).

39. Actas del Cabildo, I, 253, September 18, 1778, III, (1), 47–50, June 10, 1785.

Near the end of the Spanish period, the Cabildo quibbled with Bishop Peñalver over a proposed schedule of hours for religious services. The councillors believed that the hours the bishop wanted to assign were improper. They forwarded their objections to acting civil governor Vidal, asking that he resolve the matter. Vidal supported the council and requested Peñalver to amend the schedule to conform with the council's suggestions.[40]

Perhaps one of the best-known episodes involving the Cabildo and the church was the Sedella affair in 1790. Father Antonio de Sedella had been appointed commissary of the Holy Office of the Inquisition for Louisiana. When he was about to invoke his powers as inquisitor, Governor Miró and Auxiliary Bishop Barcelona moved to stop him. Explaining that starting the Inquisition would produce unrest in the province (Miró, with royal approval, was attempting to promote Protestant immigration to Louisiana), the governor arrested Sedella and deported him to Spain. The Cabildo's relations with Sedella, however, were excellent, and its members supported him both before and after his arrest. Sedella returned to Louisiana about the end of 1793, cleared of charges. He did not, however, act for the Inquisition. Sedella later became legendary as "Père Antoine" in the affection he won from New Orleanians. The city plunged into mourning on his death in January, 1829.[41]

The Cabildo's relations with the governor, the intendant, and the church were not always clear and precise. Exact lines of authority did not

40. *Ibid.,* IV, (3), 168–69, April 18, 1800; Morazán, "Letters," I, 106.

41. Much has been written about the Sedella affair. Clarence Bispham believes that Sedella was an agent for Madrid interests and that Miró had political motives for arresting and deporting him. See Bispham's articles, "Contest for Ecclesiastical Supremacy in the Valley of the Mississippi, 1763–1803," *LHQ,* I (1918), 155–89; "Fray Antonio de Sedella," *LHQ,* II (1919), 24–37; and "Fray Antonio de Sedella, Part II," *LHQ,* II (1919), 369–92. Heloise Hulse Cruzat's posthumous article, "Governor Estevan Miro, Fra Antonio de Sedella and the Inquisition in Louisiana," *Publications of the Louisiana Historical Society,* 2nd ser., II, (1974), 23–35, explains much about the affair. Charles Edwards O'Neill, S.J., in " 'A Quarter Marked by Sundry Peculiarities': New Orleans, Lay Trustees, and Père Antoine," *Catholic Historical Review,* LXXVI (1990), 261–68, believes it was Cirilo de Barcelona who in reality wanted Sedella out. But O'Neill does not adequately examine the governor's effort to promote immigration. On Miró's immigration efforts, see Gilbert C. Din, "The Immigration Policy of Governor Esteban Miró in Spanish Louisiana," *Southwestern Historical Quarterly,* LXXIII (1969), 155–75; and "Proposals and Plans for Colonization in Spanish Louisiana," *LH,* XI (1970), 197–213.

exist in Spanish Louisiana. Inter-agency disputes, which are probably common in any bureaucratic organization, occasionally flared up in colonial New Orleans. Nonetheless, they were exceptions, not the rule. Overall, the Cabildo maintained cordial relations with the governors, the intendants, and the church officials of Spanish Louisiana in most of their contacts. They generally cooperated to provide the colony with as good an administration as time, money, and circumstance permitted.

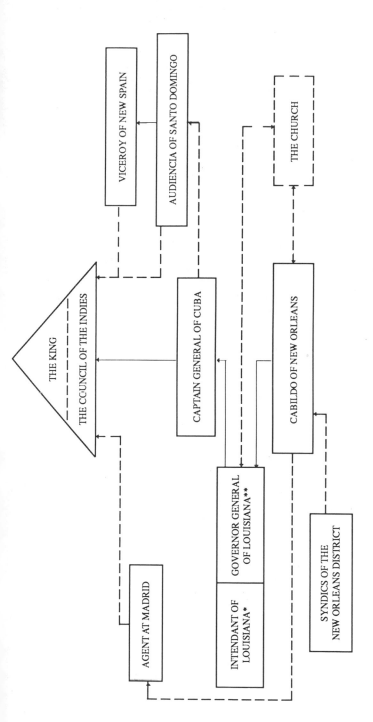

Figure 1. Administrative Flow Chart for Louisiana

* At times the offices of governor and intendant were combined.
** The governor, or his substitute including the lieutenant governor, served as president of the Cabildo.
—— Direct line of authority.
---- Peripheral, semiofficial; or theoretical connection.

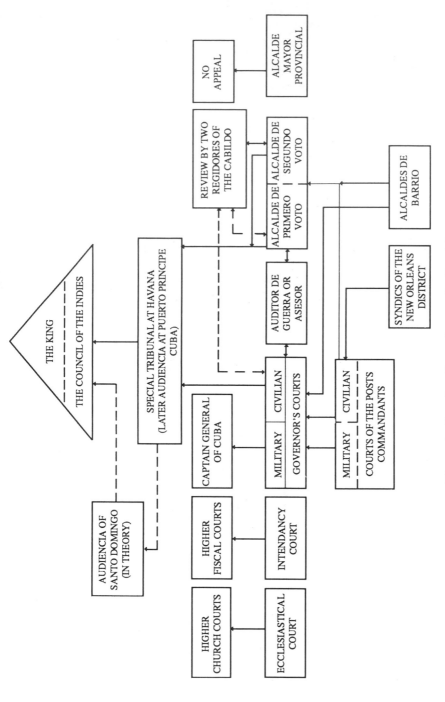

Figure 2. Spanish Court System for Louisiana

——— Direct line of authority

– – – Peripheral; semiofficial; or theoretical connection

FIVE

The Cabildo and the Spanish Legal System

I N the French and Spanish periods in Louisiana, two local governing bodies were present in New Orleans, the French Superior Council and the Spanish Cabildo, respectively. Although they have often been compared, they were not similar institutions. The Superior Council was established originally to serve as a provincial court, and only later did it acquire duties in governing the colony. It was more concerned with the province than with the city, and, overall, New Orleans under French rule suffered from neglect. The Superior Council paid little or no attention to streets, sidewalks, sanitation, markets, urban lighting, and building codes. The levee was not a city concern, and the only police present were occasional military patrols. In short, city government in New Orleans began with the Spaniards.[1]

But beyond the Cabildo's many duties in governing the city, it also had a judicial role. Two of its members, the *alcaldes ordinarios,* acted as judges in addition to their other responsibilities on the city council. Four of the original six *regidores* exercised judicial functions of importance in

---

1. Micelle, in "From Law Court," 85–107, traces the evolution of the Superior Council and notes the errors made by earlier historians of French Louisiana. For a discussion of the Superior Council's judicial duties, see Hardy, "Superior Council," 87–101.

their collateral offices. Moreover, several lesser Cabildo employees also performed legal tasks.

In November, 1769, Alejandro O'Reilly formally replaced French legal codes with the Spanish Laws of the Indies and the Laws of Castile. In reality, this change had occurred on a de facto basis with his arrival in August. To facilitate the use of Spanish laws in the colony, two lawyers, Urrutia and del Rey, compiled a summary code based on those laws, which was distributed to officials throughout the colony. The summary, named the Code O'Reilly, served to acquaint the inhabitants with Spanish laws as they were used throughout the empire; the Code O'Reilly was not a substitute for Spanish law. Spanish government administrators, army officers, and Cabildo officials in Louisiana employed the *Recopilación de leyes de los reynos de las Indias* and other Spanish legal texts. The *Recopilación* is cited frequently in official correspondence. Existing French customs in the colony, however, were allowed some status as long as they did not conflict with Spanish law or custom.[2]

The New Orleans court system changed radically with the start of the Spanish regime (see Figure 2). Under the French, the Superior Council was the court of first and last resort; the king intended for all cases to be dealt with summarily. Justice was swift and exemplary in criminal cases when perpetrators were apprehended. Civil litigation under the Superior Council was vastly out of proportion to the colony's sparse population.

2. Code O'Reilly, 154–88; Asbury, *French Quarter,* 30; Texada, "Alejandro O'Reilly," 145–46; Bjork, ed. and trans., "Documents," 563, 569; Actas del Cabildo, I, 251, July 31, 1778, I, 271–72, March 12, 1779, II, 82–87, November 9, 1781, IV, (1), 54, September 4, 1795, IV, (1), 163, November 3, 1796. For a study of the framework for Spanish law in the New World, see Joseph Thomas Vance, *The Background to Hispanic American Law: Legal Sources and Judicial Literature of Spain* (Washington, D.C., 1937).

O'Reilly also issued special decrees in February, 1770, to cover areas that had not received attention. They included his land ordinance, regulations on medicine, instructions to post commandants, and directions to commandants in upper Louisiana (regulations on land are in "O'Reilly's Ordinance of 1770; Concerning Grants of Land in Louisiana to New Settlers, Fencing of Same, Building of Roads and Levees, and Forfeiture of Strayed Cattle," *LHQ,* XI [1928], 237–40; on medicine in AGI, PC, leg. 188A; and on commandants in AGI, SD, leg. 2594). The *bandos de buen gobierno* (edicts of good government) of Governors Miró, Carondelet, and Gayoso supplemented the Code O'Reilly with laws they wanted to stress (Actas del Cabildo, III, 90–96, June 2, 1786, contains Miró's; Fortier, *History of Louisiana,* II, 149, summarizes Carondelet's; and Gayoso's in Spanish and French is in AGI, PC, leg. 197).

Civil suits were decided along formal and legal lines, except in probate cases, with little concern for mitigating circumstances or local conditions. In probate cases, however, iniquity that benefited lawyers and guardians flourished at the expense of legitimate heirs, who were unable to protect themselves. Unlike the later Spanish courts, the Superior Council did not charge for its services. One of its officers, roughly equal to a sheriff, and the troops stationed in the city enforced its judicial decisions. Several years before 1769, however, the ability of the Superior Council to execute its decrees declined considerably.[3]

Whereas the Superior Council probably heard cases when sitting as a body, the Cabildo judges heard their cases individually. The *alcaldes ordinarios* were only two of several judges in New Orleans who exercised parallel jurisdiction. The most important of the judges or courts dealt with persons who enjoyed *fueros,* or special privileges. Individuals covered by the *fueros* included military personnel, civil officers, and the religious. These courts merit a brief examination.[4]

The governor was judge in several special courts, in addition to the one that tried cases similar to those the *alcaldes ordinarios* tried in their courts. Of these special courts, the governor's military court had two principal functions. It conducted courts-martial in purely military cases and the trials of military personnel that involved civilians. For example, if a civilian sued an army officer who possessed the *fuero militar,* the latter could demand that his case be heard in the presumably sympathetic military court. In addition, the families and servants of military personnel were entitled to the *fuero.*[5]

3. Giraud, *History of French Louisiana,* Vol. II, *Years of Transition,* 87–88; Hardy, "Superior Council," 95, 96, 98, 100-101; Micelle, "From Law Court," 99; Asbury, *French Quarter,* 23–24; James D. Hardy, Jr., "Probate Racketeering in Colonial Louisiana," *LH,* IX (1968), 109–21; O'Reilly to Arriaga, No. 3, New Orleans, October 17, 1769, *SMV,* Pt. I, 99. The numerous civil court cases in New Orleans had a parallel in French Illinois (Winstanley Briggs, "Le Pays de Illinois," *William and Mary Quarterly,* 3rd ser., XLVII [1990], 45).

4. Code O'Reilly, 259, 261; François-Xavier Martin, *The History of Louisiana, from the Earliest Period* (1827; 3rd ed., Gretna, La., 1975), 209; Jefferson, "Description," 351–52; Henry P. Dart's note in Porteous, ed. and trans., "Index," *LHQ,* VI (1923), 145; Dart, "History of the Supreme Court of Louisiana," *LHQ,* IV (1921), 17; Texada, "Alejandro O'Reilly," 175.

5. Miró to Ezpeleta, New Orleans, January 15, 1784, "Dispatches," III (XII), 54. The *fuero militar* included tax exemptions and other legal privileges. It was greatly abused in New Orleans (Morazán, "Letters," I, 125–26; Porteous, ed. and trans., "Index," *LHQ,* XVI [1933],

The court of the intendancy operated much like the governor's court in matters related to the Royal Treasury, maritime affairs, and, after 1799, disputes involving land titles. It was the court for treasury and naval personnel who enjoyed the *fuero*. A legal adviser helped the intendant in the cases, although at times the judge advocate, who advised the governor, and the *asesor* were the same person. The intendant's court began functioning in 1780, when Martín Navarro became the first intendant. Before that time, he brought suits for the treasury through the governor's court. Between 1788 and 1794, when the governor was also intendant, it is uncertain whether treasury and marine cases were heard by lesser treasury officials or by the governors-intendant of that period, Miró and Carondelet.[6]

The ecclesiastical court began in Louisiana upon the arrival of Vicar General Cirilo de Barcelona in 1772, but it did not become active immediately. It had jurisdiction over marriages, annulments, divorces, and separations as well as over matters that concerned members of the clergy, church employees, and church-owned slaves. Persons connected to the church were entitled to the ecclesiastical *fuero,* which was similar to the privilege for military and intendancy personnel. Although the church court passed problems involving property settlements to the civil courts of the governor and the *alcaldes ordinarios,* it nevertheless possessed a certain amount of temporal authority. In one case, the vicar general had surgeon Juan Jassed Dorquigny imprisoned for domestic infelicity. In another instance, the ecclesiastical judge became embroiled in a jurisdictional dispute with the Cabildo. Francisco María de Reggio, the *alcalde ordinario de primer voto* and acting civil governor in 1784, insisted that he had authority over an apprehended fugitive slave belonging to the Capuchin Order and decreed that he suffer two hundred lashes. Captain General Bernardo de Gálvez of Cuba reprimanded the Cabildo for being dis-

---

387, and XX [1937], 1166–67). Militia officers enjoyed their *fuero militar* until 1800, when a royal order disallowed it (Actas del Cabildo, IV, [3], 230–31, September 5, 1800; Morazán, "Letters," II, 119–21). For an examination of this military privilege, see Lyle N. McAlister, The *"Fuero Militar" in New Spain* (Gainesville, Fla., 1957).

6. Porteous, ed. and trans., "Index," *LHQ,* VIII (1925), 310, XV (1932), 559, XVI (1933), 349–54, XVIII (1935), 456–64, XIX (1936), 537–38 and 1121–23, XXI (1938), 938, XXIII (1940), 664–65 and 945–50, XXIV (1941), 263–65.

respectful to Barcelona but not for exceeding its power. Evidently Gálvez agreed that Reggio had the right to try the fugitive.[7]

Before their numbers increased in 1797, four of the six original *regidores* exercised a role in the colony's legal system. In addition, Spanish law did not distinguish between judicial functions and law enforcement functions. All Spanish subjects were legally required to assist in law enforcement. Cabildo officials were charged with upholding the law, and the troops in New Orleans were required to assist them when asked.[8]

There has been much misunderstanding about the courts of the *alcaldes ordinarios*. The term *ordinario* should not be translated to mean "petty" as some Louisiana historians have done. The courts were not petty. *Ordinario* simply means that the courts had jurisdiction over persons who did not possess a *fuero*. It has also been claimed that Cabildo courts never handled significant criminal cases, large civil suits, or cases from outside of New Orleans. This is patently false as even a cursory examination of the judicial records indicates.[9]

Criminal trials in *alcalde ordinario* courts ranged from petty to capital

7. Actas del Cabildo, II, 219–26, III, (1), 1–4, July 2, 1784; Cirilo de Barcelona to Miró, New Orleans, August 27, 1783, *SMV,* Pt. II, 78; Gálvez to Navarro, New Orleans, October 26, 1778, "Dispatches," II, (VIII), 62; Porteous, ed. and trans., "Index," *LHQ,* XIII (1930), 355, XVI (1933), 151–57; Carrigan, "Commentary," 391–92, 401–403; Reeves, "Spanish Colonial Records," 11; Burson, *Stewardship,* 2. Light Townsend Cummins, in "Church Courts, Marriage Breakdown, and Separation in Spanish Louisiana, West Florida, and Texas, 1763–1836," *Journal of Texas Catholic History and Culture,* IV (1993), 101, explains that *divortium* (divorce) did not have the same meaning in eighteenth-century Louisiana as it does today. Then it meant "separation from bed and board," which released couples from conjugal obligations and permitted them to live apart. But the marriage was still valid before civil and ecclesiastical law.

8. Code O'Reilly, 259; Porteous, ed. and trans., "Index," *LHQ,* VI (1923), 709, XII (1929), 504; Robertson, ed., *Louisiana Under the Rule,* I, 181. In a few instances the Cabildo exercised original jurisdiction. For example, it tried Dr. La Casa for practicing medicine without a license, which the Cabildo was empowered to grant. Other minor officials who had judicial functions will be discussed below in conjunction with the lower courts.

In AGI, PC, leg. 72, there are documents between Nicolás María Vidal, the civil governor, and the Marqués de Casa-Calvo, the military governor, in which army assistance was authorized for the *alcaldes ordinarios* and *alcaldes de barrio* to assist them in carrying out their duties. The documents are for 1801, but the practice no doubt began much earlier.

9. Kate Wallach, *Research in Louisiana Law* (Baton Rouge, 1958), 210–11; Texada, "Alejandro O'Reilly," 135, 151–52; Chambers, *History of Louisiana,* I, 300, 303; Fortier, *History of Louisiana,* II, 5; Porteous, ed. and trans., "Index," *LHQ,* XXVI (1943), 1192, 1199; Actas del Cabildo, III, (1), 1–4, July 2, 1784.

offenses, including libel, petty and grand theft, receiving stolen goods, accessory before the fact, perjury, contempt of court, fugitive slaves, inciting slaves to run away, assault and battery, arson, attempted murder, manslaughter, treason, and murder. In their appellate function, however, the *alcalde ordinario* courts heard only civil, not criminal, appeals. Although several governors claimed jurisdiction over the more significant cases, these cases were not reserved solely for the governor's court.[10]

In their civil capacities, *alcalde ordinario* courts heard suits involving large sums of money, thousands and even tens of thousands of pesos in estate cases. In conjunction with the governor's court, the *alcalde ordinario* courts were superior and appellate courts for the inferior courts of the post commandants, the district syndics, and the *alcaldes de barrio*. They heard cases on appeal arising from property disputes, slave emancipations, suits for debts, and probate successions. *Alcalde ordinario* courts also assisted in notarizing contracts, recording wills, and authorizing property sales, all of which had to be done before notaries. Cases came to them from throughout lower Louisiana and as far away as Ste. Genevieve. Residents from neighboring Bayou St. John and closer were subpoenaed to appear in the *alcalde ordinario* courts while more distant witnesses made depositions before post commandants and two witnesses. Litigants in civil suits had the option of either journeying to New Orleans or appointing a *procurador* (person with power of attorney) to represent them in New Orleans.[11]

Alcalde ordinario courts heard the same kinds of cases as the governor's civilian court and even sat on some of the same cases. Civil and criminal cases passed easily from the governor's court to those of the *alcaldes ordi-*

---

10. Porteous, ed. and trans., "Index," *LHQ,* VIII (1925), 324–28, IX (1926), 334, XII (1929), 498–511, XIII (1930), 329–43, 361, XV (1932), 539–42, 687–706, XVI (1933), 157–63, 339–45, XVII (1934), 622–27, 1033–34, XIX (1936), 512–22, 1135–38, XX (1937), 860–65, 1148–66, XXIII (1940), 955–80, XXV (1942), 601–603, XXVIII (1945), 1287; Caughey, *Bernardo de Gálvez,* 224–25; Carrigan, "Commentary," 391–92; Jefferson, "Description," 352.

11. Porteous, ed. and trans., "Index," *LHQ,* VI (1923), 313, 322, 695–96, VII (1924), 145, 149–51, 185–86, 540, 541, 712, 722, VIII (1925), 155, 522–24, 530, 718–21, X (1927), 304–306, XII (1929), 527, XIII (1930), 177–93, 345, XIV (1931), 119, 132, 468–69, 610–13, 627, XVI (1933), 599, XVIII (1935), 204–12, 1033–34, XXIII (1940), 1306, XXVIII (1945), 1319, XXIII (1940), 304–307; Robin, *Voyage to Louisiana,* 59; Texada, "Alejandro O'Reilly," 137–38; Morazán, "Letters," I, 170.

narios and vice versa. The records clearly reveal that *alcalde ordinario* courts possessed concurrent jurisdiction with that of the governor.[12]

In a 1785 letter to Governor Miró, Captain General Bernardo de Gálvez made it clear that the *alcalde ordinario* courts were not inferior to the governor's court. He ruled that Alcalde Ordinario Francisco María de Reggio had been within his jurisdiction in trying fugitive slaves and condemning four of them to death. Probably with the counsel of his *auditor de guerra,* Gálvez wrote to Miró: "The jurisdiction of the *Alcaldes* is not subordinate, nor is it a step to the governor's [court]. It is subject only . . . to the Royal Audiencias, and the [*alcalde ordinario* courts of New Orleans] to the Tribunal of Appeals established by the King in [Havana]."[13]

Why the governor's court rather than the *alcaldes ordinarios* handled certain cases, however, is unclear. Most of them were criminal appeals from the *alcalde ordinario* courts and cases involving treason, foreigners, provincial security, and economic welfare. A few were so insignificant that the lowest courts could have dealt with them. Perhaps in some cases the governor wished to make an example of the criminal.[14]

Besides acting as judges, the *alcaldes ordinarios* were expected to patrol the city and investigate crimes. They enjoyed the assistance of the *alguacil mayor* (chief constable), his lieutenants, the Cabildo *escribano,* and, if necessary, citizens or troops. Various *alcaldes ordinarios* actually conducted patrols and personally made arrests, particularly in troubled times. In one example, they and other Cabildo members joined Governor Miró and a detail of dragoons to patrol New Orleans in an effort to catch an arsonist in 1791. That same year, Alcalde Ordinario de Primer Voto Juan Ventura Morales tracked down, captured, and punished a band of thieves that had

12. Porteous, ed. and trans., "Index," *LHQ,* VIII (1925), 518–25, XI (1928), 169, XII (1929), 341–48, 354, XIII (1930), 525, 528, XVIII (1935), 747–49, 757–58, XX (1937), 841–65; Caughey, *Bernardo de Gálvez,* 224–25. Dart acknowledged that the court of the *alcalde ordinario* held concurrent jurisdiction with the governor's court but he was uncertain about its origin. See his comment in Porteous, ed. and trans., "Index," *LHQ,* XIV (1931), 468–69.

13. Esteban Miró to the Conde de Gálvez, No. 135, New Orleans, October 1, 1784, AGI, PC, leg. 3A; Gálvez to Miró, Havana, April 15, 1785, AGI, PC, leg. 11.

14. Kerr, "Petty Felony," 18–19.

been plaguing the city. Both incidents occurred before the establishment of regular night watchmen.[15]

In the event of the death or prolonged absence of one of the *alcaldes ordinarios,* the *alférez real* assumed his place. The latter had no judicial functions assigned to his office, and he could either be elected *alcalde ordinario* or serve in the absence of one of them. These absences occurred on several occasions. Four of the five other *regidores* held collateral Cabildo offices with judicial duties and consequently were ineligible to serve as *alcalde ordinario.*[16]

The *alcalde mayor provincial,* the second-ranking *regidor,* exercised judicial power outside the city, mainly in its rural district, although occasionally an *alcalde ordinario* might claim jurisdiction. The *alcalde mayor provincial's* first duties involved crimes such as theft, rape, murder, and arson, among others, committed in rural locales. He could pursue criminals whose offenses occurred in urban areas if the governor or an *alcalde ordinario* was not involved. The *alcalde mayor provincial* was expected to render speedy justice, and his sentences could not be appealed. He was enjoined to conform closely to the spirit of the law and to seek legal assistance in his decisions. He was also expected to make frequent excursions into the countryside to perform his duties.[17]

As in other parts of the Spanish Empire, a Santa Hermandad (brotherhood of rural police) was created in Louisiana in 1798, primarily to pursue fugitive slaves, but it could also apprehend military deserters. The Santa Hermandad was under the *alcalde mayor provincial* and had the power to arrest runaways both within and outside the city. Whites made up the *cuadrilleros* (patrolmen) of the Santa Hermandad. Little is known about the activities of the *alcalde mayor provincial* because records of his office have not survived. He had, nevertheless, occasional conflicts of authority

15. Unzaga to de la Torre, New Orleans, July 11, 1772, "Dispatches," I, (IV), 13; Porteous, ed. and trans., "Index," *LHQ,* XII (1929), 507, XX (1937), 1153; Alliot, "Historical and Political Reflections," 146–49; Miró to Las Casas, New Orleans, July 2, 1791, "Dispatches," V, (XXIV), 42; Holmes, *"Dramatis Personae,"* 156.

16. Code O'Reilly, 256; Porteous, ed. and trans., "Index," *LHQ,* VII (1924), 148, 153, 165, VIII (1925), 706, XVIII (1935), 1031; Actas del Cabildo, I, 184, July 17, 1772, IV, (2), 158, September 22, 1798; Morazán, "Letters," I, 134, 137–38.

17. Code O'Reilly, 261–63.

with the *alcalde ordinario* courts. In 1792, upon the death of Alcalde Mayor Provincial Beauregard, the office remained vacant for six years because he had not assigned a successor and the heirs quarreled among themselves over his assets. The governor seems to have assumed the functions of the office.[18]

The office of the *alguacil mayor,* usually translated as chief constable or sheriff, was the third *regidor* in rank and the principal enforcement arm of the *alcalde ordinario* courts. The *alguacil mayor* was charged with apprehending criminals, maintaining public order, supervising the royal jail, appointing prison personnel, and overseeing the punishment of criminals. When ordered by the courts in civil suits, he executed writs, exacted payments, and seized property. His duties included visiting public places at all hours to prevent disputes, scandalous offenses, and illegal gaming. The *alguacil mayor* employed several *tenientes* (lieutenants or deputies), who did most of the legwork. In his absence, one of his assistants acted as constable but did not replace him on the Cabildo. He and his lieutenants could arrest lawbreakers but could not release them without proper authorization. When property was seized, the *alguacil mayor* received a fee called the *diezmo,* which meant a portion, not a "tenth" as some Louisiana historians have claimed. It entitled the *alguacil mayor* to receive 5 percent of the first one hundred pesos in property seized and 2 and ½ percent of anything above that. He also received twelve reales for every free person and eight reales for every slave arrested and imprisoned.[19]

18. *Ibid.;* Jefferson, "Description," 352; Morazán, "Letters," I, 134; Chambers, *History of Louisiana,* I, 299; Actas del Cabildo, III, (2), 21, April 18, 1788; Porteous, ed. and trans., "Index," *LHQ,* VI (1923), 699; Gayoso proclamation on *cimarrones,* New Orleans (1798), AGI, PC, leg. 49.

In cases of disputed jurisdiction between the *alcalde mayor provincial* and the other tribunals of the province, the governor decided cognizance in accordance with the laws (Texada, "Alejandro O'Reilly," 135, 138; Actas del Cabildo, III, [1], 107–108, October 6, 1786). In at least one instance, a criminal case was appealed from the court of the *alcalde mayor provincial* to the Cabildo, although this was contrary to the Code O'Reilly (Actas del Cabildo, IV, [4], 149, January 8, 1802).

19. Code O'Reilly, 263–64, 286, 288; Porteous, ed. and trans., "Index," *LHQ,* VI (1923), 687. *Tenientes de alguacil mayor* who served between 1770 and 1788 include Santiago Hallays, Luis Liotau, Pedro Pizania (Pizaña), [?] Bessieren, Antonio Gossom, Pedro Bertonier, Nicolás Fromentín, Bernardo Auricosti, Miguel Gómez, and Felipe Ravina. Some of these men also served in other Cabildo employments such as porter, jailer, appraiser, and assessor of court costs

The *alguacil mayor* appointed the warden of the royal jail, subject to the governor's confirmation. He could, however, dismiss the warden at his pleasure. A warden had to post a two-hundred-peso bond and be sworn in before the Cabildo. He was required to keep a logbook of the prisoners, their offenses, and under whose authority they were arrested. He was obliged to live in the jail, provide necessities to the inmates, and separate them by sex. He could not fraternize with the prisoners, under a sixty-peso fine for each infraction. He received fees ranging from one to one and one-half reales per prisoner per day. From his fees, he had to feed and care for the prisoners. In 1792 Warden José de la Peña resigned because the *carcelaje* or jailer's fee, paid at the time prisoners were released, had been canceled for white and black militiamen, and per diem to maintain the prisoners had been reduced to one real. The reductions did not permit him to pay for foodstuffs, utensils, cooking, and cleaning. Although the facility was called the royal jail and was supposedly supported by judicial fines, the Cabildo paid for the jail from municipal revenues. It spent thousands of pesos on repairs, remodeling, and a new building after the 1794 fire.[20]

The warden and the soldiers assigned to the jail were personally responsible for the security of their prisoners. On more than one occasion, when inmates escaped and the possibility of collusion existed, the warden and the guards became prisoners in their own jail. Furthermore, all their property was seized until they were cleared of complicity in the escapes. After their acquittal, they returned to their posts. Warden Antonio Gossom spent five and one-half months in prison before he was found guilty of negligence and not collusion. His penalty was the time served. The royal jail was also a military prison. Soldiers served as its guards, and some of them were quartered there.[21]

(Porteous, ed. and trans., "Index," *LHQ*, VII [1924], 152, VIII [1925], 184, 713, XII [1929], 146, 702, XIV [1931], 271–72; Actas del Cabildo, III, [2], 20, April 18, 1788).

20. Code O'Reilly, 267–68; Actas del Cabildo, IV, (1), 121–22, May 13, 1796, III, (3), 32–33, November 16, 1792; Morazán, "Letters," I, 55, II, 65.

21. Porteous, ed. and trans., "Index," *LHQ*, VIII (1925), 712, X (1927), 133–34, 137–42, XXIII (1940), 306. The royal jail was not the only military prison. Wardens of the New Orleans royal jail included Antonio Gossom, Francisco Muñoz, Francisco Sánchez, José de la Peña, Francisco Pavaña, José Antonio Ruby, and Blas Puche (*ibid.*, VI [1923], 694, XII [1929], 499,

The Cabildo employed a public executioner or hangman, who also administered the lesser physical punishment the courts decreed. He was usually, if not always, a black. He lived in the jail and received a small salary in addition to his room and board. His six-peso-per-month salary was raised to fifteen pesos in 1799 and to twenty pesos in 1803.[22]

The *depositario general* was the fourth *regidor* in seniority and the custodian of properties and funds seized by the *alguacil mayor* for the courts. His post as a public trustee required him to post a one-thousand-peso bond. For his services, he received 3 percent of the value of movable property and 5 percent of the value of real estate or other income-producing property, such as slaves, entrusted to his care. In cases in which seized property was sold at public auction, the *depositario general* made disbursements to the creditors, to the courts for costs, and, for whatever remained, to the party whose property it had been. He was the custodian of bonds posted with the Cabildo. He also served as a temporary court guardian for intestate properties until a suitable guardian could be appointed. In 1802, Dr. Jaén, the judge who conducted Miró's *residencia,* ordered the office of *depositario general* abolished and its holder reduced to a *regidor sencillo.* The records, however, do not reveal whether the Cabildo complied.[23]

The fifth *regidor* in rank was assigned the collateral office of *receptor de penas de cámara* (receiver of court fines). Its duties involved recording and safekeeping the fines imposed by the civil courts. As such, the *receptor* was a public trustee and had to furnish a one-thousand-peso surety bond. The funds in his care could be disbursed only by order of a judge, and he was accountable to the intendancy for them. The funds above the expenses of operating the judiciary were royal property, and the intendancy audited the receiver's accounts each year. The *receptor* earned a 10 percent fee for

---

XV [1942], 598; Actas del Cabildo, III, [3], 33, November 16, 1792; Morazán, "Letters," I, 132, II, 64).

22. Actas del Cabildo, III, (2), 35, September 12, 1788, IV, (2), 111, April 13, 1798, IV, (2), 145, July 20, 1798, IV, (3), 6–7, January 18, 1799, IV, (5), 96, September 30, 1803; Morazán, "Letters," II, 54.

23. Code O'Reilly, 264; Actas del Cabildo, I, 44–45, February 8, 1771; Porteous, ed. and trans., "Index," *LHQ,* VII (1924), 155, 713, VIII (1925), 183; Morazán, "Letters," II, 140. Bayle, in *Los cabildos,* 268, writes that the fee the *depositario general* received in Spanish America was 2.5 percent.

the monies he collected. From this he paid the salaries of his assistants and any other expenses incurred in collecting fines. This office fell vacant in 1789 when its holder died and the assignee was under suit by the Royal Treasury. The Spanish period ended without a new appointment, and the records do not show who assumed the office's functions. No replacement served in the Cabildo meetings.[24]

The sixth *regidor,* the *regidor sencillo,* held no collateral position and performed no regular judicial duties. His office was one of the two on the Cabildo that was compatible with the post of *alcalde ordinario.* Nicolas Forstall, who served as the sixth *regidor* from 1772, was elected *alcalde ordinario* six times. With the creation of six new *regidores sencillos* in 1797, they also became eligible, and several of them served as *alcaldes ordinarios* (see Table 3).

In addition to the *regidores,* several other Cabildo officials had judicial functions tied to their offices. The *síndico procurador general,* judicially as well as administratively, was a watchdog for the public. His primary judicial duty was to examine and ensure that the laws and municipal ordinances were observed and to report violations to the appropriate tribunal. He was not a judge, but when he encountered violations against the province, the poor, and the unprotected, he acted as a prosecutor. These cases included collecting debts owed the city, enforcing contracts made with the city, and evicting squatters from municipal property. He was also charged with prosecuting any public official who infringed on the rights of the town or the province. Another key charge was to prevent the courts from exceeding the punishment permitted by law in sentencing criminals. The *síndico procurador general'*s judicial duties gave him considerable knowledge of the law and experience with court procedures. The Cabildo put his training to use by electing many of the former officials to the post of *alcalde ordinario.*[25]

The Cabildo *escribano* had judicial duties in addition to his many administrative functions. He and another notary served as recorders for the *alcalde ordinario* courts. These courts and the governor's court exchanged

24. Code O'Reilly, 264–65; Texada, "Alejandro O'Reilly," 140–41; Morazán, "Letters," II, 5; "Digest," 21; Actas del Cabildo, IV, (3), 229, August 29, 1800, IV, (4), 213, May 21, 1802.

25. Code O'Reilly, 265–66; Porteous, ed. and trans., "Index," *LHQ,* VIII (1925), 184; Jefferson, "Description," 252; Morazán, "Letters," I, 185–87, 200.

escribanos freely to suit their convenience. The Cabildo *escribano* held a small claims court, served writs, participated in the inventorying of estates, and took depositions from witnesses for the *alcaldes ordinarios*. In conjunction with other New Orleans *escribanos,* he notarized and legitimized the sale of slaves and immovable property. He was also the official recorder of mortgages and, with the other *escribanos,* recorded contracts for the public. These papers were preserved in the Cabildo archives. The post of court recorder was considered sufficiently influential that, when the *escribano* had an interest in a case, he was expected to recuse himself.[26]

The civil courts of New Orleans employed many lesser and part-time officials. The most notable of them were the court bailiffs (*alguaciles*). In addition to their courtroom duties, the bailiffs served citations for the courts. They received fees for each citation served, but they had difficulty collecting them. When in 1792 the bailiffs first asked the Cabildo for a salary, the council refused and advised them to use the courts to collect their fees. Two years later the council relented and assigned the bailiffs a salary of ten pesos per month, to be raised from a one-peso tax on each city-owned hut and stall on the levee. In 1800, in conjunction with replacing a bailiff for bad conduct, the council raised their salaries to fifteen pesos per month.[27]

In its *capitular* sessions and in its courts, the Cabildo was expected to employ the Spanish language. Royal orders several times pointed out to Louisiana officials that the government did not wish to see documents in other languages. To comply with the royal mandate, the courts hired interpreters. Although they held only a part-time post, court interpreters possessed a commission and a title from the governor. The courts also used a public printer to make handbills and a town crier to inform the New Orleans citizenry of newsworthy events. The locally printed announcements were generally done in French and Spanish.[28]

26. Actas del Cabildo, II, 186–87, August 1, 1783; Porteous, ed. and trans., "Index," *LHQ,* VI (1923), 315, VII (1924), 529–30, 712, VIII (1925), 166–67, XI (1928), 155, 158–60, 169–71; Gayarré, *History of Louisiana,* III, 631; Morazán, "Letters," I, xxxvi, 17, 19–20.

27. Actas del Cabildo, III, (2), 198–99, April 20, 1792, III, (3), 151–52, August 1, 1794, IV, (3), 163–64, March 28, 1800. Court bailiffs and *tenientes de alguacil mayor* were either the same officials or their offices were compatible. The descriptions of their duties are nearly identical, and the word *alguacil* can be translated as *bailiff.*

28. Actas del Cabildo, I, 212, November 15, 1776; Porteous, ed. and trans., "Index," *LHQ,*

At the beginning of the Spanish regime, the courts used knowledge-able, albeit randomly selected, men as property appraisers. But by 1779, this system had produced rampant tax abuses. On the advice of Síndico Procurador General Andrés López de Armesto, the Cabildo appointed two public appraisers and tax assessors. The fees decreed by O'Reilly should have made these posts rewarding, but they were not. In 1797, both ap-praisers complained of being unable to collect their fees and requested the Cabildo to grant them a salary. The council refused and referred them to the courts. The courts also used local smiths as appraisers for precious metals until 1798, when the Cabildo appointed an assayer to evaluate them.[29]

A final judicial office was that of assessor of court costs and partitioner of properties. López de Armesto secured this post early in the Spanish period, removing its functions from the *escribano*. Later in the period, Luis Lioteau and Esteban de Quiñones served in the office. The Code O'Reilly prescribed the fees for the assessor of court costs.[30]

The *alcaldes ordinarios* used a legal adviser and consulted his opinion before rendering judgments. This method was not unique to Louisiana; the Spanish government employed it throughout the empire. The legal adviser was usually the government *auditor de guerra,* who also advised the governor, or the intendancy *asesor,* who counseled the intendant. At times the same man filled both posts. He was either a *licenciado* (lawyer) or doctor of law and often one of the few persons in the colony with formal legal education and experience. The governors were military men while the *alcaldes ordinarios* came from the planters, merchants, and Spanish civilian and military bureaucracy, all of whom lacked formal legal training. When the adviser gave his legal opinion, he, not the judge, became responsible for any irregularity or maladministration of justice that might later be found. The *alcalde ordinario* did not always follow the opinion of his ad-

---

VIII (1925), 167, XIII (1930), 522, XXVIII (1945), 573. The Spanish records fail to mention the fees or salaries that court interpreters received.

29. Actas del Cabildo, I, 284, June 4, 1779, III, (2), 129, April 29, 1791, III, (3), 71, June 14, 1793, IV, (2), 58, October 13, 1797, IV, (2), 166, November 23, 1798; Porteous, ed. and trans., "Index," *LHQ,* VII (1924), 713, XIV (1931), 273.

30. Porteous, ed. and trans., "Index," *LHQ,* X (1927), 284, XVI (1933), 569, XXV (1942), 261; Code O'Reilly, 288.

viser, but he had to assume responsibility for the decision when he over-ruled him. In this way, the judge and the adviser acted as a check on each other. *Alcaldes ordinarios,* however, did not always sit with an adviser, even in cases involving more than fifty pesos as required by law.[31]

The judge advocate and the intendancy assessor were not the only attorneys to act as advisers to the courts. When there were other *licenciados* or persons with legal experience in the province, they were frequently elected to the post of *alcalde ordinario* or asked to advise the courts. Some of them willingly obliged but others abstained.[32]

The legal advisers who served the courts received fees set by law, which were in addition to the salaries they received for their other offices. Of the approximately half dozen lawyers who acted as advisers to the Spanish civil courts of Louisiana, only the last judge advocate, Vidal, appears to have been corrupt. His questionable conduct surfaced after the departure of upright Governor Carondelet in 1797, and it became more evident after Governor Gayoso's death in 1799, when he became acting civil governor for two years. His conduct did not improve under the incompetent Governor Salcedo.[33]

31. Porteous, ed. and trans., "Index," *LHQ,* VII (1924), 539–40, XXI (1938), 321; Jefferson, "Description," 252; Burson, *Stewardship,* 204–206; Wood, "Life in New Orleans," 699; Morazán, "Letters," II, 104; Robertson, ed., *Louisiana Under the Rule,* II, 275. At times the assessor as lieutenant governor heard civil cases in the governor's court (Porteous, ed. and trans., "Index," *LHQ,* XI [1928], 152–55, XXII [1939], 1228–29, XXIII [1940], 337–38). The system of employing an adviser has been the source of criticism of the Spanish legal system, but the criticism appears unwarranted.

32. Actas del Cabildo, III, (1), 45–46, May 6, 1785, III, (1), 99, August 4, 1786, IV, (4), 119–21, July 31, 1801; Porteous, ed. and trans., "Index," *LHQ,* VIII (1925), 156, XIII (1930), 177, 339–43; Laura L. Porteous, trans., "The Documents in Lipponot's Case," *LHQ,* XII (1929), 48; Burson, *Stewardship,* 15, 218; Robin, *Voyage to Louisiana,* 59; Morazán, "Letters," II, 116; Caron-delet, "Decree of June 1, 1795," in *American State Papers, Miscellaneous Documents,* Vol. I (Washington, D.C., 1834), 379.

Félix del Rey, Cecilio Odoardo de Sayas, Juan Doroteo del Póstigo, Francisco Paula Cabas y Padilla, Manuel Serrano, and Nicolás María Vidal were all *licenciados* (lawyers) who were either the judge advocate (government lawyer) or the intendancy assessor. Vidal was also a doctor of laws. *Licenciados* José de Ortega y Díaz and José Martínez de la Pedrera held neither of these posts, although Ortega was employed by the intendancy in the royal tobacco monopoly. Anyone trained in law was called a *letrado.* For the work of lawyers in the Spanish colonies, see Javier Malagón Barceló, "The Role of the *Letrado* in the Colonization of America," *Americas,* XVIII (1961–62), 1–17.

33. Code O'Reilly, 286; Porteous, ed. and trans., "Index," *LHQ,* VIII (1925), 157; Actas del

Because of the scarcity of trained lawyers in Louisiana, virtually anyone who was reasonably intelligent, knowledgeable, and literate could act as an advocate in civil and criminal cases before the New Orleans courts. Early in the Spanish period, some of the Cabildo *regidores* performed in this capacity, and later notaries public also served as legal counselors. Persons of means, however, preferred to employ individuals designated to serve in the local courts. They were usually notaries and had knowledge of law and experience with court procedure.[34]

The first two lawyers permitted to practice before Louisiana's Spanish civil courts were Leonardo Mazange and Enrique Despres. Both of them had acted in similar capacities before the court of the French Superior Council. O'Reilly appointed them as *procuradores públicos del número* (public attorneys). These posts required royal confirmation, after which they became inheritable and salable. Appointees and purchasers, however, had to qualify to perform the duties of the office. Before the governor granted their temporary commissions, he ordered the judge advocate to examine them. There were never more than three or four *procuradores públicos del número* practicing in New Orleans at any one time. The value of this office remained modest, ranging from six hundred to one thousand pesos for most of the period.[35]

Cabildo, I, 21–22, June 12, 1770, II, 67–68, August 17, 1781; Robertson, ed., *Louisiana Under the Rule*, I, 207–208; Laussat to Decres, July 18, 1803, in Robertson, ed., *Louisiana Under the Rule*, II, 42. Berquin Duvallon and other French writers of the late Spanish period in Louisiana accuse Vidal of being corrupt.

34. Porteous, ed. and trans., "Index," *LHQ*. VII (1924), 150, 526, VIII (1925), 161, 311-13, IX (1926), 330, XII (1929), 510, XIV (1931), 271, XXI (1938), 319.

35. "Digest," 13; Wood, "Life in New Orleans," 699; Henry P. Dart, ed., "A Murder Case Tried in New Orleans in 1773," trans. Laura L. Porteous, *LHQ*, XXII (1939), 623–24; Laura L. Porteous, ed. and trans., "Index," *LHQ*, VII (1924), 148, 161, 183, XI (1928), 170, XXII (1939), 623–24, XXIV (1941), 911–15; Actas del Cabildo, I, 9–10, February 23, 1770, I, 94, December 18, 1772, I, 171, September 9, 1774, I, 179, March 13, 1775, III, (1), 18–19, September 10, 1784; Burson, *Stewardship*. 203. O'Reilly gave the rates allowed to lawyers in the Code O'Reilly, 286–87. Occasionally, a judge allowed a double fee for a particularly laborious *escrito* or *procès-verbal* (Porteous, ed. and trans., "Index," *LHQ*, VIII [1925], 328). In 1781 Procurador Público del Número Rafael Perdomo was found to be overcharging his clients, and the Cabildo forced him to conform to the fees set in the *Book of Fines* (Actas del Cabildo, II, 68, August 17, 1781; Jefferson, "Description," 352).

Persons who served as *procurador público del número* included Leonardo Mazange, Enrique Depres, Francisco Broutin, Rafael Perdomo, Francisco Rodríguez, and Antonio Méndez. Ma-

Procuradores públicos del número received all the cases in which the court appointed an attorney. This was particularly true for the prosecution of criminal cases, for which a lawyer was selected as *promotor fiscal* (royal prosecutor). The *procuradores* were also named to the position of public defender if the accused was unable or unwilling to secure counsel. Besides these court appointments, the *procuradores* also cornered the lion's share of civil cases.[36]

Although the Cabildo sought to attract Spanish lawyers to Louisiana, it had little success. The government employed almost all the trained lawyers, or *letrados*. The only one in Louisiana in January, 1803, was Vidal. In the rare instances when a lawyer ventured to the province, he did not practice there for long. High office fees and unfamiliarity with local customs and perhaps the French language seem to have restricted their practice. Furthermore, they sometimes ran afoul of the local administration. This happened to Licenciado José Martínez de la Pedrera, whom Governor Salcedo imprisoned and deported to Cuba.[37]

With the establishment of the Spanish regime in Louisiana, O'Reilly requested the crown to create a special superior tribunal in Havana to hear appeals from the Louisiana courts. He cited as reasons for the need the colony's unique position in the Spanish Empire and the need for prompt justice. The king granted the request in a royal order of January 28, 1771. The Havana tribunal of appeals consisted of the captain general, the army and navy judge advocates, and the attorney (*fiscal*) of the Royal Treasury. The tribunal was under the nominal authority of the *audiencia* of Santo Domingo, which it consulted in rare instances for rendering decisions for Louisiana. The Havana tribunal heard appeals in civil suits for more than

---

zange and Rodríguez later served as Cabildo *escribanos*. Both resigned their lawyer's commission before taking up their new post, which may indicate that the two offices were incompatible (Actas del Cabildo, II, 7, December 17, 1779; Porteous, ed. and trans., "Index," XX [1937], 1160).

36. Porteous, ed. and trans., "Index," *LHQ*, VIII (1925), 522, X (1927), 460–62, XX (1937), 1160, XXIII (1940), 955–80; Code O'Reilly, 276; Dart, ed., "Murder Case," 623; Wood, "Life in New Orleans," 699.

37. Actas del Cabildo, I, 114, September 16, 1773, III, (3), 99–100, August 4, 1786, IV, (4), 119–21, July 31, 1801, IV, (4), 168–70, February 12, 1802; Morazán, "Letters," II, 79, 81, 116; Robertson, ed., *Louisiana Under the Rule*, I, 208; Pedro de La Roche to Manuel de Salcedo, New Orleans, January 7, 1803, AGI, PC, leg. 139.

330 pesos and appeals in criminal cases. It routinely reviewed all death sentences. A civil appeal to Havana was expensive and was granted only when the appellant posted bond to guarantee payment for the costs of a new trial.[38]

Louisianians, however, rarely appealed the decisions of the Havana tribunal to the *audiencia* in Santo Domingo. In 1800 the Cabildo asked the king to permit final judgment in criminal cases to take place in a court of appeals in New Orleans and to allow the *audiencia* at Puerto Príncipe, Cuba, to handle other appeals. The crown had made the *audiencia* at Puerto Príncipe the appellate court for both civil and criminal cases from Louisiana. In 1802 appeals from the Louisiana courts were transferred from the special court at Havana to the *audiencia* at Puerto Príncipe. The court was actually the *audiencia* of Santo Domingo, which had relocated to Cuba because Spain had ceded the colony to France as stipulated in the 1795 Treaty of Basel.[39]

Appeals of civil cases from the courts of the *alcaldes ordinarios* and the governor up to 90,000 maravedís (about 330 pesos) were addressed to the Cabildo as a body. To review the appeal of the losing party, the Cabildo elected two *regidores* to sit with the original judge. This appeals court could and did reverse decisions, occasionally even over the advice of an *asesor*. A two-to-one vote was binding at this stage, but further appeal could be made to a superior court. Appeals to the Cabildo were to be made on points of law, not on facts of the case, but this was not always observed. Appeals to the Cabildo provided a relatively quick and inexpensive alternative to petitioning a higher but distant court.[40]

38. Code O'Reilly, 277–78; French, ed., *Historical Memoirs,* V, 247; Bjork, "Establishment of Spanish Rule," 151; Henry P. Dart, ed., "A Twelve Year Lawsuit in New Orleans During the Spanish Regime (1781–1792)," trans. Laura L. Porteous, *LHQ,* XVII (1933), 298–301; Unzaga to the Gentlemen of the Tribunal of Appeals, March 27, 1774, "Dispatches," I, (V), 52; Las Casas to Carondelet, May 6, 1793, "Dispatches of Carondelet," VI, (III), 358ff.; Jefferson, "Description," 352; "Digest," 72; Chambers, *History of Louisiana,* I, 300; Miró to Ezpeleta, October 29 and December 1, 1787, "Dispatches," III, (XIV), 53 and 59, respectively.

39. Porteous, ed. and trans., "Index," *LHQ,* XXIII (1940), 955, 1306; Actas del Cabildo, III, (2), 180–81, February 17, 1792, IV, (3), 198, July 11, 1800, IV, (3), 228–29, August 29, 1800, IV, (4), 1–2, September 19, 1800, IV, (5), 6, July 30, 1802; Morazán, "Letters," II, 162–63.

40. Code O'Reilly, 178–79; French, ed., *Historical Memoirs,* V, 247. Three hundred and thirty pesos was a decent yearly wage for a skilled artisan or lower-grade professional in Louisiana. At least one criminal case was appealed to the Cabildo from the court of the *alcalde*

The courts of the *alcaldes* and the governor were civilian courts of the first instance for the New Orleans area. In addition, Louisiana had several inferior courts. They were the courts, if that word can be used, attached to the offices of post commandant, district syndic, and *alcalde de barrio*. These officers each had administrative, judicial, and law enforcement functions in certain matters. Post commandants were military officials, usually regular army officers if forts were present and militia officers if they governed over primarily civilian settlements; in both instances, they had jurisdiction over the lay population. As the chief executive officer of their districts, commandants enjoyed limited judicial power and acted as notaries. They could not hear serious criminal cases (they merely gathered depositions from witnesses and sent them and the accused to New Orleans), settle lawsuits of more than twenty pesos, or probate estates that were contested. The post commandants were subject to the orders of the civil courts at New Orleans, and these courts served as superior and appellate courts for the posts.[41]

A system of rural syndics had been used by the French regime. The Spaniards initially did not use syndics in the new settlements they began, but syndics appear to have continued quietly in the older French settlements. Locally kept documents confirm their presence. In a 1790 letter, Governor Miró referred to syndics who watched over levees on the Mississippi. Governor Carondelet formally re-created the office to assist post commandants in his 1792 levee ordinance. Later, as Louisiana's rural population grew, it included many foreigners whom the authorities felt needed

---

mayor provincial. It was contrary to the Code O'Reilly, which stated that there would be no appeals from that official's judgment and that the Cabildo would not hear criminal appeals (Actas del Cabildo, IV, [4], 149–50, January 8, 1802).

41. "Instruction which Post Commandants [*Tenientes particulares*] should follow," O'Reilly, New Orleans, February 12, 1770, AGI, SD, leg. 2594; Porteous, ed. and trans., "Index," *LHQ*, VII (1924), 149, 541, XIV (1931), 627, XVI (1933), 599, XVIII (1935), 204–205; Texada, "Alejandro O'Reilly," 137–38; Robin, *Voyage to Louisiana*, 59; Carondelet, "Decree of 1795," 379; Jefferson, "Description," 352–53. Morris S. Arnold discusses Spanish law at Arkansas Post in *Unequal Laws Unto a Savage Race: European Legal Traditions in Arkansas, 1686–1836* (Fayetteville, Ark., 1985), 43–113. He notes *alcalde ordinario* participation in some Arkansas cases that reached down to New Orleans. Arnold observes that at times not all the rules of law were followed at Arkansas Post (*Colonial Arkansas, 1684–1804: A Social and Cultural History* [Fayetteville, Ark., 1991], 147–51). Probably the same occurred at other posts.

watching. Carondelet enumerated the syndics' legal duties more clearly in 1795, undoubtedly pushed to do so by the need to keep levees, roads, and bridges in good repair, the entry of numerous immigrants, Jacobin unrest, and the Pointe Coupee slave conspiracy. He ordered post commandants to nominate responsible and literate persons, usually planters, to serve as syndics subject to his confirmation. In 1797 the Cabildo began electing twelve syndics for the seven posts within fifteen miles of New Orleans. They were distributed in the following manner: three in Tchoupitoulas; two on the right bank upriver; two below New Orleans on the left bank; two outside the San Carlos Gate or suburb; one for Bayou St. John; one for Metairie; and one for Gentilly. Although the Cabildo elected them, they were still responsible to the commandants of their respective districts. Residence determined the selection of syndics. They were spaced along the principal waterways, at intervals of three leagues (approximately nine miles). They were required to make weekly reports to their respective commandants on the events and conditions within their districts.[42]

As deputies of the district commandants, syndics assumed first cognizance of all crimes committed in their jurisdictions and held hearings to settle civil disputes up to ten pesos. They passed suits involving larger sums to the post commandants. In their police duties, the syndics kept watch on strangers and suspicious activities, enforced livestock and boundary regulations, and had charge of all matters relating to slave supervision. They could impress the residents of their areas for police duty, and they had charge of slave patrols. They had the added responsibility of seeing that landowners maintained all levees, roads, and bridges. A glimpse of a syndic is seen in the election of Martín Duralde in Opelousas in 1785. His chief duty was to administer district funds for public projects. Spanish documents appear not to discuss this local taxing authority, and it prob-

---

42. Gayarré, *History of Louisiana,* II, 239; [Miró] to Monsieur Porte, New Orleans, April 30, 1792, AGI, PC, leg. 204; Laura L. Porteous, trans., "Governor Carondelet's Levee Ordinance of 1792," *LHQ,* X (1927), 513; Actas del Cabildo, IV, (2), 92, January 5, 1798; Carondelet, "Decree of 1795," 377–81; Dorothy Ida Yerxa, "The Administration of Carondelet, with an Appendix of Original Documents" (M.A. thesis, University of California, Berkeley, 1926), 30–31; Morazán, "Letters," I, 87–88, 152; "Digest," 237. Coastal syndics (*síndicos de las costas*), who assisted post commandants along the Mississippi, were also called *jueces pedaneos* (petty judges) (Actas del Cabildo, IV, [4], 149, January 8, 1802).

ably varied in the different districts where it existed. At the end of the Spanish regime in Louisiana, Dr. John Watkins noted in his 1804 report to American governor W. C. C. Claiborne that local administration had been effective under Carondelet because of his strict police measures, but it had deteriorated after he left the province.[43]

In 1779 the Cabildo divided New Orleans into two wards and elected two *alcaldes de barrio* (ward commissioners, roughly justices of the peace) from each ward to preserve order therein. The same four men were unanimously reelected to serve the following year. The Cabildo minutes mention no more elections until 1792. Possibly the offices continued without formal elections, for two of the men elected in 1792 bore the same names as two who had served earlier. Because of New Orleans' growth, Carondelet created four city wards in 1792. The wards later became seven when they included the three suburbs of Santa María, San Carlos, and Bayou St. John.[44]

The duties of the *alcaldes de barrio* included conducting a running census of their wards, particularly keeping track of newcomers to New Orleans. They were empowered to fine and jail owners of lodgings who did not inform them of new guests. The *alcaldes* could investigate crimes and imprison suspects for the higher courts. They were permitted to hear civil cases up to ten pesos. Finally, they appointed two watchmen to assist them in performing their duties.[45]

It is unclear under whose authority the ward *alcaldes* served. The Cabildo elected them, subject to the governor's approval. He gave them written instructions for fulfilling their duties. Yet, besides their judicial

43. Carondelet, "Decree of 1795," 377–81; John Watkins Report to Claiborne, February 2(?), 1804, in Robertson, ed., *Louisiana Under the Rule,* II, 318; Carl A. Brasseaux, ed. and trans., "Election of Martin Duralde as Syndic, 1785," *Attakapas Gazette,* XVI (1981), 153–54. Brasseaux compares the office of syndic to that of the modern-day parish police juror in Louisiana (or county supervisor in other states). How strict Carondelet's police measures were is subject to interpretation; they have not been thoroughly investigated.

44. Fortier, *History of Louisiana,* II, 149; Morazán, "Letters," I, 88, 152; Asbury, *French Quarter,* 39; Actas del Cabildo, I, 275–76, April 30, 1779; "Digest," 232–33; Yerxa, "Administration of Carondelet," 10–12. The four men named in 1779 were Francisco Braquier, Juan Bautista Cavelier, Juan La Costa, and José Antonio Astier. Because *alcaldes* were already present, Governor Carondelet did not begin the New Orleans system of *alcaldes de barrio* with his reform program of 1792.

45. Yerxa, "Administration of Carondelet," 10–12; Jefferson, "Description," 352.

functions, they were involved in the city's fire-fighting system, which came under the city treasury department of the *mayordomo de propios*. The Cabildo did not pay the *alcaldes* a salary, but they might have collected fees from their small claims courts.[46]

The watchmen who assisted the ward *alcaldes de barrio* were the predecessors of the *serenos,* or night patrolmen, who began serving in 1794. They were originally eight armed men under the supervision of a corporal. Their number later expanded to twelve men and two corporals. The *serenos* served in the triple capacities of preserving the peace, keeping the street lamps lit after they were installed, and sounding an alarm in case of fire. Although they had a police function, the *serenos* were employees of the lighting department and under the authority of the *mayordomo de propios.* The monthly commissioners also assisted in supervising them in their routine duties.[47]

Because the Spanish legal system was similar in many ways to French legal practices, its introduction did not greatly disturb established usage. For example, the Spaniards and French relied on judges rather than juries in court cases. In addition, their systems of interrogation and deposition were virtually identical.[48]

In civil cases, the Spanish courts preferred accommodation between litigants and, on occasion, insisted that they settle out of court. To further accommodation, the courts sometimes employed costs to bludgeon the parties into agreement. Court costs were not uniformly high, however, and in several instances they were dismissed completely for impoverished individuals. In a similar vein, the courts occasionally refused to execute judgments against the indigent but ordered them to make payment whenever they could afford it. When on rare occasions a person was imprisoned

46. Yerxa, "Administration of Carondelet," 10–12; Actas del Cabildo, III, (2), 167, January 14, 1792, III, (2), 169, January 17, 1792, III, (2), 170–71, January 28, 1792. The post of *alcalde de barrio* was not popular with many New Orleans residents. Many men either declined the post or attempted to resign once in office, usually because their duties took them away from their businesses.

47. Morazán, "Letters," I, 114–15n. Asbury, *French Quarter,* 39, states that Carondelet also instituted day patrols of armed and uniformed civil guards. They are not mentioned in the Cabildo records and, if they existed, were probably military personnel.

48. Porteous, ed. and trans., "Index," *LHQ,* IX (1926), 324–30, XII (1929), 498–511, XV (1932), 159–62, XVI (1933), 157–61, XX (1937), 1148–60; Texada, "Alejandro O'Reilly," 148–50.

for debt, a relative could secure his release by assuming the debt. As an act of charity, debtors and petty criminals were released from prison on the eves of Christmas, Easter, and Pentecost, when the judges visited the jails.[49]

Once a lawsuit began, debtors could not leave the province, sell, or otherwise dispose of their property until the debt was satisfied. If defaulting debtors lacked liquid assets, their property was seized. If they still failed to make payment or reach an agreement with their creditors, the court ordered that their assets be sold at public auction. Under no circumstances could the property of debtors be sold for less than half its appraised value. When the debtors lacked sufficient property to satisfy all their creditors, privileged creditors such as doctors, food vendors, and unpaid employees were remunerated first. The common creditors then divided the remaining cash proportionally.[50]

The Spanish regime reformed probate procedure considerably from the legalized theft that had occurred under the French. With the establishment of the Cabildo, the Superior Council office of probate attorney was abolished. Shortly thereafter, Governor Unzaga disallowed the "family meeting," which had permitted relatives and friends of the family to fleece heirs who were minors. Under the Spaniards, minors who were old enough usually chose their guardians. The guardian was then solely responsible to the courts for the management of the property in his charge. It was a vast improvement over the French system it replaced. Under the Spaniards, like the French, a minor reached majority at age twenty-five. A father or guardian, however, could emancipate his children or wards through the courts, beginning at age fourteen for boys and twelve for girls. Once emancipated, minor heirs could receive their inheritances directly.[51]

49. Porteous, ed. and trans., "Index," *LHQ*, VI (1923), 694, 695, VII (1924), 175, 526-27, 532, 537, VIII (1925), 176–77, 309, 311, 509, IX (1926), 162, 351, XI (1928), 165, XII (1929), 167, XIV (1931), 308–10, XVI (1933), 576; Code O'Reilly, 261; Texada, "Alejandro O'Reilly," 136–37.

50. Porteous, ed. and trans., "Index," *LHQ*, VI (1923), 692, VII (1924), 153–57, 545, VIII (1925), 154, 159–60, 173, 176, 322, 523, XI (1928), 161, XIV (1931), 471–74, XVIII (1935), 471–72; Henry P. Dart, ed., "A Judicial Auction in New Orleans, 1772," trans. Laura L. Porteous, *LHQ*, XI (1928), 32–38; Jefferson, "Description," 352; Texada, "Alejandro O'Reilly," 147–48.

51. Code O'Reilly, 269, 281–85; Hardy, "Probate Racketeering," 112, 120; Laura L. Porteous,

For most of the Spanish period, New Orleans' judges conducted themselves properly. Many checks against arbitrary action existed, and the records provide few examples of misconduct.[52] The closing years of the Spanish period, however, found conditions in Louisiana much changed.

Charges of corruption and inefficiency have often been raised against the Spanish officials in Louisiana, including the Cabildo. Much of the corruption in the Spanish Empire consisted of "honest graft," the usual small gratuities and bribes for services rendered by petty, low-paid officials. Because public office was sometimes acquired by purchase and

---

ed. and trans., "Governor Unzaga Decides That the Family Meeting Has No Place in Spanish Probate Procedure in Louisiana, 1771," *LHQ,* XII (1929), 293–94; Porteous, ed. and trans., "Index," *LHQ,* VI (1923), 515, 695, VII (1924), 532–33, VIII (1925), 704–707, 734, IX (1926), 162–70, 336, 341–44, XI (1928), 166, XII (1929), 352, 675, XIII (1930), 519, XXIV (1941), 604–605; Actas del Cabildo, III, (2), 104, June 11, 1790. See the Code O'Reilly, 269 and 281–85, for rules relating to testaments.

52. Justice was sometimes harsh in Spanish Louisiana when gauged by later and more humanitarian standards, but it generally fell within the norm for that age. Thomas Jefferson wrote in 1803 that he regarded Spanish law as relatively mild. Punishment for serious crimes was brutal, dramatic, and public. It was expected to serve as a deterrent to would-be criminals. Spanish law also required more definitive proof for imposing the death penalty than had French law in Louisiana. The courts dropped a significant number of criminal cases for lack of conclusive evidence (Code O'Reilly, 279–81, lists the usual punishments for specific crimes under Spanish law. Porteous, ed. and trans., "Index," *LHQ,* IX [1926], 324–27, XII [1929], 498–511, 682–703, XXV [1942], 603, XXVIII [1945], 1307–17; Laura L. Porteous, trans., "Torture in Spanish Criminal Procedure in Louisiana, 1771," *LHQ,* VIII [1925], 5–22; Burson, *Stewardship,* 208; Asbury, *French Quarter,* 44; Texada, "Alejandro O'Reilly," 148–50).

Sentences decreed by the courts included fines, exposure to public shame, imprisonment in the local jail, exile, imprisonment in Havana, serving on the public works of the province or on galleys, and death. For slaves punishment included lashing, branding, imprisonment, and death. Convicted persons were usually assessed damages in robbery and assault cases (Porteous, ed. and trans., "Index," *LHQ,* VIII [1925], 310, 372–81, IX [1926], 825–26, XII [1929], 510–11, XIII [1930], 361, XIV [1931], 339–45; XV [1932], 706, XVI [1933], 157–61, 322, XIX [1936], 322, XX [1937], 665, 1148–66; Dart, "Murder Case," 624).

In a military case, Private Juan Esgilencia was sentenced to death, presumably for a serious crime committed at an outpost, by a New Orleans court-martial. The Havana Supreme Council of War, however, reduced the sentence to ten years' imprisonment because the accused had not had the benefit of counsel when the witnesses were questioned (Miró to Las Casas, New Orleans, July 23, 1791, with enclosure of Bouligny to Las Casas, New Orleans, July 19, 1791, AGI, PC, leg. 1440B).

regarded as private property, it was normal for the officeholder to think that a profit could be derived. Overall, however, this seems not to have been true for most Cabildo officials. In any case, corruption had existed in Louisiana before the Spaniards arrived, and it continued long after they left.[53]

Many, and perhaps most, Louisianians were satisfied with the Spanish system of justice. Much of it was familiar to them. The major divergence for some French planters involved the milder treatment of slaves. Nevertheless, Louisianians generally preferred the Spanish legal system to the common law that was foisted upon them when the United States acquired the province. Understandably, the inhabitants made several attempts after 1803 to return to laws similar to the Spaniards'. Despite opposition, some success was achieved. Consequently, there was a significant carryover of

---

53. Diffie, *Latin-American Civilization,* 616; Robin, *Voyage to Louisiana,* 59; Hardy, "Probate Racketeering," 110, 112; Asbury, *French Quarter,* 21; Carrigan, "Commentary," 427–31. Spanish imperial administration, which was huge, cumbersome, and bureaucratic, was not without its flaws. Institutionalized immorality was part of the machinery by which the empire functioned; but in this, the Spanish Empire was not unique. For a study of the character of judges, see Ralph H. Vigil, "Oidores, Letrados, and the Idea of Justice, 1480–1570," *Americas,* XLVII (1990–91), 39–54.

The end of the Spanish era, with the nefarious practices of acting civil governor Vidal (1799–1801) and Governor General Salcedo (1801–1803), should be contrasted with the early Spanish period. Henry P. Dart, who worked extensively with the New Orleans court records for the first half of the Spanish regime, found no evidence of peculation. He noted that in cases where litigation was unduly prolonged, the fault rested with the litigants and not with the courts. He judged the courts to be relatively efficient (Robertson, ed., *Louisiana Under the Rule,* I, 201–202; Laussat to Decres, July 18, 1803, *ibid.,* II, 42; Claiborne to Madison, January 2, 1804, *ibid.,* 231; Alliot, "Historical and Political Reflections," I, 35; Asbury, *French Quarter,* 256–57; Le Gardeur and Pitot, "Unpublished Memoir," 73–86; Texada, "Alejandro O'Reilly," 157; Carrigan, "Commentary," 431; Wood, "Life in New Orleans," 699; Robin, *Voyage to Louisiana,* 59; Dart, "Twelve Year Lawsuit," 294–95).

There are many instances in the early court records when the courts showed no favoritism to persons of status and influence, even Cabildo councillors. Evidence on the efficiency of law enforcement shows two tendencies. Caughey (in "Louisiana Under Spain," 30, 32, 39, 64) insists that justice was well enforced, at least in the first half of the Spanish period. Chambers (in *History of Louisiana,* I, 301) states that "justice was surely and evenly administered and a respect for law [was] inculcated in the minds of the rank and file of the people." This echoes statements made by Jefferson in his "Description." Travelers and historians of the final years of the Spanish period, however, often noted a different condition present in the colony.

Spanish legal usages into the American period, and some of these practices have continued to the present.[54]

54. Morazán, "Letters," II, 215; Robin, *Voyage to Louisiana,* 161–62; Robertson, ed., *Louisiana Under the Rule,* II, 169, 180; Everett S. Brown, ed., "The Orleans Territory Memorialists to Congress, 1804," *LHQ,* I (1918), 99–102; Claiborne to Madison, October 16, 1804, in Robertson, ed., *Louisiana Under the Rule,* II, 172–75; Philip Coolidge Brooks, "Spain's Farewell to Louisiana, 1803–1821," *Mississippi Valley Historical Review,* XXVII (1940), 36; Dart, "History of the Supreme Court," 16–18; Texada, "Alejandro O'Reilly," 179–80; Hans W. Baade, "The Law of Slavery in Spanish *Luisiana,* 1769–1803," in *Louisiana's Legal Heritage,* ed. Edward F. Haas (Pensacola, 1983), 71–75.

On the controversy over the origins of Louisiana's Civil Code of 1808, which forms the basis of about half of the state's present civil code, see Russell C. Reynolds, "Alfonso el Sabio's Laws Survive in the Civil Code of Louisiana," *LH,* XII (1971), 137–47; Rudolfo Batiza, "The Louisiana Civil Code of 1808: Its Actual Sources and Present Relevance," *Tulane Law Review,* special issue, XLVI (1971), 4–165; Robert A. Pascal, "Sources of the Digest of 1808: A Reply to Professor Batiza," *Tulane Law Review,* XLVI (1972), 603–27; Rudolfo Batiza, "Sources of the Civil Code of 1808, Facts and Speculation: A Rejoinder," *Tulane Law Review,* XLVI (1972), 628–52; Joseph Modeste Sweeney, "Tournament of Scholars Over the Sources of the Civil Code of 1808," *Tulane Law Review,* XLVI (1972), 585–602; and Grant Lyons, "Louisiana and the Livingston Criminal Codes," *LH,* XV (1974), 243–72. Batiza and Sweeney find the basis of Louisiana civil law in the French Napoleonic Code, whereas Reynolds and Pascal insist that it was derived from Spanish law that governed Louisianians for a third of a century. None of the participants denies that many Louisianians wanted to return to Spanish law.

The offices of *sereno, escribano,* post commandant, *síndico procurador general,* district syndics, and a type of *alcalde* were carried over into the American period (Morazán, "Letters," I, 2–3, 20; Robertson, ed., *Louisiana Under the Rule,* II, 309–19; Vincent Folch, ed., "Regulations to Be Observed by the Syndics and Alcalds [Alcaldes] of the Jurisdiction of Baton Rouge, 30 October 1804," *LHQ,* IX [1926], 405–10; Wilson and Huber, *The Cabildo,* 81–82). Public executions were retained in New Orleans until 1853 (Asbury, *French Quarter,* 201).

Thomas N. Ingersoll, in "Old New Orleans: Race, Class, Sex, and Order in the Early Deep South, 1718–1819" (Ph.D. dissertation, University of California, Los Angeles, 1990), has argued that Spanish slave law differed little from the Code Noir. Planters insisted that the Code Noir be reintroduced in December, 1803, however, thereby suggesting that a genuine difference existed. Ingersoll errs in believing that the Spanish crown decreed the Code Noir ou Loi Municipale, when in reality two French planters, members of the Cabildo, drew it up because they wanted to restore the Code Noir to Louisiana. See Chapter Seven.

SIX

Municipal Finances

T HE Cabildo's primary financial role was to pay for the administration of New Orleans. In the early years, its efforts and authority
in taxing and services were modest. But as the Spanish era pro-
gressed, the city's obligations grew and required more revenue. Before
long the Cabildo assumed taxing prerogatives that O'Reilly had not en-
visioned and the Laws of the Indies prohibited. Similarly, it engaged in
activities for the public welfare that Spanish law forbade. But had the
Cabildo not provided needed municipal services or sought new sources of
revenue, New Orleans would not have been a fit place to live in and its
services would have been dismal. From today's perspective, the changes
the city government of New Orleans introduced meant that it was modernizing and that Spanish laws, many of them centuries old and not relevant to the city, in some cases no longer applied.[1]

Several areas in which the Cabildo innovated for the public welfare
either were related to taxing or fell under the purview of the *mayordomo
de propios*. They included a variety of disparate fields: taxation, slavery,

---

1. New Orleans was not the only city expanding its services and seeking new sources of
revenue in the eighteenth century. Cities in English North America began doing the same
several decades before New Orleans (Carl Bridenbaugh, *Cities in Revolt: Urban Life in America,
1743–1776* [New York, 1955], 219–24).

night patrols, city illumination, fire fighting, and tavern and dance hall regulation. These services that the New Orleans municipal government first provided during the Spanish period were later regarded as normal. Other cities in North America were also moving in a similar direction.

After O'Reilly established the Cabildo in 1769, he worked with the councillors to create sources of revenue to pay for the city's administration. He placed annual licensing taxes on public facilities: twenty pesos for each of the six inns and forty pesos for each of the twelve taverns and six billiard halls. He also permitted the city to impose a one-peso-per-cask duty on liquor brought into the province. He estimated conservatively that the tax would generate five hundred pesos yearly for New Orleans.[2]

The general altered the taxation on meats and gifts that the butchers had paid during the French regime. They now received a monopoly contract for supplying New Orleans with meat in return for an annual tax of 365 pesos. Moreover, the butchers agreed not to raise meat prices.[3]

In addition, O'Reilly gave the city the two blocks of royal land that flanked the Plaza de Armas. He estimated that the Cabildo would realize three hundred pesos annually from renting lots to shopkeepers. In all, municipal income would yield approximately two thousand pesos, a sum he judged adequate to pay for services, employee salaries, and other necessary expenses.[4]

Separate from the city's general revenues but under the Cabildo's supervision were the anchorage fees ships paid to moor at the city levee. The rate was three pesos for ships below two hundred tons and six pesos for larger vessels. The Cabildo designated this money for repairs because the mooring posts driven into the levee contributed to its constant deterioration.[5]

2. O'Reilly to Arriaga, New Orleans, December 10, 1769, *SMV,* Pt. I, 134–35. AGI, PC, leg. 110, contains documents for 1770 and 1771 on the sums of money collected for the Cabildo from anchorage, tavern, inn, billiard, and liquor fees. The Royal Treasury's most important duty was paying defense costs because the military consumed the greater part of the subsidy sent yearly from Mexico. Other significant expenditures included the salaries of civilian royal officials and employees, Indian affairs, immigration or settlers, customs, and administering Louisiana's mercantilist regulations.

3. O'Reilly to Arriaga, New Orleans, December 10, 1769, *SMV,* Pt. I, 134–35.

4. *Ibid.* The city owned additional land besides that on the Plaza de Armas.

5. *Ibid.;* Morazán, "Letters," I, 144–45. Under the French, money raised from licensing and taxing taverns was given to the church and the poor (Gayarré, *History of Louisiana,* II, 362).

In accordance with the Laws of the Indies, O'Reilly entrusted city finances to the annually elected *mayordomo de propios*. Aided by the Cabildo's monthly commissioners and porters, he collected the city's taxes and rents. He also made the disbursements for the city, except those belonging to the judiciary. Initially, confusion arose between his duties and those of the *depositario general*, but they were resolved by 1777. In the 1790s, the *mayordomo* received charge of the lighting department and the licensing of public facilities.[6]

The office of *mayordomo de propios* posed more problems for the Cabildo than any other elective post. Persons who possessed energy and financial acumen hesitated to serve in a position that offered only modest rewards. Under Spanish law, the *mayordomo* received a 1.5 percent fee of the monies he collected during his year in office. Because the city's revenue was initially only two thousand pesos, the *mayordomo* would earn a modest thirty pesos per year. In late 1776, Governor Unzaga and the Cabildo raised the commission to 2 percent.[7]

Despite an increase in income, it still represented a tiny payment for all of the service rendered, and finding competent persons to fill the office of *mayordomo de propios* was difficult. The annual audits of the city accounts often revealed shoddy bookkeeping. In such cases, the outgoing *mayordomo* had to resolve the discrepancies before he could relinquish the office to his successor.[8]

Because of the difficulty in securing qualified citizens to serve in the post, the Cabildo began to violate the law in 1778 by electing *mayordomos de propios* to more than two consecutive terms and without the requisite unanimous vote. As a result, Luis Boisdore, Francisco Blanche, Matías Alpuente, and Juan de Castañedo all served four or more consecutive terms. Of the nine men who filled the office during the Cabildo's thirty-

6. Code O'Reilly, 266; Actas del Cabildo, I, 223, March 1, 1777, III, (2), 103, May 14, 1790, IV, (2), 51–54, September 30, 1797, IV, (2), 77, November 17, 1797, IV, (3), 47, July 5, 1799; Texada, "Alejandro O'Reilly," 143.

7. Actas del Cabildo, I, 70, January 31, 1772, I, 75–76, March 13, 1772, III, (2), 170–75, January 28, 1792, III, (3), 44–45, January 11, 1793, IV, (3), 108–109, November 15, 1799, IV, (4), 64–65, January 30, 1801. Juan Durel served four years as *mayordomo de propios,* first in 1770 and 1771 and later in 1774 and 1775.

8. *Ibid.,* I, 147, January 28, 1774, I, 250, July 10, 1778, III, (3), 28, October 26, 1792.

four-year life, five of them held it for a total of thirty years (see Table 4 in Chapter Three).

The Cabildo elected the last *mayordomo de propios,* Castañedo, for eleven consecutive years. In 1795, after three years in office, he asked the Cabildo to raise his rate of commission to 5 percent and give him a fifty-ducat bonus. Síndico Procurador General Miguel Fortier, whom the council consulted, opined that the 5 percent fee was acceptable but the bonus should be denied because treasury funds were scarce and disbursements numerous. He added that the increase in commission should begin on the day Castañedo petitioned. Perhaps because the *mayordomo's* duties had recently increased with the creation of the lighting department, the Cabildo and Governor Carondelet permitted boosting Castañedo's fee to 5 percent.[9]

During Castañedo's eleven years as *mayordomo,* his brother José twice filled in for him with Cabildo permission. He did so first in 1793, when Juan left the province and again in 1802, when Dr. Jaén suspended him because he had become a *regidor.* In the latter case, Jaén alleged that the two offices were legally incompatible. Despite Jaén's ruling, the council reelected Castañedo as *mayordomo* in 1803. Castañedo, meanwhile, fought back. On July 16, 1802, he registered a formal protest with the Cabildo over his suspension, arrest, and "trial" by Dr. Jaén. He claimed that Jaén had acted illegally and exceeded the authority of his commission, which was to conduct Miró's *residencia,* not investigate the Cabildo. Castañedo appealed to the government to declare Jaén's proceeding null and void and to bring a criminal suit against him. He asked the governor to prevent Jaén from leaving the province so that his usurpation could be punished. There is no evidence that any of his requests were granted.[10]

By every indication, Juan de Castañedo was an able administrator. Shortly after he was first elected in January, 1793, he noted the absence of detailed instructions for fulfilling the duties of his office. Consequently, whenever in doubt, he asked the council for direction. As he demonstrated

9. *Ibid.,* III, (3), 195, January 9, 1795. Castañedo received 5 percent on regular revenues. Late in the Spanish period, revenues exceeded thirteen thousand pesos. For extraordinary services, such as handling the city's massive flour purchases and sales or collecting an eight-thousand-peso debt from Lorenzo Sigur, he received a flat rate, which ranged between 1 and 2 percent.

10. *Ibid.,* III, (3), 67–68, May 17, 1793; Morazán, "Letters," II, 139, 145–52.

his competence, the Cabildo permitted him to act on verbal orders rather than wait for certificates of authorization required by law. Following complaints from the Havana superior tribunal in 1796, the council returned to issuing written authorizations. About a year later, however, it agreed to permit Castañedo and the monthly commissioners to make disbursements of up to ten pesos without prior authorization. They simply reported the petty expenditures at the end of each month.[11]

Castañedo's repeated reelection as *mayordomo* was opposed by Andrés Almonester. In October, 1797, he presented the Cabildo with a brief criticizing Castañedo's failure to post the bond required by law and objecting to the 5 percent commission rate. In response, the council required Castañedo to furnish the bond but only forwarded the protest about his fee to the king for clarification.[12]

Not surprisingly, in the 1798 elections, Almonester voted against Castañedo, protesting that his five years of continuous service created a dangerous precedent. The other councillors, nonetheless, voted for him, and he retained the office despite the lack of unanimity. Almonester's death several months later silenced objections from that quarter. In November, 1799, Castañedo petitioned the crown for permission to charge 5 percent on his commissions. The Cabildo had agreed to pay him that amount in 1795, pending royal approval that never came.[13]

In 1801 the council members became concerned about their decision to overpay Castañedo in violation of the law. They now attempted to replace him at the legal fee rate of 1.5 percent. They elected Francisco Duplessy as *mayordomo,* but he refused the office if they reduced the commission. The Cabildo then capitulated, dumped Duplessy, and reinstated Castañedo, a proven administrator, at the rate of 5 percent.[14]

The men who held the office of *mayordomo de propios* seem to have been

11. Actas del Cabildo, III, (3), 49, February 1, 1793, IV, (1), 110–11, April 22, 1796, IV, (2), 69–71, October 27, 1797.

12. *Ibid.,* IV, (2), 62, October 20, 1797, IV, (2), 66, October 27, 1797. The October 27, 1797, minutes seem not to have been approved because they lack signatures. A month earlier, Almonester had tried to block Castañedo's purchase of his post of *regidor* on the council.

13. *Ibid.,* IV, (2), 90, January 1, 1798, IV, (3), 112, November 22, 1799; Morazán, "Letters," I, 147.

14. Actas del Cabildo, IV, (4), 64–65, January 30, 1801.

upright; no evidence of corruption among them exists. Nevertheless, to ensure honesty, in 1792 the governor and the council took steps to prevent the possibility of graft. Shortly after arriving in Louisiana, Carondelet demanded that the city's accounts be forwarded through his office to the royal accountant. At that time, the governor still held the office of intendant. Later, after Carondelet relinquished the office, the city accounts continued to be forwarded through the governor to the intendant. In 1802 the Cabildo required the *mayordomo* to place city funds in the "coffer of the three keys" at the end of each month. The safe, a cypress chest housed in the *casa capitular,* would be opened only when the governor, the *alférez real,* and the *mayordomo de propios* were all present with their respective keys.[15]

The sums handled by the *mayordomo* grew significantly during the Spanish era. The Cabildo expanded the city's revenue base in two ways: it increased several of the taxes and rents that O'Reilly had established and it imposed new taxes.

In the early years, the city's privilege of taxing the taverns and cabarets gave it control over them.[16] They quickly increased in number and had tripled by the mid-1770s. Late in 1775, the Cabildo voted to give two men, Pedro Moris (Peter Morris) and Raymond Escate (Scott?), a monopoly on the operation of taverns, cabarets, restaurants, and boardinghouses servicing the city and its suburbs. The conditions of the contract stated that the lessees pay the city 840 pesos per year; pay an additional 140 pesos for the support of Charity Hospital and 25 pesos for the lighting of the city to celebrate the birth of a royal infant; submit a list of bartenders and cabaret operators for the council's approval; restrict the locations of bars to within three-quarters of a league from the city; and post a 6,600-peso bond. Moris and Escate accepted the terms, and the Cabildo granted them

15. *Ibid.,* III, (3), 23–24, October 2, 1792, III, (3), 132–33, March 28, 1794, IV, (1), 173–74, December 16, 1796, IV, (5), 2–3, July 19, 1802; Morazán, "Letters," I, 147–48.

16. Under the French, New Orleans had six cabarets in 1745. The police regulations of 1751 permitted six taverns to sell wine and spirits to the city's inhabitants but prohibited soldiers, Indians, and blacks from purchasing them. Taverns could not sell on Sunday during holy services, had to close by 9:00 P.M., and paid a two-hundred-livre (forty-peso) fee for each license (Henry P. Dart, "Cabarets in New Orleans in the French Colonial Period," *LHQ,* XIX [1936], 578–83).

the monopoly, permitting them to increase the number of taverns to twenty-four.[17]

Sometime before 1780 and at the instigation of Governor Gálvez, the Cabildo transferred the tavern monopoly to the militia. Gálvez calculated that the transfer would raise the city's tavern revenues to 1,200 pesos and benefit the militia besides. It, however, proved to be a blunder. The militia tavern keepers quickly found ways to evade payment. They departed with the militia for service elsewhere during the war, refusing to pay their license fees; sold their licenses back and forth; used personal influence with acting governor Piernas; and blatantly invoked their military *fuero*. Although the Cabildo strengthened the *mayordomo*'s authority to collect, he reported in 1781 that the taverns were 509 pesos in arrears. Gálvez soon assumed responsibility for collecting this money and released the *mayordomo* from his obligation. In 1781 the Cabildo returned the taverns to private and competitive ownership.[18]

Over the next decade, the competitive handling of the taverns worked well. The Cabildo minutes do not mention any problems, and income from tavern licenses rose to 1,996 pesos, 2½ reales in 1789. In 1791, however, the notorious reputation of several cabarets outside the city outweighed the benefits of the revenue they produced. Síndico Procurador General Francisco de Riaño complained to the council that certain taverns had become havens for iniquitous persons, including slaves. The latter were illegally purchasing liquor and arms, sometimes with pilfered articles. Because these establishments lay beyond the city's patrols, there was little likelihood that their illicit activities would be stopped or the law-breakers apprehended. Riaño asked the Cabildo to shut down the trouble spots permanently. The council agreed and mandated a fine for violations of its order.[19]

17. Clark, *New Orleans,* 262–63; Actas del Cabildo, I, 194, October 27, 1775, I, 198–99, December 1, 1775. For a discussion of taverns in Spanish Louisiana, see Holmes, "Spanish Regulation of Taverns," 149–83.

18. Actas del Cabildo, II, 27, May 26, 1780, II, 38, October 27, 1780, II, 49, February 24, 1781, II, 56, May 25, 1781, II, 67–68, August 17, 1781, II, 85–86, November 9, 1781; "Digest," 114.

19. Dart, ed., "Account of the Credit and Debit," 586–87; Actas del Cabildo, III, (2), 134, May 27, 1791.

The closing of several bars in New Orleans, however, did not end the chronic wrongdoing of other establishments. In 1793 Governor Carondelet began taking direct action and by the next year had shut down at least six bars. In 1795 the city's revenue from the tavern tax had dwindled to 1,440 pesos. Alguacil Mayor de la Barre introduced a resolution to the Cabildo that he thought would both solve the tavern problem and improve his office's effectiveness. He requested that six of the closed bars be reopened under his supervision and that their licensing be placed under his office. He could thus increase his staff by four or five bailiffs and compel the city's bistros to operate legally. The councillors timidly waited for the governor's reaction before endorsing de la Barre's proposal. Carondelet rejected it but agreed that the taverns needed scrutiny.[20]

Carondelet's solution was to close more bars. By 1797 only ten taverns still operated. That same year, the governor's office gave the *mayordomo de propios* authority to license bars to simplify the process and eliminate confusion in collecting the tavern tax.[21]

After Carondelet left Louisiana in 1797, bars in New Orleans increased in number and again attracted vulgar patrons and illegal activities. In 1800 Síndico Procurador General Pedro Barran asked the Cabildo to close the disorderly bistros. Acting civil governor Vidal refused to shut them down, but he promised that new licenses would not be issued until the existing bars went out of business. In 1803, at the end of the Spanish era, twenty-four taverns operated in and around New Orleans.[22]

Public dance halls also provided revenue for the city. Dancing was a popular form of entertainment for all social classes, from the elite to the slaves. Private celebrations with music, such as weddings, baptisms, anniversaries, and birthday parties, had long allowed the invited guests to dance. Private dance halls existed both for whites and blacks. Documents are silent about when they first appeared, but it is known that they were present by 1780. The first public dance hall for whites in New Orleans appeared in 1792, when the Cabildo placed one on the site of the old

20. Actas del Cabildo, III, (3), 47, January 25, 1793, III, (3), 147–48, June 27, 1794, III, (3), 149–50, July 11, 1794; "Miscellaneous Documents," I (unnumbered), 26–28, December 31, 1795, III (unnumbered), 5, December 31, 1795.
21. Actas del Cabildo, IV, (1), 222, June 2, 1797; Morazán, "Letters," I, 49–50.
22. Actas del Cabildo, IV, (3), 133, February 7, 1800; Morazán, "Letters," I, 49–50.

marketplace. (Black public dance halls are discussed in Chapter Seven.) The council offered a contract calling for an individual to build a hall to the Cabildo's specifications on city land. In return, the contractor would have the rent-free use of the facility for three years. After that time, he could either rent the concession from the city at a nominal rate or he could sell the building to the city for its appraised value. During the three-year life of the contract, the city agreed to maintain the building and its sidewalks and gutters.[23]

Filberto Farge accepted the contract. He built a wooden structure eighty feet long and more than thirty feet wide. It had a wooden dance floor and several tiers of boxes for chaperons and girls too young to dance. Other seats surrounded the dance floor to accommodate the dancers. Four reales entitled patrons to dance the night away, beginning at seven in the evening and continuing until morning. Five or six musicians provided the music. For those who craved additional diversion, a gaming room adjoined the dance hall. Although gambling was forbidden under Spanish law, the authorities never made a serious attempt to enforce the prohibition. For the city's inhabitants gambling was a passion second only to dancing. Even when higher fines were imposed to stop it in the American period, illegal gambling grew rather than diminished.[24]

In 1796, Farge accepted the option of renewing his concession, paying a fee of twenty pesos per month. Under the new contract, which Farge drafted, he was responsible only for minor repairs while the city was answerable for major repairs to the building. At the end of the five-year contract, the structure would become city property.[25]

When Farge's second contract expired in 1801, the Cabildo continued

23. Actas del Cabildo, IV, (4), 137–38, September 25, 1801, III, (2), 183–84, March 2, 1792. Rowdiness and disorder occasionally occurred at the dance halls. The governor responded by using soldiers to preserve order. Municipal authorities assumed control in the American period (Le Gardeur and Pitot, "Unpublished Memoir," 86; Robertson, ed., *Louisiana Under the Rule,* I, 211–16, II, 242–43; Asbury, *French Quarter,* 80–82).

24. Robertson, ed., *Louisiana Under the Rule,* I, 211; Asbury, *French Quarter,* 80–82; Morazán, "Letters," I, 48. In 1814 gambling was legalized and the proceeds of licensing were used to benefit the poor (Morazán, "Letters," I, 42–44; John Sibley, "The Journal of Dr. John Sibley, July–October, 1802," *LHQ,* X [1927], 483; Pintard, "New Orleans, 1801," 232).

25. "Miscellaneous Documents," II, Nos. 373–75, 64–65, October 30, 1800; Morazán, "Letters," I, 48.

to rent out the building but not as a dance hall. The councillors stipulated this restriction in their contract and leased the structure through an intermediary to Francisco La Rosa at 150 pesos per month. Despite the contractual restraint, La Rosa persisted in holding dances. Soon, however, the building required extensive repairs and he insisted that the Cabildo make them. When the city threatened to refuse because of his dances, La Rosa declared that he would not honor the lease if he could not continue them. The council authorized the repairs but insisted that the terms of the agreement were clear; moreover, it refused to permit La Rosa to break the contract. He kept the lease, but he resumed the public dances, presumably receiving permission for them from either Vidal or Salcedo.[26]

By 1803 the Cabildo's role in operating the dance hall had degenerated into subservience to the governor. The councillors never formally conceded La Rosa's right to hold public dances, but they tacitly consented. For example, the council once petitioned the governor that only clean and properly attired persons be admitted to the dances and that he publish the Cabildo regulation to this effect. Several weeks later, the council agreed to help stimulate La Rosa's business by trying to influence citizens to use his facilities and catering service for private parties. The council supported him but only if he continued to pay the same rent and kept the lease.[27]

The Cabildo's problems with the liquor import tax differed markedly from those related to regulating public facilities. Although the council preserved O'Reilly's import duty on liquors until late in the Spanish era, its most compelling problem concerned tax evasion. To guard against it, the Cabildo appointed an inspector of weights and measures. In 1781 ship captains and pilots attempted to invoke their marine *fuero* to avoid paying the tax. The next year, the council requested Governor Miró's assistance to force the merchants to report all liquor introductions to the *mayordomo de propios*. In 1793 the importers claimed excessive leakage in the liquor casks to evade taxes. The *mayordomo* then wanted the Cabildo to appoint a master cooper to inspect the barrels and halt the deception. The Cabildo referred him to Governor Carondelet, but the issue remained unresolved

26. Actas del Cabildo, IV, (4), 77, March 13, 1801, IV, (4), 105, June 26, 1801, IV, (4), 106–107, July 10, 1801, IV, (4), 137–38, September 25, 1801.

27. *Ibid.*, IV, (5), 39, January 21, 1803, IV, (5) 46–47, February 4, 1803.

because the same abuse continued in 1795. That year the Cabildo limited the leakage and evaporation allowance to 10 percent. The merchants' last known major attempt to cheat occurred in 1797, when they tried smuggling liquor into the city via Bayou St. John. Alerted, the Cabildo vowed to stop them.[28]

The continual efforts of the liquor merchants to cheat on import duties might have been tied to the method of wholesale marketing. Tavern keepers bought nearly all the imported wines and liquors at public auctions, where they conspired to fix the price they paid. Although this practice allowed them to retail the beverages at a moderate price, it squeezed the profits that import merchants realized.[29]

The Cabildo made only minor changes in the liquor tax during the Spanish era. Initially, the tax was one peso per cask or small barrel (*barrica*); moreover, it was collected only on fine rums and brandies. The authorities exempted refined *aguardiente* and rum brought from Jamaica and other foreign ports. The council soon changed its policy and permitted only *aguardiente* imported from Spain and the rest of Europe to enter tax free. It raised the tariff to two pesos per pipe before 1793 and placed cheap rums on the duty list in 1796. By 1797, the liquor tax netted 2,820 pesos, 1½ reales in revenue. The only liquor that remained untaxed was rum in bond. The merchants quickly seized this loophole, and by the summer of 1801, they imported only rum bottled in bond. Mayordomo Castañedo asked the Cabildo to halt this circumvention of the liquor tax. The council, which was by then impotent, resolved only to refer the problem to Governor Salcedo.[30]

During the Spanish era, the Cabildo left O'Reilly's anchorage fee unaltered. The wars of that age on occasion contributed to the decline of port traffic and wharfage revenues. During wartime, the council had to

28. *Ibid.,* I, 103–104, March 5, 1773, II, 49, February 24, 1781, II, 137–38, October 4, 1782, III, (3), 47–48, January 25, 1793, IV, (1), 52, August 29, 1795, IV, (1), 221–22, June 2, 1797.

29. Morazán, "Letters," I, 50.

30. Actas del Cabildo, IV, (1), 121–22, May 13, 1796, IV, (4), 129, August 21, 1801; "Miscellaneous Documents," I (unnumbered), 51, December 31, 1797. Between December 10, 1769, and November 18, 1770, the tax on imported *aguardiente* yielded 955 pesos and 4 reales. It, however, fell significantly for the first half of 1771 to 141 pesos ("Noticia de las cantidades . . . ," Juan Durel, New Orleans, AGI, PC, leg. 110).

find other income to defray the upkeep of the levees. In 1800 the port captain, who was a Royal Treasury official, challenged the city's right to the income. The king had approved O'Reilly's decree assigning the tax so the captain general of Cuba upheld the city's claim. But he sent the issue to the crown for clarification. The Spanish era ended without a royal decision, and the city collected the anchorage fee into the American period.[31]

Besides changing several of O'Reilly's taxes, the Cabildo introduced new duties. They were related to slave regulation (which is discussed in Chapter Seven) and to the establishment and upkeep of the lighting department. Each of the new taxes required the approval of the local residents, the governor, and the king.

The creation of the lighting department constituted the largest sustained Cabildo initiative in taxation. In 1792 the council, perhaps at the suggestion of Governor Carondelet, agreed to establish the lighting department. Once in operation, it developed into the city's principal fire-fighting and policing agency as well. Financing its operations became a prime Cabildo concern in the 1790s, but the city's efforts in fire prevention and fire fighting had begun much earlier.[32]

In 1770 the Cabildo took its first steps in fire prevention. It commissioned two stonemasons to inspect all of the city's chimneys to guarantee that they were not fire hazards. The inspections continued throughout the Spanish period. In 1775 the Cabildo established a ten-peso fine for citizens who failed to clean their chimneys before the trice-yearly inspections. The council employed stonemasons or bricklayers as inspectors, paying them each two pesos per day. It took two men two weeks to examine the entire city at the usual cost of forty-eight pesos. These inspections later provided the city with a census for the chimney tax.[33]

In April, 1771, New Orleans experienced its first serious fire in the

---

31. Morazán, "Letters," I, 144–45; Clark, New Orleans, 267; "Miscellaneous Documents," I (unnumbered), 28–34, December 31, 1797; Actas del Cabildo, IV, (3), 199–200, July 18, 1800.

32. Actas del Cabildo, III, (3), 25–26, October 5, 1792.

33. Ibid., I, 31, September 28, 1770, I, 193, October 20, 1775, III, (3), 48–49, February 1, 1793, IV, (1), 201, March 3, 1797, IV, (2), 51, September 30, 1797, IV, (2), 88, December 22, 1797; "Miscellaneous Documents," I, No. 155, 79, February (no day), 1797; Henry P. Dart, ed., "Fire Protection in New Orleans in Unzaga's Time," trans. Heloise H. Cruzat, LHQ, IV (1921), 201–204.

Spanish era. Because few men volunteered to combat the blaze that broke out on Conti Street, the Cabildo asked the governor to ensure the availability of sufficient firefighters in future emergencies. Unzaga obliged and issued an edict that required all able-bodied carpenters and joiners to assist in demolishing structures that might allow fires to spread. The edict imposed a one-ducat fine and the threat of imprisonment for all free men who failed to help when called upon. Masters whose slaves did not respond received a five-ducat fine. Citizens had to keep ladders, buckets, axes, pickaxes, and gaffs in their homes ready for use. Fires in homes could be employed only in fireplaces having chimneys, and the chimneys needed to be kept in good repair. At that time, many one-story New Orleans houses lacked fireplaces and the residents built fires on dirt floors.[34]

With the governor's consent, the council resolved to purchase two fire pumps and a large quantity of lightweight leather buckets for the fire brigades. It took six years for the city to discover that two fire pumps were already in their midst but in disrepair. After the army engineer inspected them, the councillors purchased them for 100 pesos each. Repairing them cost another 185 pesos. The council hired a blacksmith at 5 pesos per month to keep the pumps in working order.[35]

In early 1781 an arsonist seemed to be loose in New Orleans, and the public became alarmed. Martín Navarro, who was then acting civil governor, reported to Governor Gálvez in Havana that five fires had started in the city. He attributed one to a faulty chimney, but he believed the others had been started by hand. The Cabildo then acted, presumably by inspecting chimneys. It quickly demolished seventy-five inadequate chimneys and twenty ovens.[36]

When the devastating conflagration of 1788 occurred, the city's fire pumps appeared to be operational, but the flames consumed them. That fire broke out on March 21, at the house of José Vicente Núñez on Chartres Street. Fanned by a strong southerly wind, the blaze raged out of control for several hours. By the time firefighters extinguished it, about four-fifths of New Orleans had been reduced to ashes. Among the more than 850

34. Actas del Cabildo, I, 47–48, April 19, 1771; Dart, ed., "Fire Protection," 201–204.
35. Actas del Cabildo, I, 47–48, April 19, 1771, I, 226, April 25, 1777.
36. Navarro to Gálvez, New Orleans, March 5, 1781, AGI, PC, leg. 83. Inexplicably, the Cabildo minutes do not mention any of this information.

buildings lost were the church, the presbytery, the *casa capitular,* the jail, and the public market. In addition, the fire destroyed the commercial warehouses with their provisions and trade goods. The destruction amounted to an estimated 2,595,561 pesos. In the fire's aftermath, the Cabildo, the governor, and the intendancy collaborated closely to relieve the afflicted citizens. They also appealed to the crown for long-term assistance.[37]

The Cabildo soon moved to replace the destroyed fire-fighting equipment. It commissioned Regidor Carlos de Reggio to order sixty leather buckets, two large hook-and-chain grapples, and six wooden-handled gaffs. More important, the council implored Governor Miró to request four fire pumps from the captain general in Havana. Miró made the request, but nothing came of it. Instead, in 1789 the council began buying fire pumps from private citizens. Oliver Pollock furnished the first one for 326 pesos, which included the freight charges from Philadelphia. When he made delivery, the council built a shed to house it and hired an army engineer to inspect and maintain it.[38]

To pay for two additional fire pumps in May, 1792, the councillors authorized the *alcaldes de barrio* to accept voluntary contributions from the city's four wards. The council sought to raise six hundred pesos, but the residents generously donated one thousand pesos. After paying Prospero Jerroyolo for the pumps, the Cabildo returned the remaining money pro rata to the contributors. The lighting department would pay for maintaining the pumps.[39]

In 1793 the Cabildo hired Espiritu Liotau at fifty pesos a year to care for the fire pumps, but it soon dismissed him. That spring, the Cabildo

37. Actas del Cabildo, III, (2), 12–13, March 26, 1788, III, (2), 14–15, March 27, 1788, III, (2), 16, April 4, 1788; Burson, *Stewardship,* 220; Lauro A. Rojas, "The Great Fire of 1788 in New Orleans," *LHQ,* XX (1937), 580–82.

38. Actas del Cabildo, III, (2), 64, June 19, 1789, III, (2), 65, July 3, 1789, III, (2), 69, August 21, 1789. Oliver Pollock was an American merchant living in New Orleans. He ingratiated himself to Spanish officials and used his fortune and influence to aid the American Revolution. See James Alton James, *Oliver Pollock: The Life and Times of an Unknown Patriot* (New York, 1937).

39. Actas del Cabildo, III, (2), 201–202, May 4, 1792, III, (3), 14, August 3, 1792, III, (3), 20, September 14, 1792; "Miscellaneous Documents," I, No. 169, 98 (undated), II, Nos. 265–66, 53–54 (undated).

purchased two additional fire pumps at 270 pesos apiece and more fire-fighting equipment. Funds came from the residents through the efforts of the *alcaldes de barrio*. The city also built new sheds to house the fire pumps. The destructive hurricane of August 18, 1793, however, demolished the sheds and the Cabildo had to rebuild them.[40]

The city gradually assumed responsibility for providing other fire-fighting equipment. In 1771 Governor Unzaga made the residents responsible for axes, buckets, hooks, and ladders in case of fire, but his decree was unenforceable. Therefore, the Cabildo began purchasing minor equipment and placing it throughout the city, entrusting the homeowners with its care. Ultimately, the council provided dozens of ladders, more than a hundred axes, and about six hundred leather buckets. It published regulations governing the kinds and numbers of fire-fighting tools to be distributed throughout the city. When the citizens failed to comply with the regulations, the council purchased the necessary items from city funds and instructed the *alcaldes de barrio* to distribute them.[41]

The Cabildo's efforts to provide adequate fire protection seem to have been effective. No major fires occurred between 1788 and 1794. An arsonist later identified as Juan, who was a slave belonging to Colonel Piernas, started six fires in 1791 but failed to produce a significant blaze. An anxious Governor Miró scoured the city with patrols of army troops, Cabildo members, and city employees searching for him. After Juan's arrest in July, 1791, the fires ceased. He was sentenced to six years of labor on the Havana fortifications and shipped out of Louisiana in December.[42]

The Cabildo's precautions helped when the next major fire occurred in December, 1794. Confined to a portion of the city, it nevertheless destroyed 212 buildings, at a cost greater than that of the 1788 fire. Among the city's

40. Actas del Cabildo, II, (3), 48–49, February 1, 1793, III, (3), 52, February 8, 1793, III, (3), 57, March 1, 1793, III, (3), 66, May 10, 1793, III, (3), 72, June 14, 1793, III, (3), 102, December 13, 1793.

41. *Ibid.*, I, 61, November 8, 1771, I, 235, November 28, 1777, I, 248–49, May 22, 1778, II, 51–52, April 27, 1781, II, 58–59, June 15, 1781, III, (2), 64, June 19, 1789, III, (2), 171–72, January 28, 1792, III, (2), 171, February 3, 1792, III, (3), 33–34, November 16, 1792, IV, (1), 88, January 22, 1796, IV, (1), 172, December 16, 1796, IV, (1), 201, March 3, 1797, IV, (2), 81, December 1, 1797, IV, (2), 110–111, April 3, 1798.

42. Miró to Las Casas, New Orleans, July 2 and 15, December 26, 1791, all in AGI, PC, leg. 1440.

losses were the entire flour reserve and most of its other provisions. The Cabildo again appealed to the crown for emergency relief.[43]

After the fire, the council relocated the fire pumps. Over the next few years, it moved them several times in an effort to obtain maximum protection for the city and the pumps. Eventually, the Cabildo stored them in the houses of the *alcaldes de barrio,* who became responsible for the pumps' protection and operation. The decentralized locations made the pumps more readily available in case of fire but impeded their protection, inspection, and repair. In a 1792 decree, Governor Carondelet charged the *alcaldes de barrio* to appoint a monthly fire brigade of fifteen men for each ward and to name a competent leader for each brigade. Carondelet also required that a well be dug on each city lot to furnish water for fighting fires.[44]

Following the 1794 blaze, the Cabildo had difficulty finding a reliable engineer to keep the pumps in running order. In 1795, an engineer named Francisco Chaise or Chesse was under contract to care for them at an annual salary of three hundred pesos. When he failed to service and test the pumps regularly, the council dismissed him and entrusted the monthly commissioner with inspecting them. Although the council was supposed to hire an expert to keep the pumps operational, the system proved unsatisfactory. In 1799 the Cabildo assigned another engineer, Santos Letourneau, to care for them. He had to test each pump twice monthly and keep all of them in repair. Except for paying 250 pesos in 1801 for overhauling one pump, the council had no more problems with the pumps for the rest of the Spanish period.[45]

Governor Carondelet also initiated other fire-fighting measures in the

43. Morazán, "Letters," II, 107; Asbury, *French Quarter,* 38; Clark, *New Orleans,* 256; Actas del Cabildo, III, (3), 187, December 19, 1794. The only study of the 1794 fire is Holmes, "The 1794 New Orleans Fire," 21–43.

44. Actas del Cabildo, IV, (1), 52–53, August 29, 1795, IV, (1), 55, September 11, 1795, IV, (1), 141, July 15, 1796, IV, (2), 29–30, September 1, 1797, IV, (2), 58–59, October 13, 1797, IV, (2), 71, October 27, 1797; "Miscellaneous Documents," II, Nos. 283–84, 75–76 (undated); Yerxa, "Administration of Carondelet," 10–11.

45. Actas del Cabildo, IV, (1), 52, August 29, 1795, IV, (3), 20, March 8, 1799, IV, (4), 123, August 7, 1801. The system of fighting fires that evolved under the Spaniards was retained in its essentials under American rule (Morazán, "Letters," II, 171–72; Wilson and Huber, *The Cabildo,* 62).

1790s. He started them before the 1794 fire but did not complete them until after the conflagration. In this period the lighting department began functioning under the management of the *mayordomo de propios*. Care for the city's fire-fighting equipment fell to the lighting department, which paid its expenses.[46]

Soon after he became governor, Carondelet proposed establishing a lighting system. Many of the larger cities in Europe and America were then being illuminated.[47] The baron observed to the Cabildo that New Orleans' darkened streets facilitated criminal activity. He suggested purchasing and placing lamp reflectors on corner buildings at street intersections. He offered to obtain the reflectors at a reduced price, and he believed that the city's property owners could be persuaded to contribute to their maintenance. He proposed paying for the reflectors by cutting the trees adjacent to the city; the woods furnished hiding places for malefactors and jeopardized New Orleans' security from a military standpoint. Once the land was cleared, the Cabildo had the choice of either selling the lots or fencing them in to pasture cattle. He estimated that the city could charge four reales per month per head of livestock, a fee below that demanded by owners of unfenced pasturage farther away. The councillors unanimously agreed.[48]

Carondelet patterned New Orleans' street lighting system after the one in use in Havana. It was fairly elaborate for a frontier town. The governor's initial plan for the reflectors might have been only to improve the existing lighting already provided by the residents. A delay, however, postponed establishing the reflectors. Not until 1794 did Carondelet order eighty lamps from Philadelphia and issue directions on how to hang them. The city paid 626 pesos, 5 reales, for the lamps and 521 pesos to install them. The governor also drew up rules for their use. After the council approved them, he had them printed and distributed to the judges, night watchmen, and other officials. The council negotiated annual contracts with local tradesmen to repair and maintain the lamps. The Cabildo began

46. Morazán, "Letters," II, 171–72; Actas del Cabildo, IV, (1), 52, August 29, 1795, IV, (1), 70–73, November 13, 1795, IV, (1), 79–80, December 11, 1795.

47. Philadelphia, New York City, Charleston, and Boston started to illuminate their streets at night in the 1760s and 1770s (Bridenbaugh, *Cities in Revolt*, 241–43).

48. Actas del Cabildo, III, (3), 25–26, October 5, 1792.

purchasing additional lamps made locally—artisans now manufactured them in New Orleans—as the need arose.[49]

Although watchmen lit the lamps only on nights when moonlight was insufficient, maintaining the lighting system proved expensive. The Cabildo paid more than 150 pesos for barrels to store the oil and grease used in the lamps. Repairs to the lamps amounted to several hundred pesos over the last years of the Spanish period. The lamps also consumed cotton wicks, flints and steels, and sulfur. Nevertheless, fuel for the lamps, either fish oil or bear or pelican grease, constituted the most expensive part of illuminating the streets.[50]

In March, 1796, Almonester furnished the council with an itemized estimate of the consumable materials for the lamps. He calculated lamp usage at twenty-two nights per month and fuel consumption at forty-two cans of oil per lamp per year. Each watchman was assigned seven or eight lamps, which meant that approximately ninety lamps were in use. At the rate of three reales per can of oil or five reales per can of grease, the minimum fuel expenditure would exceed 1,417 pesos per year. Almonester also estimated that the watchmen would consume yearly 288 flints, 9 pounds of cotton wicks, 9 pounds of sulfur, and 24 steels. He judged the cost of these minor items at only 15 pesos yearly.[51]

Rarely, if ever, did expenditures run less than the figure Almonester projected. In 1801 the purchase of fish oil alone cost the city 2,392 pesos. The contract for supplying New Orleans with fish oil was sold at public auction. In 1797 the Cabildo found no bidders for the contract and, consequently, commandeered all available oil in the city. Because fuel oil ran out, the next year the city employed pelican and bear grease.[52]

49. *Ibid.,* III, (3), 134, April 25, 1794, III, (3), 141–42, May 23, 1794, III, (3), 158, August 22, 1794, III, (3), 162–63, September 19, 1794, III, (3), 170–71, October 24, 1794, III, (3), 196–97, January 16, 1795, IV, (1), 148, August 5, 1796, IV, (1), 149, August 12, 1796, IV, (3), 120–21, December 20, 1799; "Miscellaneous Documents," I, Nos. 177–80, 105–106, November 24, 1797; Morazán, "Letters," II, 106.

50. Actas del Cabildo, III, (3), 180, November 21, 1794, IV, (4), 150, January 8, 1802, IV, (5), 46, February 4, 1803, IV, (1), 79–80, December 11, 1795, IV, (1), 101, March 11, 1796.

51. *Ibid.,* IV, (1), 101, 104–105, March 11, 1796.

52. *Ibid.,* IV, (2), 84, December 7, 1797, IV, (2), 87, December 22, 1797, IV, (2), 101, February 23, 1798, IV, (2), 107, March 9, 1798, IV, (2), 146–47, July 27, 1798, IV, (2), 151, August 17, 1798, IV, (2), 156, September 14, 1798, IV, (4), 62, January 23, 1801, IV, (4), 88, April 24, 1801, IV, (4), 128, August 21, 1801; "Miscellaneous Documents," I, No. 339, 86–88 (undated).

When Carondelet suggested street illumination, he outlined plans for *serenos*. They appear not to have started working until October, 1794, when the Cabildo officially appointed personnel and assigned salaries. Initially, eight watchmen and one corporal made up the corps of *serenos*. It later expanded to twelve watchmen and two corporals.[53]

Although the *serenos* were subject to the orders of the monthly commissioners, they were under the *mayordomo de propios'* immediate authority. The Cabildo furnished them with uniforms, badges of office, sabers, scabbards, iron spears (halberds), and ladders for reaching the street lamps. As employees of the lighting department, their duties included keeping the lamps fueled and lit on dark nights. In addition, they had to keep the peace and watch for suspicious activities and fires. The last duty was especially important, and anyone sounding the alarm in a fire received a twenty-five-peso reward. It was a significant sum because *serenos* received fifteen pesos monthly and corporals twenty pesos. Sereno Antonio Hojeda earned the reward in May, 1795, for alerting the city and possibly averting a major fire. At full strength the yearly payroll for *serenos* was 2,500 pesos.[54]

The corps of watchmen, however, was inadequate for meeting all the city's security needs. Bars outside New Orleans lay beyond its surveillance. Nor were the *serenos* entirely effective against fires; they failed to apprehend an arsonist in 1795. After the unknown incendiary started three fires in a short period of time, Carondelet offered a five-hundred-peso reward for the miscreant's capture. The Cabildo received responsibility for paying the reward, but the arsonist eluded apprehension.[55]

Operating the lighting department, which included the *serenos'* salaries, was expensive. The street lamps and the equipment for the watchmen initially cost 2,168 pesos. The department borrowed the funds from the city treasury. The original estimate for running the department was 3,897 pesos annually. In addition, the department had responsibility for replac-

---

53. Actas del Cabildo, III, (3), 166, October 10, 1794.

54. Morazán, "Letters," I, 114; Fortier, *History of Louisiana,* II, 165; Actas del Cabildo, III, (3), 167, October 10, 1794, IV, (1), 34–36, May 29, 1795, IV, (3), 118, December 13, 1799, IV, (3), 162, March 21, 1800, IV, (3), 186, June 6, 1800; "Miscellaneous Documents," I (unnumbered), 14–17 (undated), I (unnumbered), 165–66 (undated); II, No. 217, 17, 29 (undated), II, Nos. 291–94, 80–81 (undated).

55. Actas del Cabildo, IV, (1), 34, May 29, 1795.

ing the lamps and the fire-fighting equipment. The Cabildo needed to find a satisfactory way to finance these high costs.[56]

On establishing the lighting department in 1794, the Cabildo discussed the feasibility of imposing a frontage tax on all the lots within the city. The frontage was the length of the lot on the street. Because it did not take into consideration the depth of the lot or the value of the property on the lot, the proposed tax was regressive. The Cabildo appointed two *regidores* to estimate the costs to determine the rate of taxation. Governor Carondelet, however, disapproved of the idea and proposed a chimney tax as a suitable alternative.[57]

A chimney tax seems to have existed earlier. It was a progressive tax because residents owning larger houses with many rooms and fireplaces paid more. To avoid the full tax burden, several enterprising residents constructed houses with double and even triple fireplaces, using the same chimney to heat two or three rooms. Carondelet proposed raising the yearly chimney tax to nine reales per chimney, with chimneys servicing more than one fireplace paying double the tax. The councillors believed that this rate was more affordable by the poor and could be adjusted to meet the needs of the lighting department. They approved it and asked Carondelet to inform the public through the town crier.[58]

The new tax satisfied the lighting department's needs for 1794, but the New Orleans fire in December changed conditions. The loss of many houses belonging to wealthy residents reduced city revenue significantly. The Cabildo considered abandoning the lighting system, but Carondelet disagreed. He prevailed upon the council to raise the chimney tax on the remaining houses to twelve reales per chimney.[59]

Although owners of larger houses seem not to have protested, in the spring of 1795 several other residents complained that they were taxed out of proportion to their chimneys. The council had the *alcaldes de barrio* make a special chimney census to ensure fair and uniform taxation. Some

56. Morazán, "Letters," II, 106.
57. Actas del Cabildo, III, (3), 136, May 2, 1794, III, (3), 152, August 1, 1794.
58. *Ibid.,* III, (3), 152, August 1, 1794.
59. *Ibid.,* III, (3), 187–88, December 19, 1794, IV, (1), 31, May 22, 1795; "Miscellaneous Documents," III, Nos. 323–24, 54, April 2, 1796.

homeowners, however, continued to avoid payment. Collection of the chimney tax was 479 pesos, 2 reales, in arrears by the end of 1797.[60]

In an extraordinary cabildo meeting held in early 1798, Governor Gayoso pointed out to the councillors that the chimney tax was unsatisfactory and sometimes uncollectible. He stated that merchants had suggested an import duty on goods entering the colony. But because the impost required royal approval before it could begin, Gayoso asked the councillors for an alternate solution to secure the needed revenues.[61]

The Cabildo failed to find a satisfactory answer until the city butchers and bakers came to the rescue in April, volunteering to pay a tax to support the lighting department. Moreover, they would not ask for an increase in meat or bread prices but pay the duty from their profits. Once Vidal tentatively sanctioned the tax as legal pending royal confirmation, the Cabildo approved it.[62]

The councillors then ordered the *alcaldes de barrio* to collect the unpaid chimney taxes and announce its end. When they failed to recover the funds, the *regidores* informed the *mayordomo* to regard them as irreclaimable. They instructed him to write off the amount and close the chimney tax account. The chimney inspections for fire hazards continued unchanged.[63]

The crown responded slowly to the needs of the lighting department. Six months after the butchers' and bakers' tax went into effect, the Cabildo received royal permission to establish the lighting department and increase the chimney tax. Permission came as a command, and the Cabildo quickly responded that it could not comply. It was a perfect example of *obedezco*

60. "Miscellaneous Documents," III, Nos. 318–19, 28–35, December 31, 1797, III, No. 320, 42, December 31, 1797, I (unnumbered), 18–25, December 31, 1797, III, No. 333, 72, December 31, 1797, III (unnumbered), 36–42, December 31, 1797, III, No. 335, 76, September 14, 1798.

61. Actas del Cabildo, IV, (2), 98–99, February 14, 1798. In Gayoso's 1798 *bando de buen gobierno,* he included several provisions on fire fighting. The *alcalde de barrio* was to have in his quarter buckets, axes, and ladders that would be distributed to volunteers who assisted in extinguishing fires. Each property owner had to dig a well on his property or the city would do it for him at his expense. Each month the *alcalde de barrio* had to appoint fifteen men from his ward as axmen and fifteen more as bucketmen and provide them with axes and buckets. The *alcalde de barrio* had to appoint a competent person to direct the firefighters. If the fire spread, the *alcalde* was to obtain help from other quarters and all citizens, especially carpenters and masons, who were obliged to help (Chandler, "Life in New Orleans," 179–86).

62. Actas del Cabildo, IV, (2), 112–13, April 16, 1798, IV, (2), 114–22, April 20, 1798.

63. *Ibid.,* IV, (2), 122, April 27, 1798, IV, (2), 157, September 14, 1798.

pero no cumplo (I obey but I do not fulfill), which colonial officials employed many times in answer to royal decrees. The council appointed two *regidores* to renew its plea for a new food tax to raise the needed lighting revenue.[64]

In 1802 the king accepted the Cabildo's request. First, however, he reprimanded the council for imposing the meat and flour duty without waiting for his approval. He then permitted the Cabildo to use whichever tax was most beneficial and adjust it to meet the needs of the lighting department. The council thanked the king and sent him documents to demonstrate the advantages of the food impost.[65]

Income for the lighting department was now secure, usually exceeding six thousand pesos yearly, with the butchers and bakers each paying approximately half. Moreover, the lighting department generally had funds left over each year, which the council used to repay the city treasury's loan to establish and operate the department after the 1794 fire.[66]

The Cabildo had various other minor sources of income. It leased city-owned lots to tenants at an annual rent or tax of 5 percent of the property's value. The council made several attempts to increase the city's property holdings, which would have brought additional revenue. The king usually granted the city the lands it asked for, but the Cabildo never secured royal clarification of its land rights. In times of need, the council taxed untitled lands such as the lots on the levee used by food vendors.[67]

When the need became critical, the Cabildo had the right to impose an excise tax, pending royal confirmation. The council enacted this tax but kept the revenues separate from the city's general account until 1796. At that time, Judge Advocate Vidal opined that it was illegal to keep them apart. Although the Cabildo had earlier agreed to keep them separately, it now bowed to Vidal's judgment.[68]

The council also had charge of endowment funds for charitable insti-

64. *Ibid.,* IV, (2), 161–62, October 19, 1798.

65. *Ibid.,* IV, (4), 220–21, June 25, 1802.

66. *Ibid.,* IV, (3), 27, April 19, 1799, IV, (4), 176–77, February 26, 1802; "Miscellaneous Documents," II, No. 231, 20–42, December 31, 1800; II, No. 272, 63, December 31, 1800.

67. Actas del Cabildo, I, 225–26, April 11, 1777, II, 183–84, July 11, 1783, II, 197–98, December 19, 1783, IV, (2), 67, October 27, 1797, IV, (3), 61, August 23, 1799; Clark, *New Orleans,* 267.

68. Actas del Cabildo, IV, (1), 173–74, December 16, 1796.

tutions. Shortly after its creation, the Cabildo had a measure of financial control over the parish church. After relinquishing charge over the church, the council still retained direction of the endowments for the orphan asylum and the leper hospital. Bernardo de Gálvez had granted the orphanage the rents from seventeen government-owned houses. That income exceeded the orphanage's needs, and the surplus grew to nearly seven thousand pesos by 1801. The king permitted the city government to use the surplus to build a public granary, but it was less needed by the time permission arrived. Instead, the Cabildo loaned the money to the intendancy to cover a shortfall in royal revenues.[69]

The fund for the leper hospital operated differently from that for the orphanage. In 1786 the Cabildo enjoyed a 2,100-peso surplus from the market rents. Gálvez, now viceroy of New Spain but still exercising authority over Louisiana, ordered that the money become an endowment for the hospital. After paying for several repairs, the Cabildo loaned the remaining money to endow an income for the hospital. The borrowers, usually Cabildo members or their relatives, paid 5 percent interest and an additional customary alms of 5 percent. Moreover, the borrowers had to post a surety bond, usually mortgages on their real estate. The money consisted of two loans of one thousand pesos each, and the borrowers could use the money indefinitely as long as they maintained their bonds and paid the quarterly interest promptly. Regidor Luis Toutant Beauregard managed the fund until his death. In 1796 Mayordomo Castañedo assumed control.[70]

Although O'Reilly set a three-thousand-maravedí (ten-peso) limitation on what the Cabildo could spend without the governor's approval, the Cabildo freely exceeded the limit. Moreover, discord between the governor and the council seldom occurred for most of the period because both sought to use municipal funds in the most advantageous manner. On several rare occasions, however, a difference of opinion surfaced. Only two

69. Morazán, "Letters," II, 27.
70. Actas del Cabildo, III, (1), 123, December 22, 1786, IV, (1), 169, December 2, 1796, IV, (1), 225–26, June 23, 1797, IV, (2), 24–25, August 23, 1797, IV, (2), 33, September 7, 1797, IV, (2), 160, October 13, 1798, IV, (4), 79, March 20, 1801, IV, (5), 37, January 14, 1803; Duffy, ed., *Rudolph Matas History,* I, 261–62.

gubernatorial vetoes of Cabildo spending, both by Salcedo in 1802, are worthy of mention.[71]

Salcedo imposed his vetoes at a time when the Cabildo's power had declined. On the first occasion, the city government hired Licenciado José Martínez de la Pedrera as its legal counsel at an annual salary of five hundred pesos. The Cabildo had already clashed with Salcedo and realized that it could not obtain appropriate advice from the government lawyer Vidal. When Martínez advised the council on how to proceed in its battle with Salcedo, a vengeful governor first arrested and then deported him to Havana for trial. On his departure, Martínez asked the Cabildo to pay his salary to his family until he returned. Salcedo advised the councillors against doing so because he had not approved Martínez' appointment. The *audiencia* at Puerto Príncipe subsequently acquitted Martínez of all charges and ordered the council to pay him more than three hundred pesos in back wages. In this case, a superior tribunal overrode the governor's veto.[72]

Salcedo's second veto was closely tied to his first. The Cabildo hired Cuban attorney Domingo Piña to represent its interests at the *audiencia* in Puerto Príncipe and agreed to send him a three-hundred-peso retainer. When Salcedo read this in the council minutes, he tried to block payment, alleging that public funds were being put to private use. He ordered Mayordomo de Propios Castañedo to halt payment by whatever means necessary. He, however, replied that the money had already been shipped, and, in any case, he would have had to obey the Cabildo's order. Meanwhile, the council apprised the governor that the money was being used for public, not private, purposes and that the *audiencia* could decide the issue. If it ruled against the Cabildo, the councillors would repay the money. There is no indication that they did because Havana probably decided in the Cabildo's favor.[73]

71. Code O'Reilly, 257. In 1770 Governor Unzaga postponed paying several hundred pesos for livery and accoutrements for the Cabildo porters. He argued that frills should wait until the council attained a surplus in the city treasury. Within two years, the Cabildo purchased the regalia with Unzaga's approval (Actas del Cabildo, I, 36, November 16, 1770, I, 62–63, November 22, 1771, I, 72–73, February 21, 1772).

72. Actas del Cabildo, IV, (4), 167–70, February 12, 1802, IV, (4), 198–99, April 23, 1802, IV, (4), 211–12, May 14, 1802, IV, (5), 17–18, September 17, 1802; Morazán, "Letters," II, 79–80n, 116.

73. Morazán, "Letters," II, 161–68. The Cabildo's retention of an attorney at Puerto Prín-

Salcedo used the two vetoes to block the Cabildo from employing municipal funds for legal aid against him. In both cases, the governor's motive for barring the expenditures was political, not economic as he claimed. The two cases involved hundreds of pesos, and in both instances the governor lost. The two examples demonstrate the governor's limited veto power over municipal finances, even near the end of the Spanish period when the Cabildo was severely weakened.

The Spanish governor's inability to spend municipal revenues without Cabildo authorization was perhaps even more significant than the ineffectiveness of his veto power. Not until Carondelet's administration did a governor infringe upon the use of city funds. Early in his administration, the baron began to order things done and report his acts to the Cabildo after the fact. The councillors paid the bills because they did not object to the governor's arbitrary methods and, overall, the city benefited.[74]

Only Governor Salcedo used municipal funds without Cabildo authority. One incident best illustrates the governor's disregard of the council. In 1803 Spanish troops at New Madrid captured Samuel Mason's band of river pirates and transported them to New Orleans. Because the pirates were mainly Americans who had committed their crimes on United States soil, Governor Salcedo sent them to Natchez in the Mississippi Territory for trial. The cost for shipping them first to New Orleans and then to Natchez totaled 1,570 pesos. Salcedo wanted the city treasury to advance the money to the impecunious intendancy; American authorities would reimburse the city. He offered as collateral two thousand dollars in American banknotes, which was part of the captured loot. But the council refused his request because poor relations between the two already existed. Then in two extraordinary Cabildo meetings, Salcedo issued formal orders to obtain the money, but the councillors still balked. Faced with the Cabildo's intransigence, the governor dispatched an army officer to withdraw the money from the chest of three keys. Reluctantly, the council accepted the banknotes as collateral, declaring that its money had been

cipe followed on the heels of Salcedo's mistreatment of Martínez de la Pedrera. The Cabildo shipped the retainer a week after the governor refused to pay Martínez' salary. In Havana, the captain general already knew that Salcedo was unqualified to hold his office (Someruelos to Jerónimo Caballero, No. 248, Havana, May 12, 1802, AGI, SD, leg. 2569).

74. Actas del Cabildo, III, (3), 44–45, January 11, 1793.

seized over protest. The councillors swore that they would inform the king.[75] Salcedo's two vetoes and forced loan were the only gubernatorial infringements on municipal revenues of which the Cabildo disapproved.

City revenues increased substantially during the Spanish period, particularly toward the end. Starting at 2,000 pesos in 1770, they grew to 9,907 pesos by 1791, and to 13,145 pesos by 1795. They continued to rise because the meat and flour tax, which produced large sums of money, began after 1795.[76]

By contemporary Spanish American standards, New Orleans had a high per capita municipal income. It exceeded those of Havana, Mexico City, and Buenos Aires. Closest of the three was Havana, but New Orleans' per capita municipal income was still 50 percent greater than Havana's. Perhaps because the city government was not dominated by dynastic families in opposition to revenue enhancement, New Orleans made a greater effort to raise money than did other Spanish American cities. It worked strenuously to provide services in important areas where neglect might threaten the lives and property of the inhabitants. In 1801, near the close of the Spanish era, the chief sources of income for the city were the meat tax; the billiard, inn, and tavern tax; the liquor tax; rent from the dance hall; and the anchorage tax. Overall, these taxes were regressive. That year the city generated in income 12,587 pesos, 3½ reales, which, added to a surplus of 13,839 pesos, 4½ reales, at the end of 1800, gave New Orleans a working capital of 26,427 pesos. Expenses for 1801 amounted to 15,243 pesos, which left the Cabildo with 11,184 pesos at the end of the year.[77] The list noting the income for 1801, however, failed to include another important source of revenue, the flour tax.

New Orleans differed from other Spanish American cities in another major respect. It used its revenues more constructively than was common in the other Spanish colonial cities. Perhaps influenced by the modernizing trends then under way in the major urban centers on both sides of the Atlantic, New Orleans was developing faster than the older, isolated, and traditional Spanish American municipalities.[78]

75. Morazán, "Letters," II, 191–205; Actas del Cabildo, IV, (5), 52–53, March 7, 1803.
76. "Miscellaneous Documents," I, No. 281, 74, December 31, 1791; Actas del Cabildo, IV, (1), 119, May 6, 1796.
77. Ezquerra Abadía, "Un presupuesto americano," 686–90.
78. Clark, New Orleans, 263; Ezquerra Abadía, "Un presupuesto americano," 694, 710.

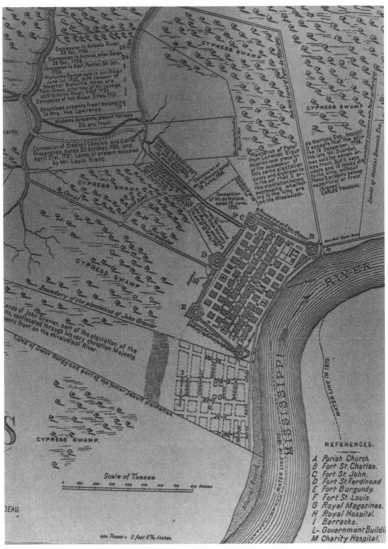

Detail of the Spanish plan of 1798 (translated) showing the city of New Orleans
and its environs
Courtesy Special Collections, University of Memphis

DON ALESSANDRO
O'REILLY

Alejandro O'Reilly, governor of the Spanish colony in 1769, who arranged for the
construction of the first *casa capitular*
Courtesy Special Collections, University of Memphis

Sketch of the first *casa capitular*. The Cabildo met in this building until it was destroyed
in the great fire of 1788.
Restorative sketch by Henry J. Krotzer, Jr., courtesy of Kock and Wilson

Esteban Miró, governor of the colony from 1782 to 1791. The Cabildo reached the zenith
of its prestige and effectiveness under Miró.
Courtesy Special Collections, University of Memphis

Barón de Carondelet, governor (1792–97) under whom the Cabildo lost its vitality
Courtesy Special Collections, University of Memphis

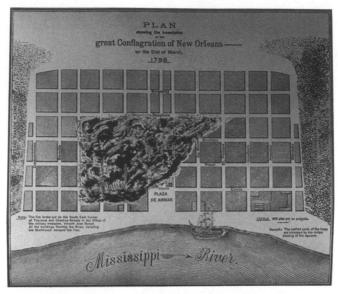

Drawing of the New Orleans riverfront, showing the area damaged by the 1788 fire
Courtesy Special Collections, University of Memphis

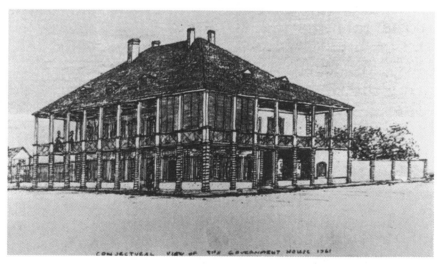

The Government House, where the Cabildo met briefly and extralegally after the
fire of 1788
Sketch by Henry J. Krotzer, Jr., courtesy of Kock and Wilson

Andrés Almonester y Roxas, a senior *regidor* in the municipal government, who in 1795 offered to finance the reconstruction of the *casa capitular*. Portrait by Salazar.
Courtesy Archdiocese of New Orleans

The second *casa capitular* at the time of the Louisiana Purchase. The Cabildo met here from 1799 through 1803.
Retrospective sketch by Joseph Pennell

SEVEN

The Cabildo and Blacks

THE New Orleans Cabildo played an important role in attempting to control Louisiana's African population. Regulating slaves and free blacks was the principal area in which the Cabildo tried to impose its authority beyond the city's immediate vicinity. Because blacks constituted approximately half of the colony's population, the Cabildo councillors, particularly those who were slave-owning planters, believed it vital to regulate Africans, both slave and free, which they attempted to do in the 1770s and 1780s. After the 1791 Haitian revolution erupted, planters felt even more apprehensive about the blacks in their midst. Moreover, a number of them detested Spain's "lenient" slave laws such as *coartación* (self-purchase by slaves), notaries granting letters of freedom, the right of slaves to complain to the authorities of abuse by masters and seek new owners, and limitations on punishment. The planters tried several times to resurrect the French Code Noir, or at least those parts that gave them more control of their slaves.[1]

---

1. Not all parts of Louisiana's 1724 Code Noir were enforced during the French regime. Among the provisions not enforced, fugitive slaves usually did not receive the punishment the code decreed; interracial cohabitation went on; and blacks and mulattoes were emancipated in violation of the law. See Mathé Allain, "Slave Policies in French Louisiana," *LH,* XXI (1980), 127–37; Carl A. Brasseaux, "The Administration of Slave Regulations in French Louisiana, 1724–1766," *LH,* XXI (1980), 139–58; and Usner, *Indians, Settlers, and Slaves,* 50. French planters,

The earliest slave problem the Spaniards encountered concerned fugitives, a carryover from the French era. Both the Cabildo and several governors attempted to deal with runaway slaves. Before O'Reilly left Louisana, Síndico Procurador General Luis Ranson presented a petition from planters proposing a fund for the capture of runaways. He wanted to create a "small police force" consisting of six free mulattoes or blacks called the Cuadrilleros de la Santa Hermandad (Patrolmen of the Holy Brotherhood). For their work, they would receive a half peso per fugitive captured in New Orleans and six pesos for each captured in the countryside. Owners would compensate the captors for blacks found on the roads without their master's permission. To pay the patrolmen for their work, slave owners living on the Mississippi from the river's mouth to the Acadian Coast would contribute one real for each slave of working age they possessed. Monies collected would be sent to New Orleans, where a governor-appointed treasurer would keep them. Owners whose slaves were killed resisting arrest or executed would receive a modest compensation. Masters living outside the district would have to pay twelve pesos for each of their slaves caught by the *cuadrilleros*.

The writers of the proposal included an unattractive provision. Any patrolman who committed an error (errors were not defined) in carrying out his duties was to serve three months without pay. A second violation meant a year of service without pay. Punishment for the hapless patrolman who committed a third error was enslavement.

The petitioners asked the governor to issue a pardon to the fugitives who returned within a month of its publication. Those who did not could suffer the punishment contained in the Code Noir (ear cropping, branding, hamstringing, and execution). Last, slaves filing complaints against their masters would have their ears cropped and be branded on the back.[2]

---

in both the French and Spanish periods, did not all agree on what the law should be, and they should not be viewed as a homogeneous group. The wealthier and more conservative planters were more likely to voice their opinions in the Superior Council, and later the Cabildo, than their poorer counterparts.

On December 7, 1769, O'Reilly issued a proclamation stating that it was against Spanish law to enslave and hold Indians captive. Owners were forbidden to part with such captives except by giving them their freedom (O'Reilly Proclamation, New Orleans, December 7, 1769, *SMV*, Pt. I, 125–26). See also Webre, "Problem of Indian Slavery," 117–35.

2. Petition of the *síndico procurador general* and the leading citizens to the governor, New

O'Reilly accepted parts of the petition but rejected others that clashed with Spanish law. He declared that the compulsory fund would apply only on the Mississippi from the German Coast to the last plantation downriver. The inhabitants would name a treasurer to work with the Cabildo's *síndico procurador general* to administer the fund. O'Reilly rejected the Code Noir punishment the petitioners wanted, except for fugitives who resisted arrest with firearms. He similarly threw out enslavement to punish patrolmen. Nor would slaves who had just complaints against their masters be punished. He issued a pardon for the runaways, giving them a month to return without fear of castigation.[3]

Although the Cabildo was not directly involved in this petition, that institution's public advocate had a major hand in it. O'Reilly's reply was probably the first knowledge the planters had that their stringent customs for dealing with Africans would not continue. But their petition came as O'Reilly was preparing to leave Louisiana. There is no evidence that the police force or the slave fund proposed were created at that time. This initiative, however, might have laid the groundwork for what came later.

Among its many functions, the Cabildo served as a sounding board for the residents' grievances. On June 21, 1771, it heard a complaint that masters permitted their unskilled slaves to hire themselves out, paying their masters a rent for granting that privilege. Hired blacks, however, often lacked the skills to earn the money to pay their rent and support themselves. To obtain money, they frequently resorted to theft and other mischief. The Cabildo swore that it would warn slave owners against facilitating this corrupt practice.[4]

Orleans, February 27, 1770, AGI, PC, leg. 110; Andreu Ocariz, *Movimientos,* 41–43; Torres Ramírez, *Alejandro O'Reilly,* 145–46. James T. McGowan, in "Creation of a Slave Society: Louisiana Plantations in the Eighteenth Century" (Ph.D. dissertation, University of Rochester, 1976), 256, note 9, says that Louis Ronson (*sic*) on May 6, 1770, called on Governor Unzaga to establish a constabulary force to apprehend runaway slaves. The governor seems not to have agreed.

The first suggestion for a slave fund in Louisiana is in Article XXXVI of the 1724 Code Noir. It stated that a slave condemned to death after being denounced by his master should be appraised by two notable citizens and the amount paid to the master. To raise the money, the article permitted a tax to be placed on every slave in the colony.

3. O'Reilly Regulations, New Orleans, February 28, 1770, AGI, PC, leg. 110.

4. Actas del Cabildo, I, 51, June 21, 1771.

The Cabildo, however, undercut its own initiative when it acted to accommodate New Orleans merchants in January, 1772. The *síndico procurador general* brought a petition from the merchants asking that they be allowed to sell to blacks on Sundays and holy days (days that slaves normally did not work). The councillors unanimously agreed to allow the merchants to open their stores at noon after religious services had concluded.[5]

In 1773 the Cabildo began its biggest effort to control fugitive slaves, many of whom committed crimes while at large. Black lawbreakers were then disturbing the colony's tranquillity and the Cabildo councillors, five of whom were planters, wanted to use their offices to curtail these activities. The need for new regulations arose because owners did not report the wrongdoing or flight of their bondsmen. This often happened in serious crimes when punishment was either death or imprisonment; slave owners only reluctantly accepted a financial loss. To raise funds to pay for expected costs, the Cabildo created the first new tax since O'Reilly's departure. It agreed to assess all slaves and compile a yearly census of them. The Cabildo would then use the revenue to compensate owners for slaves killed as fugitives or in the pursuit of fugitives. Payment initially was to equal the appraised value of the lost slaves. To benefit, the owner needed to report a slave's flight, death, or prison sentence to the *mayordomo de propios* within four days. The regulation embraced all of lower Louisiana from Balize to Natchitoches.[6]

Governor Unzaga, however, proposed holding an open cabildo first to elicit the opinions of slave owners at large. He wanted their support when the Cabildo applied for royal authorization for the tax and the fund. The *cabildo abierto* did that but modified several proposed regulations. Owners had five days to report the flight of a slave. The reward tariff for apprehending and returning runaways was based on distance: three pesos for a slave caught in New Orleans, four pesos for one apprehended up to four leagues away, six pesos for sixteen leagues, eight pesos for thirty-two leagues, ten pesos for fifty leagues, and twelve pesos for slaves caught in

5. *Ibid.,* I, 67–68, January 10, 1772.
6. *Ibid.,* I, 109–110, August 6, 1773. In the spring of 1773, several fugitives had been apprehended and punished before being returned to their masters (Unzaga to [Baltazar] de Villiers, New Orleans, April 1, 1773, AGI, PC, leg. 111).

the Natchitoches, Attakapas, and Opelousas districts. The Cabildo *escribano* proposed to publish a weekly list of fugitives. Captured runaways would be turned over to the *alcalde mayor provincial*. The slave fund was to pay the captors and reimburse the owners for any losses. Although the king delayed four years in approving these measures, the Cabildo began implementing them immediately.[7]

About six weeks after the open cabildo, the councillors agreed to use the slave fund to finance expeditions sent to catch fugitives. Expenses included personnel salaries, supplies, and incidentals. Because free blacks were more successful than whites in tracking down *cimarrones* (fugitive slaves), the council voted to pay a troop of eighteen free blacks an incentive of two pesos each for volunteering.[8]

The Cabildo immediately ran into problems when it attempted to collect money for the slave fund to indemnify the owners of dead blacks. In Pointe Coupee, Natchitoches, Opelousas, and Attakapas, slave owners refused to pay the ten-*sueldo*-per-slave tax (0.85 real, or 10 cents). There were then three dead *cimarrones* whose owners needed to be compensated. The council also modified the regulation on how much to pay owners of dead slaves. Perhaps fearing abuse, the council limited compensation to two hundred pesos. The Cabildo minutes do not reflect adequately how the slave fund operated and who was compensated. They reveal only unusual circumstances and payments made to prominent persons or council members.[9]

Recompense was not made solely on the basis of claims. On several occasions, the council refused remuneration until it received proof that the slave was a fugitive. If a slave was found dead, the Cabildo denied payment on the possibility that he or she had committed suicide. When

7. Actas del Cabildo, I, 113–14, August 27, 1773, I, 232, October 10, 1777. In 1773 Governor Unzaga sent an *expediente* on the slave fund to the crown. It stated that owners would be compensated two hundred pesos for each slave executed or mutilated (AGI, SD, leg. 2581). This was the first mention of limiting compensation for a dead slave to two hundred pesos.

8. Actas del Cabildo, I, 116, October 8, 1773, I, 139, October 15, 1773.

9. *Ibid.,* I, 142, November 19, 1773, I, 163–64, June 9, 1774, I, 146, January 14, 1774, I, 149, February 11, 1774, I, 174, December 16, 1774, I, 197–98, November 24, 1775, I, 249, May 22, 1778, II, 162, March 7, 1783, II, 163–64, March 14, 1783, II, 165, March 21, 1783, II, 195, October 31, 1783.

a runaway killed another slave, the owner of the dead slave had to prove he was killed trying to apprehend the fugitive.[10]

The council also used the slave fund for other purposes. Owners were compensated when their slaves died trying to protect their masters' homes and property. The fund financed expeditions against bands of marauding *cimarrones*. Still more expenses resulted from medical care for captured fugitives, compensation to owners for slaves injured or killed while engaged in public works, and bounties paid to Indians who killed fugitives. Finally, the fund recompensed a band of free mulattoes and blacks who assisted the militia in hunting *cimarrones*.[11]

The demands on the slave fund exceeded the Cabildo's effort to keep

10. *Ibid.*, I, 233, October 31, 1777, I, 244, March 6, 1778, III, (2), 8–9, March 7, 1788, III, (2), 49, February 20, 1789, III, (2), 103–104, June 4, 1790.

How prevalent suicides were among slaves is not known. Planters seem not to have reported suicides to the authorities, and post commandants seldom mentioned them in their dispatches to the governor. One exception, however, was the double suicide of two male *bozal* (unassimilated African) slaves living in the Galveztown area. After making a pact, one slave shot and killed the other and then killed himself with the same gun (Marcos de Villiers to Miró, Galveztown, No. 3, June 1, 1788, AGI, PC, leg. 114). For a study on slave suicides, see María Poumier Taquetchel, "El suicidio esclavo en Cuba en los años 1840," *Anuario de estudios americanos,* XLIII (1986), 69–86. The author states that slave suicides were common wherever slavery existed and that *bozales* were most inclined to take their own lives (*ibid.,* 69).

11. Actas del Cabildo, I, 116, October 8, 1773, II, 135–36, September 20, 1782, II, 136–37, September 27, 1782, II, 162, March 7, 1783, II, 195, October 31, 1783, III, (1), 6, July 30, 1784, III, (1), 34–35, January 28, 1785, II, 215–16, June 4, 1784, III, (1), 68, November 25, 1785, III, (2), 49, February 20, 1789, III, (2), 103–104, June 4, 1790, III, (2), 106, June 25, 1790; "Miscellaneous Documents," I, No. 149, 77 (undated); "Records of the City Council, 1770–1792," WPA transcription, Nos. 93–94, September 14, 1782. See also Gilbert C. Din, "*Cimarrones* and the San Malo Band in Spanish Louisiana," *Louisiana History,* XXI (1980), 237–62.

In 1781 Juan Ventura Morales, a treasury official who had been charged with collecting the slave tax, declared that the slave fund was to pay only for expeditions sent to apprehend fugitives. Governor Gálvez, however, ruled that the April 9, 1779, agreement was to indemnify owners for their runaways killed while being apprehended (Actas del Cabildo, II, 64–65, July 27, 1781). In that same meeting, it was agreed that all inhabitants (*i.e.,* slave owners) were to pay two reales per slave. The minutes of that day, however, close with "*no vale*" ("not valid"), probably because of the 1777 royal order stating that contributions had to be voluntary (*ibid.*). Morales did not long remain in charge of trying to collect the slave tax. At the August 31, 1781, meeting, he sent the Cabildo a letter stating that attention to his duties prevented him from collecting the tax. The Cabildo then named Juan Arnoul, who held the post of *regidor-receptor de penas,* to collect it, and the *mayordomo de propios* would make disbursements when the *ayuntamiento* so decreed (*ibid.,* II, 70, August 31, 1781).

it solvent. Initially, when out of money the council deferred payments until more funds became available. Later, it borrowed from the city treasury to cover shortages. Moreover, slave owners in outlying districts contributed reluctantly and the Cabildo had to badger post commandants to make them pay. In May, 1775, the council appointed two *regidores,* Forstall and Reggio, and Reggio's son Carlos, making them responsible for slave fund collections in New Orleans and two adjacent districts. The governor would name other individuals to collect monies in more distant posts.[12]

The Cabildo's intention was to assess slave owners only when claims to the fund arose. The owners had just several days to pay so as to liquidate the claims as quickly as possible. Less than two years after making the first levy, the Cabildo assessed the owners an additional half real per slave. The extra funds, however, were still insufficient because more claims arose.[13]

Although the king approved the slave tax in his orders of May 14, 1777, he decreed that it be paid freely. He also commanded the citizens throughout the province to draft a new *reglamento* for disciplining slaves. The royal orders were read in the Cabildo on October 10, 1777, and February 13, 1778. The councillors decided to use the opportunity to introduce harsh new measures for slaves that in essence meant the re-creation of the articles in the Code Noir agreeable to planters.[14]

12. Actas del Cabildo, I, 174, December 16, 1774, I, 184, May 16, 1775, I, 197–98, November 17, 1775, I, 249, May 22, 1778, III, (1), 6, July 30, 1784.

13. *Ibid.,* I, 197–98, November 24, 1775.

14. *Ibid.,* I, 184–85, May 16, 1775, I, 197–98, November 24, 1775, I, 232, October 10, 1777, I, 243, February 13, 1778, I, 249, May 22, 1778, I, 273–74, April 9, 1779.

There is a possibility that Governor Bernardo de Gálvez asked his uncle, Minister of the Indies José de Gálvez, to grant the notables of Louisiana the authority to draw up the regulations for slave conduct. That would help explain why the governor never made public the slave regulations contained in his uncle's instructions of November 25, 1776 (royal instructions to the governor of Louisiana, November 25, 1776, AGI, PC, leg. 174B). Unfortunately, no letter from Bernardo de Gálvez asking for this permission has been found.

Among the November, 1776, orders to Bernardo de Gálvez concerning blacks, masters were to treat their slaves humanely and justly, avoiding excessive punishment that produced uprisings and flight; the governor was to issue a pardon to fugitives to get them to return; persons selling blacks liquor, guns, and gunpowder and who were paid with stolen goods were to be severely punished; black nocturnal dances and assemblies in New Orleans and the countryside were prohibited; black Catholics were to marry within the church; and free female mulattoes who lived dishonestly faced deportation to Haiti. There is no evidence that Governor

On February 13, 1778, the Cabildo appointed its Alférez Real Francisco María de Reggio and Depositario General Joseph Ducros, both planters, to prepare regulations for the conduct of blacks, which were meant to restore to slaveholders the domination that Spanish laws had removed from them. After many months, the new regulations were printed in French, titled Code Noir ou Loi Municipale, and presented to the Cabildo on October 16, 1778. Reggio and Ducros had modeled them on the 1724 Code Noir. The proposed regulations significantly diminished the rights of both free blacks and slaves. As Hans W. Baade has written: "It comes as little surprise that the 1778 *projet* of a black code for *Luisiana* faithfully reflected the major repressive features of the 1724 *Code Noir*. Thus, slaves were to be incapable of holding property, of contracting, and of receiving inheritance; subject to one exception, they were to be disqualified as witnesses; and they were generally deprived of standing in civil litigation." Other provisions declared that manumissions had to be approved judicially, self-purchase was no longer valid, and notaries could not write letters of freedom. Free persons of color were relegated to an inferior position whereby they no longer enjoyed the rights of whites. Free women of color could not wear expensive clothing adorned with gold or silver. After receiving the new proposals, the Cabildo circulated them in neighboring districts and informed the notable citizens (planters) to present their ideas on slave conduct to the Cabildo or to post commandants.[15]

Gálvez issued a *bando* incorporating these orders (royal instructions to the governor of Louisiana, November 25, 1776, AGI, PC, leg. 174[b]). The instructions that Minister Gálvez issued in the name of the king owe their origin to Francisco Bouligny (see Din, *Francisco Bouligny,* 55–74). A copy of the instructions that probably once belonged to Bouligny is in the Kuntz Collection, Howard-Tilton Library, Tulane University. These instructions gave Governor Gálvez the authority to issue a pardon to fugitives, which he did belatedly on April 20, 1778. A reference to Gálvez' pardon is in AGI, PC, leg. 70 (Andreu Ocariz, *Movimientos,* 63).

15. Actas del Cabildo, I, 243, February 13, 1778, I, 255, October 16, 1778. The Code Noir ou Loi Municipale is in the Library of Congress; the Parsons Collection, Humanities Research Library, University of Texas, Austin; and elsewhere.

At least two historians have mistakenly believed that the Code Noir ou Loi Municipale represented royal legislation. See Jack D. L. Holmes, "The Abortive Slave Revolt at Pointe Coupee, Louisiana, 1795," *LH,* XI (1970), 344n; and Ingersoll, "Old New Orleans," 567, in which he attributes the law to King Charles III; and Ingersoll's article, "Free Blacks in a Slave Society: New Orleans, 1718–1812," *William and Mary Quarterly,* 3rd ser., XLVIII (1991), 180. A law professor–historian who did not err is Baade, "Law of Slavery," 64–67; the quotation is on p. 65.

The suggestions of the notables were gathered by February 19, 1779. The councillors devoted that session and the next one to reading the draft regulations and suggestions. At the February 26 meeting, the councillors invited the most notable planters and distinguished citizens of the New Orleans district to an extraordinary cabildo to be held on March 1 to give their opinions of the *reglamento*. There the final version of the new code would be drawn up.[16]

The meeting attracted a large audience, which listened to the reading of the ordinances and approved them. Those present then petitioned the king to approve the regulations and thanked the Cabildo for its work in the matter. It was here the councillors approved the Loi Municipale. But because Governor Gálvez had privately become angry at the councillors, the regulations never were sent to the king.[17]

When Gálvez signed his approval of the Cabildo minutes on March 1,

16. Actas del Cabildo, I, 266, February 19, 1779, I, 267, February 26, 1779.

17. *Ibid.,* I, 268, March 1, 1779. Those present at the extraordinary cabildo asked the king for a code "according to the laws of the kingdom *and those in use in the Province*" (emphasis added) (Bernardo de Gálvez to José de Gálvez, New Orleans, March 2, 1779, AGI, SD, leg. 2662). No final version of the Loi Municipale is extant.

The origins of the attempt to get new slave regulations began when María Juana, a slave belonging to Juan Siriray, filed a purchase-of-freedom petition in Governor Unzaga's court in 1776. Because Siriray had also filed proceedings against Jenkins, the master of a British ship, for enticing and harboring a fugitive slave (María Juana), Unzaga joined the two suits together. Much time elapsed in taking testimony, and in this period Unzaga's legal adviser, *asesor* Cecilio Odoardo, left Louisiana. Unzaga believed that he could not give a ruling without legal counsel and referred the case to Havana. There Licenciado Veranes judged that Siriray had not made good his case against Jenkins and that María Juana was entitled to her *carta de libertad*. By the time the Havana advice arrived, Bernardo de Gálvez was governor in Louisiana and he made changes.

He accepted the first part of Havana's judgment against Siriray but ruled against María Juana because the royal order cited by Veranes was directed to Cuba, not Louisiana, and customs and usages in Louisiana should not be changed without the king's consent. The second point, often cited by historians favorable to the French, was decreed when Governor Ulloa first went to Louisiana. But that changed, particularly after the 1768 insurrection and O'Reilly's imposition of Spanish law in 1769. What Gálvez was saying in 1777 was that self-purchase, a Spanish slave regulation, had no right in Louisiana even though it had existed for several years. In ruling against María Juana, Gálvez seems to have fallen under the influence of his future father-in-law, Gilbert Antoine de St. Maxent, a major slave owner, rather quickly after arriving in Louisiana. Thus the Cabildo through the Code Noir ou Loi Municipale tried to rid Louisiana of Spanish slave laws and reintroduce the Code Noir (Baade, "Law of Slavery," 62–63).

he was already hostile to the *regidores*. In a letter written the day after the *cabildo abierto* to the minister of the Indies (his uncle José), Gálvez accused them of being subversive, hostile to Spain, and unappreciative of the many benefits the king had given them. Gálvez' enmity seems to have arisen from the Cabildo's effort to take over direction of Charity Hospital, which it tried to do at the same time that it was cooperating with the planters to create a new slave code. If the council assumed control of the hospital, the governor's authority over the institution would decrease. Gálvez, however, balked at the Cabildo's clumsy attempt to expand its power at his expense, and that was the basis for his charges to Uncle José. Gálvez stated that he would write again supporting his accusations against the Cabildo, but he never did.[18]

Perhaps Gálvez developed cold feet about trying to rid Louisiana of Spanish slave laws. The arrival of a new *auditor de guerra* and *asesor,* Juan Doroteo del Póstigo y Valderrama, in June, 1779, who was well versed in Spanish laws, might have been behind the abandonment of the Loi Municipale. Gálvez never mentioned it again and the Cabildo never acted to revive it.[19]

Slave behavior, meanwhile, did not improve. In April, 1779, the *síndico procurador general* reported that fugitives were increasing in number. The governor called a new *cabildo abierto* to summon the planters to New Orleans to find a remedy to the problem. Eighty prominent planters attended. They agreed to re-create the slave fund through a voluntary contribution of four reales per slave; anyone declining to participate, however, would not be compensated for dead bondsmen. The planters further agreed

18. Bernardo de Gálvez to José de Gálvez, New Orleans, March 2, 1779, AGI, SD, leg. 2662; Stella O'Connor, "The Charity Hospital of Louisiana at New Orleans: An Administrative and Financial History, 1736–1946," *LHQ,* XXXI (1948), 18–19. See also Din, *Francisco Bouligny,* 110; and J. Horace Nunemaker, ed., "The Bouligny Affair in Louisiana," *Hispanic American Historical Review,* XXV (1945), 339–63.

19. Baade, "Law of Slavery," 66–67. Póstigo was in New Orleans by June 1, 1779, the day he presented his credentials to the Cabildo (see his title in AGI, PC, leg. 566). The Cabildo acquired a copy of the *Recopilación de leyes de los reynos de las Indias* in the summer of 1778, which might have helped to change the thinking of the *regidores.* But they still tried to get the Code Noir ou Loi Municipale adopted for the province after its acquisition. Unfortunately, much about the Cabildo's 1778–79 attempt to change the slave laws was not committed to writing.

to establish patrols and take other measures to seize fugitives. Gálvez approved their decisions and, on April 20, issued a pardon to runaways who voluntarily returned to their masters.[20]

This latest effort against maroons took place only shortly before Spain's entry in the American revolutionary war. It did little to diminish the problem of runaways and their crimes. *Marronage,* consequently, increased during the war. To survive while at large, fugitives stole foodstuffs. Plantation slaves sometimes helped them, giving or selling them food and arms and even slaughtering animals for the fugitives. In return, runaways performed plantation chores for them. Some whites employed the *cimarrones,* perhaps because of a labor shortage produced by the war that began in Louisiana in late August, 1779.[21]

Louisiana became an active theater of war against neighboring British West Florida. Slave problems retreated in priority in governing of the colony. Nothing was done about runaways for several years, and their numbers increased.[22] With the arrival of ships, crews, and soldiers for the assault on British-held Pensacola, taverns and nightlife in New Orleans

20. Actas del Cabildo, I, 273–74, April 9, 1779; Andreu Ocariz, *Movimientos,* 44; Jack D. L. Holmes's notes of the April 20, 1779, proclamation by Gálvez sent to Din. The document Holmes consulted is owned by Winston DeVille.

21. Few descriptions of *cimarrón* activity exist. One is in Bouligny to Miró, New Orleans, May 18, 1784, AGI, PC, leg. 10. Gwendolyn Midlo Hall, in *Africans in Colonial Louisiana: The Development of Afro-Creole Culture in the Eighteenth Century* (Baton Rouge, 1992), 207–12, uses data from the early 1780s to generalize, claiming that it was typical of maroon activity during the entire Spanish period. But it was not typical. Runaways increased in number during the American revolutionary war because little was done to contain them, and the slaves knew it. Maroons were still present after 1784 to the end of the Spanish era, but they were never again as menacing as they were in 1783 and 1784. When military expeditions were sent against them, the soldiers and militia destroyed the makeshift settlements and captured large numbers of maroons. Maroons did not control south Louisiana as Hall asserts.

22. The war in Louisiana is covered in Caughey, *Bernardo de Gálvez,* and J. Barton Starr, *Tories, Dons, and Rebels: The American Revolution in British West Florida* (Gainesville, Fla., 1976). McGowan, in "Creation of a Slave Society," 232–33, states that planters petitioned Governor Gálvez to return to Louisiana, and he quotes from the Cabildo minutes in English, "to check the savage negroes that may alter the order and peace of the citizens." McGowan uses this quotation to illustrate the power of blacks in Louisiana. But the Spanish version of the May 12, 1780, Cabildo meeting McGowan cites reads that Gálvez' presence was requested *"para contener los salvajes que podrían hazer irrupción"* ("to contain the savages who could start an uprising"). *"Salvajes"* clearly refers to Indians, not blacks (Actas del Cabildo, II, 25, May 12, 1780).

blossomed. The wartime gaiety caused many free blacks and slaves to flock to the city, dressed in disguises as if for Carnival, seeking merriment and dances. Worried that the enemy might seize the opportunity to infiltrate the city, the *síndico procurador general* advised interim governor Pedro Piernas on January 19, 1781, to prohibit disguises and black attendance at nocturnal dances. This, however, was really an attempt to control black behavior and not because of fear of an enemy attack. The British had been thrown back to Pensacola and constituted no immediate threat to Louisiana.[23]

In 1782 efforts to deal with the persistent problem of *cimarrones* again caught the attention of the governor and the Cabildo. Interim governor Piernas gave orders for free blacks to chase *cimarrones* in February, but they caught only two of them. In September, Piernas, again as acting governor, authorized militia captain Baptista Hugon and eight colored militiamen to pursue runaways who were hiding in the rear of Madam Le Conte's plantation. In two days of work, Hugon and his men reportedly accomplished their mission. Payment for the expeditions came from Cabildo funds.[24]

In February and March, 1783, acting governor Miró, who had taken over from Gálvez the previous year, dispatched two detachments of soldiers to apprehend fugitives who again grew numerous. They caught forty-three slaves and forced others to return to their owners. Guido Dufossat led one

23. Actas del Cabildo, II, 47, January 19, 1781. McGowan, in "Creation of a Slave Society," 233, uses a faulty translation to give the impression that the wartime conditions resulted from the presence of so many blacks. He goes on to state that nothing happened to confirm the planters' fears, and "neither did the temporary tranquillity alter their [planters'] belief that they maintained control only through the uneasy sufferance of their own slaves." McGowan again exaggerates the power of the slaves. Moreover, in the reference to wartime, the *síndico procurador general* referred to the war against England, which affected Louisiana everywhere, and he did not suggest that blacks were creating another "wartime condition" in the province as McGowan claims.

24. Actas del Cabildo, II, 97, February 15, 1782, II, 135–36, September 20, 1782, II, 136–37, September 27, 1782. A Cabildo order to the *mayordomo de propios* to pay two hundred pesos to René Huchet de Kernion in 1783 and a receipt for the same amount paid to Louis Judice, *fils,* for his dead runaway slave, dated December 21, 1784, Pointe Coupee, are in the John Minor Windom Collection, Special Collections, Howard-Tilton Library, Tulane University. To what degree the slave fund, which could function only with slave owners' contributions, was still working is unclear. Cabildo minutes between 1779 and 1784 reveal little about its operations.

of the expeditions into the "Land of Gaillarde," in the eastern part of present-day St. Bernard Parish, where maroons had established a small settlement of huts. Dufossat caught many fugitives and destroyed the structures.[25]

By 1783 Juan San Malo (Jean St. Malo) seems to have risen as the leader among the fugitives of the Land of Gaillarde. San Malo had a reputation for harsh discipline. He reputedly killed his wife or woman when she attempted to return to her master and a subordinate for refusing to slaughter a calf when ordered by San Malo. In addition, San Malo and members of his gang were involved in killing two groups of whites, totaling about eight persons. When in the spring of 1784 the murder of whites became public knowledge, coupled with more slaves running away and an increase in attacks on plantations, the Cabildo demanded action.

On April 23, the *síndico procurador general* complained of the great harm that fugitives were inflicting on plantations. The Cabildo then issued a call for a junta of notable planters to discuss ways to apprehend them and to raise money to pay for new expeditions. The slave fund appears not to have been working. Numerous citizens attended the meeting six days later to discuss the crisis. The planters accepted responsibility for the costs of an expedition against the runaways, borrowing the money from the Cabildo and imposing a tax on their slaves. The planters also composed new rules for slave conduct.[26]

The *cabildo abierto* of April 29, 1784, drafted eleven articles regulating slave conduct. The articles prohibited slaves from traveling without written passes; denied the sale of liquor, gunpowder, or shot to them; forbid them from using firearms, except when specifically permitted; forbade

25. Actas del Cabildo, II, 162, March 7, 1783, II, 163, March 14, 1783; Porteous, ed. and trans., "Index," *LHQ*, XX (1937), 841–60. At the March 14 Cabildo meeting, the council agreed to pay *Regidor* Reggio two thousand pesos for his slave Jean Luis, a sum in excess of the value of most slaves at that time.

How viable were fugitive settlements? Hall, in *Africans*, 203, argues that they were self-sustaining. In contrast, McGowan, in "Creation of a Slave Society," 238–39, 240, points out that maroons needed guns, ammunition, and foodstuffs from the outside to survive. In addition, many fugitives who fled there found life too harsh and returned to their masters. The terrain was not inviting then and even today has failed to attract substantial settlement. Moreover, when expeditions sent to pursue *cimarrones* wanted to penetrate the area, they did so at will.

26. Actas del Cabildo, II, 206, April 23, 1784, II, 207–209, April 30, 1784.

black assemblies without passes from their owners; required owners to inspect for runaways among their own slaves and prohibited owners from hiring out their slaves unless they had trades; required free blacks to carry certificates of their emancipation; and prohibited citizens from giving horses to slaves. Governor Miró soon issued his own decree to the province, which was almost identical to the Cabildo's.[27]

In May and early June, 1784, after Miró had been called away to Indian congresses in Pensacola and Mobile, the Cabildo nervously pressured acting military governor Francisco Bouligny to send out large expeditions to capture the San Malo gang. Through May the runaways continued to cause trouble, and it became evident that the new ordinances had not made life more difficult for the *cimarrones*. A Cabildo meeting on May 28 sounded hysterical after reporting that the San Malo gang had killed a party of whites; a closer examination reveals that it had occurred months before, but that did not diminish its importance. Magnifying the danger, the Cabildo alleged that plantations had been abandoned and San Malo was fomenting a slave insurrection. A week later the Cabildo again appealed for action, declaring that the planters would pay the expenses for the expeditions sent against the fugitives.[28]

Meanwhile, Bouligny was carefully sending out large and small expeditions composed of white soldiers and white and black militiamen to places informers had named. About June 7, San Malo and most of his lieutenants were captured; eventually more than a hundred *cimarrones* were caught.[29]

The captured slaves were brought to New Orleans, where Reggio as first *alcalde ordinario* took charge of the prisoners. San Malo, who had developed gangrene from a gunshot wound, confessed his crimes and

---

27. Morazán, "Letters," I, 201–202; Actas del Cabildo, II, 207–208, April 30, 1784; *bando* of Governor Miró, New Orleans, May 1, 1784, AGI, PC, leg. 3A.

28. Actas del Cabildo, II, 211–15, May 28, 1784, II, 215–17, June 4, 1784; Din, *"Cimarrones"* 249–52.

29. Din, *"Cimarrones,"* 251–54. The largest figure for captured runaways is in the service sheets of the army officers who participated in the expeditions. See Bouligny's service sheet in Holmes, ed., *Honor and Fidelity,* 98. Gilberto Guillemard's published service sheet erroneously lists 323 captured fugitives (Holmes, ed., *Honor and Fidelity,* 127), a figure that far exceeds anything in the written reports.

coaxed his lieutenants to admit theirs.[30] Reggio sentenced him and three of his henchmen to death for murdering whites. They were hanged in the Plaza de Armas before a multitude of onlookers on June 19. Other runaways received up to two hundred lashes, branding with an M for *maroon,* and wearing shackles for three months. Fugitive women received similar penalties. In August Reggio condemned four more captured fugitives to death, three of them for committing crimes while members of San Malo's gang.[31]

30. Hall, in *Africans,* 231, denies San Malo's confession, believing instead the dirge ("Ourra' St. Malo") that he kept silent. But the dirge about his capture and execution was written after the fact by person(s) who had no knowledge whether San Malo and the others confessed or not. Furthermore, it confuses San Malo's execution with that of blacks who participated in the 1795 Pointe Coupee conspiracy. The dirge can be found in George W. Cable, *Creoles and Cajuns: Stories of Old Louisiana,* ed. Arlin Turner (Garden City, N.Y., 1959), 418–19, and in Din, *"Cimarrones,"* 256–57. Hall accepts without comment other maroon confessions.

In Bouligny's letter to Miró (New Orleans, June 19, 1784, AGI, PC, leg. 10), he mentions that San Malo confessed and persuaded his confederates to admit their misdeeds too. On page 231 of *Africans,* Hall suggests "cogent reasons" for doubting the confession. Her chief reason was that Bouligny lied to defend his conduct to Miró for permitting Reggio, as *alcalde ordinario,* to try the fugitives. Miró had wanted to try them. Hall suggests that Bouligny invented the confessions to prove the *cimarrones* guilty. But as Bouligny declared in reply to the governor, Miró had not made his wish known. On having this pointed out to him, the governor graciously accepted his error. This shows that Bouligny had no need for lying.

Miró, on July 5, 1784, approved the sentences of the maroons who had been tried and punished, including the executions. He concluded his letter to Bouligny, "Friend, he who governs is exposed to being right in what is essential, and you have acted with total correctness and prudence" (Miró to Bouligny, Mobile, July 5, 1784, AGI, PC, leg. 11).

31. "Criminal proceedings against fugitive slaves for shooting at the arresting expedition & for running away from owners," fols. 196–98, August 7, 1784, Judicial Records of the Spanish Cabildo, Louisiana State Museum; Din, *"Cimarrones,"* 258–59.

Hall, in *Africans,* 231, uses the Cabildo's problems with Cirilo de Barcelona—an accusation that Bouligny cooperated with Reggio in trying the church slave Baptiste—as misconduct. Hall ignores the center of the clergy's opposition to the punishment, which was the church *fuero.* (On the Reggio-Barcelona dispute, see Barcelona to Reggio, [New Orleans], June 19, 1784, and Reggio to the Auxiliary Bishop of Cuba [Barcelona], New Orleans, June 19, 1784, both in AGI, PC, leg. 1375). Hall also mentions that San Malo had remained silent about the innocence of Prince and Baptiste in the murders of whites. But the implication is clear that San Malo had talked about *cimarrón* activities and perhaps implicated Prince and Baptiste. Finally, Hall seems unfamiliar with the Spanish legal system. She calls Reggio's questioning of the maroons "a private, one-man show" (*Africans,* 231–32). She denies that an investigation had been made.

The Spanish system of interrogating prisoners called for the presence of a scribe, two

Paying the costs of the expeditions did not come so quickly. On July 30, a list of expenses amounted to 2,261 pesos and 4 reales, but it omitted many items. Owners had not yet submitted bills for their dead slaves. Moreover, the Cabildo generously accepted payment of a thousand pesos to Regidor Charles Honoré Olivier for emancipating Bastien, who had revealed San Malo's hiding place. The slave fund, however, was broke and the Cabildo agreed to pay the expenses from regular funds until new slave revenue could be raised. Probably because of slave owners' reluctance to contribute to the fund, Miró imposed a five-real-per-slave assessment in October, 1784. How successful he was in collecting the money is unclear, but it is known that the slave fund remained in debt for some years. The system of voluntary contributions imposed by the crown had not worked.[32]

---

witnesses, and the questioner or judge. After weighing the evidence, which in this case were the *procesos* or depositions, the judge (Reggio) alone made his decision in sentencing. Spanish law normally required that death sentences pronounced in New Orleans be reviewed in Havana or Spain before being carried out. But when *cimarrones* murdered whites and the situation appeared dangerous, their leaders could be executed summarily without a review (Herbert S. Klein, *Slavery in the Americas: A Comparative Study of Virginia and Cuba* [Chicago, 1967], 71). The higher court in Havana did not criticize the New Orleans authorities for the actions they took.

Captain General Gálvez of Cuba told Miró in 1785 that Alcalde Ordinario Reggio had been fully competent to try the fugitives and that Reggio's court was not subordinate to the governor's court. The *auditor de guerra* in New Orleans, the only trained Spanish lawyer in Louisiana, also said that Reggio had acted properly. The *auditor* reviewed the *proceso*, or trial record, which proves that an investigation had been conducted (Miró to the Conde de Gálvez, No. 35, New Orleans, October 1, 1784, AGI, PC, leg. 3A; Gálvez to Miró, Havana, April 16, 1785, AGI, PC, leg. 11). Gálvez, however, told Miró that the Cabildo did not show Barcelona the respect due him and advised him that respect must be demonstrated (Gálvez to Miró, [Mexico City], December 24, 1785, AGI, PC, leg. 2360).

32. Actas del Cabildo, III, (1), 6, July 30, 1784, III, (1), 34–35, January 28, 1785, III, (1), 106, October 6, 1786, Francisco Rivas to [Miró], Fort Bute de Manchac, November 1, 1784, AGI, PC, leg. 10. In 1784, the Cabildo collected in revenue 3,407 pesos, but its expenses were 4,972½ pesos. Approximately half of the expenses went to suppressing the runaway slaves (Accounts of Alcaldes Francisco de Reggio and José Ducros, New Orleans, February 19, 1785, Windom Collection).

Cabildo minutes show that the slave fund debt declined slowly over the years. On February 9, 1787, it was placed at 1,200 pesos; on February 16, 1787, it was refined to 644 pesos, 4 reales still to be collected for the slave fund; and on May 25, 1792, 351 pesos were still owed to the *cimarrón* fund (Actas del Cabildo, III, [1], 132, February 16, 1787, III, [1], 133, February 16, 1787, III, [3], May 25, 1792). After that, the Cabildo minutes ceased referring to the debt caused by the 1784 expeditions.

In early 1787, to avoid another levy on slave owners, the council resolved to impose a one-peso tax on each slave imported into the province. The council asked Governor Miró to secure royal approval for the impost. The Cabildo opted to wait for royal confirmation before implementing the tax, one of the few times it did. With no money available, the council agreed to pay for slaves killed as *cimarrones* only when it received funds. It accepted two claims in September, 1787, one in February, 1788, and none thereafter. In 1790, the Cabildo renewed its request for royal approval for the tax because the crown had not yet replied. When two more years elapsed, the *síndico procurador general* proposed convening an open cabildo to find a solution to their money problems.[33]

In 1792 the countryside around New Orleans suffered from many crimes committed by fugitives, who, it was said, brazenly ventured into the city to perpetrate them.[34] The *síndico procurador general* proposed taking immediate measures to capture the runaway blacks. The Cabildo itself chose only to have the governor call a meeting of the inhabitants of the district around New Orleans to hear propositions and to select those most convenient. It did not propose wider participation or taking vigorous action. By this time, the councillors had given up on a fund to finance expeditions. Voluntary contributions had proved ineffective. Governor Carondelet, who was new to Louisiana, however, tried in 1792 and 1795 to reestablish a fund through contributions, and both times he failed.[35]

The new rules Governor Miró and the Cabildo issued for slave conduct in May, 1784, went unchallenged for five years. Miró added to the slave regulations with his *bando de buen gobierno,* which he proclaimed in June,

33. Actas del Cabildo, III, (1), 132–33, February 9, 1787, III, (1), 161–62, September 7, 1787, III, (1), 162, September 14, 1787, III, (2), 7, February 15, 1788, III, (2), 113–14, September 17, 1790, III, (2), 199, April 20, 1792.

34. *Ibid.,* III, (2), 199, April 20, 1792.

35. *Ibid.;* [Carondelet] to Messieurs Peyroux, Vienne, Blanc, and Cavelier, [New Orleans], August 25, 1792, AGI, PC, leg. 122B; Carondelet to [the Cabildo], New Orleans, August 14, 1792, AGI, PC, leg. 206. A *règlement* proposed by district representatives assembled in Government House on August 29, 1792, to create a slave fund is in AGI, PC, leg. 206. On Carondelet's 1795 attempt to start a slave fund, see Francisco Rivas to Carondelet, Galveztown, November 5, 1795, AGI, PC, leg. 32. Carondelet sent the proposal for the slave fund to the post commandants on July 31, 1795 (*ibid.*). The Cabildo appears not to have been consulted on this occasion.

1786. Although the cautious large planters of the New Orleans district approved these measures, they opposed lenient slave laws coming from Spain. In 1789, the crown circulated a liberal slave code for the Spanish Empire called "His Majesty's Royal Cédula on the Education, Treatment, and Occupations of Slaves" (*Real Cédula de Su Magestad sobre la Educación, Trato y Ocupaciones de los Esclavos*). When the councillors saw it early the next year, they considered some of the provisions potentially dangerous and others ruinously expensive to implement. They objected in particular to the requirements that each plantation furnish a chaplain for the slaves' spiritual needs; segregate slaves by sex even while working; permit slaves to marry; and rigidly observe Sundays and holy days as days of rest. The Cabildo first called on Governor Miró to suspend the decree's enforcement and then petitioned the crown to nullify it on the basis of its economic unfeasibility and potential danger.[36]

Because the crown did not respond to its plea about the "Royal Cédula," the Cabildo felt disheartened about being able to regulate African behavior. It retained this attitude for several years. But interest in controlling blacks revived after the Pointe Coupee slave conspiracy was uncovered in April, 1795. Several councillors voiced opinions on what they believed should be done to reduce any threat of a black insurrection. In an extraordinary meeting requested by Síndico Procurador General Miguel Fortier, he presented two letters from persons who believed that an uprising was still possible. He also claimed that many other people had talked to him about it. Fortier belonged to a faction that believed the Cabildo should participate in this crisis. He urged the council to select

36. Actas del Cabildo, III, (2), 90–91, February 26, 1790, III, (2), 107, July 23, 1790; Weston A. Goodspeed, ed., *The Province and the States: A History of the Province of Louisiana Under France and Spain and of the Territories and States Formed Therefrom* (7 vols.; Madison, 1904), I, 294–95; Wood, "Life in New Orleans," 660–61; Javier Malagón Barceló, *Código Negro Carolino (1784)* (Santo Domingo, 1974). Malagón traces the development of a black code for Santo Domingo in 1784 to the "Royal Cédula of His Majesty on Slave Education, Treatment, and Labor in all his Dominions in the Indies, and Philippine Islands" of 1789. This document of fourteen chapters called for improving the treatment of slaves. Cabildos were to have a major role in enforcing the provisions.

Under Miró, no effort was made to enforce the "Royal Cédula." But that changed when the Barón de Carondelet became governor. Much to the distress of many planters, he tried to implement a part of the Cédula. For a discussion of planters' discontent with Carondelet, see Brasseaux, "François-Louis Hector," 67–68.

four persons from the New Orleans district as *testigos de asistencia* (witnesses to interrogations), who, with four similar persons from Pointe Coupee, would assist the commandant there in his investigation of the conspiracy. He also recommended that another eight persons be selected from the New Orleans district to help determine who the colony's unruly and insubordinate slaves and free blacks were. He proposed holding investigations in all districts and arresting accused blacks and expelling them from the province.[37]

But the Cabildo was not united in support of Fortier; Alférez Real Almonester opposed certain measures. He argued that the commandant of Pointe Coupee should carry out his own investigation without outside interference. Moreover, the actions of the Cabildo would sabotage the governor's efforts to deal with problems. Bypassing Almonester's objections, the remaining members chose four *testigos de asistencia* and others to be named to investigate insubordinate blacks. Perhaps in recognition that the governor had to approve anything they did, the most outspoken councillors moderated their views and agreed to let the governor take the measures he believed appropriate.[38]

Governor Carondelet angrily denounced rumors and falsehoods that worked to undermine his authority and alleged that he favored slaves over masters. In an impassioned letter to the Cabildo, he pointed out his services to the province in bolstering its security, improving its commerce, and working against insurrection. Propaganda, he argued, was twisting facts about him and subverting his and Spanish authority in the province.[39]

Pedro María Cabaret also found himself the butt of a rumor that he had twelve hundred fusils ready at his house to distribute to blacks in an insurrection. He protested to the Cabildo, which investigated and found the rumor to be false. But efforts to determine who started the falsehood failed.[40]

On June 20, 1795, the councillors decided that it would be harmful to permit slaves who were not *bozales* (culturally unassimilated African slaves) to enter the colony. They also thought it better to suspend slave imports

37. Actas del Cabildo, IV, (1), 2–5, April 25, 1795.
38. *Ibid.,* IV, (2), 2–5, April 25, 1795, IV, (2), 10–12, May 2, 1795.
39. *Ibid.,* IV, (2), 13–19, May 2, 1795.
40. *Ibid.,* IV, (1), 28, May 9, 1795, IV, (1), 32–33, May 22, 1795, IV, (1), 39, June 12, 1795.

entirely while the war continued, a measure many residents favored. The councilmen agreed to ask the governor to publish a *bando* stating that if it was discovered within six months of the sale that newly introduced slaves were not *bozales,* the sale would be nullified. The seller would be sentenced to suffer the fine the governor imposed in his *bando.* The governor also sent the Cabildo five copies of his June 1, 1795, police measure that included rules for masters in the treatment of their slaves. He furthermore sent an *oficio* of June 5 that reproduced his letter, which was being circulated through the province, about the fifty-four slaves lost to their owners in Pointe Coupee, proposing a way to indemnify them for the loss. Later Carondelet attempted to impose a six-real-per-head tax on slaves and succeeded in collecting some money, but many more owners refused to pay. The Cabildo made no effort to indemnify owners for their executed and imprisoned slaves.[41]

The council's attitude clearly showed it no longer thought the slave fund was viable. Collecting assessments had been difficult from the outset, and the 1777 royal order making contributions voluntary doomed it. Governor Carondelet encountered the same obstinacy from slave owners in his two attempts to revive the fund in 1792 and 1795. The Cabildo as an institution cooperated minimally in the first and not at all in the second. In the remaining years of Spanish rule, fugitive slaves were occasionally pursued, and owners paid fees to the captors. By then the Cabildo no longer played a role in apprehending fugitive slaves.[42] The two remaining

41. *Ibid.,* IV, (1), 41–42, June 20, 1795. Carondelet's 1795 police regulation is in James A. Padgett, ed., "A Decree for Louisiana Issued by the Baron of Carondelet, June 1, 1795," *LHQ,* XX (1937), 590–605.

Demands by Governor Carondelet for funds are in his messages to post commandants throughout Louisiana. See, for example, Nicolas Verret to Carondelet, Lafourche Interior, August 25, 1795, and [Carondelet] to Verret, New Orleans, September 5, 1795, both in AGI, PC, leg. 211A. In 1797 Guillermo Duparc, the first white to learn about the 1795 Pointe Coupee conspiracy, stated that Carondelet's effort to raise funds by taxing slaveholders had netted only enough to buy a slave his freedom, reward two Indian women, and pay for "writings," presumably court documents. Therefore, the owners of executed and imprisoned slaves received nothing in compensation (petition of [Duparc] to the king, New Orleans, June 30, 1797, AGI, PC, leg. 131B). On the 1795 Pointe Coupee conspiracy, see Holmes, "Abortive Slave Revolt," 341–62; Andreu Ocariz, *Movimientos,* 117–77; and Hall, *Africans,* 344–74.

42. The Cabildo showed a brief interest in runaway slaves in 1799 and 1800, however. Near the end of the Spanish period, the Cabildo agreed to pay to establish a jail in Concordia,

areas in which the Cabildo continued to display interest in regulating blacks were dances and slave importations.

Dancing was a popular form of entertainment for all social classes, including Africans. Dancing in New Orleans had long taken place at private houses and at establishments not regulated by the city. Shortly after the opening of a city-owned dance hall for whites in 1792, the council authorized free blacks and mulattoes to use the facility for Saturday night dances. The partnership of Santiago Bernardo Coquet and José Antonio Boniquet received the concession. In payment for their monopoly, the partners agreed to subsidize the New Orleans theater, El Coliseo.[43]

The dances for the free people of color soon attracted both slaves and white men. The dances became known as "tricolor balls" because of the presence of whites, mulattoes, and blacks. The Cabildo had not intended this to happen because it portended trouble. Several years passed, however, before disturbances occurred that were noted in the Cabildo minutes. In January, 1796, Síndico Procurador General Gabriel Fonvergne petitioned the Cabildo to revoke the license for the black dances, explaining that slaves of both sexes attended the dances, sometimes without their owners' permission. He alleged that slaves resorted to theft so they could dress as well as free blacks. Moreover, sailors and other "disreputable whites" attending the dances informed the blacks about slave revolts in the Caribbean. The Cabildo worried that news of successful insurrections might incite local black rebelliousness. On Fonvergne's advice, the council banned slave attendance at the dances and agreed to fine Coquet one hundred pesos for each slave he admitted, including those with written permission from their owners.[44]

---

across the Mississippi from Natchez, to facilitate exchanging captured runaways with American authorities. But it was never built because the commandant at Concordia delayed in claiming the money and it was no longer available when he finally asked for it. Then a new quarrel between the council and Interim Military Governor Casa-Calvo prompted the Cabildo to abandon the project (Actas del Cabildo, IV, [3], 22–23, March 29, 1799, IV, [3], 173–74, May 2, 1800, IV, [3], 177–78, May 15, 1800).

43. Ronald R. Morazán, ed. and trans., " 'Quadroon' Balls in the Spanish Period," *LH*, XIV (1973), 310–11. As part of their concession, Coquet and Boniquet received permission to hold a public lottery. The dances for whites were on Sunday and for blacks on Saturday (Morazán, "Letters," I, 208n).

44. Actas del Cabildo, IV, (1), 88–89, January 22, 1796. The "tricolor balls" were the

Opposition to the Cabildo's restrictive measures, however, appeared from an unexpected quarter, the slave owners. The public dances had raised morale among the New Orleans slaves. Carondelet found the owners' complaints justified and concluded that a more equitable solution was to prohibit whites from attending black balls. He continued to require slaves to have written permission from their masters to be admitted. The council accepted the governor's decision.[45]

Carondelet's solution appears to have been satisfactory for the rest of his administration and that of his successor. Before his death in mid-1799, Gayoso renewed the monopoly permit for Coquet and Boniquet. Following his demise, abuses at the black dances multiplied. Síndico Procurador General Pedro Barran reported to the Cabildo that whites still attended black dances, slaves used forged notes of permission and stole to dress extravagantly, and gambling flourished on the premises. Barran petitioned the council either to close the dance hall or to enact tough measures to end abuses.[46]

Before answering Barran, the councillors conferred with acting civil governor Vidal. He refused to prohibit the dances or stop the gambling. He said it was improper for him as the acting civil governor to rescind a permit issued by Governor General Gayoso. He promised, nevertheless, to reprimand Coquet and Boniquet for abuses. The councillors accepted Vidal's decision because stopping the dances would mean closing the theater for the last part of Carnival season. They assumed the dances would cease when Lent began. Frustrated, Barran asked the council for certified copies of the proceedings as evidence that he had fulfilled his duty in the matter.[47]

Protected by their permit, Coquet and Boniquet continued the dances for blacks after Carnival season ended. Without Vidal's support, the Cabildo could not stop them, but it canceled the concessionaires' use of the

---

precursors of the later romantic "quadroon balls" of New Orleans (Robertson, ed., *Louisiana Under the Rule,* I, 216; Morazán, ed. and trans., "'Quadroon' Balls," 310; Asbury, *French Quarter,* 94).

45. Actas del Cabildo, IV, (1), 90–91, January 29, 1796.

46. *Ibid.,* IV, (3), 133–39, February 7, 1800, IV, (3), 144–45, February 21, 1800, Morazán, "Letters," I, 140–49, II, 37–41.

47. Actas del Cabildo, IV, (3), 144–45, February 21, 1800; Morazán, "Letters," II, 38.

city-owned building. Not to be outmaneuvered, Coquet side-stepped the Cabildo by purchasing a building on Conti Street, where he resumed the dances.[48]

There the abuses became more flagrant. Guards at the premises refused entry to respectable people, including an officer of the city patrol and Alcalde Ordinario Francisco Caisergues, who sought to inspect the facility. Cabildo involvement, however, was not the same now as it had been earlier when Coquet and Boniquet rented a city-owned building. With the arrival of Governor General Salcedo, the new *síndico procurador general,* Pablo Lanusse, renewed the attack on the tricolor balls. He petitioned the Cabildo to shut them down, alleging that the abuses were so outrageous that if the dances did not cease, he would place the issue before the crown. After his arrival, Governor Salcedo spent a month investigating Lanusse's allegations before permitting the dances to continue. The Cabildo took no further action against the black dances, and they persisted well into the American period.[49]

The final area in which the Cabildo took an interest concerning blacks, and which involved the entire colony, was slave imports. Planters, some of whom always held Cabildo seats, needed an ample labor supply to expand agricultural production. Lower Louisiana's chief economic activity in the late eighteenth century was agriculture. In the early Spanish period, the only export commodity that had a market abroad was tobacco. On June 30, 1770, Síndico Procurador General Luis Ranson suggested sending a proposal to the king to allow Louisiana's planters to ship tobacco to Saint Domingue and bring in return *bozales* for agricultural labor. The council named Juan Bautista Fleurian and Dionicio Braud to draft a petition.[50]

The Cabildo did nothing more regarding slave imports for several years. During the Unzaga governorship, the English provided many contraband slaves. When José de Gálvez became minister of the Indies in 1776, the Spanish government tried to shift commerce away from the English and permitted slaves to come from the French West Indies. But

48. Morazán, "Letters," I, 46; Morazán, ed. and trans., " 'Quadroon' Balls," 312–15.

49. Morazán, "Letters," I, 48, II, 37–41; Actas del Cabildo, IV, (4), 126–27, August 14, 1801, IV, (4), 135–36, September 18, 1801; Asbury, *French Quarter,* 94.

50. Actas del Cabildo, I, 24–26, June 30, 1770. A copy of Luis Ranson's June 28, 1770, letter to the Cabildo is in AGI, PC, leg. 110.

Louisiana planters had long had reservations about Creole slaves from the Caribbean; they were judged unruly, and many masters in the islands sold off their ungovernable blacks. Louisiana planters preferred *bozales*—fresh slaves imported from Africa. In 1782 the Cabildo received new trade regulations that gave Louisiana absolute freedom in the importation of slaves for ten years. In addition, the duty on slave imports was to be moderate. Spain's participation in the American revolutionary war was winding down at that time, and New Orleans accepted the news with citywide rejoicing.[51] In the 1780s, slaves entered Louisiana in large numbers, mostly from the Caribbean and brought by the English.

Governor Miró's 1786 *bando de buen gobierno,* however, prohibited the entry in Louisiana of Creole slaves from French and British Caribbean islands. He permitted owners to bring slaves for their own use as field hands on plantations or as domestics. But if the owners subsequently wanted to sell the slaves, they needed a license from the governor.[52] Whether the council had a hand in Miró's decision is unknown; the Cabildo minutes are silent about this.

In 1789 France broke out in revolution, preaching liberty, equality, and fraternity, slogans that shook the tranquillity of the French slave colonies. Two years later, Haiti's blacks rose up in rebellion against French authority. The Spanish government had already taken precautionary measures. On May 21, 1790, it issued a confidential royal order forbidding entry in the Spanish colonies of slaves, black refugees, or mulattoes from French possessions because they might be a bad influence. Miró promised to expel any who came, but he might not have been successful.[53]

Probably unaware of the royal order but cognizant that the French Revolution had made slaves throughout the Caribbean restless, on February 10, 1792, the Cabildo judged it prudent to ban slave imports from foreign Caribbean islands. It ordered the inspection of arriving slave ships to deterimine the origin of their cargoes. The monthly commissioner re-

51. Actas del Cabildo, II, 102–104, April 8, 1782, II, 105–106, April 12, 1782, II, 106–107, April 19, 1782. The regulations that affected Louisiana are in *SMV,* Pt. II, 1–5.

52. Miró's *bando,* dated June 1, 1786, is in Actas del Cabildo, III, (1), 90–96, June 2, 1786; Miró to Vicente Folch, [New Orleans], December 5, 1786, AGI, PC, leg. 12.

53. Miró to Domingo Cabello, No. 4 confidential, August 21, 1790, AGI, PC, leg. 1446.

ceived the duty of examining the cargo and informing the governor, but this procedure proved cumbersome and ineffective.[54]

In July, 1792, Síndico Procurador General Juan Bautista Poeyfarre asked for an extraordinary meeting of the Cabildo and the governor granted it. At the meeting, Poeyfarre warned about slaves coming from Guarico (Cap Français, Haiti) despite the February 10 agreement to ban all except *bozales* from entering Louisiana. He believed the governor should prevent Creole slaves from coming to the province, and he urged the council to bar slave importations from colonies where African insurrections had occurred. Ships then on the Mississippi bringing slaves under license needed to be inspected rigorously to determine if the slaves were of African or Caribbean origin. If there were illegal slaves on board, a two-hundred-peso fine per black should be imposed and the slaves returned at the shipowner's expense. All present at the meeting, including Governor Carondelet, agreed and signed the minutes. In January, 1793, the king approved Louisiana's decision to end the importation of Caribbean slaves.[55]

This remained the policy of the governor and Cabildo until the Pointe Coupee conspiracy in 1795 forced them to reconsider it. In the wake of the conspiracy, several Cabildo officials wanted to participate in the investigation to determine its origins and the blacks responsible. In addition, the cautious councillors sought to identify the insubordinate free blacks and slaves in the colony and ship them out. That, however, necessitated money to cover costs and indemnify the owners, and planters, by and large, would probably refuse to contribute. Moreover, taxing to raise the money was illegal without royal approval. Governor Carondelet, too, did not favor this Cabildo initiative that gave power to persons who were mostly planters. Instead, on June 1, 1795, he issued his own police measures on slave conduct.[56]

At the June 20 meeting, the Cabildo received copies of the governor's police regulation. No doubt aware of it beforehand, the councillors first discussed how harmful it would be to continue bringing in slaves, even

54. Actas del Cabildo, III, (2), 179, February 10, 1792.

55. *Ibid.*, III, (2), 179, February 10, 1792, III, (3), 9–10, July 16, 1792; Gayarré, *History of Louisiana*, III, 214. On the permits that individuals obtained to bring slaves to Louisiana, see Andreu Ocariz, *Movimientos*, 103–106.

56. Padgett, ed., "Decree for Louisiana," 590–606.

bozales. They judged it better not to introduce more blacks while the war with France persisted, and they asked the governor to publish a *bando* to that effect. If a shipment of *bozales* arrived, however, for which a permit had been granted, any purchaser of slaves had six months to determine if they were truly *bozales.* He could void the sale within that time if he learned they were not, and the importer would be fined according to the punishment decreed by the governor.[57]

Because individuals had recently acquired licenses to import *bozales,* Governor Carondelet did not immediately stop slave imports. He gave persons with licenses six months to use them. The governor was also concerned with his own police measures and efforts to re-create the slave fund. Resistance to contributing to the fund developed in late 1795, and by early 1796, it appeared a hopeless cause. It was at that time, on February 19, that Síndico Procurador General Fonvergne raised the question of banning all slave imports again. The councillors agreed and stated that they would petition the king via the governor to prohibit the introduction of all slaves. While waiting, they urged the governor to issue a *bando* to this effect. Carondelet accepted their petition, banned all slave importations, and sought royal approval.[58] Perhaps the decline of the two principal export crops of an earlier era, tobacco and indigo, permitted the slaveholders to accept a ban on slaves.

No sooner did those two crops fade than two new ones appeared to take their place. Cotton and sugar became important commercial exports in the late 1790s, and they kept growing in size, limited only by the available labor. Many planters, consequently, wanted to reopen the slave trade to expand their production. But there were others who were adamantly in opposition.[59]

The question of slave imports surfaced again in August, 1800. About

57. Actas del Cabildo, IV, (1), 41, June 20, 1795.

58. *Ibid.,* IV, (1), 96–97, February 19, 1796. Some slaves entered Louisiana despite the 1796 ban. For example, in 1799 Governor Gayoso permitted colonist Santiago (James) Fletcher to introduce two hundred slaves for his personal use. That act set off a heated exchange between the governor and Acting Intendant Juan Ventura Morales (Holmes, *Gayoso,* 219). Other Americans who entered the colony via the Ohio and Mississippi rivers also brought slaves with them.

59. Actas del Cabildo, III, (3), 9–10, July 16, 1792, IV, (1), 41–42, June 20, 1795; Fortier, *History of Louisiana,* II, 173–74; Morazán, "Letters," I, xlvii–l, lv–lvi, 162–88.

forty planters petitioned acting civil governor Vidal to renew the introduction of *bozales* directly from Africa. Vidal planned to support the petition, but he first forwarded it to the Cabildo for an opinion. The council
debated the issue heatedly. Síndico Procurador General Pedro Barran
spearheaded the opposition to reopening the trade. He entered an impassioned plea outlining the dangers of allowing more slaves into Louisiana
because they were already insubordinate everywhere. He claimed, "We do
not have any law to restrain and bring slaves back to their stations." He
proposed stringent rules for blacks and training runaways "to the subor-
dination that the common good and general tranquility of the province
demand, and to endow the masters with the legitimate authority that they
should have over their slaves."[60] Perhaps the real issue in Barran's opposition was not slave importations but the discipline of Africans.

The council voted six to five to sustain Barran's position, with four
planters and one merchant favoring reopening the slave trade.[61] The Cabildo, however, did not have the authority to decide, and opposition to
the vote appeared. Both Casa-Calvo and Vidal took umbrage at Barran's
argument and the inference that the Cabildo enjoyed the power to overrule
them. Casa-Calvo and Vidal declared that jurisdiction in the matter belonged to them and the intendant, and all three men favored reopening
the slave trade. The Cabildo countered with a technical argument that the
crown had approved closing the trade and that royal consent was needed
to open it. The councillors, however, failed to produce a royal order that
validated Carondelet's slave embargo. Moreover, the Cabildo majority
quickly evaporated.[62]

Intendant López issued a proclamation on December 24, 1800, that

60. Morazán, "Letters," I, 168–86.
61. Actas del Cabildo, IV, (3), 206–207, August 8, 1800, IV, (3), 208–22, August 16, 1800;
Morazán, "Letters," I, lviii, 184–86, 197. The four planters who voted for importing slaves were
French and the merchant a Spaniard. Those who voted to continue the ban were two French
planters, one French and one Spanish merchant, a Spaniard who had earlier worked for the
government and possibly was then in business, and one French Creole who was a Spanish army
officer. The latter six identified more with the safety measures of Governor Carondelet.
62. Morazán, "Letters," I, xlvii–l; Actas del Cabildo, IV, (4), 11–28, October 24, 1800. Casa-
Calvo probably knew that although the Cabildo voted against reopening the slave trade, most
Louisiana planters favored it (Paul F. Lachance, "The Politics of Fear: French Louisianians and
the Slave Trade, 1786–1809," *Plantation Society in the Americas*, I [1979], 175–77).

permitted the importation of slaves coming directly from Africa. Casa-Calvo sympathized with the planter class. He belonged to the planter elite in Cuba that also wanted black laborers to increase agricultural production on the island. He reprimanded the Cabildo for thinking it had the authority to decide this issue.[63]

Nevertheless, the Cabildo refused to recognize the proclamation's validity and appealed to the crown. The Spanish period ended before a response arrived, but in the interim the council seems to have prevailed. Intendant López departed for a new post, and Juan Ventura Morales again became acting intendant. He was against resuming the importation of slaves. But despite his opposition, some slaves continued to enter the colony both legally and illegally. After the retrocession to France had been formally announced, three shiploads of slaves quickly arrived in the colony.[64]

63. Casa-Calvo to Vidal, New Orleans, September 24, 1800, in Actas del Cabildo, IV, (4), 13–22, October 24, 1800; Vicente Fernández Texeiro to Casa-Calvo, No. 31, Ouachita, May 15, 1801, with López *bozal* slave decree of December 24, 1800, enclosed, AGI, PC, leg. 72. On the Marqués de Casa-Calvo (Sebastián Nicolás Calvo de la Puerta y O'Farrill, Arango y Arriola), see Alan J. Kuethe, *Cuba, 1753–1815: Crown, Military, and Society* (Knoxville, Tenn., 1986), 130–31, and on the Cuban elite, 113–18.

64. Morazán, "Letters," I, 162, 186–87, II, 31; Fortier, *History of Louisiana*, II, 171; Actas del Cabildo, IV, (5), 48–49, February 18, 1803, IV, (5), 50, March 4, 1803; Robertson, ed., *Louisiana Under the Rule*, I, 113, II, 244–45. On slave mutinies in Virginia, see Douglas B. Egerton, *Gabriel's Rebellion: The Virginia Slave Conspiracies of 1800 and 1802* (Chapel Hill, 1993). While the Cabildo and the governor quarreled about permitting slaves to enter by sea, they were coming into Louisiana from western American settlements. Americans were then entering the province in growing numbers, and many of them were bringing slaves. Most Americans stayed in Missouri or the northern reaches of modern-day Louisiana, and their slaves were not for resale. Nevertheless, Intendant López expressed some concern about them while he was still in Louisiana (Miguel Cantrelle to the governor, Cabahanoce, March 30, 1801, and José Vidal to Casa-Calvo, No. 114, Concordia, May 3, 1801, both in AGI, PC, leg. 72). A more serious clash between Governor Salcedo and Acting Intendant Morales occurred in July, 1802. Salcedo had given Carlos (Charles) Smith of Maryland permission to settle in Rapide (Alexandria) with his slaves. After doing so, Morales ordered Commandant Martín Duralde to seize Smith's slaves and send them to the intendancy. Instead, Duralde consulted the governor. The news disturbed Salcedo because he had given Smith permission to settle and the latter had taken an oath of loyalty. Salcedo informed Duralde not to obey the intendant on any point the governor had authorized. Nevertheless, no slaves were to be permitted who had participated in a mutiny in Virginia or were known to be vicious (Martín Duralde to Manuel Salcedo, No. 380 reserved, Opelousas, July 31, 1802, and [Salcedo] to Duralde, New

The Cabildo's efforts to control blacks in Spanish Louisiana achieved limited success. Initially, they revolved around capturing fugitives and stopping their crimes. In the 1770s and 1780s, the Cabildo was the voice of the large planters of the New Orleans district, and the councillors used their offices to pressure the governor to take measures against fugitives and adopt police regulations to control blacks, particularly slaves. The refusal of planters, especially those living beyond the immediate New Orleans vicinity, to contribute to the slave fund and the royal decree making contributions voluntary defeated this effort. The Cabildo also failed to secure tougher antiblack measures. In 1779 the councillors could blame Gálvez for deserting them. Although Miró tightened regulations against blacks in 1784 and 1786, his measures did not reach the proportions some planters favored. In addition, they heatedly opposed the crown's 1789 slave law and they did not welcome Carondelet's attempt to enforce it. Following the 1795 Pointe Coupee conspiracy, planters in the Cabildo attempted to play a role in regulating Africans, but Governor Carondelet was not amenable to their participation. He believed it was his duty, not the Cabildo's, to discipline blacks. The councillors, nonetheless, endorsed Carondelet's police measures, often described as the toughest under Spanish rule. But they were not as stringent as some modern writers have believed nor sufficiently rigorous to satisfy the planter class that wanted harsh measures. Barran's 1800 appeal to the Cabildo reveals that he and others of his persuasion favored more stringent measures. But after the Cabildo's fight on this point failed, it became passive on issues involving blacks to the close of the Spanish era.

Nevertheless, when it became known that France would recover the colony, many of these same persons demanded tougher measures, and they acted immediately after Pierre Clément de Laussat took control for France in 1803. During his twenty-day rule in Louisiana, the planters obtained the reinstitution of the Code Noir.[65] But it was a hollow victory because

---

Orleans, August 13, 1802, both in AGI, PC, leg. 138).

Although the majority of Louisianians wanted to keep it open, the slave trade closed again after the United States takeover of the colony (Robertson, ed., *Louisiana Under the Rule*, II, 254, 258–59).

65. Pierre Clément de Laussat, *Memoir of My Life,* ed. Robert D. Bush and trans. Agnes-Josephine Pastwa (Baton Rouge, 1978), 87. Laussat described the pressure he received from the

during the interregnum between the end of the Spanish regime and when American law effectively took over in the colony with the new legal codes of 1806 and 1808, Spanish law continued.[66] Moreover, certain features of Spain's slave laws persisted well into the nineteenth century, which shows that not all French planters were hostile to them.

---

planters or the Cabildo: "The members of the local government tormented me to sanction yet one more decree relative to the regulation of the Negroes. They pointed out that they daily felt an extreme need for it. They came back to the charge several times. I kept refusing on the grounds that this was on the eve of my laying down my ephemeral power. Finally, I gave in. I explained the motives for my conduct in the preamble of a decree that I drew for the purpose. A good deal of trouble was taken to hasten printing and publication (on December 17, 1803) of this decree" (*ibid.*).

66. Baade, "Law of Slavery," 72–75.

EIGHT
Food and Marketing

I N keeping with practices in Spain and its American colonies, the
Spaniards regulated the supply and price of food in Louisiana. O'Reilly
gave the Cabildo responsibilities in this area, and the city government
went beyond them to protect the public interest. It worked to prevent
food shortages and keep prices within reach of most consumers. The council's guiding principle in regulating foodstuffs was that "prices were to be
determined on the basis of the cost of the article or commodity, plus a
reasonable gain for the producer or retailer, and on the wealth of the
community." [1] Besides striving to keep food and other necessities moder-
ately priced, the Cabildo often, but not always, tried to generate revenues,
most of which paid for services.

On his arrival in New Orleans, Governor O'Reilly found the provincial
food supply in disarray. On September 17, 1769, he issued a tariff fixing
prices for most staples. It was aimed principally at New Orleans, which
was the biggest consumer of foodstuffs in the province. Violators of the
tariff would be fined ten pesos for a first offense and twenty pesos for a
second infraction. [2]

1. Moore, *The Cabildo in Peru Under the Hapsburgs,* 169, quoting the *Recopilación de leyes de
los reynos de las Indias,* libro IV, título IX, ley XXII.
2. O'Reilly, "Proclamation of September 17, 1769," *SMV,* Pt. I, 93–94.

General O'Reilly proclaimed the tariff before the Cabildo was created. Only after Governor Unzaga's administration, however, did the council begin to monitor the food supply and alter the tariff. In July, 1777, Governor Bernardo de Gálvez reissued O'Reilly's tariff, changing only the prices for rice and lard.[3]

The Cabildo's role in using a food tariff was but a small part in regulating the city's food supply. It had the additional responsibilities of assuring the accuracy of weights and measures, building and supervising the operation of public markets, guaranteeing a plentiful supply of staples, and controlling the prices and quality of staples, especially meat and bread. Usually, the Cabildo's activities in food regulation fell within the framework of Spanish colonial law, but occasionally sheer expediency dictated the measures it took.

The use of accurate and uniform weights and measures by the city's merchants and vendors constituted an important part of the council's obligation to protect consumers. Spanish American cabildos generally had an office of *fiel ejecutor* (inspector of weights and measures) attached ex officio to the sixth *regidor* in seniority. O'Reilly did not create this office in New Orleans, and for three years the Cabildo did nothing in this area. In the spring of 1773, it learned that merchants were using false measures to underpay the duties on imported liquors. It then established the office of inspector, naming Juan Escant, a master cooper, to fill the post with an annual salary of twenty pesos.[4]

The Cabildo was already moving in that direction, having acquired the first set of scales and measures in December, 1772. It now ordered others to be manufactured locally. Periodically, the Cabildo paid to recalibrate and repair the inspector's standards. Weights for the scales ranged from ounces to more than one hundred pounds, and measures went from very small containers to barrels with a capacity of 180 pounds.[5]

By 1776, several merchants again engaged in deception, which generated public discontent. The Cabildo implored Governor Unzaga to issue a public edict requiring all persons who sold goods within the city to have

3. Bernardo de Gálvez, "Proclamation Fixing Prices," July 15, 1777, *ibid.*, 239–41.
4. Morazán, "Letters," I, xxvii; Actas del Cabildo, I, 103–104, March 5, 1773.
5. Actas del Cabildo, I, 211, November 15, 1776, I, 214, December 13, 1776, IV, (2), 71, October 27, 1797; "Miscellaneous Documents," I (unnumbered), 36–37, October 27, 1797.

their weights and measures inspected at the *casa capitular*. They would then be marked so that false measures could not be substituted. Anyone selling from an unmarked weight or measure would be fined five ducats, with the proceeds to be evenly divided between the city treasury and Charity Hospital. Any merchandise in the offender's possession would be donated to Charity Hospital. Unzaga endorsed the edict.[6] This seems to have been the first attempt at a systematic enforcement of honest weights and measures in New Orleans. It worked reasonably well because the system remained intact for many years.

In 1793, the Cabildo formalized regulations on the inspection of weights and measures. It appointed Alcalde Ordinario de Primer Voto Manuel Serrano to draft a set of rules.[7] The regulations he drew up stated that the inspector was to have charge of the weights and measures, which he would compare with those used by vendors selling in the city. Those found to be accurate would be stamped with seals, and dishonest instruments would be confiscated. The inspector's fee for examining them was a half-silver real, but whenever he accompanied the judges or deputies, he would charge nothing. Fines for the first offense were twice the amount or value of the goods sold or received with dishonest or unstamped weights and measures; for a second misdeed twice that of the first fine; and for a third violation the loss of half of the offender's property.[8]

The Cabildo furnished the new inspector with the standards and an official stamp for marking the implements he examined. The council asked the governor to order all the weights and measures used in the city to be taken to the inspector's house to be examined. After the 1794 fire, the inspector of weights and measures and the monthly commissioner shared a room attached to the meat market, where the inspections took place.[9]

In 1798 a tinsmith named Juan Luis Nicolás held the office of inspector of weights and measures. He abused it by insisting that vendors buy and

6. Actas del Cabildo, I, 207, July 5, 1776.

7. Normally, the duty to draw up the law governing the inspection of weights and measures fell to the *síndico procurador general*. It is one of many instances when theory and practice did not meet. Perhaps Serrano's superior legal knowledge was the reason for selecting him.

8. Actas del Cabildo, III, (3), 62–64, April 19, 1793.

9. *Ibid.*, III, (3), 112–13, January 3, 1794, IV, (2), 55–56, October 6, 1797, IV, (2), 154, September 7, 1798; "Miscellaneous Documents," I (unnumbered), 36–37, October 27, 1797.

use only measures of his manufacture. When other metalsmiths complained about his unethical practice, the Cabildo ended it but left him in office. The following year, Nicolás quit when his contract expired.[10]

The creation of the post of inspector of weights and measures relieved the monthly commissioners of much of the drudgery of protecting the public against fraud. Still the Cabildo had to strengthen the inspector occasionally, as it did in 1792, when the council punished several bakers for selling underweight bread. Besides working to ensure accurate weights, the Cabildo had to regulate the quality of foodstuffs marketed in New Orleans.[11]

Under the French, New Orleans never had a central public market, and that omission continued during the first decade of Spanish rule. Cabildo activity in regulating the sale of foodstuffs probably was minimal during this time. But because of growing abuses in sales within the city, the council attempted to curb them in 1779. At that time, food vendors plied their edibles throughout the city and officials had difficulty inspecting them. To correct the problem, the Cabildo resolved to build a public market for the sale of certain foods. It would assist the monthly commissioners in their inspection of the provisions and the regulation of sales. Moreover, a public market would protect food from exposure. Francisco Simón de Bellislle won the contract to build a wooden structure sixty feet long by twenty-two feet wide.[12]

The public market, which was mainly for meat, enjoyed immediate success. Shortly after its completion in 1780, the councillors talked of improving and expanding it. In 1782 they built a new structure, which was more elaborate than the first one it replaced. It had cement-plastered walls, a paved brick floor and sidewalks, a gallery, and a loft with a staircase. Two years later, the Cabildo built a second market for the sale of foods other than meats; the butchers took over the 1782 facility for their sole use. The council reasoned that the two markets enabled the monthly commissioners to ensure the quality and prices of foodstuffs sold in them.

10. Morazán, "Letters," I, 10n. The office of inspector of weights and measures continued well into the American era.

11. Actas del Cabildo, III, (3), 6–7, June 22, 1792.

12. Ibid., I, 32–33, October 5, 1770, I, 40–41, January 18, 1771, I, 277–78, May 21, 1779, II, 28, June 2, 1780.

The city charged butchers fifteen pesos each per month for their shops and other vendors four pesos each per month for their smaller stalls.[13]

Not all the vendors, however, used the public facilities. Peddlers, fish sellers, and hunters, among others, still operated on their own. In the fall of 1784, the Cabildo ordered them to sell in the markets, where stalls would be assigned to them for a small fee. Those violating the decree would receive an eight-day jail sentence and a fine, or a lashing if they were slaves. The Cabildo exempted city truck-garden owners and slaves sent by their masters from neighboring plantations to sell vegetables, milk, fowl, venison, and mutton. Hunters and others who brought salt, meat, oil, suet, and pork lard by boat could continue to sell on the levee as before. First, however, officials had to inspect their wares and assign them a period of time to sell at retail, after which they could sell at wholesale. Similarly, farmers who brought rice, corn, peas, beans, and other items such as chickens and turkeys could sell them on the levee for three hours at retail. After that they could dispose of their foodstuffs at wholesale prices. Fishermen, who often left putrid fish and entrails cast upon the ground, could no longer sell their catch throughout the city. They now had to go to a designated place and sell by the pound using honest weights. Hunters would not be permitted to sell spoiled game; any found in their possession would be thrown into the river, and they would be fined.[14]

In 1786 the Cabildo tightened the administration of the meat market. It appointed one of its porters as caretaker and built a small house adjoining the market for his use. His duties were to open and close the market, watch over it during its hours of operation, guard it at night, and keep it clean. He received additional compensation for making minor repairs.[15]

---

13. *Ibid.,* II, 134–35, September 13, 1782, III, (1), 15–18, September 10, 1784, III, (1), 33–34, January 21, 1785.

14. *Ibid.,* III, (1), 15–16, September 10, 1784. Indians, who lived on the edge of the city, provided much of the game for the New Orleans market (Alliot, "Historical and Political Reflections," I, 81). Game remained plentiful, varied, and reasonable in price throughout the Spanish era (Pintard, "New Orleans, 1801," 221).

15. Actas del Cabildo, III, (1), 80, February 17, 1786, III, (1), 105, September 15, 1786, III, (1), 106, October 6, 1786; "Miscellaneous Documents," III (unnumbered), 3, July 29, 1791.

By the mid-1780s, the Cabildo had established an adequate market system for the city, but as New Orleans continued to grow the markets quickly became congested. Then the fire of 1788 devastated the public markets. Once more the Cabildo paid to put up new structures. The new and improved market that opened in 1790 cost 2,824 pesos to build. The councillors now charged each beef vendor only seven and one-half pesos per month to rent one of the ten large rooms facing the river; smaller rooms cost only two reales per day; and any small rooms left over would be rented to veal, pork, and game dealers at two pesos per month. Stalls cost two reales per day regardless of what was sold.[16]

The porter, however, found the new open-air market impossible to guard. After he complained, the city attempted to remodel the structure by placing ceilings over the stalls and strong doors at each end of the building. It also constructed rooms at each end of the market for the use of the porter and the monthly commissioner. In 1792 the building required renovation, and acting council president Vidal bypassed the councillors, who seem to have acquiesced, to hire a contractor. The next year Roberto Jones, Vidal's contractor, also repaired the building after the August hurricane struck.[17] The market escaped the 1794 conflagration because it did not reach down to the river.

In the mid-1790s, burdened with many obligations, the monthly commissioners became increasingly careless in fulfilling their duties. In 1797 the *síndico procurador general* accused them of neglecting their inspections. In defense of the *regidores,* Almonester retorted that he had always done his and that the commissioners lacked the necessary tools for proper inspections. Thereupon the council agreed to furnish the correct instruments and to repair the public market as well. Furthermore, the *regidores* resolved to perform their duties as monthly commissioners more conscientiously.[18]

16. Actas del Cabildo, III, (2), 6–7, February 8, 1788, III, (2), 99, May 7, 1790, III, (2), 114–15, September 24, 1790; "Miscellaneous Documents," I, Nos. 147–48, 76, May 14, 1790, I (unnumbered), 54–58 (undated).

17. Actas del Cabildo, III, (2), 166, January 13, 1792, III, (2), 192–93, March 23, 1792, III, (3), 15, August 11, 1792, III, (3), 33, November 16, 1792, III, (3), 84, August 20, 1793, III, (3), 87, September 13, 1793. The frequency of repairs to the 1790 market perhaps resulted from its exposed location between the river and the levee.

18. *Ibid.,* III, (3), 155–56, August 13, 1794, III, (3), 157, August 16, 1794, IV, (2), 52–53, September 30, 1797, IV, (2), 67, October 27, 1797; "Miscellaneous Documents," I (unnumbered), 36–37, October 27, 1794.

The daily duties of the monthly commissioners at the meat market were rigorous. They included being present during its hours of operation, inspecting the cattle and listing the brands, noting the number of cows slaughtered, recording the names of persons doing the rending, preventing monopolies (as in the supply of cattle), ensuring that provisions arriving after the market closed would not be sold until the next day, and inspecting the weights and measures. They also collected the rents and the taxes on each steer slaughtered and each butchering block used. These rents and imposts provided the city with approximately 250 pesos monthly.[19]

Meanwhile, the Cabildo permitted the sale of other foods in different parts of the city. As time passed, the number of stalls, shacks, and carts on the levee, teeming with foodstuffs and goods, increased. Although the Cabildo regulated their activities in 1784, it did not tax them for another ten years. It then began charging one peso per month for each shack and stall on the levee. It enacted the tax in response to Almonester's suggestion that it be used to pay the salaries of the judiciary bailiffs.[20]

In the fall of 1797, fifty city merchants led by Fernando Alzar petitioned the Cabildo to prohibit peddling on the levee. They claimed that peddlers facilitated theft and evaded the inspection of their wares. The merchants offered to compensate the city for any tax loss it experienced. The council rejected the offer and agreed only to ask Governor Gayoso to restrict the improperly licensed stands and peddlers and to have the vendors furnish a list of their goods that could be checked for theft.[21]

Two weeks later, the council entertained a motion to build a fish market that would include all the foods sold on the levee, except for vegetables. The proponents claimed that it would facilitate cleaner food, diminish spoilage from the heat, and protect the fishermen in bad weather. They projected an expense of 788 pesos, which they claimed rents would quickly amortize. A feisty Almonester led the opposition, arguing that the cleanliness of the stalls depended on whether the monthly commissioners en-

19. Actas del Cabildo, IV, (2), 52–53, September 30, 1797; "Miscellaneous Documents," I, Nos. 171–74, 99–101. These "Miscellaneous Documents" are the meat tax accounts for October through January of 1790–91. By 1802 the butchers were selling approximately thirty steers a day.

20. Actas del Cabildo, III, (3), 151–52, August 1, 1794.

21. *Ibid.,* IV, (2), 56–57, October 6, 1797.

forced the regulations. He believed the Cabildo had been wise in not building a fish market for the past twenty-eight years. Unable to reach a decision, the council left the matter pending.[22]

Only a week later, Fernando Alzar, who had earlier wanted to prohibit peddlers from selling on the levee, offered to build the market to any specification the Cabildo imposed. In return for donating the building to the city, he wanted the privilege of renting out the space in the market for two years and a guarantee that all the fish, pork, lamb, and other food vendors would have to use the facility. At the end of two years, the city would acquire the building. Although several councillors supported the proposal, the majority rejected it because they refused to permit Alzar to control the facility.[23]

The Cabildo, however, realized that something had to be done about the fish peddlers. In November, 1798, the council voted to build a public fish market at city expense, attached to the side of the existing meat market. Opposition from Almonester was gone inasmuch as he had died the preceding April 26. Bartolomé Lafond won the contract to build the market at a cost of 2,773 pesos, of which the Cabildo lent him one-third. The council appointed two *regidores* to supervise construction. After it was finished in 1799, the city spent another 245½ pesos to furnish it with large and small tables to display veal, pork, lamb, and fish and a large sunshade because of its open-air construction.[24]

Although the fish market appears to have been a success, the building and location were not. In 1803 Governor Salcedo warned that the facility was on the verge of collapse unless the city undertook immediate repairs. The market was situated on a portion of the levee that was then disintegrating.[25]

For the most part, the sale of vegetables remained outside the scope of Cabildo regulation. The city provided no facility for the fresh vegetable

22. *Ibid.,* IV, (2), 61, October 20, 1797, IV, (2), 67–68, October 27, 1797.

23. *Ibid.,* IV, (2), 77–78, November 17, 1797, IV, (2), 79, November 24, 1797.

24. *Ibid.,* IV, (2), 166, November 23, 1798, IV, (2), 176, December 15, 1798, IV, (3), 40–41, June 14, 1799, IV, (3), 73, September 20, 1799, IV, (3), 114, November 29, 1799; IV, (3), 171, April 25, 1800.

25. "Records of the City Council," Book 4088, No. 429, September 16, 1803; Morazán, "Letters," II, 226n; Pintard, "New Orleans, 1801," 229.

sellers. They appear to have operated from stands on the levee and in other parts of New Orleans. Vegetables generally sold at immoderate prices, which the city did not control.[26] Only late in the Spanish era did the Cabildo attempt to tax the vegetable peddlers. In 1798 it placed a one-real-per-week tax on the city's vegetable stands. The vegetable growers objected and fought the assessment. With Governor Gayoso's assistance, they induced the Cabildo to cancel the tax before it began. In 1800 the city believed that the consumption of greens and spoiled fruit was causing "summer illnesses." As a public duty, the council asked acting civil governor Vidal to warn both the fruit vendors and the inhabitants to discard "unhealthy fruit."[27]

An important part of the Cabildo's function in regulating food was assuring an adequate supply of beef at an affordable price. The Code O'Reilly assigned the task to the city, but the Cabildo carried it farther than its mandate suggested. Its origins rested in Spanish practices that placed it within the realm of public interest. As early as 1770, the city awarded contracts through auctions to successful bidders for time periods ranging from one to five years. The winning bidders offered the lowest meat prices and paid the highest taxes. In 1770, four butchers won the monopoly for one year by bidding a tax of 365 pesos. In addition, the Cabildo members and employees would enjoy first choice in the beef and mutton at the rate of four sueldos (four cents) per pound. Charity Hospital would also be able to buy the two meats at three sueldos per pound.[28]

The city employed this system through the 1770s, despite growing

26. Vegetables were expensive in other cities as well. François André Michaux remarked about Charleston, South Carolina, that "vegetables are dearer than meat" ("Travels to the West of the Allegheny Mountains," in *Early Western Travels, 1748–1846,* ed. Reuben Gold Thwaites [32 vols.; Cleveland, 1904–1907], III, 122).

27. Alliot, "Historical and Political Reflections," 81; Morazán, "Letters," II, 107–109; Sibley, "Journal," 460; Actas del Cabildo, IV, (2), 125, May 11, 1798, IV, (2), 130–31, June 1, 1798, IV, (2), 132, June 8, 1798, IV, (3), 194, June 27, 1800. Morazán suggests that the planters near New Orleans maintained a virtual monopoly on the production of vegetables and kept the prices high. Sibley, however, states that the planters were too involved in their commercial crops to give any attention to supplying the city with vegetables. Both Morazán and Sibley ignore the small farmers of St. Bernard and the German and Acadian coasts upriver who supplied the city with vegetables (Din, *Canary Islanders,* 52, 88; Robertson, ed., *Louisiana Under the Rule,* I, 97, 111, 117).

28. Code O'Reilly, 257; Porteous, ed. and trans., "Index," *LHQ,* VI (1923), 525.

abuses. In April, 1777, though unable to agree on a suitable alternative, the council revoked Juan Le Blanc's four-year contract two years early. That fall the Cabildo sought to find two or three butchers to make bids on a new contract. Evidently, the city had failed to find a new method and returned to using the old system.[29]

In late 1779, New Orleans faced a meat shortage, induced by Spain's entry in the American revolutionary war. To remedy the shortage, Governor Gálvez called a *cabildo abierto,* which many of the leading citizens attended, to discuss possible solutions. Most of the people in attendance preferred that the upriver settlements (the German and Acadian coasts) supply the cattle, which was adopted. The Cabildo ordered cattle owners to have 10 percent of their herds available for the city's use. They set the price for fresh meat at two reales for three pounds and salt meat and game at one-half real per pound. Because this system allowed steers to go directly from the producers to the butchers, eliminating the contractor or middleman, any profits derived from the sale of beef were to be set aside to benefit either Gálvez' soldiers or any other use the governor selected.[30]

In 1781 the Cabildo changed the system for supplying meat because the quality of beef had worsened. The council resolved that if the butchers who bought the beef monopoly failed to supply the quantity and quality of meat specified, the city would purchase it and charge the butchers. Moreover, the Cabildo extended its protection to Joseph Collette of New Iberia, who planned to drive a cattle herd to New Orleans but feared interference from the Attakapas and Opelousas ranchers. The council asked Governor Miró to warn them against obstructing Collette.[31]

Problems in supplying cattle continued, and the Cabildo stopped relying on the butchers to obtain them. It then awarded a four-year contract to George Heno in 1781. Because he failed to provide the cattle, the council

29. Actas del Cabildo, I, 191, September 22, 1775, I, 192, October 7, 1775, I, 225, April 11, 1777. One reason for the Cabildo's reluctance to change the system was the preferential treatment members received.

30. *Ibid.,* II, 7–8, December 17, 1779. On the effort of Texas to supply Louisiana with cattle during the war, see Robert H. Thonhoff, *The Texas Connection with the American Revolution* (Burnet, Tex., 1981); and Jack Jackson, *Los Mesteños: Spanish Ranching in Texas, 1721–1821* (College Station, 1986), 173–221.

31. Actas del Cabildo, II, 66–67, August 3, 1781, II, 70–71, August 31, 1781.

canceled the contract and supplied the city by seizing 10 percent of the herds in the neighboring areas. It was only a temporary expediency; the next year the Cabildo tried to interest the Attakapas and Opelousas ranchers in supplying New Orleans. It invited them to the city to bid for leases in the new meat market. Although Collette had developed a new road from the city to the west, the ranchers' interest remained low. The Cabildo again returned to the practice of a monopoly contract, but it retained the right to regulate retail meat prices.[32]

Although this system was unsatisfactory and abusive, the Cabildo kept it until January 1, 1790. In a meeting the previous September, the council declared it harmful for only one man to provide all the cattle for the city's needs. It decided to permit all ranchers who wished to sell their cattle to the New Orleans market to do so. The councillors fixed a tax on the butchers of three reales per beef slaughtered and the retail price of the meat at one-half real per pound, which represented a small reduction in the price from ten years before.[33]

But the new method of supplying meat produced fresh abuses. Cattle rustling and fraud forced the monthly commissioners to inspect all cattle brands and bills of sale. They needed to keep count of the beeves slaughtered each month, which the *mayordomo de propios* then audited and reported to the Cabildo.[34]

When Governor Carondelet girdled New Orleans with new fortifica-

32. *Ibid.,* II, 131–32, August 9, 1782, II, 140, November 8, 1782, II, 196–97, December 5, 1783, III, (1), 7, August 6, 1784. The "road" by which the cattle would be driven to New Orleans probably refers to the natural ridges that exist in the lowlands of south Louisiana (Porteous, ed. and trans., "Index," *LHQ,* XX [1937], 260–65).

In behalf of the city, Mayordomo de Propios Francisco Blanche sued Heno, claiming 1,959 pesos, court costs, and the tenth (*diezmo*). Heno lost and, unable to pay, had his property seized. Because other creditors against him also established claims, the city received only a note for 1,500 pesos from the purchaser of Heno's house. The *mayordomo's* work in this matter is notable because O'Reilly had charged the *síndico procurador general* with acting as attorney for the city to recover debts (Code O'Reilly, 265).

33. Actas del Cabildo, III, (2), 70–71, September 4, 1789.

34. *Ibid.,* III, (2), 115, September 24, 1790. The Cabildo in May, 1784, had issued a regulation requiring all livestock to be branded. The damage done by roaming livestock would be fixed by experts. There were no restrictions on the movement of livestock. The council decreed that animals had to be restrained during the harvest season and the owners of loose animals would be fined one peso (*ibid.,* II, 211–12, May 28, 1784).

tions in 1793, he appropriated the site of the city slaughterhouse. The Cabildo thereupon furnished the butchers with a new facility on a plot of city-owned land on the Bayou St. John road.[35]

Although the price of beef—and pork—fluctuated, it was usually two reales for three pounds.[36] When in 1796, four men sought a monopoly to supply New Orleans with meat, the Cabildo reconsidered the system of free competition. By then it had been in operation for seven years. In their answer to the petitioners, the council praised the free market system that had provided better meat, more efficient management, and less disease than the former methods. They resolved to keep it.[37]

Changes, however, had occurred. In the past ranchers had driven the cattle for sale to New Orleans. Now butchers were journeying to the cattle-raising districts west of the city, where they purchased prime beef at low prices. Although the drive to New Orleans and the scarcity of forage along the trail resulted in tougher and leaner steers, this method benefited the butchers.[38] When the price of beef dropped to three pounds per real, they complained that it was too low and asked for a price increase.

In 1797 the butchers petitioned to raise the price to half a real per pound. In a five-to-four vote, the council's new *regidores* agreed. The senior *regidores*, however, argued that the butchers already derived a profit from the sale of hides and entrails and that an increase in the price of meat constituted public exploitation. They were correct in their assessment.[39]

That money was made in supplying the city with beef became apparent to others. In 1798 three Chef Menteur and Attakapas residents offered to

35. *Ibid.*, III, (3), 61–62, April 12, 1793, III, (3), 77–78, July 12, 1793. A squatter named Gabriel Peyroux challenged the Cabildo's right to the land, but his appeal to the courts failed.

36. *Ibid.*, III, (3), 86, September 6, 1793, III, (3), 91–92, September 27, 1793, III, (3), 123, January 31, 1794, III, (3), 125, February 14, 1794, III, (3), 127–28, February 28, 1794, III, (3), 154–55, August 8, 1794, IV, (2), 75, November 10, 1797, IV, (2), 81, December 1, 1797.

37. *Ibid.*, IV, (1), 108, April 8, 1796, IV, (1), 131–35, June 17, 1796.

38. Alliot, "Historical and Political Reflections," I, 115.

39. Actas del Cabildo, IV, (2), 75, November 10, 1797, IV, (2), 81, December 1, 1797. Morazán explains that with the addition of six new *regidores* to the Cabildo in 1797, mercantile interests within the council became a strong force. The new members granted a 50 percent increase in price when the old rate was still marginally profitable. There is evidence from contemporary observers after 1800 that the butchers were enriching themselves at public expense. Clark also notes evidence of merchant-planter conflict of interests as early as 1788 (Morazán, "Letters," I, lviii; Clark, *New Orleans,* 271).

keep the same meat taxes and pay five thousand pesos per year in addition in return for a five-year contract. The council sent the proposal to Governor Gayoso to learn if the butchers could better the offer and to the *síndico procurador general* to inform the council how such an arrangement might affect the public welfare. The Cabildo needed money at that time because the lighting department was a heavy burden. Faced with a possible loss of their system, the butchers quickly made a counteroffer. They proposed paying four reales for each steer and two reales for each pig, calf, and sheep they slaughtered. Questioning the legality of accepting such an offer, the council consulted Vidal for his opinion. They then accepted the butchers' offer on a provisional basis while awaiting royal confirmation.[40]

This system continued until March, 1803, when conditions again changed in Louisiana. At that time, the Cabildo expected forty-five hundred French troops to arrive to take possession of the colony. It wanted to prevent speculation, hoarding, and inflation from occurring as a result of the influx of such a large number of soldiers. The council sought to have a thousand steers available for the troops outside the city. When the Cabildo received no bids on its terms, it accepted an unfavorable offer from Pedro Heno and Francisco Laudon. The French soldiers, however, never arrived because France had already sold Louisiana to the United States. In July, the Cabildo canceled the contract and allowed meat to be sold to the residents tax free. It also declared that on October 1, free competition in supplying meat to the city would resume.[41]

The proclamation caused Heno and Laudon to protest the cancellation of their contract and the prices the Cabildo set. They asked the governor to extend their monopoly through November. Salcedo referred their protest to the council, which said that the contract was contrary to public interest and had been enacted because of an expected emergency. Moreover, the thousand head of cattle would be consumed by October 11. On the advice of Vidal, Salcedo extended the contract through the end of October, 1803. The council rejected that date and the governor then set October 16 for the contract's conclusion. He proclaimed free competition to begin at

40. Actas del Cabildo, IV, (2), 104, March 2, 1798, IV, (2), 112–13, April 16, 1798, IV, (2), 114–21, April 20, 1798.

41. *Ibid.,* IV, (5), 55–57, March 11, 1803, IV, (5), 58–59, March 23, 1803, IV, (5), 78–79, July 8, 1803.

that time. He fixed the price of beef at one-half real (6¼ cents) per pound and veal at eight sueldos (8 cents) per pound. The council seems not to have challenged the governor's intrusion into the regulation of meat prices. In any case, the Spanish era was winding down and the Cabildo accomplished little in its final months.[42]

Two New Orleans butchers, Luis Elías Malbrough and Latil, also disliked the Heno-Laudon contract. They soon launched rumors alleging that the *regidores* benefited from it. The rumors incensed the councillors, who wanted to punish the responsible parties. When Governor Salcedo heard about the Cabildo's discontent, he consulted Vidal on what to do. Vidal recommended fifteen days of detention to punish and correct the butchers, and Salcedo agreed. By that time Latil and Malbrough had already been arrested and released. Because they were not then in New Orleans, they were to be rearrested on their return.[43]

Bread was, and still is, an important item in the diet of New Orleanians. For most of the Spanish period the Cabildo tried to assure the city an adequate supply of bread at reasonable prices. Because the New Orleans bakers consumed large quantities of wheat flour, merchants often attempted to profiteer in it at the expense of the residents. Similarly, bakers tried to manipulate bread prices to their advantage. The Cabildo worked to prevent abuses and control the quality of both flour and bread, but it was not always successful. In the late Spanish period, regulation intensified when the taxes on flour played an important role in funding the lighting department.

O'Reilly's 1769 food tariff left the price of bread flexible because its manufacture depended on the price of flour. Lower Louisiana did not produce flour and had to import it at costs that fluctuated. In an effort to

---

42. *Ibid.,* IV, (5), 81, July 22, 1803, IV, (5), 83–84, August 5, 1803, IV, (5), 86–88, August 19, 1803, IV, (5), 95, September 30, 1803; Morazán, "Letters," II, 225.

43. Juan de Castañedo to Salcedo, New Orleans, May 6, 1803, Pierre de La Roche and Castañedo to the Cabildo, May 6, 1803, with Salcedo's marginal notation of May 7, 1803, to send the documents to the *auditor de guerra* (Vidal), Salcedo to Castañedo and La Roche, New Orleans, May 7, 1803, and Jaime Jordá and Castañedo to Salcedo, New Orleans, July 22, 1803, all in AGI, PC, leg. 139. The Cabildo contract of April 30, 1803, with Heno and Laudon, fifteen pages long and badly eaten by ink, is attached to La Roche and Castañedo, New Orleans, May 2, 1803, in AGI, PC, leg. 103.

ameliorate this circumstance, the Cabildo enacted its first regulation governing the flour supply and the price of bread in 1770.[44]

It stated that persons dealing in flour needed to exhaust the local supply before they could buy it outside the province. Flour producers deserved a 20 percent profit on their labor and bakers a one-peso profit on each barrel of flour they converted into bread. Proceeds from the flour tax were to be equally divided among the crown, the department of justice, and the department of public works.[45]

In 1772, the Cabildo anticipated the arrival of a battalion of Spanish soldiers, which would create a flour shortage. In an effort to prevent speculation and profiteering, the council asked the governor to do whatever was necessary to prevent injury to the residents. Unzaga proposed that the Cabildo buy up all the flour at eight pesos per barrel and sell it to the bakers at the same price; the bakers continue to enjoy the same one-peso-per-barrel profit; and the price of bread be set at three pounds per real. The council endorsed the proposals and Unzaga published them. Profiteering had recently shrunk the size of bread loaves to two pounds and four ounces per real. Because few small coins circulated in Louisiana, the price of bread and other basic commodities was changed by raising or lowering the volume of the product.[46]

Because of New Orleans' uncertain flour supply, between 1774 and 1775 three flour shortages occurred. Twice the Cabildo resolved the crises by purchasing flour from Anglo-American ships despite its violation of mercantile laws and the absence of royal permission. Governor Unzaga suspended the law to make the purchases. The Cabildo sold the flour to the bakers on credit, and they repaid the city treasury after selling their bread. In the third shortage, the Cabildo reported that profiteers were exporting flour and other staples to the detriment of the colony. At the request of the council, Unzaga embargoed foodstuffs, including rice, until the city acquired an adequate supply. Prohibiting the export of rice during flour

44. See O'Reilly's tariff in *SMV,* Pt. I, 93–94.

45. Actas del Cabildo, I, 19–20, April 20, 1770. The act increased the price of cake from six sueldos and three deniers per pound to eight sueldos and one denier per pound. The bakers did not profit from the price increase because it was essentially a luxury tax on the consumption of cake.

46. *Ibid.,* I, 88–89, September 18, 1772, I, 90–91, October 30, 1772.

shortages might have been counterproductive because the rice shipped to Philadelphia paid for much of the flour imported from there.[47]

In 1777 Síndico Procurador General Enrique Despres frightened the public when he announced that spoiled flour was causing illnesses in the city. The council appointed *regidores,* Síndico Despres, the city physician, and two experienced bakers to inspect all the flour in New Orleans. They ordered the unfit flour found dumped in the river but later amended their decree to storing it until the owners shipped it out of the province. In 1792 and 1793, the Cabildo again dealt with bad flour, on these occasions choosing to throw the spoiled barrels into the Mississippi.[48]

In 1779 another flour shortage occurred caused by merchants over-exporting the commodity and by the arrival of new army recruits and many immigrants from the Canary Islands, Málaga, and Granada. The councillors resolved to buy and hold in the city warehouses the provisions they believed necessary to supply the residents. They set aside five hundred pesos for purchases and assured the flour owners of reasonable prices.[49]

In the 1780s, after the war ended, New Orleans' flour supply became more certain. Governor Bernardo de Gálvez initially permitted Americans to enter Louisiana during and immediately after the war. In 1784, however, he began to regard them as security risks and changed his mind about letting them enter the province. His decision resulted from American claims to territory that Spain had conquered in the war. Although Spain closed the Mississippi River to American commerce by that year and despite Gálvez' ruling, local officials continued to allow American immigrants who wished to settle and become Spanish subjects to enter. They often made their way down the Ohio and other rivers to the Mississippi, bringing flour with them, which the Spaniards agreeably purchased. In 1787 the Cabildo asked Governor Miró to release confiscated American flour that came downriver, arguing that a shortage would arise if it ceased to come. Following the 1788 New Orleans fire that destroyed much of the

47. *Ibid.,* I, 164, June 17, 1774, I, 180, March 3, 1775, I, 204, February 23, 1776, I, 197, November 24, 1775; Carmelo Richard Arena, "Philadelphia–New Orleans Trade" (Ph.D. dissertation, University of Pennsylvania, 1959), 49–51.

48. Actas del Cabildo, I, 229–30, June 20, 1777, III, (3), 6, June 22, 1792, III, (3), 68, May 17, 1793.

49. *Ibid.,* I, 271, March 12, 1779.

city's food supply, Governor Miró sent ships and money to Philadelphia to bring flour.[50]

In the early 1790s, flour arrived in New Orleans from North American Atlantic ports by sea and from western American settlements via the Mississippi. Direct trade with the United States that Miró started in 1788 continued, permitted by the crown in a 1789 decree that let American goods paying a tax and settlers come down the Mississippi. Although the flour supply became more assured, other problems arose. In 1793 clever merchants were buying flour from royal officials at ten pesos per barrel and selling it to the bakers for twelve pesos per barrel. The council entrusted Síndico Procurador General Juan Sarpy to work out a sliding scale to adjust the price of bread to that of flour. That would enable the Cabildo to regulate the price of bread quickly and fairly. At that time, the bakers protested that they could not profit when they bought flour at ten pesos a barrel and sold forty-ounce loaves at one real. The Cabildo allowed them to trim the loaf to thirty-six ounces temporarily.[51]

After several months, Sarpy produced a tariff and the flour-to-bread ratio based on the standard 180 pound barrel. When the bakers converted the flour to bread, the weight increased to 216 pounds, or 3,456 ounces. Bakers could earn a profit ranging between 16 and 20 reales (2 to 2½ pesos) per barrel of flour. The council accepted Sarpy's tariff and agreed to enforce it. Sarpy, however, failed to take into account the costs for other ingredients: lard or butter, milk, yeast, and salt. Moreover, firewood to heat the ovens, losses caused by waste and spoilage, labor costs, equipment for their shops and ovens, and rent reduced the bakers' profit margin. Overall, the bakers earned about the same profit they made in 1770. Good bakers used approximately fifty barrels of flour per month, which netted them about fifty pesos in profit, or twice the monthly salary of a lower-echelon civil servant.[52]

50. Clark, *New Orleans,* 206–14; Actas del Cabildo, III, (1), 158–61, August 31, 1787; Piernas to Miró, Natchez, May 31, 1783, Miró to Felipe Treviño, New Orleans, September 15, 1783, Treviño to Miró, Natchez, October 17, 1783, all in AGI, PC, leg. 9B. See also Gilbert C. Din, "Spain's Immigration Policy and Efforts in Louisiana During the American Revolution," *Louisiana Studies,* XIV (1975), 255–57; and "Proposals and Plans for Colonization," 205.

51. Actas del Cabildo, III, (3), 91–92, September 27, 1793. For the tariff, see *ibid.,* III, (3), 82, August 9, 1793.

52. *Ibid.,* III, (3), 68, May 17, 1793, III, (3), 80–82, August 9, 1793, III, (3), 91, Septem-

The tariff gave the councillors a formula by which they could adjust the price of bread, but they were not always prompt in doing so. In August, 1794, Governor Carondelet did it for them, but even then the bakers had found a way to make their own modification. They started to mix good and bad flour in their bread. Alerted, the Cabildo warned the bakers to cease. Punishment for a first offense was having all their bread cast into the river; a second violation would deprive them of baking and selling bread for a year. In 1795 the Cabildo again delayed raising bread prices to meet rising flour costs. The bakers once more resorted to using bad flour, but there is no evidence that they were punished for doing so.[53]

The 1794 fire destroyed the city's flour reserve, the flour in private hands soared in price, and the Cabildo raised the price of bread. Carondelet ordered the importation of flour and loaned the Cabildo 8,442 pesos from the Royal Treasury to purchase it once it arrived. These measures prevented flour and bread prices from rising even more.[54]

In 1796 there was a serious flour shortage, and Governor Carondelet took extraordinary measures to assist the New Orleans residents. He banned the export of flour, corn, and rice, and when an examination of existing supplies in the city revealed even less than expected, he dispatched a ship to Veracruz to bring flour. He seized four hundred barrels of corn, which the city paid for, from two ships anchored in the river. To stretch the flour supply, the bakers, with Cabildo permission, innovated by making bread from a mixture of half flour and half rice. It proved unpalatable, and the bakers reduced the rice to one-third before they judged the bread edible. A thirty-ounce loaf cost one real.[55]

Before long the Cabildo began to err grievously in dealing with the flour problem. Fearing a continued shortage of flour, the Cabildo forced Santiago (James) Fletcher to sell to the city 397 barrels at eighteen pesos

ber 27, 1793, IV, (2), 144, July 20, 1798, IV, (2), 150, August 17, 1798; Morazán, "Letters," I, 129–30n.

53. Actas del Cabildo, III, (3), 152–53, August 1, 1794, IV, (1), 59, October 2, 1795, IV, (1), 82, December 18, 1795.

54. Clark, New Orleans, 256; Actas del Cabildo, III, (3), 182, December 12, 1794; "Miscellaneous Documents," IV, No. 357, 88–90 (undated).

55. Actas del Cabildo, IV, (1), 112, April 22, 1796, IV, (1), 113–15, April 26, 1796, IV, (1), 115–16, April 27, 1796, IV, (1), 116–18, April 28, 1796.

per barrel, which was an exorbitant price. Later the Cabildo had the flour inspected and found that eighty barrels were spoiled. When the councillors attempted to return them to Fletcher, he filed suit against the city. The court investigated to learn when the flour had spoiled. The result must have gone against the Cabildo because it paid Fletcher for seventy-eight of the barrels. The council ordered the flour from these barrels made into hardtack and sold so as not to suffer a total loss. The councillors, however, expected another flour shortage in January, 1797.[56]

This shortage did not materialize, and the city found itself burdened with a quantity of expensive flour that it had difficulty selling. The council asked the bakers to buy it, but they bid only ten pesos per barrel. The councillors nevertheless accepted the bid so as not to be burdened with flour that had depreciated in value. How much money the city lost between May, 1796, and January, 1797, is difficult to calculate. It is known that it spent 30,960½ pesos during that time. The loss might have amounted to 10,000 or 12,000 pesos.[57]

In 1798 the Cabildo became more diligent in overseeing the regulation of flour distribution and the activities of the bakers. Early in the year, the bakers, along with the butchers, volunteered to assume a tax to aid in financing the lighting department. They agreed to pay four reales per barrel on all the flour they used, but the council had to keep track of it so as to collect the tax.[58]

That same year, the merchants and bakers conspired to derive a greater profit at public expense. Because the price of bread was related to the cost of flour in the 1793 tariff, the confederates manipulated the price of flour by raising it through purchase, sale, and repurchase, the price rising with each transaction. In the final sale, the bakers bought it at an inflated price and surreptitiously received a rebate from their merchant-cohorts. The bakers passed the final sale price of the flour to the consumers through the higher cost of the bread. The Cabildo ended the practice by assessing the monthly flour consumption for each baker based on his statement of

56. *Ibid.,* IV, (1), 124–25, May 24, 1796, IV, (1), 125–26, June 3, 1796, IV, (1), 160–61, October 21, 1796, IV, (1), 162, November 3, 1796, IV, (1), 164, November 11, 1796.

57. *Ibid.,* IV, (1), 195–96, January 20, 1797; "Miscellaneous Documents," IV, No. 357, 91–97 (undated).

58. Actas del Cabildo, IV, (2), 112–13, April 16, 1798.

how much bread he sold each month. Despite some adjustments, the system ended most of the fraudulent practices and facilitated the collection of the flour taxes.[59]

Nevertheless, a few persons tried to evade the system. In response, the city developed a method that was more difficult to dodge. It required payment based on records, with the bakers having to prove any deductions that would decrease their tax burden.[60]

In 1800 the Cabildo enacted its last regulation on bread sales. The price and the quality of bread had begun to fluctuate greatly. To impose some degree of uniformity, the council ordered the bakers to make two grades of bread, one from superior flour and another from common flour. The council fixed the rates for both types of bread in a tariff, which it published.[61] Although this was the last regulation on bread, it was not the last crisis.

In 1803 Síndico Procurador General Prevost declared that the available flour supply was small, old, and wormy. The reason was acting intendant Morales' suspension of the right of deposit that Americans had enjoyed in New Orleans and Governor Salcedo's ending food importation from the United States. The Cabildo, which had a continuing fight with the governor, resolved only to take such steps as were dictated by prudence. It bypassed the governor and prevailed upon Morales to exempt foodstuffs from his prohibition. He complied.[62]

Besides flour, the Cabildo occasionally took an interest in regulating rice and corn, staples consumed by poor people. When the two commodities were in short supply in the colony, the council often purchased them from Anglo-American ships on the river. The Cabildo also considered building a public granary in 1796, particularly for the storage of rice.[63]

59. *Ibid.,* IV, (2), 137, June 28, 1798, IV, (2), 144, July 20, 1798, IV, (2), 150, August 17, 1798, IV, (3), 27, April 19, 1799.

60. *Ibid.,* IV, (3), 72, September 13, 1799, IV, (3), 74, September 20, 1799.

61. *Ibid.,* IV, (3), 203–204, August 1, 1800.

62. *Ibid.,* IV, (5), 42–45, February 1, 1803; Morazán, "Letters," II, 190; Clark, *New Orleans,* 246. Earlier, in 1781, the Cabildo had also worked through the intendancy. It induced Intendant Navarro to permit French ships, which were carrying lumber from Louisiana, to bring in food and merchandise that were desperately needed (Actas del Cabildo, II, 67–69, August 17, 1781).

63. Actas del Cabildo, I, 180, March 13, 1775, II, 2–3, October 1, 1779, IV, (1), 103–104, March 11, 1796, IV, (1), 106–107, April 1, 1796, IV, (1), 112, April 22, 1796, IV, (3), 168, April

Granary construction in the late eighteenth century was widespread in Mexico, where periodic food shortages occurred. In New Orleans, the storage of grain, especially rice, had been a problem in the past. Warehouse owner Filberto Farge stored rice for the city and sold it when a need arose. The city neither taxed the sale of rice nor profited from it. The king granted the Cabildo permission to build a granary, assigned an endowment of 4,925 pesos for construction, and donated the land on which to erect it. The royal funds were to come from surplus revenues that had accumulated in the fund for orphan girls. The Cabildo delayed in construction and only after Governor Gayoso's death did the councillors discover that he had been using the money; the city did not recover it from his estate until 1801. But it did not keep the money. Because of delays in the shipment of royal funds to Louisiana, the intendancy was in desperate need of money. Governor Salcedo urged the council to loan the funds to the Royal Treasury, which it did. As a consequence, the city never started construction of the rice granary.[64]

Firewood and game were the only other basic provisions that received Cabildo attention. During the winter, when freed from agricultural chores, slaves engaged in cutting firewood. After it dried, they transported the wood to New Orleans for sale. In addition, Indian women gathered deadwood and hawked it in the city streets. The price for firewood was set in the 1769 tariff and remained unchanged until late in the Spanish era.[65]

In 1796 the Cabildo prohibited woodcutters from felling trees on public lands. In 1801 wood sellers were gouging the public. The council tried to end the abuse by granting a monopoly to supply the city and imposing a ceiling of 3½ pesos per cord. The monopoly proved unsuccessful because slaves continued to sell firewood above the fixed rate. The Cabildo's efforts to enforce the monopoly seem to have been fruitless, and in 1803 firewood sold in the city at four pesos per cord.[66]

18, 1800, IV, (5), 39–41, January 21, 1803; "Miscellaneous Documents," I, No. 159, May (no day), 1797.

64. Actas del Cabildo, IV, (2), 1–2, July 14, 1797, IV, (3), 55–57, August 3, 1799, IV, (4), 114–15, July 17, 1801; Morazán, "Letters," II, 92n.

65. Alliot, "Historical and Political Reflections," I, 59, 83, 85; O'Reilly, "Proclamation of September 17, 1769," SMV, Pt. I, 93–94.

66. Actas del Cabildo, IV, (1), 141–42, July 15, 1796, IV, (4), 141–42, November 13, 1801, IV, (5), 41, January 21, 1803.

Besides trying to assure a supply of necessary staples and fix prices that all residents could afford, the Cabildo at times tried to impose regulations on merchants who attempted to gouge the public by creating artificial shortages. In the spring of 1781, several merchants were buying goods from ships downriver before they arrived in New Orleans. The merchants were trying to raise prices by creating shortages. The council asked the governor to stop this abuse.[67]

In the summer of 1782, the Cabildo suspected the established merchants of conspiring to exclude new competitors from operating in New Orleans. The local business community resented the intrusion of foreign merchants. At that time, Governor Miró questioned the loyalty of the city council more than he did that of the merchants. He answered the Cabildo from Natchez, where he had gone to reinforce the post against a possible British attack, that he suspected its members of attempting a power play to subvert the loyalty of the merchants. He told them that he would not abet them in their nefarious scheme. The councillors protested and alleged that they were only endeavoring to perform their duty. Differences between the merchants and planters diminished after 1782 because of the new rules on trade. But not until after the 1788 fire did Miró side with the planters, who were dominant on the Cabildo and who favored open competition among all the merchants.[68]

One final area of Cabildo regulation in the late Spanish period concerned mules. They were important in the rising sugarcane industry in Louisiana. Through its actions the Cabildo showed that it had moved away from favoring monopolies that protected the public welfare and produced a fixed revenue for the city to a system of free competition in the supply of foodstuffs at competitive prices and improved quality. The Cabildo revealed its devotion to this principle in 1800.

That year Claudio Francisco Girod planned an expedition to Texas to acquire three hundred mules for use in Louisiana. Mules in New Orleans

67. *Ibid.,* II, 52–53, April 27, 1781.
68. *Ibid.,* II, 127–28, July 19, 1782, II, 128–30, August 2, 1782, II, 133–34, September 6, 1782. On the background of Miró's trip to Natchez and the reason for going, see Gilbert C. Din, "Loyalist Resistance After Pensacola: The Case of James Colbert," in *Anglo-Spanish Confrontation on the Gulf Coast During the American Revolution,* ed. William S. Coker and Robert R. Rea (Pensacola, 1982), 161–66.

were then worth between two hundred and three hundred pesos. Therefore, the herd that Girod proposed to bring had a potential value of between sixty thousand and ninety thousand pesos. He sought Cabildo support for his project, which he needed to win the approval of the viceroy
of New Spain. The council readily endorsed Girod's petition but declared
that it would support anyone else who sought to import mules from Texas.
The Cabildo wanted to avoid any possibility that Girod might be trying
to obtain a monopoly.[69]

In attempting to regulate staples and prices, the New Orleans Cabildo
tried to ensure an ample supply of foodstuffs at fair prices. It labored
strenuously to avoid either natural or artificial conditions that would have
permitted profiteering and gouging the needy. Although the results did
not always meet with success, the Cabildo worked vigorously to achieve
beneficial results, particularly up to the time of Gayoso's death in mid-
1799. Thereafter, the Cabildo's struggle with Vidal and Salcedo severely
limited its effectiveness.

69. Actas del Cabildo, IV, (3), 154–55, March 14, 1800; Sibley, "Journal," 479.

NINE

Medicine and Health Regulation

EIGHTEENTH-CENTURY New Orleanians had great need
for medical care and sanitation. Located near the Gulf of Mexico
and with a subtropical climate, the city was literally a hothouse for
disease and insects. Moreover, it was surrounded by water, below the level
of the Mississippi, and often deluged by torrential rains. In this inauspi-
cious setting, New Orleanians had only primitive medicine to help them
overcome the assorted ills that plagued them. Besides the physicians and
surgeons described here, poorer residents of New Orleans and rural Louisiana often resorted to folk medicine that consisted mostly of herbs and
prayers for the many little-understood afflictions of that age. Even the
trained medical community possessed only limited knowledge of the "arts"
they exercised. Nevertheless, New Orleans probably differed little from
other cities on the Gulf of Mexico, the Caribbean, and the eastern seaboard
of North America in the health care available.[1]

1. For discussions of medicine in colonial Louisiana, see Duffy, ed., *Rudolph Matas History*,
I; and O'Conner, "Charity Hospital," 1–109. For a comparison of the activities of another cabildo
in the area of public health, see Della M. Flusche, "The Cabildo and Public Health in Seventeenth Century Santiago, Chile," *Americas*, XXIX (1972–73), 173–90.
    For a view of medicine in a North American city, see Benjamin Rush, "An Inquiry into
the Comparative State of Medicine, in Philadelphia, Between the Years 1760 and 1766, and

Into this environment, the New Orleans Cabildo brought several centuries of Spanish legislation to guide it in its actions. It participated actively in colonial Louisiana's health needs. Spanish law assigned some of its duties, O'Reilly's regulations designated others, and the Cabildo added more health responsibilities on its own initiative. The major areas of Cabildo activity in health care consisted of regulating medical practices, maintaining hospital facilities, combating contagious diseases, and improving sanitation.[2]

The Cabildo's regulation of medical practitioners in Louisiana falls into several categories. The city councillors were expected to help enforce O'Reilly's decrees on medicine and pharmacy. In addition, the Cabildo expanded the general's provisions for medical and pharmaceutical examinations. On occasion, the council also prosecuted nonlicensed health practitioners. The Cabildo steadily increased its authority in these areas until the late 1790s, when it gradually began to cede jurisdiction to the governor.

The Cabildo's authority over medical practitioners had its origin in O'Reilly's medical decree of February 12, 1770. Although the decree di-

the year 1805," *Medical Inquiries and Observations,* 2nd ed. (Philadelphia, 1805), IV, 364–405, republished in *The Rising Glory of America, 1760–1820,* ed. Gordon S. Wood (New York, 1971), 219–36. Among the many illnesses Rush listed were cholera morbus; fevers including yellow, scarlet, and bilious; pneumonies; rheumatisms; inflammatory sore throats; catarrhs; influenza; colica pictonum or dry gripes; and smallpox. Among the medicines or cures employed were mercury, lead, zinc, arsenic, digitalis, bloodletting, horseback riding for invalids, opium to ease pain, and spiritus minereri and spirit of sweet niter to induce sweating. He called cold air, cold water, and ice "among the new remedies of [the] modern practice" of medicine. The presence of the many privies Dr. Rush mentions no doubt contributed to polluted water and illnesses. On the positive side, cowpox vaccination had replaced inoculation with the smallpox virus as the way to prevent the disease.

2. Cabildos in Spanish America regularly examined the medical practitioners who wanted to work in their cities. See Frederick B. Pike, "Public Work and Social Welfare in Colonial Spanish American Towns," *Americas,* XIII (1956–57), 361–75. See also John Tate Lanning, "The Illicit Practice of Medicine in the Spanish Empire in America," in *Homenaje a Don José María de la Peña y Cámara,* ed. Ernest J. Burrus, S.J., and George P. Hammond (Madrid, 1969), 140–79. Lanning states that a serious shortage of physicians existed in Spanish America, thereby leading to the widespread use of *curanderos* (medicine men), who were largely charlatans. New Orleans in the late Spanish era, by comparison, had a fair number of surgeons and physicians in addition to practitioners of folk medicine.

vided the medical profession into two categories, physicians and surgeons, its primary concern was regulating the activities of surgeons.[3]

The two principal motives behind O'Reilly's decree were to curb surgeons' claims of their abilities, thus keeping them subordinate to university-trained physicians, and to protect the public from charlatans. Because Louisiana lacked an adequate number of physicians in the early Spanish era, the decree permitted surgeons to practice internal medicine for ten years. O'Reilly's decree required all medical practitioners to be examined for competence before they could be licensed to practice in the province. The decree also called for punishing all nonlicensed practitioners and persons who concealed useful medical knowledge.[4] Medical practitioners were expected to share their learning.

To be admitted to practice, a surgeon first had to be a Roman Catholic. He could then take an examination by presenting himself, his instruments, books, certificates of study, character references, and any other relevant documents to the king's (army) physician. The examining physician verified the petitioner's credentials and administered an oral examination. A special register recorded the examination results. The governor next approved the applicant's certificates, and the Cabildo *escribano* registered them in his office. If an applicant failed his first examination, he had to serve a six-month apprenticeship at Charity Hospital before being reexamined. A second failure barred him from practicing medicine in Louisiana.[5]

3. "Le premier soin d'un Gouvernement sage, étant de fixer a chacun les bornes de ses propriétés & de veiller a la conservation de Citoyens, j'ai cru devoir établir comme dans tous le États polices, les Règlements suivants, concernant l'exercice de la Médicine & la chirurgie," O'Reilly, February 12, 1770, AGI, PC, leg. 188A.

4. *Ibid.* Physicians enjoyed a higher reputation than surgeons (Flusche, "The Cabildo and Public Health," 173–90). Lanning states about the lower standards in surgery over those in medicine in Spanish America: "Because it was so low in the scale of prestige, the Spaniards did approximate this solution in surgery; they allowed men to practice once they had assisted and observed a surgeon for five years. The majority of these, unhappily, had to be examined without the prerequisite certificate of blood purity or not at all. So deep-seated was *curanderismo* that these licensed romance surgeons eased inexorably over into the practice of internal medicine until, as the legitimate physicians bewailed, they 'reached the execrable extreme of holding consultations.' Even they found quackery more profitable and prestigious than legitimate practice" ("Illicit Practice," 179).

5. Douglas Crawford McMurtrie, ed., "A Louisiana Decree of 1770 Relative to the Practice of Medicine and Surgery," *New Orleans Medical and Surgical Journal,* LXXXVI (1933), 7–11.

Only surgeons and physicians possessing royal and military commissions were exempted from examination. For example, in 1779 Dr. Juan Vives of Denia, in the province of Valencia, Spain, was hired by the governor to attend to the Canary Islanders settled on Bayou Lafourche. There Vives served the Isleños, other bayou residents, and militia units. Medical practitioners who wanted to work in the city, however, had to pass the examination and then serve gratis for six months in the city's hospitals. This enabled them to prove further their competency before establishing private practices. Even after beginning their practices, surgeons had to donate time and services to Charity Hospital. Once admitted to practice, surgeons could not engage in the mechanical arts or business under penalty of losing their licenses. Medical doctors were required to be married or to marry within fifteen months after being licensed.[6]

O'Reilly's medical decree contained regulations that obliged doctors to report any knife or gunshot wounds they treated. Surgeons were required to obtain the consent of masters, parents, or guardians before they treated slaves or minors, especially girls. Surgeons needed to itemize their bills to patients; the courts would rule on disputed charges, upon the advice of a physician. The decree stipulated that surgeons who broke any law would lose their licenses "so as to be brought to justice."[7]

O'Reilly's decree further stipulated that surgeons meet on the first Monday of each month in the presence of a physician to confer on diseases relevant to the locale and the season. Each doctor was obliged to enter the discourse in turn. These conferences were expected to broaden the surgeons' knowledge and benefit the public. The surgeons were encouraged to train suitable women as midwives, after which they needed to pass an oral examination.[8]

6. *Ibid.;* Din, *Canary Islanders,* 69.

7. McMurtrie, ed., "Louisiana Decree of 1770," 7–11.

8. *Ibid.* This decree was similar to the one issued under the French regime in 1723 and reissued in 1743. See Heloise H. Cruzat, trans., "Cabildo Archives: Ordinance of the Superior Council Regulating the Practice of Medicine, Surgery and Obstetrics," *LHQ,* III (1920), 86–88. In 1808 the Orleans Territorial Legislature passed "An Act Concerning Physicians, Surgeons and Apothecaries," which was also similar to the Spanish medical regulations (Morazán, "Letters," I, 13–15n).

Medical doctors were privileged creditors under Spanish law, and they sometimes used the courts to collect debts from recalcitrant patients and the estates of deceased patients. Dr. Robert

O'Reilly gave the provincial magistrates and the royal physician in New Orleans responsibility for enforcing his medical decree. He did not specifically mention the Cabildo. For two years after O'Reilly's departure, no person or agency enforced the decree. Then, in the absence of medical supervision, the Cabildo intervened. On May 8, 1772, Síndico Procurador General Juan Bautista Lacosta presented the Cabildo with a memorandum on the poor relationship existing between medicine and surgery. To acquaint the councillors with O'Reilly's by-laws for practicing medicine, the Cabildo *escribano* read them. The councillors then instructed the *escribano* to inform the physicians and surgeons about the requirements and to present themselves with their medical credentials within a week. They would be questioned about their professions, and the governor would be informed of the results to act as he saw fit.[9] Thus "the Cabildo ruled that the matter of certification rested in its own hands, but no certificates would be granted until the candidates had satisfied the examining physician or physicians."[10] As in O'Reilly's decree, Cabildo involvement in regulating doctors referred only to those in private practice and not to army or government doctors.

Although the Cabildo took charge of medical licensing, doctors already practicing in the colony seem not to have complied with its resolution. The council might have enforced its decree, however, for it retained its interest in the medical examination and extended its influence in that area. Departing from O'Reilly's decree, which required the royal physician to examine the candidates, now that the Cabildo was in charge, "it became the custom to set up an examination board of several medical men."[11] The Cabildo usually appointed two of its members to serve on the board.

The council, however, seems not to have enforced meticulously

---

Dow, a Scottish physician, was long regarded as one of New Orleans' more capable practitioners of internal medicine. But an examination of the drugs he used, listed in his bill against the estate of Santiago Lemelde, raises questions about his ability. Dow administered hemlock, mercury, sarsaparilla, opium, camphor, alum, and myrrh, among other things, to his hapless patient (Porteous, ed. and trans., "Index," *LHQ*, VIII [1925], 179; and *ibid.*, XXIII [1940], 343–47).

9. McMurtrie, ed., "Louisiana Decree of 1770," 11; Actas del Cabildo, I, 77–78, May 8, 1772; Duffy, ed., *Rudolph Matas History*, I, 179.

10. Duffy, ed., *Rudolph Matas History*, I, 181.

11. *Ibid.*

O'Reilly's decree. In April, 1777, Esteban Henriques Mora received a license as a physician because New Orleans allegedly had none.[12] In that year, surgeon Santiago Vincente acquired a license after he presented his credentials, which included his 1756 title from a French medical school in Montpellier, a license from the Madrid medical community, and documents from his service as a ship's surgeon. When the physician Jean Rouelles presented his certificate, he was admitted to practice upon taking the customary oath. In 1779 the Cabildo admitted surgeon Santiago Cursol to practice after inspecting his credentials and without requiring a professional examination. The same year, the council licensed Luis Dunoyer to practice when he presented the written recommendations of two Louisiana physicians.[13]

Change came in 1788, however, when the Cabildo formalized its method of licensing health practitioners. It arranged for two Cabildo councillors, two physicians, and all of the city's surgeons to conduct the examination. The first candidate examined was Joseph Labru de la Gardelle. Thereafter, the procedure continued through 1796 with only minor variations. A simple diploma, even from a Spanish school, no longer entitled a medical doctor to be licensed.[14]

The only instance when the Cabildo granted an examination to an applicant without a diploma involved Domingo de Fleitas. In 1792, as chief surgeon of the Royal Hospital, he petitioned Governor Carondelet for an examination. The governor referred the petition to the Cabildo. Fleitas had lost his diploma when his ship sank in the wartime expedition against British-held Mobile in 1780. He produced in its stead certificates from several Louisiana physicians. The Cabildo appointed a committee to examine him so as to admit him to private practice.[15]

12. Actas del Cabildo, I, 224–25, April 11, 1777.

13. Ibid., I, 235–36, December 11, 1777, I, 245–46, March 27, 1778, I, 272, March 12, 1779, I, 289, August 27, 1779.

14. Ibid., III, (2), 10, March 14, 1788.

15. Ibid., III, (3), 202–203, May 18, 1792. Lanning, in "Illicit Practice," 156, tells of former Louisiana governor Carondelet attempting to promote medicine in Quito, Ecuador: "President [of the Audiencia of Quito, Barón de] Carondelet tried to get financing for the chair of medicine that had been authorized in the University of San Fernando; but, as one Pedro Agüayo had never produced the eight hundred peso endowment he promised, and the available property in haciendas yielded only thirty-three pesos, he had to give up. Thirty-three pesos to start a chair of medicine!"

In 1800 the Cabildo again revised the examination procedure. Acting civil governor Vidal informed the council that the current system violated Spanish law, and he outlined the correct procedure for medical examinations. In addition to the oral examination, applicants needed to examine patients at the Royal Hospital. They were to take patients' temperatures, diagnose ailments, and fill prescriptions. The candidates then had to undress and redress a wound or ulcer in the surgical ward. They needed to perform the practical tests to the satisfaction of a medical panel. Vidal's instructions did not mention Cabildo participation in the examination. The council passed a resolution accepting Vidal's opinion and excluding its members from the board of examiners.[16]

The civil governor's instructions had come in response to a petition from George Pfeiffer, who requested to be licensed in both medicine and surgery. He was examined in the two fields, although O'Reilly had not provided for such a contingency. Moreover, because Pfeiffer did not speak Spanish, he was examined by Pedro Pedesclaux, the Cabildo scribe who also acted as interpreter. Pfeiffer was the first of several doctors who attempted to qualify in both areas of medicine. After qualifying, his admittance was noteworthy in another respect. The Cabildo permitted Pfeiffer to practice despite his Protestant religion and allowed him to swear by God and the Bible instead of taking the customary oath. In this instance, the city government displayed growing tolerance toward the religion of many of its new inhabitants.[17]

The Cabildo as a body prosecuted a nonlicensed medical practitioner only once, reaching out beyond the city to a provincial settlement. When a smallpox epidemic erupted in Natchitoches in 1778, the council feared that the community lacked medical assistance, and it dispatched New Orleans physician Jean Rouelles to aid the residents. On his arrival, he found surgeon Francisco La Casa treating the afflicted. Upon his return to New Orleans, Rouelles asked that La Casa be prosecuted for practicing medicine without a license.

16. Actas del Cabildo, IV, (3), 127–28, January 17, 1800, IV, (3), 129, January 24, 1800.
17. Henry P. Dart, ed., "Spanish Procedure in Louisiana in 1800 for Licensing Doctors and Surgeons," trans. Laura P. Porteous, *LHQ,* XIV (1931), 204–207; Morazán, "Letters," I, 13. For other persons who were examined as both physician and surgeon, see Actas del Cabildo, IV, (4), 137, September 18, 1801, IV, (4), 206–207, April 30, 1802.

The Cabildo claimed jurisdiction and tried La Casa *in absentia*. Joseph Mantaigiel, who had La Casa's power of attorney, represented him. The council technically found La Casa guilty and fined him five pesos, assigning the money to Charity Hospital. Nevertheless, at the same meeting the councillors granted La Casa his license to practice medicine on the basis of certificates he presented in his defense. Among them were a statement in his behalf from Joseph Montegut, who was the royal surgeon in New Orleans, and testimonials from Natchitoches residents attesting to his skill as a medical practitioner. The Cabildo also exhorted Dr. Rouelles to be more open-minded in the future. This is the only known example of the council investigating and licensing a medical doctor outside the immediate New Orleans area.[18]

Nevertheless, it is possible that the Cabildo helped to license physicians and surgeons who practiced in the province. On April 1, 1787, on giving Captain José López de la Peña instructions on what he should do as political and military commandant of Natchitoches, Governor Miró included a provision that he watch over medical practitioners. The governor warned that charlatans and quacks, "aided by several cures that accidentally give them the character of able physicians or surgeons, [are] destroying the health of the inhabitants." Miró instructed López de la Peña to permit only the physicians and surgeons "approved in this city [New Orleans]." Anyone trying to practice medicine without the governor's permission was to be sent to New Orleans.[19]

After its slow start, the city's medical licensing policy seems to have been adhered to for some years. Toward the end of the Spanish era, however, after Vidal curtailed the Cabildo's authority in administering the medical examination, enforcement became lax. By August, 1801, a report accused six unlicensed medical practitioners of plying their arts. The council notified five of them to cease practicing until they satisfied the qualifications.[20]

The Cabildo nonetheless permitted the sixth man, a free black named

18. Actas del Cabildo, I, 254, September 25, 1778; Duffy, ed., *Rudolph Matas History,* I, 180.

19. "Instructions which Dn. José López de la Peña should follow in command of the political and military post of Natchitoches," [Miró], New Orleans, April 1, 1787, AGI, PC, leg. 118.

20. Actas del Cabildo, IV, (4), 126, August 14, 1801.

Santiago Derum (James Durham), to continue his medical treatments, but only for the throat, a specialty in which he had enjoyed great success over a period of years. Durham was born a slave in Philadelphia in 1762. He learned his knowledge about throat maladies at a young age from an expert in the field, Dr. John Kearnsley. Later Dr. Robert Dow of New Orleans bought Durham, but the budding healer soon purchased his freedom at age twenty for five hundred pesos. He has been described as the first known licensed African American physician in what is now the United States.[21]

A week after the Cabildo's warning, Joseph Fabre, one of the other five unlicensed individuals, petitioned for an examination, and the council arranged it for him. The illness of Governor Salcedo on Fabre's examination day forced a rescheduling because the examining doctors were attending to him. The other four men, meanwhile, continued their medical practices despite the warning. The council soon cautioned them again, after which the governor could act in the matter.[22]

The example of the Cabildo granting a limited license to the freedman Durham was not without precedent. In 1789 Peter Paulus petitioned the council for permission to treat all venereal diseases. The councillors discussed the success he had had in treating these diseases and readily granted his request. They limited his practice to venereal disease.[23]

In 1803 the Cabildo acted to stop a French physician from practicing without a license. Dr. Paul Alliot, a refugee from Haiti and a political suspect, had been plying his arts for three months when authorities arrested him late one night at his home. An *alcalde ordinario* authorized breaking down his door and dragging him off to jail. Although he turned

21. Hanger, "Personas de varias clases," 119–20. See also Charles B. Roussere, *The Negro in Louisiana: Aspects of His History and His Literature* (New Orleans, 1937), 9–10.

22. Actas del Cabildo, IV, (4), 128–29, August 21, 1801, IV, (4), 130–31, August 29, 1801.

23. *Ibid.*, III, (2), 78–79, November 20, 1789; Duffy, ed., *Rudolph Matas History,* I, 182. Duffy insists that Peter Paulus' cures could not have been of venereal disease, and he is probably correct. Paulus seems to have been a jack-of-all-trades. He first arrived in New Orleans in March, 1789, after having conducted thirty-four Anglo-Americans to Natchez. He soon presented himself to Governor Miró professing to be able to bring thousands of immigrants to Louisiana. Miró thought that he might be useful, gave him 350 pesos for his expenses, and encouraged him to bring settlers. Back in New York, Paulus crowed that he had hoodwinked Miró out of the money and did nothing about the settlers. The governor probably never heard about Paulus' boasts and allowed him to stay unmolested after he returned to Louisiana (Din, "Proposals and Plans for Colonization," 206–207).

out to be politically harmless, Alliot had alienated the New Orleans medical community by failing to secure a license. The council rejected his defense of ignorance of the law and found him guilty. Governor Salcedo then assumed jurisdiction and deported Alliot to France.[24]

The medical examination that doctors took to practice in New Orleans was demanding. A number of applicants failed it and had to be reexamined six months or a year later. Applicants who wanted to practice as both physician and surgeon occasionally passed one examination but failed the other. This happened to Theofilo Elmer in 1802. The following summer he passed the surgeon's examination that he had initially failed. Not all petitioners needed to wait six months to be reexamined. In 1796 Luciano Abadie became unnerved and incapable of answering questions during his examination. The Cabildo chose not to count it as an examination and allowed him one month to compose himself before trying it again. He then passed it and received his license to practice surgery.[25]

Once a surgeon or physician was licensed, he was not beyond the reach of the Cabildo. During the 1802 smallpox epidemic, the council charged Dr. Luis Giovellina with criminal neglect in the vaccination and isolation of a slave child belonging to Monsieur Otrayen. The councillors claimed that Giovellina wanted the disease to spread, and they asked Governor Salcedo, who presided at the meeting, to punish him. On the same day of the Cabildo's action against Giovellina, March 5, 1802, Salcedo told Almonester's widow, Luisa de La Ronde, who was now administrator of Charity Hospital, to name another surgeon for the facility. Salcedo had arrested Giovellina, but his incarceration was brief. By March 9, he was free and again in charge of Charity Hospital, a post he retained until he left for Europe about 1804. The accusations of the Cabildo's councillors against him appear to have been spurious. The councilmen who favored

24. Alliot, "Historical and Political Reflections," 183–84; Morazán, "Letters," I, 14n. Alliot had his revenge for being deported by writing deprecatingly, in the work cited above, about both the Cabildo and the physicians and surgeons of New Orleans. Alliot's allegations against the New Orleans medical community, especially against Dr. Montegut, were unwarranted. Montegut was well respected in New Orleans. Unfortunately, undiscerning writers sometimes accept Alliot's charges as accurate.

25. Actas del Cabildo, IV, (1), 144, July 22, 1796, IV, (5), 13, August 20, 1802, IV, (5), 76, June 17, 1803, IV, (5), 80, July 15, 1803; Duffy, ed., *Rudolph Matas History,* I, 182.

Giovellina's removal did so because he was an Almonester appointee at Charity Hospital. Perhaps they still harbored illusions of controlling the institution.[26]

By 1803, the Cabildo's role in regulating medical examinations had completed a full circle. Although O'Reilly's medical decree did not include the city council's involvement, it gradually assumed control of examining physicians and surgeons, filling a vacuum no one else claimed. Then late in the Spanish era, the Cabildo relinquished control to the governor's office and by 1803 no longer participated in the examination.

Although the Cabildo had not been named to regulate the city's physicians and surgeons, its involvement in watching over the practice of pharmacy in New Orleans began earlier. In November, 1769, Jean Peyroux requested a permit to open an apothecary shop in the city. The royal physician, François Le Beau, examined Peyroux and gave him a provisional license. The Cabildo confirmed the certificate on January 12, 1770, making him the first licensed pharmacist in New Orleans.[27]

In conjunction with his examination of Peyroux, Dr. Le Beau drew up seven rules, conformable to Spanish law, to be observed by New Orleans pharmacists. The regulation required them to keep a register of the drugs sold and their purchasers. Pharmacists could buy imported drugs only after the public had an opportunity to purchase them from the importers. Pharmacists had to sell their drugs at reasonable prices and in accordance with a tariff. Pharmacists needed to follow the prescriptions ordered by the doctors and compound their drugs in conformity with the Code of Paris, as observed in the Spanish Empire, insofar as their knowledge of these formulas permitted. They could not compound drugs on their own initiative. Finally, the king's physician could examine and reject their drugs if they were old and unfit.[28]

O'Reilly approved Le Beau's regulations on November 25, 1769, and

26. Actas del Cabildo, IV, (4), 180, March 5, 1802; Morazán, "Letters," I, 14n, 190n; [Salcedo] to Luisa de La Ronde, New Orleans, March 5 and 9, 1802, both in AGI, PC, leg. 138A.

27. Duffy, ed., *Rudolph Matas History,* I, 185–86.

28. *Ibid.* The tariff Le Beau mentioned might have been a posted list of one pharmacy's drug prices. It was not a rate schedule set by the government. The Cabildo never issued such a tariff.

forwarded them to the Cabildo shortly afterward. The council and Governor Unzaga confirmed the pharmaceutical code on January 12, 1770, when they licensed Peyroux.[29]

For the next fifteen years, Cabildo minutes did not mention pharmacy regulation until the examination of Carlos Lubier in 1785. At that time, the established pharmacists were participating in the examination of new applicants, along with all the city's medical doctors. A few years later, a strictly pharmaceutical board was created to license new pharmacists and regulate their standards. This method, however, appears not to have been effective because five unlicensed druggists plied their wares in New Orleans in 1798.[30]

One of the five lawbreakers, Felipe Serben, ran a store for his absent pharmacist brother Federico. The Cabildo ordered him to shut down the business until he was examined. Either then or at a later time, Felipe Serben became a pharmacist because he was working as one in New Orleans in 1817. The council scheduled examinations for the other four more than a month later. It appointed an examination board of two councillors, one druggist, one surgeon, and one physician. The Cabildo's ruling in this case returned the examining procedure to what it had been in 1785.[31]

In 1799 the pharmacists requested that physicians and surgeons be prohibited from supplying drugs to their patients. The council referred the matter to the *síndico procurador general*. After nearly two months, he ruled in favor of the pharmacists. Doctors would be permitted to sell drugs only on their house calls in the countryside or in emergencies. The pharmacists would be allowed to sell all nonpoisonous medical preparations without a doctor's prescription. The *síndico procurador general* also recommended that a committee, consisting of the Cabildo monthly commis-

29. Actas del Cabildo, I, 17, January 12, 1770.

30. *Ibid.,* IV, (2), 147–48, July 27, 1798; Duffy, ed., *Rudolph Matas History,* I, 189–91.

31. Actas del Cabildo, IV, (2), 147–48, July 27, 1798, IV, (2), 152, August 31, 1798. Bertram Wallace Korn, in *The Early Jews of New Orleans* (Waltham, Mass., 1969), 66, mentions a Philippe Zerban, who was undoubtedly the same Felipe Zerben. One member of that family had been working in the city from at least 1792. In April of that year, a pharmacist (*boticario*) named Mr. Zerbane was attacked and robbed in his store. He lost 5,200 pesos in money and two gold watches (Carondelet to Gayoso, New Orleans, April 10, 1792, AGI, PC, leg. 18).

sioner, the Cabildo *escribano,* a Royal Hospital physician, and a druggist selected by the monthly commissioner, inspect the pharmacies every four months.[32]

The restrictions on drug sales seem to have been enforced to some extent. Surgeon Juan Bautista Canrotte petitioned the Cabildo not to implement the measure. He stated that its enforcement would ruin him financially. The *síndico procurador general* advised the council to allow Canrotte to sell drugs that he did not manufacture. The Cabildo rejected the suggestion and referred the matter to Vidal for a legal recommendation. On his advice, the councillors granted the surgeon eight months to dispose of his stock and withdraw from the pharmaceutical business.[33]

By 1803, although the Cabildo still arranged examinations for pharmacists and administered oaths to those who passed them, the governor's office was again issuing the licenses. As in the case of the physicians and surgeons, O'Reilly's decree guided the licensing of pharmacists. There is no evidence, however, that the Cabildo regulated midwives. Surgeons delivered most babies and midwives would have come under their supervision.[34]

The Cabildo had a measure of control over three of New Orleans' four hospitals in the Spanish era: Charity Hospital, the lepers' hospital, and the smallpox hospital. It had no connection with the Royal Hospital, which was a military establishment.[35]

The oldest hospital in the city was Charity Hospital, which was founded by the French in 1736. Under the French system, distinguished

32. Actas del Cabildo, IV, (3), 78, September 27, 1799, IV, (3), 111–12, November 22, 1799; Duffy, ed., *Rudolph Matas History,* I, 190–91. Duffy believes that the 1799 regulations were never enforced but the prohibition on doctors selling drugs was.

33. Actas del Cabildo, IV, (3), 115–16, December 6, 1799, IV, (3), 117, December 13, 1799; Duffy, ed., *Rudolph Matas History,* 191–92. Duffy states that by 1799 the drug trade had become big business. Berquin-Duvallon claims that by the end of the Spanish era New Orleans surgeons were again selling drugs (Robertson, ed., *Louisiana Under the Rule,* I, 201–202).

34. Actas del Cabildo, IV, (5), 77, June 17, 1803, IV, (5), 80, July 15, 1803; Robertson, ed., *Louisiana Under the Rule,* I, 201–202.

35. Robertson, ed., *Louisiana Under the Rule,* I, 201–202; O'Connor, "Charity Hospital," 23. Little has been published on royal hospitals in Spanish America. In 1776 Minister of the Indies José de Gálvez issued a *reglamento* for the operation of royal hospitals, which included the New Orleans facility. For the regulations, see A. P. Nasatir, ed., "Royal Hospitals in Colonial Spanish America," *Annals of Medical History,* 3rd ser., IV (1942), 481–503.

members of the community and the parish vicar constituted a board of ten members. They met every three years to examine the hospital's accounts, revise policies, and appoint four directors, one of whom would have charge of the hospital. Several of the board members also served on the Superior Council.[36]

When the Spaniards assumed control of Louisiana, they modified control of Charity Hospital. The governor supervised the facility, although the vicar general remained the nominal head. To oversee its routine operations, the governor appointed an administrator, who after 1769 was sometimes the Cabildo *síndico procurador general*. The French *regidores* on the Cabildo, however, seethed with resentment at their exclusion from running the hospital, which they regarded as a city institution and which they claimed should not have been taken over by the Spanish government. In September, 1778, at a time when the councilmen believed Governor Gálvez to be favorable to them, they attempted to seize control of the establishment. They nominated a hospital administrator and treasurer who would report directly to them. They acted without first securing the approval of either Vicar General Cirilo de Barcelona or Governor Gálvez.[37]

The vicar general complained to the governor in a long letter, in which he stressed that Gálvez was being deprived of the authority to name the hospital's superintendent and treasurer. Gálvez thereupon immediately forbade the council from continuing with its plans and terminated any further discussion of the issue. The *regidores,* however, did not give up so easily. They waited three years before proceeding.

In the interim, the hospital suffered gravely from the hurricanes of 1779 and 1780 that reduced the structure to a kitchen and storehouse, with room for only six beds. Gálvez, meanwhile, left Louisiana in mid-1781 to continue prosecution of the war against Great Britain. In January, 1782, he named Esteban Miró as acting governor, a post he took over by March 1. On February 15, the councillors wrote directly to Gálvez, complaining that the hospital's administrator, López de Armesto, had not sent them the hospital accounts and was neglecting its care. Again presuming to be

36. Burson, *Stewardship*, 217–18; Porteous, ed. and trans., "Index," *LHQ*, IV (1923), 323–24; John Salvaggio, *New Orleans' Charity Hospital: A Story of Physicians, Politics, and Poverty* (Baton Rouge, 1992), 14.

37. O'Conner, "Charity Hospital," 18–19.

entitled to administer the facility, they argued that it had never been part of French royal administration and could not have been transferred to the Spanish king in 1763. Engaging in hyperbole, a characteristic of that age, they lamented that the indigent sick were dying unattended in the streets. Their letter neglected to mention the provisional hospital or their inaction in this "crisis." They also presumed that they were entitled to examine the administrator's accounts. Gálvez replied on August 18, 1782, that the governor and the vicar general alone had authority over the hospital. Moreover, he instructed Miró to take whatever measures were needed to repair and renovate the facility. If the Cabildo genuinely sought to alleviate suffering, it should present its plans to Miró.[38]

What the councillors really were objecting to was that Andrés Almonester y Roxas, a onetime government employee and scribe, had offered to rebuild the hospital. He had made money in New Orleans by acquiring property on both sides of the Plaza de Armas and building stores. In addition, his numerous other real estate transactions had given him a sizable fortune by New Orleans standards. In early 1782, with Miró's blessing, Almonester began to rebuild the hospital and that was when the councillors wrote to Gálvez. But despite being rebuffed by the absent governor, they tried again to regain what they regarded as their prerogative. Led by Alférez Real Francisco María de Reggio, in December of the same year, they objected to Miró about the clandestine manner in which "usages and customs" had been disregarded. They again stubbornly insisted that the hospital's administration was vested in them as agents for the public. They labeled Almonester's efforts to rebuild the hospital a "violation of their prerogatives."[39]

The Cabildo men now claimed that Almonester intended to employ the usable debris from the old hospital to construct the new building. They alleged that the new structure would interfere with a street they were planning to make. Miró waited nearly three months before replying. On March 20, 1783, he rebuked the council for its "attitude of injustice and ingratitude." He referred to the 1778 letters of Barcelona and Gálvez, and he rejected their mention of "usages and customs" inasmuch as the

38. *Ibid.,* 19–20.
39. *Ibid.,* 20–21.

hospital had been administered in the same way since the start of the Spanish era. He pointed out that the Cabildo's interest in the facility began only when Almonester started to rebuild the hospital. The acting governor emphasized that only his and the vicar's permission was needed for Almonester to do his work. He rejected as false their claim that the building interfered with a proposed street; no other structures were present in the vicinity and the street could be placed anywhere.[40]

Almonester rebuilt the hospital, completing it in October, 1786, at a cost of 114,000 pesos. It was a large "H"-shaped structure erected in the rear of the city. It served only whites. The fires of 1788 and 1794 spared it, but another blaze in 1809 consumed the facility.[41]

Almonester had not rested easy with the assurances of support from Gálvez and Miró. In May, 1784, on requesting royal permission to rebuild the hospital, he asked to serve as its patron and director. The king agreed and sent his royal order to Gálvez to forward. When he did so, Gálvez advised Miró to show the royal order widely to thwart any interference with Almonester's work. The new patron named the facility the Charity Hospital of St. Charles, in honor of the king. As patron and benefactor, Almonester submitted rules for its management, and the Council of the Indies approved them.[42]

Despite the passage of years and the death of Francisco María de Reggio, the Cabildo still hungered for jurisdiction over the hospital. In 1786, Almonester provided the facility with an income of fifteen hundred pesos yearly from rental property. By 1793, however, Síndico Procurador General Sarpy pointed out to the council that the rental income netted the hospital only 1,248 pesos, yet its expenses had grown to 1,830 pesos yearly. At Sarpy's request, the Cabildo asked Almonester to increase the hospital's endowment.[43]

40. *Ibid.,* 21–22.

41. Col. John Pope, *A Tour Through the Southern and Western Territories,* . . . (1792; rpr. New York, 1971), 39; Sibley, "Journal," 479; Wilson and Hubert, *The Cabildo,* 63; O'Connor, "Charity Hospital," 23.

42. Actas del Cabildo, III, (3), 93–94, October 18, 1793; O'Connor, "Charity Hospital," 22–23. See also Andrés Almonester y Roxas, *Constitution for the New Charity Hospital,* trans. Wiley D. Stephenson, Jr., Survey of Federal Archives in Louisiana (N.p., 1941).

43. Actas del Cabildo, III, (3), 93–94, October 18, 1793.

Almonester, a member of the Cabildo since 1790, having purchased the office of *alférez real* from the son of his old nemesis Reggio, knew the source of the criticism. He lashed out angrily in reply. He declared that sufficient funds existed, that Sarpy harbored malicious motives, and that, though not obligated to furnish additional funds, he would ensure that the hospital had ample financial support. Confronted with Almonester's vitriolic reply, the other councillors dropped the question of increasing the endowment.[44]

The anti-Almonester councillors, nevertheless, managed to procure Governor Carondelet's ear soon after he arrived in Louisiana. Without examining the origins of the conflict, Carondelet intervened and named Gilberto Leonard as administrator for the hospital even though it was Almonester's right. The dispossessed patron had to sue and petition the king before he regained control in 1795.[45]

After the clash with Almonester, the only Cabildo involvement with Charity Hospital came in the late 1790s. The hospital had traditionally enjoyed a monopoly in selling coffins, but the high prices charged for them created a hardship for the poor. Moved by a complaint from the *síndico procurador general,* the Cabildo terminated the hospital's monopoly and allowed the public to buy caskets from whomever they pleased.[46]

Contagious diseases periodically struck colonial New Orleans, and Charity Hospital did not treat them. As early as 1780, physicians suspected that an unknown illness in the region was leprosy. By 1785 the son of François Roquigny was diagnosed as having the disease. This solitary case resulted in a facility for quarantining lepers.[47]

Shortly after the completion of Charity Hospital, Almonester designed and built the San Lázaro (St. Lazarus) Hospital for lepers. It was a small structure with four rooms that separated patients by race and sex. Al-

44. *Ibid.,* IV, (3), 114–20, January 11, 1794. Almonester took his seat on the Cabildo on March 16, 1790; the crown confirmed his post on November 19, 1790. How much he paid for it is unknown, but the post was appraised at 1,200 pesos. See his *asiento* in AGI, PC, leg. 538B.

45. O'Connor, "Charity Hospital," 27.

46. Actas del Cabildo, IV, (2), 34, September 7, 1797.

47. *Ibid.,* III, (1), 66, November 18, 1785; Duffy, ed., *Rudolph Matas History,* I, 259–60; Burson, *Stewardship,* 198. For the care given to infectious diseases in eighteenth-century North American cities, see Bridenbaugh, *Cities in Revolt,* 326–30.

monester built it on his farm near the edge of the city and on the bank of a canal, with access to bathing for the patients. Contrary to popular belief that Almonester donated the building and its grounds to the city, the Cabildo paid him the appraised value of both. The city treasury then assumed the administration of the San Lázaro Hospital.[48]

On the orders of Viceroy Bernardo de Gálvez, the Cabildo funded the leper hospital with an endowment of twenty-one hundred pesos. After deducting slightly more than one hundred pesos for minor repairs, the nearly two thousand pesos remaining were lent at 5 percent interest. Usually, two loans of one thousand pesos each were made to persons of substance, who provided a mortgage bond on real estate. As long as the borrower paid the interest promptly, the loan could be extended indefinitely. Another 5 percent donation above that stipulated in the loan might have been informally required of borrowers. The hospital also collected minor donations in an alms box located at the gate of the hospital grounds. Food seems not to have been a major expense. In 1795 the *mayordomo de propios* spent an average of one real per day to feed patients. The total food cost for that year was 51 pesos, 1½ reales.[49]

After a flood damaged the leper hospital in 1797, the Cabildo decided to sell it. Only a year later, however, another person was diagnosed with leprosy. The Cabildo gave Dr. Estevan de Pellegrue, who treated the patient, a house in the city to isolate lepers. By the next year the number

48. Actas del Cabildo, III, (1), 42–43, April 22, 1785; Duffy, ed., *Rudolph Matas History*, I, 259–60; "Records of the City Council," No. 101, April 20, 1785; Morazán, "Letters," I, 191–92n.

In the 1760s, Governor Ulloa allegedly isolated a number of lepers in Balize. His action created discontent among the French population, and the practice was discontinued (Gayarré, *History of Louisiana*, III, 167). Gayarré also states that the location of the 1785 facility was behind the city on a ridge of land that became known as Lepers' Land. Eventually, the patients declined in number, the hospital fell into decay, and vegetation took over. It became part of the suburb of Treme in the nineteenth century (Gayarré, *History of Louisiana*, III, 168).

49. Actas del Cabildo, III, (1), 123, December 22, 1786, IV, (1), 169, December 2, 1796, IV, (2), 24–25, August 23, 1797, IV, (2), 33, September 7, 1797, IV, (2), 160, October 13, 1798, IV, (4), 79, March 20, 1801, IV, (5), 37, January 14, 1803; "Miscellaneous Documents," II (unnumbered), 43–44, January 27, 1798; Duffy, ed., *Rudolph Matas History*, I, 261–62; Morazán, "Letters," I, 192n; "Relación de Miguel Álvarez," January 1 to December 31, 1795, New Orleans Municipal Records, Records of the Cabildo.

of patients had risen to five. An army corporal cared for them and kept them secluded.[50]

In 1800 Dr. Giovellina, who treated the leprosy patients, requested that the Cabildo repair and enlarge the San Lázaro Hospital. He believed that public donations would pay for the renovations. He further confided that the city's doctors would contribute their services and pay for a black couple to nurse the afflicted. It is unknown whether the Cabildo repaired the facility. By 1803 the San Lázaro Hospital held at least twenty patients.[51]

The hospital continued briefly in the American era. In 1804 an examination of the five residents showed that they were free of leprosy. Instead, they were thought to be suffering from African yaws. Possibly a legitimate case of leprosy in Louisiana never occurred during the Spanish regime.[52]

Of the contagious diseases and fevers that afflicted New Orleans, none was more easily recognized nor more dreaded than smallpox. In the several occasions during the Spanish period when smallpox struck, the Cabildo attempted to work in concert with the governors and the doctors to minimize the effects of the contagion. The smallpox epidemics of 1779 and 1802 were the worst of the era, and they best demonstrate the range and scope of the Cabildo's activities to safeguard public health.[53]

In late 1777 smallpox was in the province among the Indians. It struck the Europeans first at Natchitoches in 1778 and then spread quickly to New Orleans. The Cabildo sent Dr. Jean Rouelles to Natchitoches in the hope of keeping the disease from spreading, but he failed. At that time, isolation was the only weapon known in the Spanish colonies for combating smallpox. In New Orleans, Governor Gálvez responded by isolating smallpox patients on the opposite side of the river. He convened an open cabildo to discuss what steps to take in this emergency. The persons at-

50. "Miscellaneous Documents," II, No. 203, 9–10, December 3, 1797, II, No. 247, 44–45 (undated); Actas del Cabildo, IV, (2), 87–88, December 22, 1797; Duffy, ed., *Rudolph Matas History*, I, 261–63.

51. Morazán, "Letters," I, 191–93n; Alliot, "Historical and Political Reflections," 97.

52. Duffy, ed., *Rudolph Matas History*, I, 259, 263; Morazán, "Letters," I, 192n.

53. The example of the smallpox epidemic in Galveztown, a new settlement formed largely of Canary Island immigrants who had recently arrived, best conveys the deadliness of the disease. See Din, *Canary Islanders*, 33–35. For a general study of smallpox in the past, see Donald R. Hopkins, *Princes and Peasants: Smallpox in History* (Chicago, 1983).

tending the meeting agreed to isolate all individuals showing symptoms of the disease for fifteen days. Those afflicted would remain secluded until they were free from the disease. The city residents in attendance at the *cabildo abierto* pledged to report smallpox cases to ensure isolation, and they thanked the governor and the Cabildo for their prompt action to arrest the contagion.[54]

The facility built to house the smallpox patients on the opposite side of the Mississippi from New Orleans did not merit the name *hospital*. It resembled an isolation and detention center because patients received no treatment and it had no regular staff. The Cabildo refused to erect the structure Gálvez wanted and instead used a small rented house as circumstances warranted.[55]

Nearly a decade later, smallpox surfaced in the New Orleans area again. Governor Miró confronted Cabildo opposition when he sought to provide housing to isolate the victims. The council judged the houses Miró proposed to buy too expensive and threatened an appeal to the king if he persisted. The governor relented, and the Cabildo authorized Santiago Copperthway (James Copperthwaite) to build a small cottage across the river for the smallpox victims. The council's solution cost a modest fifty pesos, a tiny sum when contrasted with Miró's plan to purchase costly houses.[56]

---

54. Actas del Cabildo, I, 264–65, February 8, 1779; Duffy, ed., *Rudolph Matas History,* I, 199; De Mézières to Unzaga, Natchitoches, November 7, 1777, AGI, PC, leg. 112; see also Peter H. Wood, "The Changing Population of the Colonial South: An Overview by Race and Region, 1685–1790," in *Powhatan's Mantle: Indians in the Colonial Southeast,* ed. Peter H. Wood, Gregory A. Waselkov, and M. Thomas Hatley (Lincoln, Nebr., 1989), 83. Mexico also experienced a smallpox epidemic in 1779, which killed nine thousand persons in Mexico City alone. Inoculation or variolation (giving persons smallpox, which was usually a mild case) was then introduced. See Donald Cooper, *Epidemic Disease in Mexico City, 1761–1813* (Austin, 1965); Alexander De Humboldt, *Political Essay on the Kingdom of New Spain,* trans. John Black (2 vols.; 1811; rpr. New York, 1966), I, 11; and Angela T. Thompson, "To Save the Children: Smallpox Inoculation, Vaccination, and Public Health in Guanajuato, Mexico, 1797–1840," *Americas,* XLIX (1992–93), 432.

55. Morazán, "Letters," I, 36n.

56. Actas del Cabildo, III, (1), 150–51, June 8, 1787, III, (1), 163, October 5, 1787; Duffy, ed., *Rudolph Matas History,* I, 202; Burson, *Stewardship,* 119. In December, 1784, and January, 1785, Galveztown experienced another outbreak of smallpox when eighteen persons died in two months. Prompt action by Governor Miró in sending Dr. Dow with medications prevented

When not used for medical purposes, the Cabildo rented the smallpox "hospital" to private individuals. The rent helped to defray maintenance costs. In February, 1792, the council evicted its tenant Carlos Douney when it needed the cottage to quarantine forty-three slaves, who arrived from Havana on the ship *Rosalie*. The councillors compensated Douney with fifty pesos and permitted him to harvest his crops from the surrounding farmland.[57]

The Cabildo also issued an ordinance requiring the monthly commissioners to inspect all incoming slave ships for disease. The inspection board later included a surgeon, and in 1799 acting civil governor Vidal issued a decree giving it more formal status. Nevertheless, it seems to have functioned only during crises. In 1802, when another epidemic struck New Orleans, Governor Salcedo created a permanent board of health.[58]

Despite efforts at maintenance, the smallpox hospital became dilapidated when it was not in use. In 1797 Andrés López de Armesto, the facility's administrator, spent one hundred pesos of his own money on repairs. The Cabildo repaid him from the city treasury and stipulated that the hospital would reimburse the city when funds became available.[59]

The 1802 smallpox epidemic was the most serious of the medical emergencies during the Spanish regime. The outbreak produced a clash between the Cabildo and Governor Salcedo over the proper course of action. At a meeting on February 12, the Cabildo resolved to use isolation until the number of smallpox cases climbed to twelve, when the councillors would regard the disease to be of epidemic proportions, requiring inoculation. They forwarded a copy of their resolution to the governor. He did not respond immediately and, when he did, ordered that isolation be continued.[60]

---

the disease from claiming more lives and from spreading. The 1787 smallpox scare was present throughout lower Louisiana (Din, *Canary Islanders,* 38, 76).

57. Actas del Cabildo, III, (2), 177, February 3, 1792, III, (2), 184–85, March 3, 1792, III, (3), 52, February 8, 1793.

58. Morazán, "Letters," I, 37n; II, 87–88. Salcedo's initiative was as close as Spanish Louisiana came to establishing a board of health, which would act when confronted with a medical crisis. Many large cities, however, had done little to prepare for medical emergencies.

59. Actas del Cabildo, IV, (1), 225–26, June 23, 1797, IV, (2), 16, August 4, 1797.

60. *Ibid.,* IV, (4), 170, February 12, 1802, IV, (4), 171–73, February 19, 1802.

The governor's disagreement with the Cabildo involved variolation, or the direct inoculation of a person with the microorganisms from the pus of a smallpox victim. This method of immunization had been used for more than a century and could drastically reduce the disease's mortality rate. A liability to this procedure in disease prevention, however, was that the inoculated person became a carrier during the time he or she had what was usually a mild case of smallpox. But smallpox contracted from such a carrier was as virulent as that contracted from anyone who had become afflicted naturally. Failure to understand this or isolate the carriers could systematically spread the disease. For this reason several Anglo-American colonies had outlawed variolation in the eighteenth century.[61]

In 1779 isolation was the main weapon used to battle smallpox. In 1787 Miró permitted variolation, which was the first time that it was used in Louisiana. But not all persons accepted it. Nevertheless, deaths from smallpox were far fewer in 1787 than in 1779.[62]

In 1802 Governor Salcedo was probably not aware of the problem of contagion in the use of variolation. He claimed that he wanted to avoid placing the financial burden of a general inoculation on the poor. His real motives in opposing inoculation perhaps stemmed from religious scruples and pressure from the New Orleans clergy who opposed inoculation.[63]

The Cabildo delayed in responding to Salcedo's countermanding its decree. Spanish Louisiana had only recently learned about Dr. Edward Jenner's new treatment against smallpox, vaccination or inoculation with cowpox. His report was published in England in 1798 and translated into

61. See John Duffy, *Epidemics in Colonial America* (Baton Rouge, 1953), particularly p. 38, which discusses the background and relative effectiveness of the variolation treatment to prevent smallpox and the infectiousness of the carrier.

62. Morazán, "Letters," II, 82n. Inoculation is described by Thompson ("To Save the Children," 436): "It consisted of taking matter from a pustule of a person infected with smallpox and placing it into a skin puncture on a healthy person, usually on the arm or on the hand between two fingers. The recipient usually developed a mild form of smallpox, allowing the development of antibodies that gave lifelong immunity to the disease. Quite dangerous by today's standards, inoculation caused death in 1 to 3 per cent of cases, while contracting smallpox naturally resulted in around 25 per cent mortality. Nevertheless, an inoculated person could infect others, so the entire population at risk had to be inoculated simultaneously; otherwise, inoculated patients had to be strictly isolated. Only with organization and aggressive leadership was this possible."

63. Morazán, "Letters," I, li–liii; II, 83–84.

several languages by 1801. But no one in New Orleans knew the procedure. The Cabildo heard a rumor that the cowpox vaccine was in Natchez, but it proved to be false. The councillors then permitted Santiago Livaudais to try to derive a serum from his cattle that were infected with cowpox. This, too, failed when most of the eight slaves, on whom the vaccine was tested, came down with a severe pox, which was thought to be smallpox.[64]

During the incubation period of the test vaccine, the Cabildo neutralized Salcedo's financial argument against a general inoculation. The council established a schedule of compensation for the doctors treating the disease. It limited fees to two reales per person and four reales per household and exempted the poor from payment. Charity Hospital would treat any persons who presented themselves, and the city treasury would pay the cost of treatment beyond what the hospital could absorb. The councillors also agreed that inoculation would be compulsory once it began. If a head of household refused inoculation, he would have to relocate his family at least three leagues into the countryside.[65]

In the meantime, Salcedo decided to reestablish the defunct board of health for the inspection of incoming ships. He planned to appoint two Cabildo *regidores,* a surgeon, the customs inspector, an interpreter, and the Cabildo *escribano* to the board. To cover expenses, he imposed an inspection fee of four pesos on each vessel arriving at the city. He asked the council to submit the names of two of its members, a surgeon, and an interpreter, and he would issue their certificates of appointment. The Cabildo sug-

64. Actas del Cabildo, IV, (4), 171–73, February 19, 1802, IV, (4), 182–83, March 5, 1802, IV, (4), 191–92, March 22, 1802; Thompson, "To Save the Children," 442–43. In St. Louis in upper Louisiana, smallpox broke out in April, 1801. Dr. Antoine Saugrain took immediate action and used *inoculación* to prevent the disease from spreading. The only fatality Commandant Carlos Dehault Delassus reported was an old man, who refused any medication other than *tafia* (Dehault Delassus to Casa-Calvo, No. 102, St. Louis, August 3, 1801, AGI, PC, leg. 72. See also Samuel E. Dicks, "Antoine Saugrain [1763–1820]: A French Scientist on the American Frontier," *Emporia State Research Studies,* XXV [1976], 5–26).

It was not until 1802 that the Spanish physician Francisco Savier de Balmis introduced the cowpox vaccine into Mexico and other parts of the Spanish Empire. See Michael Smith, *The "Real Expedición Marítima de la Vacuna" in New Spain and Guatemala* (Philadelphia, 1974); and José G. Rigau-Pérez, "The Introduction of Smallpox Vaccine in 1803 and the Adoption of Immunization as a Government Function in Puerto Rico," *Hispanic American Historical Review,* LXIX (1989), 393–425.

65. Actas del Cabildo, IV, (4), 183–85, March 8, 1802.

gested instead that one councillor be permanently appointed, who would be assisted by one of the two monthly commissioners. The council also agreed to rotate inspection duty among the city's surgeons.[66]

Before March 5, the doctors could inoculate slave children who either had smallpox or had been exposed to it. When Dr. Giovellina failed to inoculate four slave children who had been playing near the cradle of a smallpox victim, the Cabildo reacted hysterically. The councillors induced Salcedo to arrest Giovellina for spreading the disease. The real motive seems to have been to remove Almonester's appointee.[67]

As the incubation period neared its end, a number of prominent residents petitioned to start the inoculations. On March 22, the Cabildo called an emergency session and invited all the city's physicians and surgeons to attend. At the meeting, the doctors reported that more than thirty persons had been stricken with smallpox and that immediate inoculation was necessary to stop the spread of the disease. The council also learned about the failure to produce cowpox serum. In response, it decreed a general variola inoculation for the city, conformable to the rates agreed upon earlier. Salcedo offered no opposition and signed the minutes of the meeting.[68]

It is difficult to determine the damage caused by Salcedo's delay of inoculation or its efficacy once it began. The more than thirty cases announced at the meeting probably refer only to the city's white inhabitants. Estimates of the number of persons who died in the 1802 epidemic vary between six and twelve hundred. By the following summer, the disease had run its course.[69] What is significant about the smallpox epidemic of 1802 was the Cabildo's attempt to provide the community with the best available protection and in an equitable manner.

New Orleans also suffered from epidemic diseases other than smallpox during the Spanish period. The city's residents, including doctors and government officials, usually did not understand the nature or the causes of such diseases. For example, yellow fever raged in New Orleans periodically, but it was not positively identified until 1796. That year it took

66. *Ibid.,* IV, (4), 175–76, February 26, 1802; Morazán, "Letters," II, 83.
67. Actas del Cabildo, IV, (4), 180, March 5, 1802.
68. *Ibid.,* IV, (4), 190–92, March 22, 1802; Morazán, "Letters," II, 82n, 95.
69. Morazán, "Letters," II, 82; Robertson, ed., *Louisiana Under the Rule,* I, 205; Alliot, "Historical and Political Reflections," 63; Duffy, ed., *Rudolph Matas History,* I, 216.

more than two hundred lives, not counting blacks, Protestants, and rural victims.[70]

Despite inaccurate and confused scientific knowledge about diseases, New Orleanians knew that illnesses increased in proportion to certain conditions. These conditions included hot weather, standing water, and decaying matter in the city streets. The Cabildo could do nothing about the heat, but it tried to eliminate or reduce the refuse and standing water.

The council's efforts to free the city streets of garbage and litter had only limited success. New Orleans' continuing growth and inconsistency in enforcing municipal regulations were two important reasons. Nevertheless, the Cabildo's attempt to provide a clean environment achieved more success than the descriptions left by early nineteenth-century visitors to the city suggest.[71]

The council's attention was first called to the filth in the streets in the spring of 1779. The *síndico procurador general* presented a memorandum reporting conditions that included hogs roaming freely through the streets and rooting through debris for food. The councillors decided that the existing laws were being violated and formally resolved to enforce them.[72]

Trying to force the residents to keep the city clean achieved only partial success, and six years later, the problem again became serious. To improve hygienic conditions, the Cabildo organized a street-cleaning brigade consisting of six convicts directed by an army sergeant. The Cabildo assigned the sergeant a salary of twelve pesos per month to supervise the cleanup.[73]

As the city grew in the 1790s, this system, too, became inadequate. In the summer of 1798, at Governor Gayoso's suggestion, the Cabildo initiated regular garbage collection. Toward this end, it purchased a mule and a wagon. The councillors also agreed to hire a black to clean the streets.

70. Morazán, "Letters," I, 22n. Governor Carondelet's brother was among those who died of yellow fever in New Orleans (Carrigan, "Commentary," 413). For an eye-witness account of yellow fever in New Orleans in 1796, see Holmes, "New Orleans Yellow Fever Epidemic," 205–215; and Carrigan, "Pestilence of 1796," 27–36.

71. Duffy, ed., *Rudolph Matas History,* I, 222, 227–29; Pintard, "New Orleans, 1801," 224. In the eighteenth century, dirty cities were generally the rule, not the exception, although some North American cities adopted measures before 1800 to improve conditions (Bridenbaugh, *Cities in Revolt,* 239–41).

72. Actas del Cabildo, I, 272, March 12, 1779.

73. *Ibid.,* III, (1), 43, April 29, 1785.

Sergeant Francisco Pérez, who supervised the convicts, had authority over the garbage collector. The council auctioned a one-year contract for the post of garbage collector and accepted an offer at twenty-five pesos a month.[74]

The next year Gayoso tried to increase garbage collection during the summer. He planned to supplement the regular collection with three additional wagons. Although two Cabildo councillors believed one more wagon was sufficient, the majority approved the governor's plan. Pablo Díaz' bid of twenty-five pesos per month won the contract, but it never began.[75]

On January 24, 1800, Síndico Procurador General Pedro Dulcido Barran appealed to the council to act to improve sanitary conditions in and around the city. He complained about low-lying streets and lots that permitted water and filth to accumulate. They needed to be filled in. He and others believed that the sun's rays helped in decomposition, but decomposition emitted noxious gasses injurious to public health. He recommended throwing refuse farther out in the river, not from the batture, which allowed debris to wash back on shore. Refuse was not to be dumped outside the St. John Gate. Barran urged that greater care be taken in burying the dead, particularly non-Catholics. He suggested that sick persons coming to New Orleans be detained in a hospital outside the city to determine if they had contagious diseases.[76]

Several weeks later, the Cabildo acted to enforce a citywide general cleanup under the supervision of the ward commissioners. The city resolution provided for the cleaning, filling, and grading of yards; the dumping of garbage farther away from the city; the burial of dead animals; and the planting of willow trees to shade the cemeteries and the garbage dump. It further provided for the inspection of all ships downriver at Fort San Felipe de Placaminas. That summer the city council began employing a

74. *Ibid.,* IV, (2), 125, May 11, 1798, IV, (2), 140–41, July 6, 1798, IV, (2), 142–43, July 13, 1798, IV, (3), 130, January 24, 1800; Holmes, *Gayoso,* 207.

75. Actas del Cabildo, IV, (3), 21–22, March 29, 1799, IV, (3), 28, April 19, 1799, IV, (3), 197, July 11, 1800.

76. Morazán, "Letters," I, 22–38 and notes; Laura L. Porteous, trans., "Sanitary Conditions in New Orleans Under the Spanish Regime, 1799–1800," *LHQ,* XV (1932), 610–17.

second wagon and garbage collector to aid in keeping the streets clean.[77] Barran's petition seems to have resulted in positive measures in all areas.

In the summer of 1801, Juan Lugar's contract for collecting garbage expired and he returned the horse and equipment to the Cabildo. A month elapsed before the council arranged a new contract with Andrés Lavigne. He furnished his own wagon for year-round collection at twenty-four pesos per month and a second wagon during the six warmest months at twenty-six pesos per month. Although Lavigne's contract expired the following summer, he continued to collect the city's refuse.[78]

The Cabildo's efforts to tidy up New Orleans extended beyond street cleaning. The city installed an enclosed public privy on the waterfront. In 1790 spring floods caused the public toilets to overflow. Although the records are silent about how the problem was solved, complaints ended. That same spring other city toilets also overflowed, putrefying the streets. The council passed a regulation that required outhouses, which were usually built behind the city's residences, to be located at a specified distance from property lines. It was the only Cabildo regulation on outhouses.[79]

The city earnestly attempted to provide some means of sewage disposal in the late Spanish era. In 1798 two commissioners supervised the construction of four ditches to carry filth to the rear of the city. Workers built three of the sewers successfully, but they graded the fourth ditch improperly and it carried slime into the city. The councillors agreed to flood the ditch and use it as a canal for a small skiff to carry waste to dump behind the city. The Cabildo appropriated money for the skiff and a lock and chain to secure it when not in use.[80]

77. Actas del Cabildo, IV, (3), 151–54, March 14, 1800, IV, (3), 196–98, July 11, 1800; Duffy, ed., *Rudolph Matas History,* I, 212, 227–29; Morazán, "Letters," I, 22–38.

78. Actas del Cabildo, IV, (4), 108, July 10, 1801, IV, (4), 117, July 24, 1801, IV, (4), 124, August 7, 1801, IV, (5), 16, September 10, 1802, IV, (5), 18, September 17, 1802; Morazán, "Letters," I, 29–30n, 140. Pintard, who wrote unfavorably about New Orleans' streets in 1801, might have arrived there when street cleaning had been temporarily suspended (Pintard, "New Orleans, 1801," 224).

79. Actas del Cabildo, III, (2), 108–109, August 6, 1790; "Digest," 149. The Cabildo also set aside land for a public bath for New Orleans, but there is no evidence that it was built (Actas del Cabildo, IV, (1), 197, January 27, 1797).

80. Actas del Cabildo, IV, (2), 152–53, August 31, 1798, IV, (2), 155, September 14, 1798, IV, (2), 159–60, October 13, 1798, IV, (3), 26–27, April 19, 1799.

The Cabildo was also concerned that burials in the city's cemetery not become a sanitation problem. An unidentified visitor in New Orleans in 1799 described the difficulty in burying the dead: "In digging the graves for the dead, before they are dug sufficiently deep, they are filled with water, and the coffins are generally held just below the surface until a quantity of sand and gravel is thrown in to sink them to the bottom."[81] Because the coffins were not buried very deep, floodwaters often disinterred the dead.

The Cabildo's efforts to improve burials in the cemeteries led to disputes with the church over jurisdiction. The Cabildo twice succeeded in moving the cemetery farther away from the heart of New Orleans. In both instances, the old facility had proved unsuitable because of the difficulty of burying the dead and putrefying corpses. The governors furnished prisoners to move the remains, and the Cabildo paid to fence in each new cemetery. In 1800 the Cabildo provided a cemetery for non-Catholics, who had previously been buried randomly in the countryside. There were even instances of Protestants being left unburied.[82]

Besides these sanitation concerns, the Cabildo made numerous efforts to rid New Orleans of standing water by maintaining levees, grading streets, and providing drainage canals (these problems are discussed in Chapter Ten). Although the city did not resolve the drainage difficulty because of the abundant rainfall, floods, low elevation, and limited technology of that age, it made significant progress.

Overall, the Cabildo achieved only qualified success in trying to create a healthy environment for New Orleanians. Several travel accounts from the last years of Spanish rule comment unfavorably on the city's filthy and

81. "Notes of a Voyage from Pittsburgh to New Orleans, Thence by Sea to Philadelphia, in the Year 1799, Made by a Gentleman of Accurate Observation, a Passenger in a New Orleans Boat," in *Early Western Travels, 1748–1846*, ed. Reuben Gold Thwaites (32 vols.; Cleveland, 1904–1907), IV, 367.

82. Actas del Cabildo, III, (1), 8–9, August 27, 1784, III, (2), 36, October 17, 1788, III, (2), 63, June 5, 1789, IV, (1), 143, July 15, 1796, IV, (1), 156, September 16, 1796, IV, (2), 53–54, September 30, 1797, IV, (3), 153, March 14, 1800, IV, (4), 93–94, May 29, 1801, IV, (4), 99, June 12, 1801, IV, (4), 156–57, January 29, 1802, IV, (4), 167, February 12, 1802. Obstructionist tactics complicated the second cemetery move, as did flooding at the new site. An Englishman named Howard provided a plot of land for a Protestant cemetery outside the city before 1791 (Pope, *Tour*, 40–41).

unhealthy streets, but Dr. John Sibley, writing in 1802, said nothing about this topic. Although he was there during the sickly summer season, the inhabitants appeared healthy to him. He and fellow physician William Flood both thought that New Orleans was a healthier place to live in than Charleston, South Carolina.[83]

If New Orleans was as dirty and unhealthy as Berquin-Duvallon claimed, it was not because of Spanish rule or the Cabildo's ineffectiveness. Little in the way of sanitation had been attempted by the French before 1769, and the conditions existing at the close of the Spanish regime continued into the American period. As late as 1822, New Orleanians persisted in casting their refuse into the streets. Black convicts continued to carry out the city's limited cleanup, a practice first employed by the Spaniards.[84]

83. Sibley, "Journal," 478, 483. Eighteenth-century North American cities were not appreciably cleaner than New Orleans. For example, filth and dirt thrown on Philadelphia's streets in the eighteenth century raised their level two to three feet (Bridenbraugh, *Cities in Revolt,* 31).

84. Morazán, "Letters," I, 30n; Asbury, *French Quarter,* 78.

TEN
Public Works

P UBLIC works programs in New Orleans and adjacent areas played an important role in the development of the city and the colony. Although Spanish law did not assign it public work re sponsibilities, the New Orleans Cabildo became involved in the construction and care of levees, roads, bridges, and street gutters despite O'Reilly's 1770 land decree that forbade the Cabildo to conduct these projects at city expense. The decree charged most of these obligations to the inhabitants whose lands fronted on them. Similarly, the Code O'Reilly prohibited the Cabildo from using municipal monies to maintain the city's gutter system. The code limited the council's responsibility to keeping up only those facilities that fronted on municipal-owned or public lands. In the case of private lands, the Cabildo possessed the right—but not always the means—to force owners to keep the facilities in good repair. The city government, however, did not abide by these mandates, and it furnishes another example of the divergence between theory and practice in the administration of Spanish Louisiana. With the possible exception of maintaining the lighting department, public works constituted the largest expenditure of city funds during the Spanish period.[1]

1. O'Reilly's land decree can be found in *American State Papers, Miscellaneous Documents (1789–1823)* (2 vols.; Washington, D.C., 1834), I, 377; Code O'Reilly, 226; Actas del Cabildo, III, (2), 186–87, March 9, 1792.

Protecting the city from floodwaters was the Cabildo's most important effort in public works. The Mississippi, vital in commerce and communications, was also New Orleans' chief natural adversary. "Old Muddy" had formed much of the levee naturally by depositing sediment along its banks. The natural levee, however, contained low spots and vulnerable points that broke when tested by floodwaters. Moreover, burrowing crawfish that infest the rivers of lower Louisiana frequently weakened the embankments that collapsed under the pressure of high waters. The natural levees required man-made assistance to prevent the river from surging over them during the spring runoffs. The French began the monumental task of trying to contain the Mississippi in 1727, and the work has continued to the present. In the Spanish period, the river's levees were earthen barriers rising approximately fifteen feet above the level of the surrounding ground and about thirty feet wide at the base. At the end of the eighteenth century, when plantations had become numerous, the levees stretched from 30 miles below New Orleans to Pointe Coupee, a distance of more than 150 miles.[2]

The Cabildo's maintenance of the levee began gradually. In March, 1770, the council forbade the driving of carts on the levee fronting the city, including those that unloaded cargo from ships. The Cabildo declared that the carts hauling goods weakened the levee and that other cart owners abused the privilege. In 1772 it spent 503 pesos, 3 reales, in public funds to dump 4,837 cartloads of dirt to reinforce the levee facing the city. It was the first municipal intervention to conserve the levee, and it exempted property owners whose lots fronted on the river, to whom O'Reilly had bestowed responsibility.[3]

2. Pope, *Tour,* 37; Sibley, "Journal," 480; Morazán, "Letters," II, 4n, 7n; Gayarré, *History of Louisiana,* I, 381. In 1732 French governor Etienne Périer ordered landowners in the vicinity of New Orleans to build a six-foot-wide and two-foot-high levee that would also serve as a foot and bridle path (Davis, *Louisiana,* 85). New Orleans had started to build a levee in the 1720s but had little success because it was inadequate in size (Giraud, *History of French Louisiana,* Vol. V, *The Company of the Indies, 1723–1731,* trans. Brian Pierce [Baton Rouge, 1991], 206–10).

3. Actas del Cabildo, I, 68–69, March 1, 1770, I, 79, May 15, 1772. The strip of land between the first row of houses and the levee was of uncertain ownership. In the late Spanish period, both the Royal Treasury and the Cabildo claimed it. It is unclear whether the owner of this strip of land or the owners of the first row of houses should have been responsible for

Spring floods in 1774 made the Cabildo aware of New Orleans' vulnerability. Although uncertain of its authority, it decided to strengthen the embankment facing the city. Andrés Jung of Bayou St. John won the construction contract at auction. The Cabildo paid him in installments as he completed segments of the work. Jung finished the project in the spring of 1776, at a cost of two thousand pesos.[4]

The Cabildo did not confine its interest to the levee adjacent to the city. In 1781 it appointed two councilmen to check for weak spots and cave-ins on the levees and roads above and below the city on both banks. When crevasses in the levee occurred, floodwaters poured onto more than one plantation and sometimes reached the city. They could inflict extensive damage to crops and city property. Preventing ruptures in the levees was a legitimate community concern.[5]

The city, however, was limited in its authority to compel landowners to repair the levee where frequent flooding occurred. The Juan Bautista Macarty and Leonardo Massange lands in the Tchoupitoulas district four leagues above New Orleans illustrate the Cabildo's impotence. The owners abandoned their lands to the public domain when they exhausted their financial ability to repair the levees. The neighboring planters then tried to improve the Macarty-Massange levees to stop the floodwaters from reaching their own lands, but the costs proved prohibitive. Years passed with little being done. In addition to the flood damage, the community

---

the upkeep of the levee fronting the city. Because a breach would flood the whole city, the Cabildo felt justified in using city funds to maintain the levee.

4. *Ibid.*, I, 165–66, August 6, 1774, I, 173, November 11, 1774, I, 179–80, March 3, 1775, I, 192, October 7, 1775, I, 198, December 1, 1775; I, 205, March 15, 1776; New Orleans Municipal Records, Records of the Cabildo, "Estado de los viajes hechos a la calzada or Levee, 1774." Andrés Jung (Juen) was a contractor and merchant in New Orleans. He was the chief contractor for settling Canary Island families in Barataria in 1779. Born in Bordeaux, France, he was in New Orleans by 1750. When he died on September 4, 1784, Jung left a sizable amount of property, including a plantation on Bayou St. John, a New Orleans residence, forty slaves, several thousand pesos in coin, and other personal items. He had no legitimate children from his late-in-life marriage, but he provided for his three mulatto offspring in his will (Edna B. Freiberg, *Bayou St. John in Colonial Louisiana, 1699–1803* [New Orleans, 1980], 116, 166–67, 271–74; Din, *Canary Islanders*, 47, 51).

5. Actas del Cabildo, II, 76, October 12, 1781, III, (1), 65, October 7, 1785.

realized that standing water caused by flooding contributed to illnesses and deaths. After the 1789 spring floods again inundated much of the Tchoupitoulas district, Governor Miró asked the Cabildo to become involved.[6]

The councillors appropriated 3,480 pesos for the "permanent repair" of the levee. The Cabildo imposed a "contribution" on all the inhabitants to reimburse the city treasury, which was still depleted because of expenses stemming from the 1788 fire. To protect themselves from a royal rebuke for contravening the laws, the councillors sent the Council of the Indies a detailed explanation of the circumstances that led to their decision. Both the repair of the levee outside the city with Cabildo funds and the direct tax on the inhabitants violated Spanish law, the Code O'Reilly, and custom.[7]

The Cabildo also tried to find new owners to maintain the levees of abandoned lands. Twice the council attempted to sell the Macarty-Massange lands at public auction. A clause in the auction contract, stating that the new owners could sell the lands only if the levee was in good repair, might have inhibited potential buyers. The Cabildo next tried to give the lands to persons willing to maintain the levees. When that failed, the councillors deemed it prudent to inform the Council of the Indies about their efforts.[8]

Shortly afterward, the spring floods of 1790 destroyed the newly built levees on the abandoned Macarty-Massange lands. To stop the floodwaters, the Cabildo first commandeered slaves in the vicinity and then employed free blacks and convicts. The workers received three reales per day plus meals. The council appointed Regidores de la Barre and Ducros to supervise the repair of the levee, which was finished in late summer.[9]

---

6. "Miscellaneous Documents," I, No. 129, 70 (undated), I, No. 135, 71, January 22, 1790; Actas del Cabildo, III, (2), 89, February 19, 1791, III, (2), 123, January 14, 1791; Burson, *Stewardship,* 267. The Cabildo furnished 666½ pesos of food and supplies to the workers repairing the levee at Tchoupitoulas.

7. Actas del Cabildo, III, (2), 86, January 22, 1790, III, (2), 89, February 19, 1790; "Miscellaneous Documents," I, No. 135, 71, January 22, 1790.

8. Actas del Cabildo, III, (2), 89, February 19, 1790, III, (2), 91–92, March 5, 1790.

9. *Ibid.,* III, (2), 96–97, April 9, 1790, III, (2), 99, May 7, 1790; "Miscellaneous Documents," I (unnumbered), 58, 61, 65, June 8, 1790, I, No. 175, 103 (undated), I, No. 1, 88

The work cost 7,481 pesos, 1½ reales, which the city did not have. Governor Miró lent the Cabildo the funds from a special account erected to assist victims of the 1788 fire. Royal approval for the loan came the next year, at which time the Cabildo repaid four thousand pesos.[10]

Again in 1792, floodwaters burst the levee abutting the abandoned lands. In August the Cabildo ordered new cartloads of dirt sent to the breach and petitioned the governor for help. Carondelet appointed Regidor Ducros to supervise repairs here and elsewhere on the levees, an appointment that might have exceeded the Cabildo's authority. At this time, the governor was trying to make landowners along the Mississippi mend the levees because repairs were needed at many different places. The hurricane of August 18, 1793, caused further damage to the levees. Carondelet's formal recognition of rural syndics and their use throughout lower Louisiana was another effort to get landowners to comply with the terms under which they had received their lands.[11]

In 1791, when Miró secured the royal loan for Cabildo repairs to the levees on the abandoned lands, he endorsed an eight-thousand-peso loan to Lorenzo Sigur to improve the same levee if he accepted title to the property. Actually, Miró as intendant loaned Royal Treasury funds to the money-short Cabildo. Sigur in turn technically borrowed the money interest-free from the Cabildo for six years. A year later, the Cabildo advanced Sigur a short-term loan of 3,252½ pesos for more repairs to his levees.[12]

(undated), I, No. 166, 96, July 12, 1790, I, No. 175, 102, June 20, 1790.

Miró asked the slave owners of Tchoupitoulas to send their slaves with five or six days of rations to work on the crevasse and for a white to direct them ([Miró] to the inhabitants of Bayou Tchoupitoulas, New Orleans, April 27, 1790, AGI, PC, leg. 204).

10. "Miscellaneous Documents," I, No. 166, 97, July 12, 1790; Actas del Cabildo, III, (2), 149, November 18, 1791.

11. Actas del Cabildo, III, (3), 18, August 31, 1792, III, (3), 45, January 11, 1793, III, (3), 73, June 28, 1793, III, (3), 85–86, September 6, 1793; Porteous, trans., "Governor Carondelet's Levee Ordinance," 513–15 in English and 515–16 in French. The ordinance makes clear that syndics already existed. A 1790 letter by Governor Miró mentions them at that time; see [Miró] to Monsieur Porte, New Orleans, April 30, 1790, AGI, PC, leg. 204. Syndics were present under the French, and the older rural districts probably continued their use. Areas settled under the Spaniards, however, did not have them until the mid-1790s.

12. Actas del Cabildo, III, (2), 149, November 18, 1791, III, (3), 53–54, February 15, 1793, III, (3), 55, February 22, 1793; Carondelet to Nicolas Verbois, New Orleans, July 1, 1792, AGI,

Sigur's efforts, however, were insufficient. Even after he spent the money to reinforce the levee, problems continued. His inability to repay the short-term loan prompted the *mayordomo de propios* in 1796 to begin collection proceedings against him in the courts. Although Sigur lost in New Orleans, he appealed to the superior tribunal in Havana. Then, early in 1797, his eight-thousand-peso loan became due and the Cabildo requested payment. The councillors gave Sigur an extension of time on condition that he obtain one for the city from the Royal Treasury. Otherwise, the Cabildo would have to repay the Royal Treasury immediately.[13]

Acting Intendant Morales granted the Cabildo an eight-month extension if the council was satisfied that Sigur's motives were honest. After giving the extension, the Cabildo learned about Sigur's duplicity. He had included the eight-thousand-peso loan in his appeal to Havana and was trying to wheedle his way out of paying it. The council first hired a lawyer to represent its interests in Havana and then warned Sigur to withdraw his appeal or repay the loan immediately.[14]

Sigur refused because, he claimed, his contract had been violated. Unconvinced, the Cabildo ordered the *mayordomo* to take legal action against him. Within five months he capitulated and repaid the entire eight thousand pesos with money he borrowed from Andrés Almonester. The Cabildo immediately repaid the Royal Treasury. Presumably Sigur also repaid the city for the short-term loan.[15]

Although it recovered the money, the Cabildo still had the levee problem because Sigur abandoned the land. In 1799 another flood in the same area damaged the surrounding crops and portions of the city. Governor Gayoso informed the Cabildo that he had ordered repairs to be made, which the city had to pay. The councillors thanked Gayoso and informed

PC, leg. 215A, in which Carondelet gave absentee owners until November to repair their levees or face a one-hundred-peso fine.

13. Actas del Cabildo, IV, (1), 126–27, June 3, 1796, IV, (1), 202–203, March 3, 1797, IV, (1), 212, March 24, 1797, IV, (2), 26–27, August 23, 1797; "Miscellaneous Documents," III (unnumbered), 59, November 13, 1797.

14. Actas del Cabildo, IV, (1), 222, June 2, 1797, IV, (2), 26–27, August 23, 1797, IV, (2), 29, September 1, 1797.

15. *Ibid.*, IV, (2), 26–27, August 23, 1797, IV, (2), 29, September 1, 1797, IV, (2), 94, January 19, 1798, IV, (3), 80, September 27, 1799, IV, (3), 98–99, October 18, 1799.

him that the landowners would reimburse the city treasury for these expenses.[16]

The councillors correctly judged the willingness of landowners to contribute to levee repairs. A number of them donated funds without being asked. Within the city, the *alcaldes de barrio* collected whatever the residents contributed. These donations covered all but 292 pesos, 5½ reales, of the expenses. In January, 1800, the Cabildo absorbed the remaining amount from public funds, pending any final contributions from landowners.[17]

Other landowners also abandoned their lands because of frequent crevasses, and the Cabildo lacked the means to force them to maintain their levees. In 1792 Francisco Bernoudy requested the Cabildo to grant him a ten-thousand-peso loan to rebuild his levee on lands across the river. He declared that without the money, he would be forced to surrender the lands. The Cabildo referred his petition to Síndico Procurador General Riaño to investigate and render an opinion.[18]

Riaño reported that the petitioner's facts were accurate. If the levee were not reinforced, high waters would destroy the crops on between twelve and fourteen leagues of land. Nevertheless, Riaño could not recommend a loan because the city treasury lacked the money and the large sum required royal approval. At Riaño's suggestion, the Cabildo advised Bernoudy to apply to the Royal Treasury.[19]

In another example, Joseph Xavier de Pontalba abandoned twenty arpents of land to the public domain. Pontalba had purchased the estate of Pedro Bonne to acquire his slaves. When Pontalba found it difficult to

16. *Ibid.,* IV, (3), 42, June 21, 1799. A fragment of a document by nineteen inhabitants of Tchoupitoulas asked for assistance in 1799 for a levee break on lands that Sigur had abandoned (Nicolás María Vidal *et al.,* New Orleans, [month not legible] 24, 1799, AGI, PC, leg. 204). Acting Governor Francisco Bouligny asked for a census of slaves in the Tchoupitoulas district on August 26, 1799, and he wanted to know how best to repair the levee on the lands Sigur abandoned. See his *minuta* in AGI, PC, leg. 216A.

17. Actas del Cabildo, IV, (3), 45, July 1, 1799, IV, (3), 130–31, January 24, 1800. Technically, Governor Gayoso was personally responsible for the debt because he had ordered repairs to be made without Cabildo approval. But he had died the preceding July and his estate was in debt, so the Cabildo accepted payment.

18. *Ibid.,* III, (3), 7, June 22, 1792.

19. *Ibid.,* III, (3), 11–12, July 20, 1792.

maintain the levee on the estate, he deserted the land. Bartolomé Le Breton purchased it at public auction. He quickly learned that he, too, could not keep the levee in a good state of repair and asked the governor to allow him to abandon only that part of the land endangered by the weak levee. Carondelet forwarded the request to the Cabildo for a decision.[20]

In November, 1793, the councillors ruled against the partial abandonment and any future partial abandonments. They feared that granting permission would set a dangerous precedent and all weak levees would become a public burden. They petitioned the governor to reject any forfeiture of titles except for those that included the entire tract of the person making the request.[21]

Aside from the problem of land abandonments caused by weak levees, the Cabildo directed extensive levee repairs in various areas, particularly during the years 1793 to 1796. For these repairs the labor of free blacks and convicts was used at city expense. By 1796 Governor Carondelet had successfully diminished the possibility of injury to New Orleans from floodwaters. He had ordered the construction of six floodgates near the city, which would divert floodwaters, especially when the levee at Tchoupitoulas broke. Accomplished with donated labor and completed in June, 1796, the job cost the city only 120 pesos.[22]

20. *Ibid.,* III, (3), 97–98, November 11, 1793. See also Carondelet to Luis Macarty, New Orleans, February 21, 1793, AGI, PC, leg. 123, which states that Bonne had not built a levee on his lands. Syndic Macarty ordered Bonne to build the levee or abandon the land to the king. Apparently, he sold it to Pontalba.

21. Actas del Cabildo, III, (3), 97–98, November 11, 1793. See also a fragment of a document in AGI, PC, leg. 123, without names or dates, but which appears to be an opinion by the *auditor de guerra* on land abandonments. He ruled against Pontalba renouncing four arpents of land, which belonged to a larger landholding. The crown assumed charge of sixteen arpents of front, and Pontalba retained twenty-eight arpents of front.

22. Actas del Cabildo, III, (3), 161, September 12, 1794, III, (3), 186, December 19, 1794, III, (3), 202, February 6, 1795, IV, (1), 53, August 29, 1795, IV, (1), 75, November 27, 1795, IV, (1), 106, April 1, 1796, IV, (1), 127, June 3, 1796.

In his first year in office, Governor Carondelet issued a levee ordinance. He appointed district syndics and told the inhabitants to obey their orders; persons failing to do so would be fined. The syndics were to examine the levees in their districts and inform the landowners to make repairs after the harvest season, which coincided with low waters in the river. Carondelet also prohibited animals from roaming loose from the time of planting to harvest. Horses, mules, cows, oxen, and pigs found on the levee without an owner would be confiscated and

Repairs to the levees at city expense thereafter became less frequent and less costly. Only one major break in the levee occurred before 1802. Minor ruptures, however, aggravated by the careless anchoring of boats and ships, continued along the city's waterfront. In 1799 the Cabildo ordered the destruction of dangerous anchorages and it appealed to the king to revoke existing royal permits for anchorages along the levee.[23]

To improve anchorage and ensure the levee's safety, the Cabildo had two small wharves constructed and extra pilings installed in 1798. It also projected the construction of a large brick wharf on the waterfront. Besides protecting the levee and facilitating the loading and unloading of cargoes, the wharf would provide a place where garbage could be dumped into the river. Garbage dumped from the end of the wharf would not wash back on the levee and spoil the city's waterfront recreation area. The councillors contacted the city's commercial association (*consulado*) to enlist its support for the project and to request suggestions for daily wharfage fees for the ships using the facility. The merchants failed to support the project, and

---

the owner of the levee indemnified if damage had been done. In places subject to crevasses, owners had to have a deposit of pickets, planks, Spanish moss, and other materials necessary for levee repair or pay a one-hundred-peso fine. If the district lacked blacks to do the labor, the syndic was to inform the governor, who would then supply them.

Persons unable to keep up their levees because they lacked slaves or resources would be required to sell their lands at the end of the harvest. The government would collect the fines the syndics reported, with half going to the Royal Treasury and the other half to Charity Hospital. The syndics were to assemble the residents of their districts, read the new regulations to them, and allow them to make copies (Porteous, trans., "Governor Carondelet's Levee Ordinance," 513–16).

Breaches in the levee, even those in the neighboring countryside, could flood the city to a depth of more than four feet, causing extensive damage (Alliot, "Historical and Political Reflections," 63; Pope, *Tour,* 37).

Carondelet's 1792 levee decree was not an immediate success; numerous and costly floods continued, primarily because the syndics failed to do their duty. Carondelet corrected the problem in his general police decree of 1795 in which he repeated the 1792 provisions and added that syndics who did not fulfill their responsibilities would be held accountable for any repairs and damages resulting from their negligence (Carondelet, "Decree of June 1, 1795," 379–80, *American State Papers, Miscellaneous Documents,* I, 377–81).

23. Actas del Cabildo, IV, (1), 211, March 24, 1797, IV, (2), 85, December 7, 1797, IV, (2), 104, March 2, 1798, IV, (2), 124, May 4, 1798, IV, (3), 70, September 6, 1799, IV, (3), 120, December 20, 1799, IV, (4), 152, January 15, 1802, IV, (4), 180, March 5, 1802.

the Cabildo retained the antiquated method of posts for anchorage. Periodic repairs to the city levee continued.[24]

In 1802 the threat of a levee washout occurred near Los Naranjos (Orange Grove), at the lower end of the city. Twice in the preceding three years, the Cabildo had repaired a crevasse there. On this occasion, six residents petitioned the governor to have the Cabildo improve the levee, suggesting that earlier repair work had been defective and the council's negligence endangered the city. Perhaps there was some truth to their allegation because the two earlier repair jobs had been rushed. In 1799 two *regidores* had subcontracted the work, supervising it themselves to save time. In 1800, the Cabildo permitted the sinking of three barges to help fill in the crevasse.

The *regidores*, however, denied any shoddy work at Los Naranjos. They urged Governor Salcedo to reprimand the petitioners for their insinuations. The councillors, however, took the precaution of appointing two *regidores* to inspect the levee in conjunction with army engineer Gilberto Guillemard. The three men reported that because of high waters and the approach of the hurricane season repair work could not be done until later in the year.[25] Unfortunately, nothing more is known about the levee at Los Naranjos.

The levees remained a Cabildo concern to the end of the Spanish era. In November, 1803, after it had lost power and prestige and was marking time until the French takeover, the Cabildo took steps to repair a crevasse. The councillors ordered the use of the temporary method of "fascine and pickets." This last act closed out the minutes of the New Orleans Cabildo.[26]

Problems involving the Mississippi River extended beyond the levees. One of them was standing water because of inadequate drainage. When the river was in flood stage, its level rose above the city, held back only by the levee. First-time visitors to the Crescent City today are often amazed to see ships on the river riding above street level. The presence of

---

24. *Ibid.,* IV, (2), 178–79, December 20, 1798, IV, (4), 117, July 24, 1801, IV, (4), 122, July 31, 1801, IV, (4), 124, August 7, 1801, IV, (4), 129, August 21, 1801.

25. *Ibid.,* IV, (5), 11–12, August 9, 1802, IV, (5), 67, April 22, 1803; Morazán, "Letters," II, 153–56, 155n.

26. *Actas del Cabildo,* IV, (5), 100, November 18, 1803.

so much water in, as well as on, the ground has been a constant quandary since the city's founding in 1718. Because of health concerns, as early as the eighteenth century New Orleans residents struggled to provide the city with adequate drainage.

In the French era, a system of ditches and gutters carried surface water away from the river toward the rear of the city. When O'Reilly took possession of the colony, he stipulated that responsibility for constructing and maintaining New Orleans' gutters rested with the individuals whose property fronted on the streets along which the gutters ran. In his code, O'Reilly specifically forbade the Cabildo to maintain the gutter system with public funds. The council's only duties regarding the gutters were to conserve those fronting on public property and to ensure that individual property owners preserved theirs.[27]

The gutters ran along both sides of the city's earthen streets. They were dug in a V shape, with wooden planks lining the two sides of the opening. Additional planks covered the opening on top and butted up against the sidewalk. The covering planks gave added width to the walkway and were particularly valuable at street intersections where the sidewalks stopped. Until 1799 the Cabildo called the covered gutters *puentes* (bridges), a term that has confused readers of the Cabildo minutes.[28]

In the first years of the Spanish period, the council paid little attention to the gutters or to drainage in general. It accepted O'Reilly's dictum that responsibility for their upkeep rested with the residents. It appointed two *regidores* to inspect and oversee work on the gutters. Eventually, this system gave way to letting private contractors repair and clean the gutters.[29]

City intervention to maintain the gutters began when property owners failed to do so. When they refused after being warned to repair them, the council auctioned the task to the lowest bidder and then charged the

27. Morazán, "Letters," I, 69; Code O'Reilly, 266.

28. Sibley, "Journal," 478; Actas del Cabildo, IV, (3), 9–10, January 30, 1799. On the confusion of the term *bridges* for gutters in the Cabildo records, see, for example, Texada, in "Alejandro O'Reilly," 143, who speculated that they might be toll bridges.

29. Actas del Cabildo, I, 165–66, August 6, 1774, I, 185, June 2, 1775, I, 193, October 20, 1775, I, 272–74, March 24, 1779, I, 285, June 19, 1779. Cabildo minutes do not explain the size of a gutter. Each gutter was probably the length of an individual lot. It has been suggested that each gutter was a block long, but references made to lot owners paying for individual gutters would rule this out.

property owners. When work for individual owners was done in conjunction with that for city gutters, or for several owners under the same contract, the owners were charged on a *pro rata* basis. This method for maintaining the gutters lasted into the mid-1780s.[30]

In the spring of 1785, after many gutter repairs the previous summer, Captain General Gálvez informed the Cabildo through Governor Miró that the city would have to assume the cost for cleaning and repairing the streets, including the construction and upkeep of gutters. To finance this added burden, Miró proposed a tax of two reales per month on all carts. The councillors remonstrated that they would assume the responsibility if ordered to—if indeed they were able to—but they appealed to Gálvez to reconsider his decision.[31]

Gálvez relented in part, changing his order to read that the Cabildo would pay for repairing or replacing all of the damaged gutters. Thereafter, responsibility would revert to the property owners. He justified his decision on the basis of misfortunes inflicted on the residents by the war with Great Britain and by recent hurricanes. The Cabildo accepted his charge but extended the time of the city's responsibility until all property owners had received equal exemption for gutter repairs.[32]

The financial burden for maintaining the city's gutters was considerable. From 1785 to the mid-1790s, it cost slightly more than five pesos to repair each existing gutter and about thirty pesos to construct each new gutter. Frequently the city built thirty to sixty new gutters at one time, and the bills for them ran as high as 1,650 and 1,750 pesos. The 1788 fire destroyed many of the city's gutters. The Cabildo authorized payments for new gutters on June 6 and 20, 1788. But after the 1794 fire, the property owners, not the city, replaced the gutters.[33]

Following the 1794 blaze, the gutters rebuilt by property owners failed

30. *Ibid.,* I, 193, October 20, 1775, II, 26, May 19, 1780, II, 178, May 23, 1783, III, (1), 20–21, September 17, 1784.

31. *Ibid.,* III, (1), 41–42, April 15, 1785.

32. *Ibid.,* III, (I), 54–55, August 26, 1785. Gálvez' order appears to have come from Mexico, where he became viceroy on June 17, 1785.

33. *Ibid.,* III, (1), 66–67, November 18, 1785, III, (1), 102, August 17, 1786, III, (1), 134, February 16, 1787, III, (2), 27, June 20, 1788, III, (2), 28, June 27, 1788, III, (2), 99, May 7, 1790, III, (3), 167–69, October 10, 1794, III, (3), 180, November 21, 1794.

to drain properly. The standing water aggravated health hazards. To correct the problem and ensure proper drainage, the Cabildo hired engineers Gilberto Guillemard and Nicolás de Finiels to grade the gutters.[34]

By 1795 the Cabildo seems to have accepted responsibility for the routine maintenance of the city's gutters. That year the councillors accepted bids on a six-year monopoly contract for their upkeep in the belief that it would be cheaper. The contractor would repair existing gutters and construct new ones as they were needed at a set fee. Because of the risk involved, however, no contractor bid on it. The council then tried to make the contract more attractive by accepting a flat bid for maintaining the existing gutters and paying twenty-five pesos for each new one built. The city needed twenty new gutters at that time.[35]

Roberto Jones, a master carpenter and contractor, successfully bid eight hundred pesos per year. The city agreed to pay the fee in three installments of 266 pesos after the annual commissioners inspected his labor. The Cabildo paid him until the spring of 1797, when Síndico Procurador General Caisergues reported that Jones's work failed to meet standards and that he had built only one of twenty required gutters. The councillors agreed to make him furnish a bond within eight days. When he failed to do so, the Cabildo canceled his contract.[36]

The city auctioned the gutter contract again, awarding it this time to Bartolomé Lafond. After paying Lafond 450 pesos, the councillors discovered that his work on the gutters, too, fell below specifications. When they demanded an explanation, Lafond complained that he had not received a copy of the contract or the specifications. The councillors provided them and gave him a month to comply. If he failed to do so, they would revoke the agreement and charge him for the alterations.[37]

Lafond, however, claimed that a loophole in the contract exempted him

34. *Ibid.,* IV, (3), 12–13, February 15, 1799. On Finiels, see the introduction in Nicolas de Finiels, *An Account of Upper Louisiana,* ed. Carl J. Ekberg and William E. Foley, trans. Carl J. Ekberg (Columbia, Mo., 1989).

35. Actas del Cabildo, III, (3), 202–203, February 6, 1795, III, (3), 205, February 20, 1795, III, (3), 211, March 28, 1795.

36. *Ibid.,* IV, (1), 44–45, July 3, 1795, IV, (1), 51–52, August 29, 1795, IV, (1), 139, July 1, 1796, IV, (1), 163, November 3, 1796, IV, (1), 173, December 16, 1796, IV, (1), 201–202, March 3, 1797, IV, (1), 206, March 17, 1797.

37. *Ibid.,* IV, (2), 23, August 11, 1797, IV, (2), 55, October 6, 1797.

from repairing the old gutters. The councillors next tried to negotiate with him. When they failed to reach an accommodation, they canceled his contract. But they appear not to have charged Lafond for the alterations that his shoddy work required.[38]

In 1799, following the failure of the monopoly contract, the Cabildo reassessed the problem of gutter maintenance. It discussed a return to the pre-Gálvez system of the residents maintaining the gutters but then rejected it as unenforceable. Because city maintenance of the gutters violated Spanish law and Gálvez' 1785 order for Cabildo responsibility was a temporary expedient, the councillors appealed to the crown to let them assume permanent charge. Governor Gayoso granted temporary approval, but he warned that if the king disapproved the residents would have to reimburse the city treasury. The Spanish period ended without a royal reply.[39]

The city, nevertheless, had to find a way to reduce expenditures for gutters. Its solution was to construct new gutters made of brick and cement, with wooden covers. Two prototypes were to be built first, and the councillors awarded the contract for their construction to Bartolomé Lafond by renewing his 1797 contract. On this occasion, Lafond acted properly and furnished one sample gutter for twenty-five pesos. But then the Cabildo suspended the project because it needed the funds to repair the levees.[40]

When in early 1800 the Cabildo again turned its attention to the gutters, it amended its resolution of the previous year. At Lafond's suggestion, the councillors stipulated that the gutters be made of stone rather than brick; stone was both cheaper and more durable. The existing wooden gutters, however, were to be repaired until the new stone gutters replaced them.[41]

Juan María Dujarreau built the two stone gutter prototypes on Royal Street with materials furnished by the Cabildo. He charged only twenty-

38. *Ibid.,* IV, (2), 59–60, October 13, 1797, IV, (2), 74, November 10, 1797, IV, (2), 97, February 3, 1798, IV, (2), 100, February 16, 1798.

39. *Ibid.,* IV, (3), 8–10, January 30, 1799; Morazán, "Letters," I, 70n.

40. Actas del Cabildo, IV, (3), 12–13, February 15, 1799, IV, (3), 37–38, May 31, 1799, IV, (3), 45–46, July 1, 1799.

41. *Ibid.,* IV, (3), 164, March 28, 1800; Morazán, "Letters," I, 188n.

five pesos, seven reales for his labor. Encouraged by his fee, the city offered Dujarreau thirteen pesos per gutter for the rest of the city, with the Cabildo providing the materials, but he declined.[42]

New Orleans' gutters deteriorated badly during the last five years of Spanish rule. That period was one of rapid growth for the city, and the Cabildo did little to keep the gutters functioning properly. The councillors realized that the gutters needed massive repairs, but they feared that using municipal funds might cause them legal difficulties. They resolved again to ask the king to transfer responsibility to the Cabildo.[43]

A week after their resolution, acting civil governor Vidal perfunctorily ordered the councillors to begin construction of the gutters using city funds. But deep-seated aversion to Vidal made them recalcitrant. They refused to use municipal monies, saying the residents should pay, and told Vidal to take the opportune measures for resolving the gutter problem.[44]

The Cabildo thereafter undertook no initiatives on new gutters and only minimally repaired the wooden gutters. Moreover, the *síndico procurador general* replaced the *mayordomo de propios* as the city official in charge of gutters. In early 1801, the new *síndico procurador general,* Pablo Lanusse, informed the councillors what they probably already knew: the city desperately needed new gutters. He opined that the Cabildo should pay for them because the new meat and flour taxes were bringing in ample revenue. When Vidal supported Lanusse's opinion, the council again accepted responsibility for the city's drainage system.[45]

Within a year, the Cabildo repaired or replaced all of the city's gutters at a cost of 3,514 pesos, ½ real. In the last two years of the Spanish regime, the Cabildo repaired only those gutters that bordered on public property. But this was not because the gutters held up. Several months of excep-

42. Actas del Cabildo, IV, (3), 197, July 11, 1800, IV, (3), 200, July 18, 1800, IV, (4), 6, October 3, 1800, IV, (4), 7–8, October 10, 1800. The Cabildo never converted the city's wooden gutters to stone. In 1822, after nearly twenty years of American rule, New Orleans still used wooden gutters (Asbury, *French Quarter,* 78).

43. Actas del Cabildo, IV, (4), 10–13, October 24, 1800.

44. *Ibid.,* IV, (4), 29–31, October 31, 1800.

45. *Ibid.,* IV, (4), 42–43, December 12, 1800, IV, (4), 67–70, February 6, 1801; "Miscellaneous Documents," I, Nos. 260–62, 51–52, December 11, 1800.

tionally heavy rains in 1802 severely deteriorated the city's gutters. The Cabildo ignored the problem pending the expected change in government.[46]

In addition to the street gutters, Spanish New Orleans had several ditches that facilitated drainage of water in the city. In 1779 the Cabildo authorized a ditch to be dug along the base of the levee fronting the city to catch water seeping through the barrier. Much later Carondelet had six emergency canals dug to improve drainage efficiency. In 1798, the Cabildo opened up four sewage ditches that also removed standing water. Without doubt, the Carondelet Canal that ran from the city to Bayou St. John and was the major construction project of the Spanish era also helped drainage.[47]

The Cabildo confronted formidable problems in trying to drain the city of standing water. What the city fathers attempted to do was nearly impossible, given New Orleans' limited financial resources, the technology of the era and in a frontier setting, the frequent rainstorms and occasional torrential hurricanes, and the proximity of the Mississippi River with its tendency to overflow. Moreover, the residents all too frequently used the drainage facilities as refuse dumps, which exacerbated problems. Solving the drainage difficulties was not easy, and they persisted well into the nineteenth century. Even today, New Orleans still has its low spots that fill with water whenever downpours occur.[48]

In addition to drainage, the Cabildo assumed limited responsibilities for the care of the surrounding rural roads and, to a lesser degree, the Carondelet Canal and the Bayou St. John drawbridge. The Cabildo acted only sporadically and inconsistently in these areas, which makes it difficult to determine what its real responsibilities were.

Shortly after its establishment, the Cabildo confronted the problems of street repair that the French government seems to have ignored. In one of its first acts, the council required cart owners operating in the city to

46. Actas del Cabildo, IV, (4), 150, January 8, 1802, IV, (4), 155–56, January 29, 1802, IV, (4), 160, February 5, 1802, IV, (5), 30, November 26, 1802; Morazán, "Letters," II, 4n, 48n; Robin, *Voyage to Louisiana,* 31–32.

47. Morazán, "Letters," II, 4; Sibley, "Journal," 481; Actas del Cabildo, I, 272–73, March 24, 1779, IV, (1), 106, April 1, 1796, IV, (2) 126–27, June 3, 1798.

48. Robin, *Voyage to Louisiana,* 30; Asbury, *French Quarter,* 78, 209-10.

aid in filling holes and low places in the streets by depositing two cartloads of dirt each week. They had to report to the Cabildo the locations where they dumped their loads. To enforce this regulation and achieve equitable participation by cart owners, the Cabildo required the vehicles to be numbered and registered.[49]

In 1778 the Cabildo exercised the right of eminent domain in creating the River Road. At the request of Síndico Procurador General Lacosta, the councillors issued a regulation requiring residents whose property fronted on the river to clear a roadway parallel to the river. Property owners needed to keep the highway clear to permit crews of ships to throw lines to tie up to the bank or move upriver.[50]

In 1795 the Cabildo went farther in issuing regulations on the cutting of new streets through private property and worked to ensure that individuals did not disrupt traffic. The council permitted Joseph Xavier de Pontalba, Miguel Fortier, Esteban Bore, and Roberto Montreult (or Montreuill) to cut a street through their property. In granting the request, the council dictated that only brick houses with flat roofs should be built along the new roadway. It was part of the Cabildo's new building regulations made after the 1794 fire.[51]

When the construction of Daniel Clark's twine factory blocked access through Royal Street into the second ward in 1801, the Cabildo compelled him to reopen the street immediately. The next year, high water near the property of Doña Luisa de La Ronde obstructed the Bayou Road. The councillors instructed the *síndico procurador general* to consult with the governor and institute proceedings to restore transit on the road.[52]

The Cabildo also forced the inhabitants of the suburbs and the surrounding countryside to maintain their roads. These included the residents of Gentilly, persons living along the river both above and below the city, and the residents on the Bayou St. John road. The Cabildo resolved that the residents whose property fronted the Bayou St. John road dig a ditch two feet deep by three feet across at a distance of eight feet from the road's

49. Actas del Cabildo, I, 7–8, December 9, 1769, I, 19, March 16, 1770.

50. *Ibid.*, I, 242, February 6, 1778, I, 287, July 16, 1779. The road ran along the base of the levee and not on the levee.

51. *Ibid.*, III, (3), 205, February 20, 1795.

52. *Ibid.*, IV, (4), 121, July 31, 1801, IV, (4), 221, June 25, 1802.

scarping. The dirt removed from the ditch was to be used to build up the roadbed. The road's large holes were to be filled in with small bundles of wood before they were covered with dirt. Low areas that could not empty into the bayou were to be drained to the rear of the owner's property.[53]

In 1784 the Cabildo published a regulation requiring all the inhabitants of the New Orleans district to repair their roads within six days. It further required all carts to be licensed for a one-peso fee, which entitled owners to paint the license numbers on their carts. A register at the *casa capitular* would record the license numbers. Owners of unlicensed carts would be fined ten pesos.[54]

In the spring of 1785, the Cabildo accepted responsibility for cleaning and maintaining the city streets. Captain General Gálvez issued the order in the same decree that made the city temporarily responsible for maintaining the gutters. The Cabildo thereafter retained upkeep of the streets until the Spanish era ended.[55]

Because of the constant need to repair the streets, by 1792 the Cabildo had assigned several carts to bring dirt to fill in holes. The cart drivers worked six days a week, supervised by Francisco Pérez, who received an eight-peso-per-month salary from the Cabildo. Because of a need to build up the streets and sidewalks, the *síndico procurador general* requested the revenue produced from the sale of the merchandise brought by the French royal ship *Trucha* in 1788 to assist fire victims; the government had either not used any of the proceeds or only a part of them to assist the fire victims. Using the money as the *síndico* suggested, however, required royal approval, and the Cabildo delayed asking for it. Nevertheless, the council assigned slaves and convicts to labor on the streets when they were not involved in emergency work on the levees. The owners received the pay for their slaves while the convicts earned one real daily, which was applied equally to purchase their food and clothing. The laborers spread the dirt and filled in the large troublesome holes with surplus ballast rocks discarded by ships on the waterfront.[56]

53. *Ibid.*, II, 159–60, February 14, 1783; "Digest," 188–89.
54. Actas del Cabildo, II, 211–12, May 28, 1784.
55. *Ibid.*, III, (1), 41–42, April 15, 1785; Gálvez to Miró, Havana, March 4, 1785, *SMV*, Pt. II, 123.
56. Actas del Cabildo, III, (2), 176, February 3, 1792, III, (3), 16, August 11, 1792, IV, (1),

By 1801 the street-filling process needed additional supervision. Because ten carts were then working to fill the streets with dirt, the councillors suspected fraud. They ordered the drivers to register the vehicles and mounted numbered plates on each one to keep track of them. They instructed the regular supervisor and the ward commissioners to direct the workers to ensure their efficiency. They also ordered the destruction of any cart that carried only partial loads of dirt.[57]

The haphazard system used to fill in the streets had unwelcomed side effects. Careless work often blocked the drainage of water to the rear of the city, which the residents seized as an excuse for not repairing their sidewalks. The Cabildo then graded the streets to reestablish drainage and facilitate sidewalk repair.[58]

In 1799 the city purchased wooden stakes for grading the streets. The Cabildo, however, did not use them until 1802, when it employed Bartolomé Lafond to grade the streets. The city supplied him with a seventy-five-peso water level for his work and instructed the residents to furnish him with two hundred additional stakes and the labor of two slaves.[59]

Either Lafond never completed the work or performed it inadequately. In early 1803, the new *síndico procurador general* requested that the residents rebuild their sidewalks and the streets that fronted on their property in four months. If they failed to do so, he suggested that the city do it and charge the owners. The councillors replied that this method had already been tried by both the council and the governor, but it had not been enforced. They then forwarded the *síndico*'s petition to the governor, with the request that he punish the property owners who had not complied with the earlier ultimatum.[60]

There is little doubt that New Orleans' streets were unpaved in the

---

53, August 29, 1795, IV, (4), 130, August 29, 1801, IV, (4), 182, March 5, 1802, IV, (5), 46, February 4, 1803; "Miscellaneous Documents," I, No. 346, 95, December 31, 1797. The Spanish government seems to have taken charge of the goods brought by the royal French ship *Trucha* to help the fire victims of 1788. It sold the goods and used the funds (Actas del Cabildo, III, [2], 176, February 3, 1792).

57. *Ibid.,* IV, (4), 72–74, February 27, 1801.

58. Morazán, "Letters," II, 4n.

59. Actas del Cabildo, IV, (3), 117–18, December 13, 1799, IV, (4), 150, January 8, 1802, IV, (4), 182, March 5, 1802, IV, (4), 209–10, May 7, 1802; Morazán, "Letters," II, 174n, 175.

60. Actas del Cabildo, IV, (5), 41, January 21, 1803.

late Spanish period. Visitors to Spanish New Orleans, however, left an inconsistent picture of the city's streets. Colonel John Pope described them in 1791 as being broad and regular, some well paved with bricks. In 1802 Dr. John Sibley claimed that the streets were paved with tile but only along the walkways. The city's unpaved streets proved a formidable challenge when it rained. Vehicles had to have wheels six to eight inches wide to avoid sinking. C. C. Robin noted in 1803 that the streets were nearly impassable because of holes and ruts. Residents told him that the expected change in government had halted street repairs. In contrast to Robin, later the same year Governor William C. C. Claiborne informed James Madison that he found the principal streets of New Orleans well built and compared them favorably to those of Baltimore a few years before. In contrast to these descriptions, the Cabildo records provide a far more accurate picture of their condition and note the efforts to improve them.[61]

When the Cabildo began functioning in December, 1769, it moved almost immediately to make property owners comply with the Spanish law to furnish sidewalks, *banquetas,* parallel to the city streets. The French regime had done little or nothing about sidewalks. The French word for New Orleans' sidewalks, *banquettes,* seems to be derived from the Spanish word.[62] At the Cabildo session of December 9, 1769, the councillors required the construction of sidewalks five feet wide and sloped one inch per foot toward the streets to drain them into the gutters. They also required that awnings be hung ten feet above the walkways. Three days later, on December 12, Governor Unzaga issued a decree for the laying of sidewalks in the city.[63]

After this decree, the few Cabildo references to the sidewalks were in

---

61. Pope, *Tour,* 37; Sibley, "Journal," 478, 480; Robin, *Voyage,* 31–32; Claiborne to Madison, December 27, 1803, in Robertson, ed., *Louisiana Under the Rule,* II, 229; Morazán, "Letters," I, 23n.

62. Morazán, "Letters," I, 69. *Harrap's New Collegiate French and English Dictionary* (London, 1982), Pt. Two, 70, explains *banquette* as bench, seat, form, verge; (foot)path (of bridge or tunnel). For sidewalk, the equivalent French word is *trottoir. Ibid.,* Pt. One, 751.

By comparison, Boston had no sidewalks in 1760, an inconvenience that jeopardized the lives of pedestrians because of horse-drawn wagon and cart traffic. Charleston acquired its first sidewalks in 1762 (Bridenbaugh, *Cities in Revolt,* 243–44).

63. Actas del Cabildo, I, 7–8, December 9, 1769; Porteous, ed. and trans., "Index," *LHQ,* IV (1923), 160.

conjunction with streets or gutters. The records mentioned that the city paid for the construction and repair of sidewalks adjoining public property. Generally, the council did not encounter the same degree of resistance in making owners maintain the sidewalks as it did regarding gutters.[64]

New Orleans' wooden sidewalks suffered from constant deterioration and from the 1788 and 1794 fires. After the fires, the sidewalks, like the gutters, were rebuilt without uniformity. Many were only four feet wide and some so low that mud often covered them. Because the streets and gutters were in poor condition, some of the residents refused to repair their sidewalks in the late Spanish period. They argued that it was useless to do so unless the streets were properly graded.[65]

Through the Spanish period, the Cabildo genuinely sought to restore high-quality and uniform sidewalks in the city. The councillors commissioned Lafond to grade the streets and, in conjunction, ordered sidewalks constructed for the entire city. They expected the city treasury to finance this major project and the residents to reimburse the city. To make the plan viable, they allowed poor people more time to pay.[66]

Both the street and sidewalk projects stalled because the inhabitants resisted paying and Spanish law did not force compliance. In 1803 the new *síndico procurador general* tried to get the Cabildo to enforce its earlier rulings. The councillors merely transmitted his petition to Governor Salcedo, with their request that he punish recalcitrant property owners. The last year of Spanish rule saw little activity to secure compliance.[67]

Among the improvements that Governor Carondelet initiated were the canal that received his name and the Bayou St. John drawbridge. The Cabildo had only minor responsibilities for these two public facilities, which were constructed late in the Spanish period and located outside the city.

A canal to connect New Orleans to Lake Pontchartrain via Bayou St. John had been proposed and attempted from early in the French regime,

64. "Digest," 208; Actas del Cabildo, III, (3), 84, August 20, 1793, IV, (1), 102, March 11, 1796, IV, (4), 29, October 31, 1800, IV, (5), 30, November 26, 1802.

65. Morazán, "Letters," I, 69n, II, 4n; Actas del Cabildo, IV, (3), 14, February 15, 1799.

66. Actas del Cabildo, IV, (3), 117–18, December 13, 1799, IV, (4), 150, January 8, 1802, IV, (4), 182, March 5, 1802, IV, (4), 209–10, May 7, 1802.

67. *Ibid.,* IV, (5), 41, January 21, 1803; Robin, *Voyage,* 31.

but resources and determination were insufficient until the Spanish era. The first canal built in 1794 was one and one-half miles long and about six feet in width. Its enlargement in 1796 widened the canal to fifteen feet by six feet deep and made it big enough to accommodate small ships. It had an eight-foot path on each side to facilitate travelers and horses pulling flatboats. The canal also went around large trees. The city's convicts and 150 slaves from plantations within a radius of fifteen miles performed the labor. Besides providing a shorter water route to Mobile and Pensacola via Lakes Pontchartrain and Borgne, the canal helped New Orleans' drainage problem.[68]

After the canal's completion, the councillors named it for the governor as a gesture of their gratitude. They placed a marble plaque with an inscription engraved in Spanish, French, and English on an outside wall of Charity Hospital, adjacent to the San Fernando Gate, which opened onto the basin at the head of the canal. The inscription was repeated in Spanish beneath a portrait of Carondelet, which the Cabildo commissioned and hung in the *sala capitular*.[69]

The city paid the minor expenses incurred in hiring professional contractors to complete the canal. It also appointed a caretaker to watch over the passageway. For the first year, Pedro Herrera served in this position, after which José Antonio García replaced him. Because the post was not salaried and produced no fees, García petitioned the Cabildo in 1800 for a small parcel of land on which to build a house for himself. He asked that the lot be situated near the canal so he could continue his work. The Cabildo seems not to have complied, and that probably disinclined him to continue his volunteer service. By 1802 debris and vegetation clogged the canal and rendered it intransitable except for pirogues.[70]

68. Morazán, "Letters," I, 94–95n; Sibley, "Journal," 479–81; Yerxa, "Administration of Carondelet," 13–14; Martin, *History of Louisiana,* 263.

69. Actas del Cabildo, IV, (1), 150–51, August 19, 1796. The canal ran to the basin in the rear of the city, where boats anchored. Carondelet used the Cabildo's decision to name the canal after him as justification for asking the Prince of the Peace (Godoy) to separate Louisiana and Florida from Cuba and create a separate captaincy general with him as the head. He offered to serve in Louisiana for five more years at no extra pay. His offer was not accepted (New Orleans, August 22, 1796, AHN, Est., leg. 3900).

70. Actas del Cabildo, IV, (1), 163, November 3, 1796; Morazán, "Letters," I, 93–97n; Robin, *Voyage,* 30.

The drawbridge that spanned Bayou St. John involved the Cabildo far more than the canal. Carondelet ordered its construction and Regidor Nicolas Forstall supervised the work, which cost the city 1,697 pesos, 2½ reales. Originally, plans called for a horse to operate it, but the bridge was so well balanced that two men could raise it in less than a minute.[71]

Shortly after it began functioning, the councillors informed the governor that misuse was damaging the drawbridge. They asked that a soldier be stationed at the bridge to protect it from abuse. They offered to pay him one real per day over his military pay and furnish him with a small hut. The governor appointed a sentry, and the Cabildo built a hut for one hundred pesos. Several months later, the councillors supplemented the soldier's pay with two pesos a month during the winter to provide firewood. They also agreed to compensate him for minor repairs to the drawbridge.[72]

Repairs, however, did not remain minor and amounted to several hundred pesos between 1798 and 1803. A toll the Cabildo imposed on ships passing the bridge paid for its repairs and the soldier's salary. Until 1801, the syndic of the Bayou St. John district collected the tolls. The council then considered ending the toll system and polled the residents to determine if they would contribute to a fund to maintain the bridge. There is no record of the poll results, but the toll fee continued.[73]

As occurred in other areas of Cabildo administration, the councillors lost control of the Bayou St. John drawbridge. Although the bridge stayed under the management of the *mayordomo de propios,* by 1803 the governor ordered repairs for the bridge whenever they were needed. On Salcedo's instructions, the *mayordomo* paid for them with city funds. The governor reported the repairs to the Cabildo after they had been made.[74]

Perhaps nowhere did the Cabildo exceed its instructions in the Code

71. "Miscellaneous Documents," III, No. 327, 60, November 13, 1797, IV, No. 356, 69–89, September 3, 1796; Actas del Cabildo, IV, (1), 163–64, November 3, 1796, IV, (1), 165, November 11, 1796; Sibley, "Journal," 418.

72. Actas del Cabildo, IV, (1), 206, March 17, 1797, IV, (1), 211–12, March 24, 1797, IV, (2), 84, December 7, 1797.

73. *Ibid.,* IV, (1), 206, March 17, 1797, IV, (2), 5, July 21, 1797, IV, (2), 70, October 27, 1797, IV, (2), 145, July 20, 1798, IV, (2), 178, December 20, 1798, IV, (3), 63, August 31, 1799, IV, (3), 205, August 1, 1800, IV, (4), 126, August 14, 1801.

74. *Ibid.,* IV, (5), 68, April 22, 1803, IV, (5), 79, July 8, 1803.

O'Reilly more than in the realm of public works. Experience convinced the councillors that they had to go beyond their mandated power for the good of the community. As a consequence, they embraced responsibilities for levee repair, drainage, and street and sidewalk maintenance. As long as capable governors were present who concurred in the Cabildo's objectives, the institution continued its positive work. With the arrival of Salcedo, however, which coincided with the Cabildo's concerns about exceeding its mandate, the councillors yielded, and their service to the city declined precipitously.

ELEVEN
Cabildo Land Grants and Building Regulations

UNDER O'Reilly's land decree of February 18, 1770, the Cabildo received only minor duties in granting land.[1] The traditional practice in the Spanish Empire was for a cabildo to award land in the king's name, subject to royal confirmation. Until the land was granted, a cabildo exercised control of royal lands. A cabildo's authority theoretically extended to the jurisdiction of the next city possessing a municipal government. Because only New Orleans had a cabildo, its jurisdiction technically embraced all of Louisiana and, after 1783, West Florida. Before the creation of the New Orleans Cabildo, a 1754 royal order governing the viceroyalty of New Spain gave the intendancy the sole authority to dispense land.[2]

O'Reilly, however, vested power for granting land in the governor because an intendancy did not then exist in Louisiana. As he explained to

---

1. O'Reilly's land decree, *American State Papers, Miscellaneous Documents*, I, 376–77; it can also be found in "O'Reilly's Ordinance of 1770; Concerning Grants of Land in Louisiana to New Settlers, Fencing of Same, Building of Roads and Levees, and Forfeiture of Strayed Cattle," *LHQ*, XI (1928), 237–40. O'Reilly's printed land decree in French is in AGI, PC, leg. 189B. See also Francis P. Burns, "The Spanish Land Laws of Louisiana," *LHQ*, XI (1928), 557–81, and *American State Papers, Public Lands (1789–1837)* (8 vols.; Washington, D.C., 1832–61), V, 631–775.

2. Morazán, "Letters," I, 96; Burns, "Spanish Land Laws," 563.

the Spanish first secretary, the Marqués de Grimaldi, he held a junta in New Orleans of fourteen experienced persons, who were known for their good judgment in land matters. They told him that under the French both the governor and the *commissaire-ordinateur* had to agree before grants could be made. Because the two men often dissented, concessions were paralyzed. O'Reilly consequently let the governor monopolize land grants. He believed that the land rules the junta established and he proclaimed would benefit the great majority of the province's population and industry.[3]

In 1780 the crown created the office of intendant for the province but left the right to grant land in the governor. The crown continued to ignore the anomaly until October, 1798, when at last it extended the 1754 royal order for New Spain to Louisiana.[4] Juan Ventura Morales was acting intendant when the news arrived in the province. He drew up a long list of rules for granting land and had many copies printed for circulation. He even asked Governor Gayoso to place troops under his authority so he could enforce his decrees. Implored by the nervous planters and the Cabildo, the governor refused. What they objected to was Article 35, which transferred to the intendant absolute power in granting land. Síndico Procurador General Félix Arnaud directed a plea to the Cabildo to defend "the rights of the inhabitants." He denied Morales' claim to exclusive jurisdiction over land grants and quoted various laws to prove that the Cabildo had the right to grant lands for city revenue, public use, and other purposes. He also pointed out that the city was a property holder and thus might suffer if the intendant's regulations were implemented.[5]

Gayoso had opposed Morales' rules, but he died shortly after their publication. Morales and the Cabildo then laid their respective cases before the crown. Although the king eventually decided in favor of the inten-

---

3. O'Reilly to Grimaldi, No. 33, New Orleans, March 1, 1770, AGI, SD, leg. 2594.

4. Burns, "Spanish Land Laws," 563.

5. Actas del Cabildo, IV, (3), 63–69, August 31, 1799. Morales challenged the governor for authority in land concessions. He waited until Carondelet had left Louisiana before presenting his case to the new governor, Manuel Gayoso de Lemos, citing existing laws. Gayoso appealed to Spain and lost. See Morales to Gayoso, New Orleans, August 29 and 30, 1797, Gayoso to Morales, and Morales to Pedro Varela y Ulloa, New Orleans, October 16, 1797, all in AHN, Est., leg. 3902.

dancy, both the acting civil governor, Vidal, and Governor General Salcedo failed to enforce Article 35 of Morales' land regulations. In the meantime, Manuel Serrano, the intendancy *asesor,* died in December, 1802, leaving the disposition of land claims in an even more confused state. Morales, who was again acting intendant, took charge of the land office and closed it. The question of unconfirmed land titles, which constituted about 70 percent of all grants in Louisiana, had not been resolved when the Spanish regime ended, and the tangle of land claims extended into the American period.[6]

Royal confirmation of O'Reilly's 1770 land decree made it law and left the Cabildo in an anomalous position regarding land grants. It limited the Cabildo's authority to the *bienes municipales* (municipal property) that produced revenue for the city and to the *bienes comunales* (lands held as commons, or *ejidos,* for city residents). The distinction between the two types of city-owned lands became blurred, and Spanish American cities, including New Orleans, generally used both kinds of land as they saw fit.[7] No official or agency in New Orleans ever defined the extent of city-owned lands, and the Cabildo never attempted to exercise full authority in this area.

Nevertheless, the council acted in many ways on land issues. It granted urban lots for private and public purposes. It even issued formal titles to urban and rural grants that O'Reilly had made. It reclaimed city property when owners failed to pay assessments. It advertised and sold unclaimed lots. On one occasion, the Cabildo purchased a city lot from Alcalde Ordinario Pedro Piernas to erect a public scale on it. Within these narrow limits, the council's authority theoretically exceeded that of either the governor or the intendant.[8]

6. Morazán, "Letters," I, 97; Burns, "Spanish Land Laws," 564.

7. Morazán, "Letters," I, 96. Besides the limitations that O'Reilly placed on the Cabildo's landholding authority, the transition from French to Spanish rule possibly added to the confusion. The French inhabitants might not have understood the Spanish concept of municipality. Clark makes a partial case for this point when he writes that the Superior Council was totally provincial in its orientation and made no distinction between local and provincial affairs (*New Orleans,* 156–57).

8. Actas del Cabildo, I, 34, October 19, 1770, I, 43–44, February 8, 1771, I, 49, May 10, 1771, I, 52, June 28, 1771, I, 86, August 7, 1772, I, 188–89, August 5, 1775, I, 204, March 1, 1776, I, 225, April 11, 1777, I, 287, July 16, 1779, III, (1), 78–79, January 27, 1786; "Records of

Although it occasionally granted or sold land to individuals as home sites, these grants are rare in the Cabildo records. When residents asked for them, the council sometimes refused to grant them. The paucity of requests for city lots for home sites in Cabildo documents indicates that the governors probably received and disposed of them. This is what happened under Governor Carondelet, who granted city lands without consulting the council.[9]

More often than for private use, individuals sought city land to introduce a needed or beneficial facility or industry in the community. The Cabildo rejected most of these requests, usually because the petitioners wanted the land between the levee and the river road. The council and the governors had agreed that it was in the public interest to keep this strip clear of obstruction.[10]

The Cabildo's awards of city-owned land contributed useful facilities or businesses to New Orleans. For example, Alexandro Baudin constructed a brickyard and tile kiln on such a grant. Dr. Pellegrue used a city lot with a vacant building as a leper hospital in 1798. Urbano Gaignie set up

---

the City Council," No. 38, June 28, 1775; "Digest," 131–32.

On February 12, 1770, O'Reilly issued a mortgage regulation on real estate. It required post commandants to give notice to the Cabildo *escribano*, with date and circumstances, so he could enter the information in a book he kept for that purpose ("Instruction to which particular lieutenants of the coast constituted by me should conform and who depend immediately on the general government of this province on everything in regard to politics and the administration of civil as well as criminal justice," O'Reilly, New Orleans, February 12, 1770, AGI, SD, leg. 2594). This regulation was ahead of its time for the rest of Spanish America. Post commandants carried out its instructions, at least in lower Louisiana. Although the order was sent to all posts in the colony, the St. Louis district never complied and kept records locally. Natchitoches, however, did comply (Baade, "Real Estate," 686–91). On November 3, 1770, Governor Unzaga issued an ordinance that required the transfer of land and slaves to be executed before notaries. Within the New Orleans district, the ordinance was followed, but it is unclear how it operated at the posts. Commandants sometimes acted as notaries, and verbal agreements before two witnesses were also made (Gayarré, *History of Louisiana,* III, 631–32; Baade, "Real Estate," 697).

9. Actas del Cabildo, I, 204, March 1, 1776, I, 210–11, October 11, 1776, III, (2), 20, April 18, 1788, III, (3), 209, March 13, 1795, IV, (1), 100, March 11, 1796, IV, (2), 178, December 20, 1798, IV, (1), 221, June 2, 1797, IV, (2), 67–68, October 27, 1797. On the Cabildo's claim that Carondelet granted city lots on his sole authority, see *ibid.,* IV, (2), 74, September 20, 1799, which is the Cabildo's letter to the king, New Orleans, September 13, 1799.

10. *Ibid.,* IV, (4), 97–98, June 5, 1801; Morazán, "Letters," II, 15–18, 18n.

a sawmill in 1801 on a grant although it was on the strip between the road and the levee. The public dance hall and Protestant cemetery were both built on land the city provided.[11]

An exception to the Cabildo pattern of granting lands for public facilities occurred in August, 1792. Hurel Dupre petitioned Governor Carondelet for a city lot on which to build a rice mill. Carondelet acquiesced to his request and informed the council after the fact. Despite the governor's usurpation of a Cabildo prerogative, the councillors approved it without comment.[12]

Because the Cabildo's rights over city lands were unclear, it occasionally ran into problems. In a complicated case in 1783, Guido Dufossat declared that two royal warehouses rested on part of a lot that belonged to him. The Cabildo sent a message to Intendant Navarro, asking for clarification of ownership because the intendancy was using the warehouses. Navarro believed that because the buildings were on the list of property the French government surrendered to the Spanish crown, the buildings and the land they were on belonged to the king. He argued that the land belonged to the buildings, not the buildings to the land. Dufossat tried to resolve the conflict and extricate himself from the dispute by ceding the land to the city in 1786. Intendant Navarro, however, then claimed that renounced lands reverted to the king. Unable to make a judgment in this dispute, Governor Miró forwarded the case to Madrid. Two years later, the king informed the city that he had decided to retain the lot for the Royal Treasury.[13]

The crown did even more than that and granted city-owned lands. O'Reilly had included the front lots on both sides of the Plaza de Armas (Jackson Square) as municipal land under the Cabildo's authority. Andrés Almonester later received these lots by a direct royal grant. Royal grants did not need the council's confirmation as land given by a governor supposedly required.[14]

---

11. *Actas del Cabildo*, III, (3), 208–209, March 13, 1795, IV, (1), 100–101, March 11, 1796; Duffy, ed., *Rudolph Matas History*, I, 261; Morazán, "Letters," II, 12–13.

12. *Actas del Cabildo*, III, (3), 15, August 11, 1792.

13. *Ibid.*, II, 183–84, July 11, 1783, II, 197–98, December 19, 1783, III, (1), 78–79, January 27, 1786, III, (2), 5, January 18, 1788; C. Richard Arena, "Landholding and Political Power in Spanish Louisiana," *LHQ*, XXXVIII (1955), 29.

14. Morazán, "Letters," I, 96; Asbury, *French Quarter*, 31–32; "Digest," 177. The land ad-

Another case that illustrates the Cabildo's confusion about land rights involved Francisco Bermúdez, who in 1797 requested a city lot to construct a wax factory. The Cabildo refused, claiming it was not authorized to make such a concession. Bermúdez, however, petitioned again, this time asking for three square arpents of land outside the city for a combined apiary and laboratory for bleaching wax. On the advice of Síndico Procurador General Francisco Caisergues, the councillors endorsed his petition and forwarded it to the crown. They also agreed that should the grant be made, he must leave a right-of-way along Carondelet Canal for a road.[15]

When the crown's answer arrived more than two years later, it carelessly granted Bermúdez a plot three arpents square, not the three square arpents he had requested. Furthermore, the crown's nine-square-arpent grant included parts of the Protestant cemetery and the Carondelet Canal that the Cabildo had already awarded. The council believed these uses were more important than the proposed apiary and wax factory. Bermúdez accepted the *regidores'* argument and asked for a substitute land grant the size the crown had decreed. Síndico Procurador General Félix Arnaud agreed providing that the substitute concession met all the provisions of the royal grant and the facility benefited the community as Bermúdez claimed it would. If it did not, the land would revert to the city. The Cabildo, however, again denied that it had the right to award such a concession or alter a royal grant. It advised Bermúdez to apply to the king again. Although he did, the Spanish era ended before an answer arrived. In the Bermúdez case, the city government used fine points of procedure to nul-

---

joining the Plaza de Armas had been the site of barracks for French soldiers. New barracks, however, were built for them at the lower end of the city before the Spaniards arrived.

15. Actas del Cabildo, IV, (1), 221, June 2, 1797, IV, (2), 1, July 14, 1797, IV, (2), 6–7, July 21, 1797. Bermúdez appears to have asked Governor Gayoso for land next to the city and its fortifications. The governor recommended that the land be farther removed from the city (Holmes, *Gayoso,* 215, and AGI, Indiferente General, leg. 1344). The type of wax factory Bermúdez proposed to establish was myrtle wax of the bayberry or waxberry tree (*Myrica cerifera*) (see Jack D. L. Holmes, "Louisiana Trees and Their Uses: Colonial Period," *Louisiana Studies,* VIII [1969], 49–51). Bermúdez was a notary public. In July, 1797, he presented the Cabildo with his royal appointment as *escribano real* and *notario público.* He had already been examined and approved by Auditor de Guerra Vidal (Actas del Cabildo, IV, [2], 11, July 28, 1797).

lify a royal grant. But a question can be raised as to whether Cabildo opposition helped or hindered the city's and the province's development.[16]

In October, 1788, the council turned its attention to the city cemetery, which was described as full. It was difficult to open a new grave without encountering bodies. Inasmuch as the cemetery was near the center of the city, there was fear that its crowded condition might jeopardize public health. The councillors agreed that with the vicar general's consent, they would establish another cemetery farther away and enclose it with a fence of stakes. They would suspend burials in the old cemetery and inter the dead at the new site. The medical community and the vicar general endorsed the Cabildo's decision. Land for a new cemetery was found outside the city walls, behind the new Charity Hospital, on a plot of ground three hundred feet by three hundred feet. The old cemetery would remain undisturbed until the city received crown permission to build on it.[17]

Royal consent arrived in August, 1789, but nothing was done about the old cemetery. The councillors decided not to move the bodies until putrefaction had been completed, which required several years more. Meanwhile, burials went on at the new cemetery. In June, 1795, Filberto Farge petitioned to acquire two of the twelve lots of the old cemetery. He wanted to establish warehouses on them for government and private use. The Cabildo, however, responded that it could not yet accept bids. Despite the passage of seven years since the last burial, the council seemed unwilling to risk disinterring the dead.[18]

In July, 1796, a problem arose with the new cemetery, located near the basin at the head of Carondelet Canal, which had just been completed and opened. Waters from the canal were damaging the cemetery. Moreover, the fence around the cemetery had deteriorated. The Cabildo agreed to fix the problems using convict labor. Work in repairing the canal and re-

16. Actas del Cabildo, IV, (3), 148, February 28, 1800, IV, (3), 165–66, April 4, 1800, IV, (3), 186–87, June 6, 1800; Morazán, "Letters," I, 95–96.

17. Actas del Cabildo, III, (2), 36–37, October 17, 1788, III, (2), 37–38, October 24, 1788.

18. Ibid., III, (2), 68–69, August 14, 1789, IV, (1), 42, June 20, 1795. The royal order of Aranjuez, May 2, 1789, which authorized the construction of buildings on the cemetery site, seemed to indicate that the land belonged to the Cabildo.

placing the fence was completed by November, at a cost of 297 pesos, 5 reales.[19]

In 1797, the *síndico procurador general* raised questions about burials in New Orleans. In July, he warned that it was unhealthy to bury persons inside the cathedral. Moreover, he advised the Cabildo that some people were using the old cemetery for burials. The yellow fever epidemic of the year before had caused numerous deaths. The *síndico procurador general* stated that many persons wanted to reopen the old cemetery, but he argued that public health demanded that it not be. The councillors agreed to prohibit interment in the cathedral and the old cemetery. They also advised ventilating the church building by opening its doors and windows. Burials, however, continued in the cathedral despite the Cabildo's action.[20]

In September the *síndico procurador general* inquired about the brick fence that had formerly enclosed the old cemetery. He explained that the fence had been demolished and the bricks hauled away. Anyone could now enter the cemetery, including animals and transients, treading freely through it. He said that the public had built the fence, the well-to-do donating money and materials and the poor providing their labor. He advocated fencing in the old cemetery immediately at the expense of the person who had used the bricks. The councillors, however, demurred, explaining that they had given Almonester permission to use the bricks in the construction of the new cathedral; therefore, they would pay for the fence. The next month, Almonester suggested moving the dead from the old cemetery, arguing that it was in wretched condition. Water was opening up graves and uncovering bodies, which birds and dogs then ate. The Cabildo agreed to discuss the move with church officials.[21] Despite the deplorable description given of the old cemetery, nothing was done for three years. Almonester probably had exaggerated grossly in portraying its condition.

19. *Ibid.,* IV, (1), 143, July 15, 1796, IV, (1), 163, November 3, 1796.
20. *Ibid.,* IV, (2), 4–5, July 21, 1797. On yellow fever epidemics in New Orleans, see the works by Jo Ann Carrigan, "Impact of Epidemic Yellow Fever on Life in Louisiana," *LH,* IV (1963), 5–34; and "Pestilence of 1796," 27–36. Almonester was buried in the cathedral in 1798 and Francisco Bouligny in 1800 (Samuel Wilson, Jr., "Almonester: Philanthropist and Builder in New Orleans," in *The Spanish in the Mississippi Valley, 1762–1804,* ed. John Francis McDermott [Urbana, Ill., 1974], 243–45; Din, *Francisco Bouligny,* 224).
21. Actas del Cabildo, IV, (2), 53–54, September 30, 1797, IV, (2), 66, October 27, 1797.

In November, 1800, Bishop Peñalver inquired about ownership of the old cemetery. He seemed as interested in renting out the land as the Cabildo because both wanted the revenue. This request initiated a dispute over rights, with both sides vehemently insisting they owned the land. By 1801 they were appealing to the crown for confirmation of their ownership. The councillors even ran an auction in which they assigned the twelve lots that made up the old cemetery to private individuals. When the lots were given out, Vidal, who sided with the church, advised the Cabildo to keep any money received in rent in a separate account because the city might lose its appeal. But construction on the lots could not proceed because the dead had not yet been removed from the grounds. Two requests to the acting bishop for permission to move the remains went unanswered. When at last he replied to a third request, he refused to grant permission. The Spanish era in Louisiana ended before the crown decided the issue.[22]

In July, 1796, the Cabildo became concerned about the uncertainty of its authority over public lands when Síndico Procurador General Gabriel Fonvergne complained that firewood cutters abused the public domain. He recommended that the Cabildo determine which lands belonged to the city, and going farther, he advised that persons without proper land titles be dispossessed. His statement implied that illegal grants of city land had been made in both the French and Spanish regimes. He requested that all such grants be repudiated. The council forwarded a petition to Governor Carondelet, asking him to issue a judicial decree with the measures it wanted.[23]

Carondelet appears to have ignored the Cabildo's petition for clarification of its land rights. In October, 1797, soon after he left Louisiana, the council asked his successor, Gayoso, to define the status of the lots Caron-

---

22. *Ibid.,* IV, (4), 33–36, November 7, 1800, IV, (4), 37–41, November 14, 1800, IV, (4), 91–92, May 22, 1801, IV, (4), 92–94, 95–96, May 29, 1801, IV, (4), 101–105, June 26, 1801, IV, (4), 145, December 4, 1801, IV, (4), 156–57, January 29, 1802, IV, (4), 167–68, February 12, 1802, IV, (4), 189–90, March 18, 1802, IV, (4), 194, April 2, 1802, IV, (4), 195–96, April 9, 1802; Morazán, "Letters," I, 32–33, 96, II, 18–19. Vidal also doubted that the new cemetery, which was *extramuros* (outside the city walls), was on city-owned property. His uncertainty pushed the Cabildo to reopen its investigation of the city limits and landholdings.

23. Actas del Cabildo, IV, (1), 141–42, July 15, 1796.

delet had granted to individuals in two city wards. The councillors believed that the lots belonged to the city and were taxable. As in most cases of uncertain jurisdiction, they placed the matter before the king. They asked to be allowed to grant these lots in perpetuity to their current tenants at the annual rate of 5 percent of their appraised value.[24]

In 1799, tired of not knowing the precise limits to city lands and its authority, the Cabildo acted. It appointed Regidores Luis Darby Danycan and Francisco de Riaño to determine both questions. Danycan, however, soon resigned from the city government. That same year, the council petitioned the king to extend New Orleans' boundaries at the upper and lower ends of the city. It wanted to include within its jurisdiction the lands owned by both the crown and private individuals. It sought clear title to the properties to enable it to grant lands or tax those already granted. The intendancy, however, opposed the Cabildo and petitioned the king not to alienate the land in question from the royal domain.[25]

In January, 1802, the problem of the Cabildo's land rights remained unresolved. The councillors charged the annual commissioners and Riaño to resume the investigation to determine the city limits. Former *regidor* Danycan submitted the documents from his earlier investigation to the new committee. There is no evidence that the council cleared up this issue before the Spanish period ended.[26]

Another important area that involved the Cabildo was building regulations. The majority of the building permits and regulations issued by the Cabildo concerned land grants and fire hazards. Still other decrees dealt with specific infringements on the public domain or affronts to the Cabildo's power and prestige. Because the councillors' interests at times conflicted with the crown's, consistency in the framing or enforcement of building regulations rarely existed. Most of the Cabildo's decisions that were enforced had the effect of setting precedent.[27]

24. *Ibid.,* IV, (2), 67–68, October 27, 1797.

25. *Ibid.,* IV, (3), 61, August 23, 1799, IV, (3), 71–72, September 13, 1799, IV, (4), 100, June 19, 1801, IV, (4), 216–17, June 4, 1802. Acting Intendant Morales' attempt to assert control over rural land grants in Louisiana in the summer of 1799 might have been a factor in the Cabildo's desire to clarify its authority in awarding lands.

26. *Ibid.,* IV, (4), 57, January 29, 1802, IV, (4), 216–17, June 4, 1802; "Digest," 64.

27. Actas del Cabildo, III, (2), 82, December 11, 1789, IV, (2), 131, June 1, 1798.

Only gradually did the New Orleans Cabildo recognize a need for building regulations to reduce the likelihood of fire. Two catastrophic conflagrations finally made the councillors consider the materials used in construction, particularly cypress wood. In colonial days cypress trees flourished throughout lower Louisiana. Its abundant supply, ease in working, and resistance to rot made cypress lumber a favorite in construction in New Orleans. Greatly disadvantageous, however, was its highly flammable character that turned New Orleans into a tinderbox. Trying to prevent fires in the city through building regulations, consequently, became a prime Cabildo objective. In the colonial cities of English North America, city governments favored brick and stone buildings with slate or tile roofs and decreed the periodic cleaning of chimneys. As in New Orleans, laws in the colonial English cities were not always enforced.[28]

The New Orleans blaze of 1794 produced efforts to avert the spread of fires. Shortly after this fire, the *síndico procurador general* attempted to destroy several wood and straw huts belonging to the Capuchin priests because they did not meet Cabildo regulations. They were built too close together, were uncared for, and had recently caught fire. The huts had been erected hastily under emergency conditions after the 1788 fire, with a special two-year permit that had long since expired. The church, however, continued to collect rent from them. In addition, the *síndico procurador general* suggested that the Almonester houses, located on the upper and lower sides of the Plaza de Armas, be demolished because they, too, were fire hazards. At the next meeting, the councillors asked the governor to destroy the houses or make them conform to the safety requirements that two Cabildo-appointed engineers approved.[29]

28. Robertson, ed., *Louisiana Under the Rule,* I, 167; Bridenbaugh, *Cities in Revolt,* 99. See also John Hebron Moore, "The Cypress Lumber Industry of the Lower Mississippi Valley During the Colonial Period," *LH,* XXIV (1983), 25–47.

29. Actas del Cabildo, III, (2), 13, March 26, 1788, III, (3), 184–85, December 16, 1794, III, (3), 187–89, December 19, 1794. A question can be raised about the Cabildo calling Almonester's houses a fire hazard because some of the *regidores* obviously did not like him.

The huts on church property had been built by the people who lived in them. In 1789, when the bishop's assistant levied a high rent on them, the tenants petitioned the Cabildo for title to the land. They asked the Cabildo to take their cause to the king. The council seems not to have acted on their petition ("Records of the City Council," No. 170, November 2, 1789).

Nearly a year later, Governor Carondelet reported his concern about the fire danger posed by large wooden structures, and he asked the Cabildo to take action. The *síndico procurador general* agreed to investigate and submit a report at the next meeting. On the basis of his report and recommendations, the councillors and governor issued a short building code. All two-story houses or duplexes were to be constructed of brick or adobe and plastered over with cement at least one inch thick. Their roofs had to be either tile or brick. Existing wooden houses were to be stuccoed with cement and were not to extend into the lot more than thirty feet. Only houses whose lot frontage measured less than thirty feet across could be built with the rear or sides facing the street.[30]

The new regulations appear not to have been enforced. In July, 1796, the *síndico procurador general* recommended similar measures to the Cabildo. He advised that wooden houses be placed in the rear of lots, be one story, have tile or otherwise fireproof roofs, and be separated from other structures by at least twenty feet. He urged a six-month deadline for houses to comply with the regulations. The councillors resolved to request an edict from the governor.[31]

The regulations, however, were still being ignored in August, 1797, when Síndico Procurador General Fortier requested the destruction of the huts on the levee because they were a hazard. Since their condemnation in December, 1794, they had not been fireproofed as the law required. In August, 1797, when Gayoso assumed the governorship, the council asked him to enforce its 1794 resolution.[32]

Governor Gayoso and his successor Casa-Calvo both seem not to have responded vigorously to Cabildo efforts to enforce the fire regulations. In April, 1800, the councillors noted that the ordinances, particularly those requiring fireproof roofs, were neither complied with nor enforced. The

---

30. Actas del Cabildo, IV, (1), 58–59, October 2, 1795, IV, (1), 61, October 9, 1795; Chandler, "Life in New Orleans," 181–82. New Orleans residents resisted using bricks in construction because they were expensive. Moreover, those of local manufacture were soft and sandy and did not hold up well against the excessive moisture of the area. Therefore, they had to be plastered over with cement, which added to their already high construction cost (Robertson, ed., *Louisiana Under the Rule,* I, 169).

31. Actas del Cabildo, IV, (1), 146–47, July 29, 1796.

32. *Ibid.,* IV, (2), 25–26, August 23, 1797.

councillors could not decide how to do it, but they agreed that they must implement the edicts and compel the use of fireproof roofs. At the same time, the *alguacil mayor* attempted to halt the construction of a cabaret in a forbidden area that lacked a fireproof roof. He wanted to condemn the building and do the same to any structure built in prohibited zones. The other councillors agreed.[33]

As the public protector, Síndico Procurador General Pedro Dulcido Barran tried to gain acceptance for the construction laws, especially in building houses. He requested an extraordinary session to ensure the presence of all Cabildo members. The councillors agreed, but acting civil governor Vidal called off the meeting. Citing the Code O'Reilly, he argued that only he could call an extraordinary session. He added that he was then too busy to involve himself in Cabildo affairs.[34]

The council responded to Vidal by rejecting his decision. It requested a clarification from higher authority on whether a cabildo could meet in an extraordinary assembly when asked by the *síndico procurador general*. Vidal then yielded and called a meeting for May 26, but he did not know if his duties would permit him to attend.[35]

The extraordinary session produced less than satisfactory results. At the meeting, each attending member gave his opinion on how to deal with fire hazards. They all recognized that the main problem was noncompliance with the existing laws. At the meeting's close, they agreed to forward a copy of the minutes to Vidal for him to take "whatever action" he chose.[36]

After receiving the minutes of the extraordinary meeting, Vidal waited three weeks before replying. He argued that enforcement of the building laws would work unjustified hardship on the majority of the city's residents because they could not afford the high price of tile. He added that even if house owners could afford tile, they should be given several months

33. *Ibid.,* IV, (3), 169–70, April 18, 1800. The inhabitants of English colonial cities also frequently evaded fire regulations. For example, a fire in Charleston in 1745 destroyed nearly all of the city's seventeenth-century buildings. It resulted in regulations that permitted the construction of only stone or brick buildings and prohibited the use of wooden shingles. Residents, however, dodged compliance (Bridenbaugh, *Cities in Revolt,* 18–19).

34. Actas del Cabildo, IV, (3), 176, May 2, 1800, IV, (3), 178–79, May 16, 1800. Vidal rarely attended Cabildo sessions after April 18, 1800.

35. *Ibid.,* IV, (3), 180–81, May 23, 1800, IV, (3), 181–85, May 26, 1800.

36. *Ibid.,* IV, (3), 181–85, May 26, 1800.

to comply with the edicts. He agreed to destroy some shacks that constituted a hazard, but further action had to await the arrival of the new governor general, who was expected soon. A few structures located between the levee and the road were demolished before June, 1801.[37]

Despite Vidal's reasoning, the Cabildo remained dissatisfied. It supplied the *síndico procurador general* with copies of all the documents related to fire regulation. He used them to draft an appeal to the crown for redress from the *auditor de guerra*'s nonenforcement of the fire laws. The government had not answered the appeal when the Spanish period ended. No doubt in this case Vidal was at least partially right.[38]

Other matters concerning building regulations also exacerbated relations between the Cabildo and Vidal. In February, 1802, the council tried to stop the construction of a small house between the levee and the Plaza de Armas on land disputed between the Royal Treasury and the city. Carondelet had earlier granted the lot to Sergeant Major Guillemard at a tax or rent of two pesos monthly. Upon learning that Guillemard had failed to pay the rent regularly, the Cabildo ruled that the building he was constructing had to be demolished. In addition, it ordered the razing of two other construction projects that violated the same laws. It justified its decree on the basis that indifference would set a dangerous precedent and encourage wholesale violations of the law.[39]

Although Vidal had initially agreed with the Cabildo, he soon reversed himself and allowed Guillemard to resume paying rent on the disputed property. Faced with Vidal's duplicity, the Cabildo consulted its newly engaged legal counselor. Attorney Martínez opined that the house must be torn down. He added that the *auditor de guerra* should be informed through an official letter and, if necessary, an appeal made to the superior court. The councillors accepted his advice, but the retrocession occurred before the issue was resolved.[40]

Vidal's refusal to cooperate with the Cabildo on building and zoning codes becomes less understandable in view of a protest he made in 1797.

37. *Ibid.,* IV, (3), 188–90, June 14, 1800, IV, (4), 98, June 5, 1801.
38. *Ibid.,* IV, (3), 100, June 19, 1801.
39. *Ibid.,* IV, (4), 178–79, February 26, 1802, IV, (4), 180–81, March 5, 1802, IV, (4), 185–88, March 12, 1802, IV, (4), 189, March 18, 1802.
40. *Ibid.,* IV, (4), 189–90, March 18, 1802, IV, (4), 193, March 26, 1802.

At that time he demanded that a house and shop being built by black-smith Juan Dumaine be demolished. Dumaine was constructing them between Vidal's residence and the levee. Vidal argued that noise from Dumaine's forge would cause him discomfort and interfere with his duties as judge advocate. To support his charges, he cited legal reasons: clear access on the levee was a necessity in case of fire, and buildings in that area aided smugglers and thieves. He further claimed that Gayoso's permit to Dumaine was unlawful because only the king could grant such lands.[41]

The *auditor de guerra* added that the shacks built on the levee after the 1788 fire were illegal. Because the Cabildo regarded the levee as city property, the *mayordomo de propios* should be charging owners more rent (or tax) than one peso monthly per shack. Vidal then widened his attack to include all persons who had served as *síndico procurador general* for their failure to act responsibly in these matters. He concluded his tirade by citing Dumaine's alleged "lack of patriotism" during the recent war with France. Gayoso forwarded Vidal's petition to the crown without comment.[42]

Vidal's inconsistency in enforcing building and zoning regulations was truly remarkable. From advocating strict adherence to the building regulations in 1797, Vidal shifted three years later to become the major obstacle to Cabildo enforcement of the same laws. His selectivity in fulfilling his duties as well as his disreputable character thwarted the council's efforts in fire prevention.

Despite Vidal's—and later Salcedo's—opposition, Cabildo efforts to protect New Orleans from fire hazards had some effect, although not as much as it would have liked. Eye-witnesses in New Orleans tell differing stories about compliance with city fire regulations. Alliot states that they were neither obeyed nor enforced after Carondelet left the colony in 1797, which suggests that they were complied with up to that time. Sibley observed in 1802 that New Orleans houses had flat roofs made of slate, tile, or cement despite the expense. But he seems not to have visited the entire city and based his description on the houses near the river. A third eye-witness, James Pitot, who was probably more accurate, wrote in 1802

41. Jack D. L. Holmes, "Vidal and Zoning in Spanish Louisiana, 1797," *LH,* XIV (1973), 271–82.
42. *Ibid.*

of the city's 1,000 to 1,200 buildings, "700 to 800 houses are still of frame construction." The houses closer to the river generally complied with the building codes, but they were the city's more expensive structures and owned by the wealthier citizens.[43]

That the Cabildo did not achieve full compliance with its building regulations and codes is not surprising. In the last years of Spanish rule, the city government lost the support of its superior officials, Vidal and Salcedo. Moreover, enforcement of rigid and expensive building codes favored by the council could come only with time and improvement in the economic status of many of the city's inhabitants.

43. Alliot, "Historical and Political Reflections," 93; Sibley, "Journal," 478; Pitot, *Observations,* 109. Clark estimates the number of the city's houses at about 1,600 in 1800, "mostly of brick or stone covered with tile or plaster" (*New Orleans,* 253). Although the number of houses is perhaps accurate, their composition is not.

Moore, in "Cypress Lumber Industry," 46, based on François Marie Perrin du Lac's *Travels,* 89–92, states that brick was more popular by 1801. Moore then adds, "Despite the rising popularity of brick, however, a very large quantity of cypress was utilized to repair the losses incurred in these two fires." Therefore, it may be surmised that more wooden than brick houses were constructed in New Orleans despite the building regulations.

TWELVE

Liaison and Ceremonial Functions

VISITORS to New Orleans in the late eighteenth century often commented on the Cabildo's ceremonial activities. If they were in the city at the right time, they could have witnessed the festivities that greeted Governor General Carondelet on his arrival and the celebrations held upon the accession of Carlos IV to the Spanish throne (described in Chapter One). The Cabildo participated in these celebrations because it played an integral role in the life of the city. According to the thinking of the time, the councillors demonstrated by example to the other subjects the gratitude, loyalty, and devotion owed to their king and his secular and religious representatives for the benefits the city received.

Besides this visible ceremonial role, but not as evident to visitors, was the Cabildo's liaison function to assist citizens when calamities befell them and to obtain support for worthwhile projects. The city council was the natural conduit through which citizens could petition the government for relief or assistance. Although some of these activities were routine, others were vital to the well-being of the colony. The residents conveyed their needs and desires through the council to the proper authority.[1] Both the

---

1. Many of the Cabildo's liaison functions have already been discussed. Virtually each time the council requested a change in policy or regulation to benefit residents, it was exercising its liaison role.

liaison and ceremonial functions reflected the Cabildo's position as an important link in the chain of colonial administration.[2]

Among its functions, the Cabildo furnished the crown and the Council of the Indies with information on a variety of subjects relative to the province's welfare. Paramount among them were justifications and requests for liberalizing trade regulations, the issue and withdrawal of paper money, and the distribution of royal relief after major fires and hurricanes.

Communications with the crown followed several steps. The *síndico procurador general,* acting as the people's representative, described in writing the problem at hand to the council and proposed recommendations for dealing with it. The councillors then discussed it, and if they approved, the annual commissioners drew up a formal petition. The council forwarded the completed petition through the proper channels, usually the governor, to the crown. The king might then take up to three years to respond, and he might never answer.

Commerce was central to the well-being and even the survival of the colony. With planters constituting a majority of its members through most of its existence, the Cabildo not surprisingly constantly advocated in favor of liberal trade laws. When France ceded Louisiana to Spain in 1763, the colony was already in desperate economic straits. France had subsidized the province with approximately 800,000 livres (160,000 pesos) annually. Because this sum was insufficient, smuggling became rampant in the final years of French Louisiana. Initially, the Spanish takeover did not improve conditions. O'Reilly's trade regulations failed to provide adequate markets for Louisiana's products and reduced the already meager subsidy to 115,000 pesos.[3]

2. On this issue, see Marzahl, "Creoles and Government," 638.

3. Clark, *New Orleans,* 149, 166, 221; Caughey, *Bernardo de Gálvez,* 4, 34, 51, 70-71; Allen Christelow, "Proposals for a French Company for Spanish Louisiana," *Mississippi Valley Historical Review,* XXVII (1941), 603–611; C. Richard Arena, "Philadelphia–Spanish New Orleans Trade in the 1790s," *LH,* II (1961), 429–45; Nasatir, ed., "Government Employees and Salaries," 886; King, "Social and Economic Life," 170; Jack D. L. Holmes, "Some Economic Problems of the Spanish Governors of Louisiana," *Hispanic American Historical Review,* XLII (1962), 527; Arthur Preston Whitaker, ed. and trans., *Documents Relating to the Commercial Policy of Spain in the Floridas, with Incidental Reference to Louisiana* (Deland, Fla., 1931), and "The Commerce of Louisiana and the Floridas at the End of the Eighteenth Century," *Hispanic American Historical Review,* VIII (1928), 190–203.

Only several months after the general left Louisiana in early March, 1770, the Cabildo first requested a relaxation of his trade policy that restricted Louisiana's commerce to Spain and Cuba. At the request of Síndico Procurador General Luis Ranson, the council petitioned the crown for permission to export tobacco duty free to Cap Français in return for slaves. They argued that the colony needed a larger labor force to boost its productivity. The king approved the request.[4]

A year later, Síndico Procurador General Santiago Toutant Beauregard reported that the province was headed toward economic ruin, primarily because of restrictions that severely impeded commerce. At Beauregard's suggestion, the council resolved to inform the king of the colony's deplorable condition and ask him to take whatever action he deemed appropriate for its relief. It appointed the annual commissioners Francisco María de Reggio and Francisco Olivier de Vezin to draft the formal request to the king.[5]

In the first years of Spanish rule, the crown granted Louisiana only minor trade concessions. The greatest benefit came from Governor Unzaga's blind eye to smuggling. Starting in 1776 with José de Gálvez as minister of the Indies, Spain began permitting Louisiana to trade with the French West Indies and indirectly with France and later the United States. By 1778 the *síndico procurador general* reported to the Cabildo that the inhabitants wanted to show the king their gratitude. The council sent him a letter of appreciation for the many favors that encouraged the province's growth and development. The councillors pointed out in their report

---

4. Actas del Cabildo, I, 22, 25–26, June 30, 1770, I, 27–28, July 6, 1770.

5. *Ibid.*, I, 55, August 16, 1771, I, 56, August 23, 1771, I, 58–59, October 4, 1771. Trade in Spanish Louisiana was initially so restricted that until February, 1772, it was uncertain if New Orleans was permitted to trade with other portions of the colony. Minister of the Indies Julián de Arriaga gave permission for this trade and ordered the return of impounded property to persons who had been caught engaging in it (Arriaga to Altarriba, February 20, 1772, "Confidential Dispatches of Don Bernardo de Gálvez," 4–5).

A lengthy delay followed because none of the councillors was fluent in Spanish. They finally made their representation in French, pointing out that their use of this language was owing to ignorance of Spanish and did not imply lack of respect to the Spanish monarch and nation (Actas del Cabildo, I, 58–59, October 4, 1771).

the increase in population and prosperity that they attributed to the king's favors.[6]

Spain's war with Great Britain (1779–1783), however, disrupted the colony's growing commerce. After the conquest of British West Florida ended in the spring of 1781, the council asked that trade restrictions be lifted. It wrote directly to the king and the Council of the Indies, bypassing Governor Gálvez, who had recently departed from Louisiana. Perhaps the councillors knew that Gálvez was then supporting his father-in-law, St. Maxent, who was in Spain to secure extensive Indian trading privileges. The Council of the Indies soon gave Louisiana provisional permission for trade with Haiti. Although Gálvez had addressed a similar request to the crown and had earlier permitted trade with the French colony, the Cabildo's independent spirit annoyed him and he reprimanded it for exceeding its authority. The Cabildo replied that it had not intended to be insubordinate and cited Book VIII, Title 16, Laws 76 and 77, of the Laws of the Indies that permitted direct communication with the crown. If the laws had been superseded, the governor needed only to inform them and they would refrain from further insubordination.[7]

Gálvez instructed the Cabildo not to violate the policies he had laid down for the province's trade in French vessels from Haiti. Because the council believed that it had been following his policies, it requested specific rules for trading in French ships. Before Gálvez replied, the crown issued new policies that extended trade. Intendant Martín Navarro also made a detailed evaluation of Louisiana's economic needs and potential. After St. Maxent received his trading privileges in 1781, the crown revised its decision and allowed all its subjects to participate in the "free trade" decree of January 22, 1782, so as not to appear to be favoring the governor's relative St. Maxent.[8]

6. Actas del Cabildo, I, 237, December 19, 1777, I, 243, February 13, 1778, I, 245, March 13, 1778.

7. *Ibid.,* II, 67–68, August 17, 1781, II, 80–81, October 26, 1781, II, 82–87, November 9, 1781.

8. *Ibid.,* II, 89–90, December 7, 1781; Burson, *Stewardship,* 88–89. The commercial privileges of January 22, 1782, are in *SMV,* Pt. II, 1–4. They also granted Louisiana certain exemptions from the free trade regulation of October 12, 1778 (*ibid.,* 4–5). In his introduction to the privileges of 1782, the king referred to the influence of Gálvez and St. Maxent in making the regulations.

The free trade decree, which was not completely free, opened commerce between Louisiana and designated Spanish and friendly or neutral ports. With few exceptions, trade was to be conducted in Spanish or Louisiana ships. Louisiana was not to export specie, except in exchange for slaves. All trade was subject to a 6 percent import-export tax, save the West Indies trade, which was taxed at only 2 percent. The decree exempted Louisiana's ships from several taxes for two years to stimulate the growth of the colony's merchant fleet. The other decrees were to last for ten years.[9]

Long before the free trade edict expired, the Cabildo requested extensions for an additional ten years. A royal order of May 28, 1791, continued the trade concessions until the crown formulated new regulations. In September, 1793, the Cabildo received a royal letter that modified the free trade privileges. It increased the import-export duties, which prompted the Cabildo to petition several times for their reduction. The crown, however, did not reply.[10]

Because Spain abandoned its pro-monarchist European allies and joined Republican France in an alliance in 1796, war erupted with Great Britain which severely hurt Spanish shipping. On November 18, 1797, the Spanish government permitted its subjects in America to use neutral foreign ships to import and export their goods. The order benefited Louisiana greatly. On April 20, 1799, however, the king revoked the decree, producing protests in nearly every quarter in Louisiana. The Cabildo joined with the city's commercial corps and the civil and military governors in urging acting intendant Morales to suspend its enforcement. Besieged, Morales yielded and sent representations from the Cabildo, the merchants, Casa-Calvo, and Vidal to support his action. Until he heard from the king, the royal order of April 20, 1799 would remain suspended.[11]

9. Burson, *Stewardship,* 88–89. Although the decree did not sanction free trade in the modern sense of the term, it greatly liberalized existing policies. It was also ambiguously worded and left loopholes which the colonials immediately seized.

10. Actas del Cabildo, III, (1), 36–37, February 25, 1785, III, (1), 143, April 20, 1787, III, (2), 16, April 4, 1788, III, (2), 44–45, January 16, 1789, III, (2), 142–43, September 16, 1791, III, (3), 88–89, September 16, 1793, III, (3), 105–108, December 13, 1793, III, (3), 154, August 8, 1794, III, (3), 167–69, October 10, 1794, IV, (1), 206–10, March 17, 1797.

11. *Ibid.,* IV, (3), 79–80, September 27, 1799, IV, (3), 89, October 4, 1799, IV, (3), 89–97, October 8, 1799; Morales to Miguel Cayetano Soler, No. 354, New Orleans, November 30, 1799, with enclosures, in "File [*expediente*] on the enlargement of rules for the government of Louisiana through neutrals," AHN, Est., leg. 3892 *bis,* exped. 1.

It was at this time that the council appointed Síndico Procurador General Félix Arnaud, rather than the annual commissioners, to compose its own representation to the crown. Arnaud secured the help of an unnamed friend to draw up the document. The Cabildo was sufficiently pleased with the results of the representation that it voted the anonymous author a one-hundred-peso reward for his efforts.[12]

The Cabildo also often sought government assistance when disasters occurred. Aid sometimes came in the form of edicts liberalizing trade. Two years before the 1782 free trade edict, a hurricane had inflicted severe damage to the city, ships on the river, and crops throughout lower Louisiana. Intendant Navarro sent the crown a lengthy report on the injury inflicted on the colony. In reply, the king promised to send aid.[13]

Following the 1788 fire, the Cabildo requested royal assistance again. The intendant provided food and other supplies for the city's immediate need from the crown's warehouse. He also supported the council's requests for royal aid to enable the city to recover and rebuild. The Cabildo's petition asked for an extension of the free trade privilege to stimulate the colony's commerce; a large interest-free royal loan for rebuilding the city to be repaid over ten years; and the withdrawal from circulation of paper money, which hurt the colony's commerce. The council forwarded the petition to the crown through Governor Miró.[14]

In the fall of 1794, the Cabildo cited a series of misfortunes to justify liberalizing commerce. Three hurricanes had hit the colony within the past thirteen months. The council, however, wrote too soon because the greatest calamity that year occurred in December—the 1794 New Orleans fire. The city's disasters totaled two large fires, five hurricanes, and the occasional flooding caused by the Mississippi River, all in the space of fifteen years. The Cabildo again asked for a reduction of import duties to 6 percent and a ten-year, one-million-peso loan for rebuilding the city. Although the crown replied that it would assist the city, a loan was not part of the help granted.[15]

12. Actas del Cabildo, IV, (3), 109–10, November 15, 1799, IV, (3), 113, November 22, 1799.
13. *Ibid.,* II, 59–60, June 15, 1781.
14. *Ibid.,* III, (2), 12–13, March 26, 1788, III, (2), 16–19, April 4, 1788.
15. *Ibid.,* III, (3), 167–69, October 10, 1794, III, (3), 187–89, December 19, 1794, IV, (1), 46–47, July 17, 1795.

The Cabildo also voiced its opinion about the circulation of paper money, which first appeared in 1780 during the war against Great Britain. After the war, the crown failed to send specie to redeem the paper money that had depreciated 70 percent by 1785. Because it interfered with commerce, the Cabildo petitioned the king to retire the paper money. Two years later, after no answer came, the Louisiana government needed specie desperately. The Cabildo asked the intendant to issue more treasury notes to acquire the needed silver. Navarro agreed to do so, and the council again petitioned the king on the same subject. In October, 1788, the crown consented and ordered the total withdrawal of paper money in the colony. Then, in an unexpected move, the government seized 170,000 of the 200,000 pesos earmarked to redeem the paper money for the personal use of the Condesa de Gálvez (the former governor's widow), who was living in Madrid. Louisiana's paper money remained in circulation for several more years.[16]

In 1797 the Cabildo asked for a new issue of paper currency. A new war with Great Britain that began in October, 1796, had cut off shipment of the Mexican subsidy, and the colony needed money. Because the return to paper currency would injure Louisiana merchants in competing with their American counterparts, the council asked the king to lower the import-export tax to 2 percent on silver and 4 percent on merchandise. The crown appears not to have replied to the request.[17]

The Cabildo's liaison activities in trade carried over into slave importations and slave control. This has already been discussed in Chapter Seven.

Besides making Louisiana's desires known to the monarch, the Cabildo was responsible for disseminating royal directives to the inhabitants. This was done primarily through the town crier and the printing of posters and flyers. Initially, the Cabildo had employed and controlled both the

---

16. *Ibid.*, III, (1), 37, February 25, 1785, III, (1), 143, April 20, 1787, III, (1), 136, March 2, 1787, III, (1), 137, March 9, 1787, III, (2), 18–19, April 4, 1788, III, (2), 44–45, January 16, 1789; Coutts, "Martín Navarro," I, 197–98.

The use of paper money carried hazards other than inflation and depreciation. In 1783 Alexander Greydon and William Jones of the Natchez district were found guilty of counterfeiting. Miró sentenced them to death and exiled two of their accomplices (Porteous, ed. and trans., "Index," *LHQ*, XIX [1936], 825–26).

17. Actas del Cabildo, IV, (1), 207–209, March 17, 1797.

town crier and the public printer. In 1781 the council dismissed the printer to reduce expenses, and it subsequently lost control of the town crier. The government, however, revived the office of printer and though the office-holder still bore the title of printer for the king and Cabildo, he and the town crier were under the governor's control. In the late Spanish period, when the council wanted to inform the public about an event, it had to ask the governor to make the news known through the printer or town crier.[18]

Despite its loss of control over announcements, the Cabildo retained some responsibility for informing the public of the royal will in specialized areas. For example, when in 1792 the king established a college in Granada for the sons of Spanish American nobles, the Cabildo published the news. In a related area, the king issued several edicts requiring children in Louisiana's schools to be taught Spanish. The Cabildo was responsible for promulgating these orders and their enforcement. It also ensured that papal bulls sent to the colony were read to the public at Sunday masses.[19]

Besides the liaison services already mentioned, the council functioned in more practical areas. It occasionally arranged for the lodging of officers and troops coming to the colony. It worked with the intendancy, borrowing royal money in times of need or lending city funds when surpluses permitted. When the king imposed a war donation on the colony in 1796, the Cabildo encouraged the inhabitants to display their loyalty by contributing generously.[20]

The council used the open cabildo to permit leading citizens to discuss issues of vital importance to them. *Cabildo abierto* resolutions, however,

18. *Ibid.,* II, 66, July 27, 1781, IV, (3), 194, June 27, 1800. New Orleans acquired its first newspaper in 1794, when Governor Carondelet allowed the public printer to publish *Le Moniteur de la Louisiane.* The printer also published ordinances, primers, and catechisms for the schools and government forms. He could sell copies of public proclamations to individuals who wanted their own (Robertson, ed., *Louisiana Under the Rule,* I, 189; O'Reilly Proclamation of September 7, 1769, *SMV,* Pt. I, 93; Morazán, "Letters," I, 92).

19. Actas del Cabildo, III, (3), 19, September 7, 1792, IV, (2), 18, 21–22, August 5, 1797, III, (3), 126, February 14, 1794. Technically, the king had control of the church in the Spanish colonies in all matters except doctrine and religious discipline. The crown dispatched papal bulls to the colonies through royal officials (Haring, *Spanish Empire in America,* 167).

20. Actas del Cabildo, III, (2), 195–96, March 30, 1792, IV, (1), 124, May 24, 1796, IV, (3), 18, March 1, 1799.

were not binding. Among the problems discussed in these meetings were slavery, the meat supply, natural disasters, fires, and health measures. By accepting the opinions and recommendations from the *vecinos* (leading residents), the council secured support for measures that it approved.[21]

The Cabildo exercised its liaison capacity at other times. When the council opposed Morales' land regulations in 1799, it petitioned the king to act favorably in behalf of the colonists. Again, when Morales suspended the American right of deposit at New Orleans, the Cabildo first got Morales to exempt American foodstuffs and later appealed to the crown to rescind the suspension entirely.[22]

The Cabildo also performed the minor liaison function of providing personal endorsements for the inhabitants. These testimonials were supposed to include certification of nobility and the purity of blood, but because the French regime had not kept such records and the 1788 fire destroyed many relevant documents, the Cabildo was unable to furnish these certificates. It could only provide civilian officials and clergy who asked for them with written testimonials of their character, service, and status in the colony. Except in a few instances when the person requesting the endorsement was petitioning for a favor, it is unknown how these documents were used.[23]

Part of the criticism that both contemporary observers and historians have leveled at the Cabildo has been the honorary nature of its offices and the petty quibbling and pomposity the council members indulged in. Although these criticisms have some validity, especially in the late Spanish period, the New Orleans Cabildo was much less ceremony-oriented than other cabildos of the late Spanish Empire. Possibly the presence on the

---

21. *Cabildos abiertos* are treated in the preceding chapters. See also Charles Chapman, *Colonial Hispanic America: A History* (New York, 1933), 132–33; and Diffie, *Latin-American Civilization,* 618.

22. Actas del Cabildo, IV, (3), 77, September 13, 1799; Clark, *New Orleans,* 246; Whitaker, *Mississippi Question,* 189–96.

23. Actas del Cabildo, III, (3), 6, January 25, 1788, III, (2), 100–101, May 7, 1790, III, (2), 130, May 6, 1791, III, (2), 203–204, May 18, 1792, III, (3), 45, January 11, 1793, III, (3), 71–72, June 14, 1793, III, (3), 95, October 25, 1793, III, (3), 130, March 14, 1794, IV, (1), 38–39, June 12, 1795, IV, (1), 154–55, September 9, 1796, IV, (2), 84, December 7, 1797, IV, (3), 26, April 19, 1799, IV, (3), 100–101, October 18, 1799; Morazán, "Letters," I, 77–82; "Dispatches of Carondelet," IV, (IV), 135–36, 139, 151.

council of French members who loathed spending for Spanish celebrations was one reason. New Orleans' frontier setting might have been another inhibiting factor. Certainly, the press of finances for worthwhile projects such as street lighting, fire protection, levees, drainage, and streets was instrumental in keeping ceremonial and festival spending to a minimum. The Cabildo expended considerably more for public works and other essential services and concomitantly less for ceremonial purposes than was generally true in Spanish America.[24]

Ceremonial spending in Spanish New Orleans was usually politic, customary, and relatively reasonable. It included activities related to the royal family, the governor general, religious services, regalia for Cabildo members and employees, accouterments of the *casa capitular,* or some combination of these. Examination of the Cabildo's expenditures illustrates its usual frugality and occasional lavishness.

The Cabildo first ventured into ceremonial spending in 1770, when it provided formal livery for its two porters. Although livery was customary throughout Spanish America, Governor Unzaga suspended the council's purchases because the city treasury lacked funds. When the treasury showed a surplus a year later, Unzaga approved the purchase of these uniforms. The costumes cost only 119 pesos, 2 reales, but the porters' silver badges cost an additional 447 pesos, 7 reales. Later the same year, the council purchased a royal standard for 174 pesos, 4 reales. These items represented heavy expenditures for the city's then modest revenues, but overall the Cabildo was not yet involved in substantial public spending.[25]

In 1774 the Cabildo decorated its chambers with portraits of Carlos III and the Prince of Asturias, the heir to the Spanish throne. The annual commissioners authorized the portraits and hung the finished works in the *sala capitular.* The results pleased the council, and the next year it provided additional portraits and decorations for the *sala capitular.* The total expense for these additions was 234 pesos, 6 reales.[26]

Shortly after the councillors decorated their meeting room, they dressed

24. Ezquerra Abadía, "Un presupuesto americano," 694.
25. Actas del Cabildo, I, 36, November 16, 1770, I, 62–63, November 22, 1771, I, 72–73, February 21, 1772, I, 76–77, March 27, 1772, I, 83, July 3, 1772.
26. *Ibid.,* I, 150, February 18, 1774, I, 156, April 15, 1774, I, 189, August 5, 1775, I, 196, November 3, 1775.

the town crier, Nicolas Jourdain, in a suit of clothes befitting his position. Although the members agreed to employ frugality, they did not follow through. When the *mayordomo* reported the cost of the uniform, he included it with an expenditure for a bench for the church, which collectively cost 487 pesos, 5 reales. It can be safely assumed that the uniform cost considerably more than the bench.[27]

Religious expenses constituted an important part of the Cabildo's ceremonial spending. Before 1778, the council's religious costs had been only for a church bench and a Eucharistic canopy. That year, however, the council advanced 209 pesos, 4 reales for the purchase of a cross and a second canopy to be used in the parish church. The Cabildo authorized the use of city funds in the expectation that Vicar General Cirilo de Barcelona would reimburse the council. Unexpectedly, he refused to repay the money, and, although the Cabildo authorized the *síndico procurador general* to take whatever steps were necessary to collect the debt, he seems not to have done so. On the contrary, two months later Father Cirilo appeared before the council and requested that, in conformity with the custom in other metropolises of the Spanish Empire, the city pay for a pair of portable altars to be used in the processions of the feast of Corpus Christi. The councillors agreed and appointed one of the annual *regidores*, Nicolas Forstall, to commission and supervise the work.[28]

After the 1788 fire, when Andrés Almonester pledged to build a new church for the city, he requested the Cabildo to set a date for the ceremony to lay the cornerstones for the new edifice. The Cabildo appointed two councillors, Alcalde Ordinario José de Ortega and Alférez Real Carlos de Reggio, to lay two of the cornerstones. Presumably, Almonester, as patron of the church, and the governor, as royal vice patron, laid the other two stones. When the church neared completion, Almonester, who had purchased the office of *regidor-alférez real* from Carlos de Reggio, received the task of ordering church chairs for the Cabildo members. They cost the city 857 pesos, 6½ reales. Additional seats were added in 1797, when the

---

27. *Ibid.,* I, 156, March 18, 1774, I, 157, April 22, 1774.
28. *Ibid.,* I, 83, July 3, 1772, I, 262–63, January 29, 1779, I, 270, March 5, 1779, I, 276–77, May 7, 1779.

council grew by six *regidores*. All the chairs were covered in damask at a cost of 46 pesos, 3 reales.[29]

The Cabildo's ceremonial relations with the church were not always amicable. For example, in 1796 Louisiana's new bishop, Luis de Peñalver y Cárdenas, sent the Cabildo a pointed letter inviting the members to attend the Sunday afternoon Lenten services at the cathedral. The council demurred, stating coolly that its custom was to attend as a body only those functions required by law. It added, nevertheless, that any of its members in the city might attend as individuals, both to please the bishop and to set an example for the populace.[30]

The Cabildo also entered into other ceremonial activities when circumstance or good politics warranted. In 1778 the council attended a Te Deum of thanksgiving for the favors that the king had bestowed on Louisiana. When Carlos III learned of the city's activities, he sent the council a flowery letter of appreciation.[31]

On April 14, 1782, the Cabildo ordered a day of rejoicing to celebrate the royal *cédula* of that year, which liberalized commerce and permitted trade between New Orleans and France, including the French colonies. The ceremonies in the city consisted of parades, illumination of houses, decoration of ships in the river, and cannon salutes fired by the vessels.[32]

In February, 1784, New Orleans celebrated the peace treaty between Spain and England. The Cabildo published the royal *cédula* announcing the peace, and the officials attended a solemn high mass, which was followed by the traditional Te Deum. The council decreed the customary observance, illuminating the city for three nights.[33]

The Cabildo followed similar procedures upon notification of the birth of royal children. It complied with the instructions contained in the royal orders. Municipal expenditures were slight on these occasions. For a

29. *Ibid.,* III, (2), 48, February 13, 1789, III, (3), 183, December 12, 1794, IV, (1), 27, May 9, 1795, IV, (2), 56, October 6, 1797, IV, (2), 62, October 20, 1797.

30. *Ibid.,* IV, (1), 91–92, February 5, 1796. On the Catholic church in Louisiana and the Floridas in the Spanish era, see Michael J. Curley, *Church and State in the Spanish Floridas (1783–1822)* (Washington, D.C., 1940).

31. Actas del Cabildo, I, 257, December 11, 1778.

32. Clark, *New Orleans,* 244–45.

33. Actas del Cabildo, II, 202–203, January 30, 1784; Burson, *Stewardship,* 258.

prince, the Cabildo illuminated only the *casa capitular* and its gallery. For a princess, the council did less and limited celebration to a high mass and a Te Deum. When the Cabildo learned in March, 1785, of the birth of a royal princess the previous October, however, it held the usual Te Deum after mass on Sunday, which was followed by the illumination of the private residences of the *regidores* and prominent citizens. Not as much was done for a royal grandson. When the wife of the Prince of Asturias, the royal heir, gave birth to a son in 1780, the king ordered the colonies to thank the Almighty. This was done on December 8, 1780, probably with a Te Deum.[34]

Another occasion for ceremony was the arrival of a new governor to the city. The custom of welcoming governors with a celebration began in Louisiana with Carondelet in December, 1791. The two ranking *regidores,* Andrés Almonester and Rudolfo Ducros, greeted him on the river below the city. The council gave Carondelet a formal reception in its temporary chambers, where Miró accepted the new governor's order of appointment and administered the oath of office. In doing this, Miró usurped the prerogative of the Cabildo's *alférez real.*[35]

At the end of Carondelet's administration, the council paid him a special tribute. The *síndico procurador general* presented it with a request from the people for a description and the publication of the baron's good works to incoming Governor Gayoso, the judge of Carondelet's *residencia*. The Cabildo willingly acceded to their wish. Moreover, it met in a special session to charge the annual commissioners with bidding an official farewell to the departing governor.[36]

34. Actas del Cabildo, I, 68–69, January 10, 1772, II, (2), 40–41, December 15, 1780, III, (1), 38–39, March 18, 1785, III, (2), 81, December 11, 1789, III, (3), 29–31, October 31, 1792, III, (3), 32, November 16, 1792. When the Princess of Asturias, the wife of the crown prince, gave birth to a daughter in 1775, the Cabildo spent 25 pesos, 3 reales for illumination. Another expenditure at the same time for unspecified *fiestas reales* (royal celebrations) cost 234 pesos, 6 reales (*ibid.,* I, 196, November 3, 1775; New Orleans Municipal Records, Records of the Cabildo, two statements of November 3, 1775, Juan Bautista Garic).

35. Actas del Cabildo, III, (2), 146, October 29, 1791, III, (2), 153–54, December 30, 1791. O'Reilly and Unzaga arrived in Louisiana together in 1769, before the creation of the Cabildo, to crush the French revolt. Gálvez and Miró were both serving as acting governors when their permanent appointments came in 1779 and 1785, respectively.

36. *Ibid.,* IV, (2), 30–31, September 1, 1797, IV, (2), 31–32, September 4, 1797. The Cabildo also honored Carondelet on the dedication of the Carondelet Canal. See Chapter Nine.

The councillors' fondness for ceremony and the trappings of office grew over time. In 1787 they added golden-headed staffs of authority, similar to those of the *alcaldes ordinarios,* to the regalia of the Cabildo porters. They also changed the city's official crest. In the summer of 1798, the newly enlarged council asked that its members be accorded military honors, rank, and uniforms. The annual commissioners wrote the request and forwarded it to the king, who did not respond.[37]

By mid-1801 the Cabildo's fancy for ceremonial prerogatives clashed with the views of acting military governor Casa-Calvo. The appointed governor general, Manuel Juan de Salcedo, was expected to arrive soon. Both the Cabildo and Casa-Calvo wanted to give Salcedo a reception on the afternoon of his arrival. Casa-Calvo refused to alter his plans, but he permitted the Cabildo to use the Government House for its reception at another time. The council refused his offer and held its reception in the *casa capitular* the day of Salcedo's induction into office. The governor general obligingly attended both receptions on succeeding days.[38]

Before long, however, protocol and prestige spawned difficulties between the Cabildo and Governor Salcedo. Paramount among their problems was the theater box controversy. It originated in the standing animosity between Nicolás María Vidal and Colonel Francisco Bouligny, the regimental commandant, that stretched back to the early 1790s. On the death of Gayoso in July, 1799, the two men became respectively the acting civil and the acting military governors of Louisiana. When Bouligny soon fell sick, Vidal seized the opportunity to humiliate him. Under Gayoso the theater box had been divided by a partition, one part for the Cabildo and the other for the governor. To spite Bouligny, Vidal removed the partition and presented the entire box to the Cabildo.[39]

By January, 1802, Governor Salcedo had ordered the partition restored to divide the theater box again between the Cabildo and the governor.

37. Burson, *Stewardship,* 209; Davis, *Louisiana,* 133; Actas del Cabildo, IV, (2), 131, June 1, 1798.

38. Actas del Cabildo, IV, (4), 86–87, April 24, 1801; Morazán, "Letters," II, 10–11.

39. Actas del Cabildo, IV, (3), 51–52, July 27, 1799. On Bouligny's problems with Vidal, see Din, *Francisco Bouligny,* 184, 188–91, 199–200. The military governor was senior to the civil governor because the former was in charge of more important areas such as defense, foreign affairs, and Indian relations.

But instead of giving the councillors the large section they had previously enjoyed, Salcedo kept it for his own use and relegated the council to the small section. Outraged, the councillors sent the governor a written protest requesting that he remove the partition. He, however, replied in a scathing letter that he was within his rights under the existing royal orders and precedents and adamantly refused to alter his ruling.[40]

The councillors thereupon quit attending the theater performances and requested the opinion of Licenciado José Martínez de la Pedrera. He wrote a letter of mock epic proportions, citing laws and precedents and defending the Cabildo's right to the theater box. Armed with Martínez' advice, the councillors sent another official communication to the governor, protesting both his conduct and the pain this disagreement had caused them. They requested that the governor order the theater manager to make the proper changes in the seating arrangements.[41]

Acting on the advice of his legal expert Vidal, Salcedo refused. He sent the entire controversy to his superiors in Havana while the Cabildo appealed to the Council of the Indies. The dispute was still unresolved when the Spanish era ended. What began as a petty squabble initiated by Vidal grew into a larger struggle between the governor general and the council that contributed to the demoralization and decline of the Cabildo.[42]

Finally, the council was involved in various other aspects of New Orleans' life. Anyone assuming a civil office or being licensed to practice a profession swore a formal oath before the council. In addition, the councillors took an active role in the city's social life. As its individual members and other government officials did, the Cabildo held its own balls, but virtually nothing is known about them. Neither the council nor the governor, however, sponsored the annual Carnival (Mardi Gras) festivities.[43]

The ceremonial functions of the Cabildo did not play a vital role in

40. Actas del Cabildo, IV, (4), 152–53, January 15, 1802, IV, (4), 154–55, January 29, 1802; Morazán, "Letters," I, 41–42.

41. Actas del Cabildo, IV, (4), 160–66, February 5, 1802.

42. Ibid., IV, (4), 167–70, February 12, 1802; Morazán, "Letters," II, 79.

43. Raymond J. Martinez, Pierre George Rousseau, Commanding General of the Galleys of the Mississippi: With Sketches of the Spanish Governors of Louisiana (1777–1803) and Glimpses of Social Life in New Orleans (New Orleans, 1964), 32; "Digest," 4. See Actas del Cabildo, I, 81, June 4, 1772, for a sample oath taken by incoming regidores.

the community's welfare, but they were an integral part of the council's activities. They were visible and perhaps even appeared exotic to outsiders. This might explain the generally unflattering descriptions left by contemporary and ethnocentric foreign observers, most of whom were unfamiliar with the customs and practices of Spanish Louisiana. Although the ceremonies might have repelled American and French visitors, expenditures for them were few and comparatively frugal by contemporary Spanish standards. In 1793, when the council had already grown ceremony-oriented, Vidal commented that New Orleans' celebrations were minimal when compared to his previous experience in Colombia.[44]

44. Vidal to Las Casas, New Orleans, January 23, 1793, "Dispatches of Carondelet," V, (II), 413.

Conclusion

THE New Orleans Cabildo lost power and prestige during the final years of the Spanish regime in Louisiana. Governors Vidal and Salcedo's antagonistic relationship with the institution was the immediate cause for its decline. Underlying factors, however, that stretched back more than a decade also played an important role in its degeneration.[1]

The Cabildo reached its apogee during Governor Miró's administration in the 1780s. Although good relations continued during the governorships of Carondelet and Gayoso, the city government's power weakened severely in the early 1790s. Its inability to muster a quorum to conduct business contributed significantly to its decline. Frequent illnesses plagued the councillors, and two of the six *regidor* seats fell vacant because of deaths. Unable to fulfill their duties, the councillors gradually yielded decision making to the indefatigable Governor Carondelet.[2]

---

1. See Morazán, "Letters," I, xliv–lxi, and "The Cabildo of Spanish New Orleans," 591–605; Burson, *Stewardship,* 63; Carrigan, "Commentary," 426; and Ezquerra Abadía, "Un presupuesto americano," 681.

2. Actas del Cabildo, IV, (1), 168, November 25, 1796; Arthur Preston Whitaker, *The Spanish-American Frontier, 1783–1795: The Westward Movement and the Spanish Retreat in the Mississippi Valley* (1927; rpr. Gloucester, Mass., 1962), 18. The post of *regidor-alcalde mayor provincial* was filled in February, 1798, after six years, when Pierre de La Roche acquired it.

During this same period, the economic power structure in Louisiana changed drastically. Until the end of Miró's administration, the planters constituted the economically and politically dominant class in the colony. Overall, they enjoyed good relations with the merchants. In the early 1790s, however, conditions changed markedly and severely injured the planter class. By then Louisiana's commercial agricultural crops of indigo and tobacco had declined precipitously. Several years elapsed before cotton and sugarcane rose to replace them. At the same time, merchants achieved unprecedented prosperity as commercial opportunities for them widened. More important, as Ronald R. Morazán points out, the interests of the two dominant economic classes began to diverge. When the crown added six *regidor* seats to the Cabildo in 1797, merchants purchased four of them and became an important force on the council.[3]

Of the original six *regidor* seats on the Cabildo in 1797, two were vacant, one was held by Almonester, a nonplanter, and only three were then held by planters, de la Barre, Ducros, and Forstall. Of the six new *regidores* on the Cabildo, three were Spanish merchants, Francisco de Riaño, Jaime Jordá, and perhaps Juan de Castañedo. Castañedo had worked as a store-keeper for the Spanish government until about 1792. He was probably involved in commerce in some way. The fourth merchant was Luis Darby Danycan. The two remaining new *regidores* were army officers, Captain Gilberto Andry, whose father had also been an army officer, and Adjutant José Leblanc, whose father was a planter.

Only two years later, with the death of Governor Gayoso, Vidal became the acting civil governor. His and Salcedo's administrations represented continuity because their conduct toward the council was basically identical. During Vidal's two years as acting civil governor, a noticeably changed attitude toward the Cabildo emerged. That change persisted when Salcedo took office. He was either grossly incompetent, inexperienced, or approaching senility.[4] Whichever is correct, he permitted a tiny

3. Clark, *New Orleans,* 92, 188–89, 219–20, 244, 271–72; Morazán, "Letters," I, xliii, lv–lix; Arena, "Landholding," 26; Arena, "Philadelphia–Spanish New Orleans Trade," 40; Actas del Cabildo, IV, (3), 109–10, November 15, 1799. It is also notable that seven of the eleven *regidores* in 1799 held commissions in either the army or militia, and perhaps the governor's office exerted pressure on them.

4. Captain General Someruelos (Salvador de Muro, Marqués de Someruelos) of Cuba did

clique composed of his older son Domingo, Vidal, and López de Armesto to assume direction of the colony's government. With Vidal as his legal adviser, Salcedo made most of the administration's decisions regarding the city council. Thus the attitude of confrontation between the governor and the Cabildo initiated by Vidal persisted.

As governors, Vidal and Salcedo were clearly inferior to their predecessors in ability and leadership. They appeared unwilling to work closely with the Cabildo. Possibly corruption played a role in their recalcitrant conduct although evidence for their malfeasance is circumstantial. More concretely, it can be said that Vidal was overly legalistic, egocentric, and ambitious whereas Salcedo was unquestionably inept. It is known that Vidal wanted to increase his importance in the colony and that led to clashes with other officials. Moreover, he was born in Colombia, where he had served the crown for twenty years, and his experience there had made him aware that royal officials often dictated to cabildos and kept them subordinate. Vidal seemed to want to do the same in Louisiana.[5]

The issues in dispute between Vidal and Salcedo, on one hand, and the Cabildo, on the other, ranged from trivial matters like the theater box controversy and Cabildo observance of religious festivities, to serious questions such as smallpox inoculations and the renewal of slave importations. Vidal, and later Salcedo, boycotted Cabildo meetings and humiliated the council whenever possible. The councillors responded by insisting on their petty prerogatives, refusing to cooperate with the two governors, hiring a legal adviser, and appealing disputed issues to higher authority. Caught in the middle, the New Orleans community was held hostage by the Cabildo's and the governors' intransigence.[6]

---

not believe in Salcedo's ability. In March, 1802, Salcedo petitioned for promotions for his two sons, who were army officers in Louisiana. He wanted his older son, a brevet captain, advanced to lieutenant colonel and the other to captain. Someruelos attached a note to the petition stating, "This is irregular in all its parts." It was not customary for a governor to make such a petition, and he added, "the governor lacks the necessary talent for that command" (Salcedo to Someruelos, No. 90, New Orleans, March 17, 1802, with Someruelos' note attached, AGI, PC, leg. 1553).

5. Davis, *Louisiana*, 126; Robertson, ed., *Louisiana Under the Rule*, I, 203, 205, 207–208, 231, II, 41–42, 231; Gardeur and Pitot, "Unpublished Memoir," 80; Actas del Cabildo, IV, (4), 80–83, April 17, 1801, IV, (4), 197–99, April 23, 1802; Morazán, "Letters," II, 116–17; Din, *Francisco Bouligny*, 188, 199–200.

6. Morazán, "Letters," I, xlv–liv, lx–lxi. Although the theater box episode can be labeled

Vidal and Salcedo apparently felt confident to break with the councilmen, even though other governors, who were of greater ability and influence, had preferred to work with the council. Perhaps the two men did so because the war against Great Britain that began in 1796 had isolated Louisiana from Spain to a large degree, and the Spanish government under Carlos IV and his first secretary Godoy was corrupt. Perhaps, too, factionalism in the Cabildo gave them the confidence to attempt to dominate it.[7]

More surprising than Vidal and Salcedo's combative relations with the council was that they did so with impunity. As we have seen, the Cabildo endeavored to fight back with the tactics at its disposal: passive resistance, obstruction, and appeals to higher authority.[8] Although these tactics had worked in the past, a series of factors beyond the Cabildo's control rendered them ineffective now.

Among these were changes in personnel, structure, and policies in Spain's colonial administration, which combined to rob the New Orleans Cabildo of the time and support it needed. Change in leadership began when the able Carlos III died in 1788 and was succeeded by his mediocre son Carlos IV. Furthermore, two major revisions in colonial administration happened about this time and brought further upheaval. When Minister of the Indies José de Gálvez died in June, 1787, the responsibilities of his office were divided between two cabinet ministries, the minister of the marine and the Indies and the minister of justice and patronage. In 1790

---

trivial, it nonetheless diminished the identity and estimation of the councilmen in a society that was very class conscious. See Salcedo's lengthy explanation of his side of the affair in an *expediente* called "The Cabildo and the Theater Box in the Casa de Comedias," February 24, 1802, enclosed in Salcedo to Someruelos, New Orleans, March 2, 1802, AGI, PC, leg. 1553.

7. Although Stafford Poole was writing about sixteenth-century Spanish *letrados,* his comments apply to Vidal in Louisiana. Poole described them as often turbulent, aggressive, and ambitious. He continues, "They came to the New World to make their fortune. They were strong, assertive, and often combative personalities, inclined to bend or violate laws passed by a government thousands of miles away, determined to seize the opportunities afforded by life in a new land. They hungered for financial gain and social advancement at the same time that they often strove for efficiency or the rule of law" ("Institutionalized Corruption in the Letrado Bureaucracy: The Case of Pedro Farfan (1568–1588)," *Americas,* XXXVIII (1981–82), 150.

8. Marzahl, in "Creoles and Government," 655, shows how the cabildo of Popayán, Ecuador, fought back against its governor.

the affairs of the former office of the Indies were further divided, this time among five ministries: commerce, war, marine, finance, and justice.[9] The loss of friends in powerful places and the dissipation of colonial authority probably hurt the Cabildo in its complaints and appeals. Many of its pleas in the last years went unanswered.

Even more damaging was a shift in attitude regarding Louisiana. Spain's principal reason for accepting the colony in 1762 was to acquire a buffer zone for tenuously held Texas and mineral-rich Mexico. Louisiana, however, proved to be expensive and burdensome. With the rise of Manuel Godoy as first secretary and Spain's realignment with France in 1796 in the continuing European wars, this attitude changed. Godoy wanted to restore Louisiana to France because of the advantages he believed would ensue. As Spain's ally, France could serve as a buffer in Louisiana, with responsibility for maintaining a vigorous military establishment that Spain could no longer afford. On June 27, 1796, Godoy tried to negotiate a secret treaty in which he offered to exchange Louisiana for Haiti and French possessions in Italy. Although French diplomats agreed, the Directory in Paris rejected the treaty because it was too favorable to Spain.[10] More to the point, Godoy wished to rid himself of Louisiana, and other Spanish officials, taking their cue from him, lost interest in the colony's welfare.

When Godoy finally achieved his objective with the secret Treaty of San Ildefonso on October 1, 1800, the planned retrocession to France plunged the Cabildo further into limbo. Because the treaty was not a well-kept secret, Louisianians learned about it the next year. The knowledge that the province would be given up weakened Spanish authority in Louisiana, including the Cabildo's.[11]

As the city government's hopes for redress in Spain in its struggle with the office of governor faded, its position in the colony worsened. Most of the petty squabbling between the council and the governor was more

9. Bjork, "Establishment of Spanish Rule," 152–53; Robertson, ed., *Louisiana Under the Rule,* I, 243–45; Whitaker, *Spanish-American Frontier,* 18; Morazán, "Letters," I, 165–66.

10. Marshall Sprague, *So Vast, So Beautiful a Land: Louisiana and the Purchase* (Boston, 1974), 268. See also Alexander DeConde, *This Affair of Louisiana* (New York, 1976); and E. Wilson Lyon, *Louisiana in French Diplomacy, 1759–1804* (1934; rpr. Norman, Okla., 1974).

11. Gardeur and Pitot, "Unpublished Memoir," 75; Asbury, *French Quarter,* 41.

symptomatic than causal in the deterioration of relations. Nevertheless, the blatant opposition that spewed from Vidal, Casa-Calvo, and Salcedo severely damaged the Cabildo. When the councillors realized their impotence, it had an enervating effect on them although the results were not immediately apparent. Moreover, two other occurrences served further to divide and demoralize the council. The first was the issue of reopening the slave trade in 1800, as we have already seen in Chapter Seven.[12] The second was Miró's *residencia*.

The legal inquiry into Miro's conduct while governor had even worse consequences for the Cabildo than the slave-importing controversy. Dr. Luis de Jaén, a lawyer of the Cuban *audiencia*, arrived in New Orleans in April, 1802, to conduct the belated investigation. Although Jaén eventually absolved the deceased governor of the charges lodged against his administration, he found fault and irregularities in the Cabildo's operations. By exceeding his authority vis-à-vis the council, Jaén dealt it a lethal blow. In July, he charged four *regidores* (Forstall, de la Barre, La Roche, and Castañedo) with malfeasance and suspended them from office. Governor Salcedo then exacerbated the suspensions by arresting and jailing them. Although the officials soon gained their release, the Cabildo nearly ceased functioning in the wake of this wretched episode. Thereafter, the demoralized members performed only minimal routine duties until the Spanish period ended.[13]

In the spring of 1803, the time for the retrocession drew near. On March 26, Colonial Prefect Pierre-Clément de Laussat arrived in New Orleans and communicated his mission to the Spanish authorities, including the Cabildo. Salcedo and Casa-Calvo (who had returned to Louisiana to assist

12. Morazán considers the slave importation issue as the "point of no return" in the deterioration of Cabildo-governor relations. Much the same can be said about the Cabildo's vitality and solidarity. *Ayuntamientos* (council meetings) from late 1800 became irregular because the members frequently failed to muster a quorum despite their increased numbers (Morazán, "Letters," I, lviii; Actas del Cabildo, IV, [3], 108–10, November 15, 1799, IV, [4], 49–51, December 19, 1800, IV, [4], 137–41, September 25–November 6, 1801, IV, [4], 194–95, April 2, 1802, IV, [5], 23–30, October 2–November 26, 1802).

13. Actas del Cabildo, IV, (5), 1–3, July 19, 1802; Morazán, "Letters," II, 113; Burson, *Stewardship*, 292–93, 299; Ezquerra Abadía, "Un presupuesto americano," 685–86. Jaén, like Vidal, was a *letrado*, and he seemed to think that he held power to correct irregularities he perceived in the Cabildo.

the governor in the transfer and to mark the new boundary with the United States) issued a joint proclamation on May 18, informing the inhabitants about the retrocession. Eight days later they sent a copy of the royal order authorizing the transfer to the Cabildo.[14]

The formal transfer of Louisiana to France awaited the arrival of French general Claude Perrin Victor. Because warfare resumed in Europe after the Truce of Amiens expired, Victor never came. Then Napoleon violated his pledge to cede Louisiana only to Spain and sold the province to the United States. To satisfy the formality of French ownership, Louisiana would be turned over to Laussat, who would quickly surrender it to American officials.[15]

Salcedo and Casa-Calvo transferred possession of the colony to Laussat on November 30, 1803. That same day, the Frenchman abolished the Cabildo and replaced it with a municipality patterned along French Republican lines. The only remaining duty for the councillors was to complete an inventory and prepare their records for the turnover to the new regime. They completed this last obligation on December 10. After the transfer of records, the Cabildo of New Orleans existed only as the name for the *casa capitular* that faced the former Plaza de Armas.[16]

An evaluation of the Cabildo's thirty-four-year life is not easy. New Orleans' location on the frontier, adjacent to a dangerous river and in a subtropical climate, necessitated that the city government work to furnish

14. Robertson, ed., *Louisiana Under the Rule,* I, 375; Morazán, "Letters," II, 208–21. For an examination of Laussat in Louisiana, see Robert D. Bush, "Colonial Administration in French Louisiana: The Napoleonic Episode, 1802–1803," *Publications of the Louisiana Historical Society,* 2nd ser., II (1974), 36–59.

15. Morazán, "Letters," II, 208; Sprague, *So Vast,* 279, 361–62. See also E. Wilson Lyon, *Bonaparte's Proposed Louisiana Expedition* (Chicago, 1934).

16. Actas del Cabildo, IV, (5), 96–97, October 7, 1803; "Surrender of the Documents of the Archives of the Cabildo to the Municipality Established by the Colonial Prefect," December 10, 1803, Document No. 461, Colonial History section of the Vertical File, Special Collections, Louisiana State University Library; André Lafargue, "Pierre Clement de Laussat, Colonial Prefect and High Commissioner of France in Louisiana, Proclamations and Orders," *LHQ,* XX (1937), 168–69; Fortier, *History of Louisiana,* II, 246; Laussat, *Memoirs of My Life;* and Robert D. Bush, "Documents on the Louisiana Purchase: The Laussat Papers," *LH,* XVIII (1977), 104–107. During France's twenty-day reign in Louisiana, Laussat placed Charity Hospital under municipal control. In this way, the city government finally achieved the power it had sought for twenty-five years (Bush, "Colonial Administration," 50).

a variety of services to its residents. In doing so, the members and employees of the city council rendered valuable assistance in the areas of police, fire, and levee protection; justice; slave regulation; market system; food supply; medical and health regulations; sanitation; and public works. The Cabildo occasionally furnished city lands for private projects that were expected to benefit the community. The council also either provided or helped provide many of the average inhabitants' basic necessities: food, beverages, clothing, and tools, among other things. Last, the Cabildo made available various channels of communication to higher authority and sometimes regaled the community with pageantry and entertainment.

In its Spanish American context, the New Orleans Cabildo was advanced for its time. It was more active in welfare and public works than was the rule throughout Spanish America. One of its principal duties was the never-ending task of safeguarding public interests. Many operators of businesses in the city required constant vigilance and often succeeded in hoodwinking inspectors. Among them were bakers, tavern keepers, peddlers, and a variety of users of weights and measures. The Cabildo, reflecting Spanish law, labored in favor of fair prices and reasonable profits and against forestalling in business practices. With the American takeover, the maxim "Let the buyer beware" shifted responsibility to the consumer and replaced Spanish concepts in the marketplace whose origins were medieval.[17]

In its last days, the Cabildo lacked the manpower to safeguard adequately the public welfare in the areas where it had long labored. As important as these matters were, the bulk of the council's attention and funds shifted to public works programs. Although local citizens might have complained about deplorable streets, lighting, drainage, sanitation, and levees and lamented the inadequate police and fire protection, it was the visitors to the city who committed their observations to paper. But in the process, these authors usually failed to note Cabildo activities in the areas they complained about.[18] Thus the city government did not receive the appreciation it deserved for its efforts, only the general condemnation that not enough or nothing was being done. Moreover, it should be kept

17. Clark, New Orleans, 261. See also Chapter Eight, above.
18. Clark, New Orleans, 261.

in mind that all the areas mentioned required money, of which there never was enough. But in addition to providing services in numerous sectors, the city often needed funds to recover from natural disasters such as fires and storms that repeatedly struck New Orleans in the late eighteenth century.

Nevertheless, these expenditures that benefited the city's residents doubtless helped to avoid the wastefulness of lavish ceremonial spending. New Orleans devoted almost all of its high per capita revenues, when compared to other Spanish American cities, to the community's well-being. Perhaps in this, the Cabildo was more akin to municipal governments in the United States than to Spanish America. At comparable stages in their respective developments, five coastal North American cities (Boston, Newport, New York, Philadelphia, and Charleston) had similar problems and experienced similar frustrations in providing services and protection to their residents. In many respects, the New Orleans Cabildo differed little from these municipal governments.[19]

Admittedly, the Cabildo failed in some of its endeavors, but more important, it succeeded in many more. When it succeeded, it generally had the support of the governor and the intendant. This cooperation was largely responsible for New Orleans' ability to rebound after each of the city's many natural disasters. The council's failures were largely caused by inadequate financial and technological resources. Nevertheless, when viewed on balance, the Cabildo was a "reasonably efficient organ of government."[20]

Under the Spaniards, the small village they found on the Mississippi's bank developed into a genuine city. It grew in population, attracted professionals and artisans in varied occupations, increased in commerce, and serviced a vast hinterland. The Cabildo devoted nearly all of its energy to urban rather than provincial concerns.[21] As the only genuine city with the

19. Ezquerra Abadía, "Un presupuesto americano," 694; Bridenbaugh, *Cities in Revolt*, 215–49.

20. Clark, *New Orleans*, 256.

21. Micelle, "From Law Court," 88; Clark, *New Orleans*, 156–57, 170, 261; Robin, *Voyage to Louisiana*; Asbury, *French Quarter*, 62–63; Wilson and Huber, *The Cabildo*, 81–82. The French Superior Council devoted most of its attention to the province and provided few services to the city.

only cabildo in Louisiana, its authority theoretically embraced the entire province. But practical limitations of transportation, communications, and finances restricted the effective exercise of authority to lower Louisiana, which contained the preponderance of the colony's population during the Spanish period.[22] Even within lower Louisiana, the council restricted most of its activity to New Orleans and its immediate neighboring district. In matters such as slave importation and operation of the slave fund, however, the hand of the Cabildo embraced a wider area.[23]

Although the council had only limited ability to defy successfully a governor or intendant, under certain circumstances and with sufficient support from higher authority, it occasionally challenged even these officials. For most of the life of New Orleans' first city government this was not necessary because the aims of the governor and the council were compatible. Only Vidal and Salcedo effectively disregarded the Cabildo. Even then they did so only after Godoy as first secretary in Spain had virtually abandoned the colony and warfare had disrupted communications.

Although the Cabildo's popularity cannot be separated from that of the overall Spanish regime in Louisiana, there is considerable evidence that most Louisianians at the time of cession preferred Spanish rule to that of the United States. This feeling was strong enough that many inhabitants planned to migrate to other Spanish dominions, and, indeed, some of them did.[24] At the same time, there was fear that before American

22. "Census of Louisiana, September 2, 1771," *SMV*, Pt. I, 196; United States Congress (Census of Louisiana for 1803), Appendix No. 6 to "Digest of the Laws of Louisiana," *American State Papers, Miscellaneous Documents*, I, 384.

In the late Spanish period, St. Louis was growing rapidly although it never acquired a city government. For discussions of its development at this time and in the immediate post-Spanish era, see Dora P. Crouch, Daniel J. Garr, and Axel I. Mundigo, *Spanish City Planning in North America* (Cambridge, Mass., 1982), 116–55; Wade, *Urban Frontier*, 3–7, 59–64.

23. Technically, judicial review could be included, but because the judges, the *alcalde ordinario* and two *regidores* who made up the review board, represented the Spanish legal system and not the Cabildo, it is not counted here.

24. Probably more inhabitants would have left Louisiana if the Spanish government had immediately granted them permission to leave. The government, however, held out hope that it would recover the colony and told them to wait, renewing their petitions if the United States retained possession (Pedro Cavallo to the Marqués de Casa-Calvo, Aranjuez, January 15, 1805, AGI, PC, leg. 176B). The nearest Spanish colony to Louisiana was Texas, and it was one of the easiest to reach. But only in September, 1809, were former Spanish subjects from Lou-

troops arrived, law and order might break down because of pro-Spanish sentiment. American mismanagement immediately after the transfer enabled Louisianians to spice their complaints and appeals for redress with fulsome praise of the Spanish regime. This pro-Spanish sentiment lingered on into the American period.[25]

The American-style city government that replaced the Cabildo benefited from that body's more than thirty years of experience to guide it in its operations. Moreover, in many areas of city government, there was both short- and long-term continuity of practices initiated by the Cabildo. Although it is usually not recognized by many New Orleanians, the institution introduced by Governor O'Reilly left behind a legacy far greater than that of the *casa capitular*. Today that building continues to stand overlooking the former Plaza de Armas, but its real significance lies as a monument to the Cabildo's existence. For all of its successes and failures, the New Orleans Cabildo was an integral part of colonial Louisiana's political, economic, and cultural landscape.

---

isiana admitted directly into Texas (Bernardo Bonavía to the commandant general [Nemesio Salcedo], San Antonio de Bexar, September, 1809, and his reply enclosed, AGI, Audiencia de Guadalajara, leg. 114).

25. Robertson, ed., *Louisiana Under the Rule,* I, 55, 193, II, 51; Robin, *Voyage,* 162; William E. Beard, ed., *Tennessee Old and New* (Kingsport, Tenn., 1946), 357–58; Dart, "History of the Supreme Court," 17–18; Brown, "Orleans Territory Memorialists," 99–102; Brooks, "Spain's Farewell," 30–31, 36.

Bibliography

MANUSCRIPTS, ARCHIVES, AND DOCUMENTARY COLLECTIONS

Archivo General de Indias, Seville
  Audiencia de Guadalajara
    Legajo 114
  Audiencia de Santo Domingo
    Legajos 2531, 2542, 2543, 2569, 2581, 2586, 2589, 2594, 2662
  Indiferente General
    Legajo 1344
  Papeles Procedentes de la Isla de Cuba
    Legajos 3A, 9B, 10, 11, 12, 18, 30, 31, 32, 49, 50, 70, 71A, 72, 73, 83, 103, 110, 111,
      112, 113, 114, 118, 122B, 123, 131B, 138A, 139, 174B, 176B, 180A, 188A, 189B,
      191, 197, 199, 204, 205, 206, 211A, 215A, 216A, 538AB, 566, 600, 633, 700,
      1054, 1375, 1377, 1394, 1440B, 1441, 1442, 1443AB, 1444, 1446, 1447, 1550, 1553,
      2357, 2360
Archivo General de Simancas, near Valladolid
  Sección de Guerra Moderna
    Legajo 6912
Archivo Histórico Nacional, Madrid
  Sección de Estado
    Legajos 3882, 3883, 3892bis, 3899, 3900, 3902
Biblioteca Nacional, Madrid

Sección de Manuscritos
  Colección de documentos para la historia de la Florida y tierras adjuntas. 2 vols.
Hill Memorial Library, Louisiana State University, Baton Rouge
  New Orleans Municipal Records. Records of the Cabildo.
  Vertical File
    Colonial History.
  Works Progress Administration transcripts in English
    "Alphabetical and Chronological Digest of the Acts and Deliberations of the
      Cabildo, 1769–1803. A Record of the Spanish Government in New Orleans."
      In the introduction to the WPA English translation of the Actas del Cabildo
    "Confidencial Dispatches of Don Bernardo de Gálvez."
    "Dispatches of the Spanish Governors, 1766–1792." 7 vols.
    "Dispatches of the Spanish Governors of Louisiana: Messages of Francisco Luis
      Héctor, El Barón de Carondelet."
Howard-Tilton Library, Tulane University
  Special Collections
    Cruzat Family Collection.
    Rosemond E. and Emile Kuntz Collection.
    Windom Collection.
New Orleans Public Library
  Actas del Cabildo, 1769–1803. 10 vols. Microfilm of WPA transcripts in Spanish.
  "Miscellaneous Spanish and French Documents, 1789–1816." 4 vols., 1937. Trans-
    lated by Joseph Albert Gutiérrez for the WPA.
  "Petitions, Letters and Decrees of the Cabildo." 3 vols.
New Orleans State Museum Library
  Judicial Records of the Spanish Cabildo.
  "Records of the City Council of New Orleans and Documents Pertaining to the
    Government of Louisiana, Translated from the Spanish and French." Book Num-
    ber 4088.

THESES, DISSERTATIONS, AND UNPUBLISHED PAPERS

Arena, Carmelo Richard. "Philadelphia–New Orleans Trade." Ph.D. dissertation,
  University of Pennsylvania, 1959.
Bjork, David Knuth. "The Establishment of Spanish Rule in the Province of Loui-
  siana, 1762–1770." Ph.D. dissertation, University of California, Berkeley, 1923.
Caughey, John Walton. "Louisiana Under Spain, 1762–1783." Ph.D. dissertation, Uni-
  versity of California, Berkeley, 1928.
Coutts, Brian E. "Martín Navarro: Treasurer, Contador, Intendant, 1766–1788: Politics

and Trade in Spanish Louisiana." Ph.D. dissertation, Louisiana State University, 1981.

Din, Gilbert C. "The Gálvez-Bouligny Affair Revisited." Unpublished paper.

Greene, Karen. "The Ursuline Mission in Colonial Louisiana." M.A. thesis, Louisiana State University, 1982.

Guest, Florian F. "Municipal Institutions in Spanish California, 1769–1821." Ph.D. dissertation, University of California, Los Angeles, 1961.

Hanger, Kimberly S. "Personas de varias clases y colores: Free People of Color in Spanish Louisiana." Ph.D. dissertation, University of Florida, 1991.

Ingersoll, Thomas N. "Old New Orleans: Race, Class, Sex, and Order in the Early Deep South, 1718–1819." Ph.D. dissertation, University of California, Los Angeles, 1990.

Kerr, Derek Noel. "Petty Felony, Slave Defiance and Frontier Villainy: Crime and Criminal Justice in Spanish Louisiana, 1770–1803." Ph.D. dissertation, Tulane University, 1983.

King, Ameda Ruth. "Social and Economic Life in Spanish Louisiana, 1763–1783." Ph.D. dissertation, University of Illinois, 1931.

Lemieux, Donald. "The Office of Commissaire Ordonnateur in French Louisiana, 1731–1763." Ph.D. dissertation, Louisiana State University, 1972.

McGowan, James T. "Creation of a Slave Society: Louisiana Plantations in the Eighteenth Century." Ph.D. dissertation, University of Rochester, 1976.

Morazán, Ronald R. "Letters, Petitions, and Decrees of the Cabildo of New Orleans, 1800–1803." Ph.D. dissertation, Louisiana State University, 1972.

Texada, David Ker. "The Administration of Alejandro O'Reilly as Governor of Louisiana, 1769–1770." Ph.D. dissertation, Louisiana State University, 1968.

Wall, Helen. "The Transfer of Louisiana from France to Spain." M.A. thesis, Louisiana State University, 1960.

Yerxa, Dorothy Ida. "The Administration of Carondelet, with an Appendix of Original Documents." M.A. thesis, University of California, Berkeley, 1926.

BOOKS

Almonester y Roxas, Andrés. *Constitution for the New Charity Hospital.* Translated by Wiley D. Stephenson, Jr. Survey of Federal Archives of Louisiana. N.p., 1941.

Altamira y Crevea, Rafael. *Historia de España y de la civilización española.* 4 vols. Barcelona, 1909.

———. *A History of Spain.* Princeton, N.J., 1949.

American State Papers, Miscellaneous Documents (1789–1823). 2 vols. Washington, D.C., 1834.

American State Papers, Public Lands (1789–1837). 8 vols. Washington, D.C., 1832–61.

Andreu Ocariz, Juan José. *Movimientos rebeldes de los esclavos negros durante el dominio español en Luisiana*. Zaragoza, Spain, 1977.

Arnold, Morris S. *Colonial Arkansas, 1684–1804: A Social and Cultural History*. Fayetteville, Ark., 1991.

————. *Unequal Laws unto a Savage Race: European Legal Traditions in Arkansas, 1686–1836*. Fayetteville, Ark., 1985.

Arthur, Stanley Clisby. *Old New Orleans*. Edited by Susan Cole Dore. 1936; rpr. Gretna, La., 1990.

Asbury, Herbert. *The French Quarter: An Informal History of the New Orleans Underworld*. New York, 1936.

Bailey, Helen M., and Abraham P. Nasatir. *Latin America: The Development of Its Civilization*. Englewood Cliffs, N.J., 1960.

Baily, Francis. *Journal of a Tour in Unsettled Parts of North America in 1796 & 1797*. Edited by Jack D. L. Holmes. Carbondale, Ill., 1969.

Baudier, Roger. *The Catholic Church in Louisiana*. New Orleans, 1939.

Baudry des Lozières, Louis Narcisse. *Second Voyage a la Louisiane, faisant suite au premier de l'auteur de 1794 a 1798*. 2 vols. Paris, 1803.

Bayle, Constantino. *Los cabildos seculares en la América española*. Madrid, 1952.

Beard, William E., ed. *Tennessee Old and New*. Kingsport, Tenn., 1946.

Berquin-Duvallon. *Travels in Louisiana and the Floridas in the Year 1802*. Translated by John Davis. New York, 1806.

————. *Vue de la colonie español du Mississippi, ou des provinces de Louisiane et Floride occidentale*. 1803. 2nd ed. Paris, 1804.

Billington, Ray Allen. *Westward Expansion: A History of the American Frontier*. 4th ed. New York, 1974.

Bolton, Herbert Eugene, and Thomas Maitland Marshall. *The Colonization of North America, 1492–1783*. New York, 1920.

Brasseaux, Carl A. *Denis-Nicolas Foucault and the New Orleans Rebellion of 1768*. Ruston, La., 1987.

————. *The Founding of New Acadia: The Beginnings of Acadian Life in Louisiana, 1765–1803*. Baton Rouge, 1987.

————. *"Scattered to the Wind": Dispersal and Wanderings of the Acadians, 1755–1809*. Lafayette, La., 1991.

Bridenbaugh, Carl. *Cities in Revolt: Urban Life in America, 1743–1776*. New York, 1955.

Burson, Caroline Maude. *The Stewardship of Don Esteban Miró*. New Orleans, 1940.

Bushnell, Amy Turner. *The King's Coffer: Proprietors of the Spanish Florida Treasury, 1565–1702*. Gainesville, Fla., 1981.

Cable, George W. *Creoles and Cajuns: Stories of Old Louisiana.* Edited by Arlin Turner. Garden City, N.Y., 1959.

Castillo, Antonio de. *La Luisiana y el Padre Sedella.* San Juan, Puerto Rico, 1929.

Caughey, John Walton. *Bernardo de Gálvez in Louisiana, 1776–1783.* 1934; rpr. Gretna, La., 1972.

Chambers, Henry E. *A History of Louisiana: Wilderness, Colony, Province, State, People.* 3 vols. Chicago, 1925.

Chapman, Charles. *Colonial Hispanic America: A History.* New York, 1933.

Clark, John G. *New Orleans, 1718–1812: An Economic History.* Baton Rouge, 1970.

Coleman, James Julian, Jr. *Gilbert Antoine de St. Maxent: The Spanish-Frenchman of New Orleans.* New Orleans, 1968.

Collot, Victor. *A Journey in North America.* Translated by J. Christian Bay. Florence, 1924.

Cooper, Donald. *Epidemic Disease in Mexico City, 1761–1813.* Austin, 1965.

Crouch, Doris P., Daniel J. Garr, and Axel I. Mundigo. *Spanish City Planning in North America.* Cambridge, Mass., 1982.

Cruz, Gilbert R. *Let There Be Towns: Spanish Municipal Origins in the American Southwest, 1610–1810.* College Station, Tex., 1988.

Curley, Michael J. *Church and State in the Spanish Floridas (1783–1822).* Washington, D.C., 1940.

Curtis, Nathaniel Cortlandt. *New Orleans, Its Old Houses, Shops and Public Buildings.* Philadelphia, 1933.

Dánvila y Collado, Manuel. *El poder civil en España.* 6 vols. Madrid, 1885–86.

Davis, Edwin Adams. *Louisiana: A Narrative History.* 3rd ed. Baton Rouge, 1971.

Dawson, Joseph G., III, ed. *The Louisiana Governors: From Iberville to Edwards.* Baton Rouge, 1990.

DeConde, Alexander. *This Affair of Louisiana.* New York, 1976.

De Humboldt, Alexander. *Political Essay on the Kingdom of New Spain.* Translated by John Black. 2 vols. 1811; rpr. New York, 1966.

Diffie, Bailey W. *Latin American Civilization, Colonial Period.* Harrisburg, Pa., 1945.

Din, Gilbert C. *The Canary Islanders of Louisiana.* Baton Rouge, 1988.

————. *Francisco Bouligny: A Bourbon Soldier in Louisiana.* Baton Rouge, 1993.

Din, Gilbert C., and A. P. Nasatir. *The Imperial Osages: Spanish-Indian Relations in the Mississippi Valley.* Norman, Okla., 1983.

Duffy, John. *Epidemics in Colonial America.* Baton Rouge, 1953.

————, ed. *The Rudolph Matas History of Medicine in Louisiana.* 2 vols. Baton Rouge, 1958–62.

Eccles, W. J. *The Canadian Frontier, 1534–1760.* New York, 1969.

————. *France in America.* New York, 1972.

Egerton, Douglas B. *Gabriel's Rebellion: The Virginia Slave Conspiracies of 1800 and 1802.* Chapel Hill, N.C., 1993.

Ekberg, Carl J. *Colonial Ste. Genevieve: An Adventure on the Mississippi Frontier.* Gerald, Mo., 1985.

Finiels, Nicolas de. *An Account of Upper Louisiana.* Edited by Carl J. Ekberg and William E. Foley. Translated by Carl J. Ekberg. Columbia, Mo., 1989.

Fisher, Lillian Estelle. *The Intendant System in Spanish America.* Berkeley, 1929.

Folmer, Henri. *Franco-Spanish Rivalry in North America, 1524–1763.* Glendale, Calif., 1953.

Fortier, Alcée. *A History of Louisiana.* 2 vols. 2nd ed. Edited by Jo Ann Carrigan. Baton Rouge, 1966–72.

Freiberg, Edna B. *Bayou St. John in Colonial Louisiana, 1699–1803.* New Orleans, 1980.

French, Benjamin Franklin, ed. *Historical Memoirs of Louisiana from the First Settlement of the Colony to the Departure of Governor O'Reilly in 1770: With Historical and Biographical Notes.* 5 vols. New York, 1853.

Gálvez, Bernardo de. *Diario de las operaciones contra la plaza de Panzacola, 1781.* 2nd ed. Madrid, 1959.

Gayarré, Charles. *History of Louisiana.* 4 vols. 3rd ed. New Orleans, 1885.

Gibson, Charles. *Spain in America.* New York, 1966.

Giraud, Marcel. *Histoire de la Louisiane française.* 5 vols. Paris, 1953–87.

————. *A History of French Louisiana.* 5 vols.

Vol. II, *Years of Transition, 1715–1717.* Translated by Brian Pierce. Baton Rouge, 1993.

Vol. V, *The Company of the Indies, 1723–1731.* Translated by Brian Pierce. Baton Rouge, 1991.

Gold, Robert L. *Borderland Empires in Transition: The Triple-Nation Transfer of Florida.* Carbondale, Ill., 1969.

Goodspeed, Weston A., ed. *The Province and the States: A History of the Province of Louisiana Under France and Spain and of the Territories and States of the United States Formed Therefrom.* 7 vols. Madison, 1904.

Hall, Gwendolyn Midlo. *Africans in Colonial Louisiana: The Development of Afro-Creole Culture in the Eighteenth Century.* Baton Rouge, 1992.

Haring, C. H. *The Spanish Empire in America.* New York, 1947.

Herring, Hubert. *A History of Latin America from Its Beginnings to the Present.* 3rd ed. New York, 1968.

Hinojosa y Naveros, Eduardo. *Estudios sobre la historia del derecho español.* Madrid, 1903.

Holmes, Jack D. L. *Gayoso: The Life and Times of a Spanish Governor in the Mississippi Valley, 1789–1799.* Baton Rouge, 1965.

————, ed. *Honor and Fidelity: The Louisiana Infantry Regiment and the Louisiana Militia Companies, 1766–1821.* Birmingham, Ala., 1965.

Hopkins, Donald R. *Princes and Peasants: Smallpox in History.* Chicago, 1983.

Jackson, Jack. *Los Mesteños: Spanish Ranching in Texas, 1721–1821.* College Station, 1986.

James, James Alton. *Oliver Pollock: The Life and Times of an Unknown Patriot.* New York, 1937.

King, Grace. *Creole Families of New Orleans.* 1921; rpr. Baton Rouge, 1971.

————. *New Orleans: The Place and the People.* New York, 1907.

Kinnaird, Lawrence, ed. *Spain in the Mississippi Valley, 1765–1794.* 3 parts. Washington, D.C., 1949.

Klein, Herbert S. *Slavery in the Americas: A Comparative Study of Virginia and Cuba.* Chicago, 1967.

Korn, Bertram Wallace. *The Early Jews of New Orleans.* Waltham, Mass., 1969.

Kuethe, Alan J. *Cuba, 1753–1815: Crown, Military, and Society.* Knoxville, Tenn., 1986.

Latrobe, Benjamin Henry. *Impressions Respecting New Orleans: Diary and Sketches, 1818–1820.* Edited by Samuel Wilson, Jr. New York, 1951.

Laussat, Pierre Clément de. *Memoir of My Life.* Edited by Robert D. Bush. Translated by Agnes-Josephine Pastwa. Baton Rouge, 1978.

Le Gardeur, René J., Jr. *The First New Orleans Theatre, 1792–1803.* New Orleans, 1963.

Lynch, John. *Spanish Colonial Administration, 1782–1810: The Intendant System in the Viceroyalty of the Rio de la Plata.* London, 1958.

Lyon, E. Wilson. *Bonaparte's Proposed Louisiana Expedition.* Chicago, 1934.

————. *Louisiana in French Diplomacy, 1759–1804.* 1934; rpr. Norman, Okla., 1974.

MacCurdy, Raymond R. *A History and Bibliography of Spanish-Language Newspapers and Magazines in Louisiana, 1808–1949.* Albuquerque, 1951.

McAlister, Lyle N. *The "Fuero Militar" in New Spain.* Gainesville, Fla., 1957.

Malagón Barceló, Javier. *Código Negro Carolino (1784).* Santo Domingo, 1974.

Martin, François-Xavier. *The History of Louisiana, from the Earliest Period.* 1827. 3rd ed. Gretna, La., 1975.

Martinez, Raymond J. *Pierre George Rousseau, Commanding General of the Galleys of the Mississippi: With Sketches of the Spanish Governors of Louisiana (1777–1803) and Glimpses of Social Life in New Orleans.* New Orleans, 1964.

Montero de Pedro, José. *Españoles en Nueva Orleans y Luisiana.* Madrid, 1979.

Moore, John Preston. *The Cabildo in Peru Under the Bourbons: A Study in the Decline and Resurgence of Local Government in the Audiencia of Lima, 1700–1824.* Durham, N.C., 1966.

————. *The Cabildo in Peru Under the Hapsburgs: A Study in the Origins and Powers of the Town Council of Peru, 1530–1700.* Durham, N.C., 1954.

————. *Revolt in Louisiana: The Spanish Occupation, 1766–1770.* Baton Rouge, 1976.

Morazzani de Pérez Enciso, Gisela. *La intendencia en España y América.* Caracas, 1966.

Nasatir, Abraham P., ed. *Spanish War Vessels on the Mississippi, 1792–1796.* New Haven, 1968.

Parry, John H. *The Sale of Public Office in the Spanish Indies Under the Hapsburgs.* Berkeley, 1953.

Perrin du Lac, François Marie. *Travels Through the Two Louisianas, and Among the Savage Nations of the Missouri; Also, in the United States, Along the Ohio and Adjacent Provinces, in 1801, 1802 & 1803.* . . . London, 1807.

Phelps, Matthew. *Memoirs and Adventures of Captain Matthew Phelps.* Vermont, 1802.

Pitot, James. *Observations on the Colony of Louisiana from 1796 to 1802.* Translated and introduction by Henry C. Pitot. Baton Rouge, 1979.

Pittman, Captain Philip. *The Present State of the European Settlements on the Mississippi.* Introduction by Robert R. Rea. 1770; rpr. Gainesville, Fla., 1973.

Pope, Col. John. *A Tour Through the Southern and Western Territories.* . . . 1792; rpr. New York, 1971.

Recopilación de leyes de los reynos de las Indias. 3 vols. 1791; facsimile rpr. Madrid, 1942.

Robertson, James Alexander, ed. and trans. *Louisiana Under the Rule of Spain, France and the United States, 1785–1807.* 2 vols. Cleveland, 1911.

Robin, Claude Cesar. *Voyage to Louisiana by C. C. Robin, 1803–1805.* Edited and translated by Stuart O. Landry, Jr. New Orleans, 1966.

Robinson, Lura. *It's an Old New Orleans Custom.* New York, 1948.

Rodríguez Casado, Vicente. *Primeros años de la dominación española.* Madrid, 1942.

Roussere, Charles B. *The Negro in Louisiana: Aspects of His History and His Literature.* New Orleans, 1937.

Salvaggio, John. *New Orleans' Charity Hospital: A Story of Physicians, Politics, and Poverty.* Baton Rouge, 1992.

Schlarman, J. H. *From Quebec to New Orleans.* Belleville, Ill., 1929.

Simmons, Marc. *Spanish Government in New Mexico.* Albuquerque, 1968.

Smith, Michael. *The "Real Expedición Marítima de la Vacuna" in New Spain and Guatemala.* Philadelphia, 1974.

Sprague, Marshall. *So Vast, So Beautiful a Land: Louisiana and the Purchase.* Boston, 1974.

Starr, J. Barton. *Tories, Dons, and Rebels: The American Revolution in British West Florida.* Gainesville, Fla., 1976.

Sterkx, H. E. *The Free Negro in Antebellum Louisiana.* Cranbury, N.J., 1972.

Texada, David Ker. *Alejandro O'Reilly and the New Orleans Rebels.* Lafayette, La., 1970.

Thonhoff, Robert H. *The Texas Connection with the American Revolution.* Burnet, Tex., 1981.

Torres Ramírez, Bibiano. *Alejandro O'Reilly en las Indias.* Seville, 1969.

Usner, Daniel H., Jr. *Indians, Settlers, and Slaves in a Frontier Exchange Economy: The Lower Mississippi Valley Before 1783.* Chapel Hill, 1992.

Vance, Joseph Thomas. *The Background to Hispanic American Law: Legal Sources and Judicial Literature of Spain.* Washington, D.C., 1937.

Villiers du Terrage, Marc de. *Les dernières années de la Louisiane Française.* Paris, 1903.

Wade, Robert C. *The Urban Frontier: The Rise of Western Cities, 1790–1830.* Cambridge, Mass., 1959.

Wallach, Kate. *Research in Louisiana Law.* Baton Rouge, 1958.

Weber, David J. *The Spanish Frontier in North America.* New Haven, 1992.

Weddle, Robert S. *Wilderness Manhunt: The Spanish Search for La Salle.* Austin, 1973.

Whitaker, Arthur Preston. *The Mississippi Question, 1795–1803: A Study in Trade, Politics, and Diplomacy.* 1934; rpr. Gloucester, Mass., 1962.

―――. *The Spanish-American Frontier, 1783–1795: The Westward Movement and the Spanish Retreat in the Mississippi Valley.* 1927; rpr. Gloucester, Mass., 1962.

―――, ed. and trans. *Documents Relating to the Commercial Policy of Spain in the Floridas, with Incidental Reference to Louisiana.* Deland, Fla., 1931.

Williams, John Lee. *A View of West Florida.* 1827; rpr. Gainesville, Fla., 1976.

Wilson, Samuel, Jr., and Leonard V. Huber. *The Cabildo on Jackson Square.* New Orleans, 1973.

Worcester, Donald E., and Wendell G. Schaeffer. *The Growth and Culture of Latin America.* New York, 1956.

ARTICLES AND ESSAYS

Aiton, Arthur S. "The Diplomacy of the Louisiana Cession." *American Historical Review,* XXXVI (1931), 701–20.

―――. "Spanish Colonial Reorganization Under the Family Compact." *Hispanic American Historical Review,* XII (1932), 269–80.

Allain, Mathé. "Slave Policies in French Louisiana." *Louisiana History,* XXI (1980), 127–37.

Alliot, Paul. "Historical and Political Reflections on Louisiana." In *Louisiana Under the Rule of Spain, France, and the United States, 1785–1807,* edited by James Alexander Robertson. 2 vols. 1910–11; Freeport, N.Y., 1969.

Andreu Ocariz, Juan José. "Los intentos de separación de la capitanía general de Luisiana de la de Cuba." *Estudios* (Universidad de Zaragoza), No. 78 (1978), 397–431.

Arena, C. Richard. "Landholding and Political Power in Spanish Louisiana." *Louisiana Historical Quarterly,* XXXVIII (1955), 23–39.

————. "Philadelphia–Spanish New Orleans Trade in the 1790's." *Louisiana History*, II (1961), 429–45.

Artiles, Janaro. "The Office of Escribano in Sixteenth Century Havana." *Hispanic American Historical Review*, XLIX (1969), 489–502.

Baade, Hans W. "The Formalities of Private Real Estate Transactions in Spanish North America: A Report of Some Recent Discoveries." *Louisiana Law Review*, XXXVIII (1978), 655–745.

————. "The Law of Slavery in Spanish *Luisiana*, 1769–1803." In *Louisiana's Legal Heritage*, edited by Edward F. Haas. Pensacola, 1983.

————. "Marriage Contracts in French and Spanish Louisiana: A Study in 'Notarial Jurisprudence.'" *Tulane Law Review*, LIII (1979), 3–92.

Batiza, Rudolfo. "The Louisiana Civil Code of 1808: Its Actual Sources and Present Relevance." *Tulane Law Review*, special issue, XLVI (1971), 4–165.

————. "Sources of the Civil Code of 1808, Facts and Speculation: A Rejoinder." *Tulane Law Review*, XLVI (1972), 628–52.

Beerman, Eric. "Un bosquejo biográfico y genealógico del General Alejandro O'Reilly." *Hidalguía: La revista de genealogía, nobleza y armas*, XXIV (1981), 225–44.

————. "The French Ancestors of Felicité de St. Maxent." *Revue Louisiane/Louisiana Review*, VI (1977), 69–75.

Bispham, Clarence. "Contest for Ecclesiastical Supremacy in the Valley of the Mississippi, 1763–1803." *Louisiana Historical Quarterly*, I (1918), 155–89.

————. "Fray Antonio de Sedella." *Louisiana Historical Quarterly*, II (1919), 24–37.

————. "Fray Antonio de Sedella, Part II." *Louisiana Historical Quarterly*, II (1919), 369–92.

Bishop, W. J. "Notes on the History of Medical Costume." *Annals of Medical History*, n.s., VI (1934), 193–218.

Bjork, David K., ed. and trans. "Documents Related to the Establishment of Schools in Louisiana, 1771." *Mississippi Valley Historical Review*, XI (1925), 561–69.

Brasseaux, Carl A. "The Administration of Slave Regulations in French Louisiana, 1724–1766." *Louisiana History*, XXI (1980), 139–58.

————. "François-Louis Hector, Baron de Carondelet et Noyelles." In *The Louisiana Governors, from Iberville to Edwards*, edited by Joseph G. Dawson III. Baton Rouge, 1990.

————, ed. and trans. "Election of Martin Duralde as Syndic, 1785." *Attakapas Gazette*, XVI (1981), 153–54.

Briggs, Winstanley. "Le Pays de Illinois." *William and Mary Quarterly*, 3rd ser., XLVII (1990), 30–56.

Brooks, Philip Coolidge. "Spain's Farewell to Louisiana, 1803–1821." *Mississippi Valley Historical Review*, XXVII (1940), 29–42.

Brown, Everett S., ed. "The Orleans Territory Memorialists to Congress, 1804." *Louisiana Historical Quarterly,* I (1918), 99–102.

Burns, Francis P. "The Spanish Land Laws of Louisiana." *Louisiana Historical Quarterly,* XI (1928), 557–81.

Bush, Robert D. "Colonial Administration in French Louisiana: The Napoleonic Episode, 1802–1803." *Publications of the Louisiana Historical Society,* 2nd ser., II (1974), 36–59.

————. "Documents on the Louisiana Purchase: The Laussat Papers." *Louisiana History,* XVIII (1977), 104–107.

Carondelet, Baron de. "Carondelet on the Defense of Louisiana, 1794." *American Historical Review,* II (1897), 474–505.

————. "Decree of June 1, 1795." In *American State Papers, Miscellaneous Documents,* Vol. I, Washington, D.C., 1834.

Carrigan, Jo Ann. "Commentary." In Alcée Fortier, *A History of Louisiana.* Vol. II, 2nd ed.; Baton Rouge, 1972.

————. "Government in Spanish Louisiana." *Louisiana Studies,* XI (1972), 215–29.

————. "Impact of Epidemic Yellow Fever on Life in Louisiana." *Louisiana History,* IV (1963), 5–34.

————. "The Pestilence of 1796—New Orleans' First Officially Recorded Yellow Fever Epidemic." *McNeese Review,* XIII (1962), 27–36.

Chandler, Richard E. "Life in New Orleans in 1798." *Revue de Louisiane/Louisiana Review,* VI (1978), 179–86.

Christelow, Allen. "Proposals for a French Company for Spanish Louisiana." *Mississippi Valley Historical Review,* XXVII (1941), 603–11.

Clark, John G. "The Role of the City Government in the Economic Development of New Orleans: Cabildo and City Council, 1783–1812." In *The Spanish in the Mississippi Valley, 1762–1804,* edited by John Francis McDemott. Urbana, Ill., 1974.

Corbitt, Duvon Clough. "The Administrative System in the Floridas, 1781–1821." *Tequesta,* I (August, 1942), 41–62.

Cruzat, Heloise H. "Governor Esteban Miro, Fra Antonio de Sedella and the Inquisition in Louisiana." *Publications of the Louisiana Historical Society,* 2nd ser., II (1974), 23–35.

————, trans. "Cabildo Archives: Ordinance of the Superior Council Regulating the Practice of Medicine, Surgery and Obstetrics." *Louisiana Historical Quarterly,* III (1920), 86–88.

Cummins, Light Townsend. "Church Courts, Marriage Breakdown, and Separation in Spanish Louisiana, West Florida, and Texas, 1763–1836." *Journal of Texas Catholic History and Culture,* IV (1993), 97–114.

————. "Luis de Unzaga y Amezaga, Colonial Governor, 1770–1777." In *The Louisiana Governors: From Iberville to Edwards,* edited by Joseph G. Dawson III. Baton Rouge, 1990.

Dart, Henry P. "Cabarets in New Orleans in the French Colonial Period." *Louisiana Historical Quarterly,* XIX (1936), 578–83.

————. "Courts and Law in Colonial Louisiana." *Louisiana Historical Quarterly,* IV (1921), 255–70.

————. "Fisher's *The Intendant System in Spanish America.*" *Louisiana Historical Quarterly,* XIII (1930), 304–306.

————. "History of the Supreme Court of Louisiana." *Louisiana Historical Quarterly,* IV (1921), 14–112.

————, ed. "Account of the Credit and Debit of the Funds of the City of New Orleans for the Year 1789." Translated by Laura L. Porteous. *Louisiana Historical Quarterly,* XIX (1936), 584–94.

————, ed. "The Adventures of Denis Braud, First Printer of Louisiana, 1764–1773." Translated by Laura L. Porteous. *Louisiana Historical Quarterly,* XIV (1931), 349–84.

————, ed. "Fire Protection in New Orleans in Unzaga's Time." Translated by Heloise H. Cruzat. *Louisiana Historical Quarterly,* IV (1921), 201–204.

————, ed. "A Judicial Auction in New Orleans, 1772." Translated by Laura L. Porteous. *Louisiana Historical Quarterly,* XI (1928), 32–38.

————, ed. "A Murder Case Tried in New Orleans in 1773." Translated by Laura L. Porteous. *Louisiana Historical Quarterly,* XXII (1939), 623–41.

————, ed. "Public Education in New Orleans in 1800." Translated by Laura L. Porteous. *Louisiana Historical Quarterly,* XI (1928), 244–52.

————, ed. "Spanish Procedure in Louisiana in 1800 for Licensing Doctors and Surgeons." Translated by Laura L. Porteous. *Louisiana Historical Quarterly,* XIV (1931), 204–207.

————, ed. "A Twelve Year Lawsuit in New Orleans During the Spanish Regime (1781–1792)." Translated by Laura L. Porteous. *Louisiana Historical Quarterly,* XVII (1933), 294–305.

Dicks, Samuel E. "Antoine Saugrain (1763–1820): A French Scientist on the American Frontier." *Emporia State Research Studies,* XXV (1976), 5–26.

Din, Gilbert C. "*Cimarrones* and the San Malo Band in Spanish Louisiana." *Louisiana History,* XXI (1980), 237–62.

————. "The Death and Succession of Francisco Bouligny." *Louisiana History,* XXII (1981), 307–15.

————. "Domingo de Assereto: An Adventurer in Carondelet's Louisiana." *Louisiana History,* XXXIV (1993), 69–85.

————. "The Immigration Policy of Governor Esteban Miró in Spanish Louisiana." *Southwestern Historical Quarterly,* LXXIII (1969), 155–75.

————. "The Irish Mission to West Florida." *Louisiana History,* XII (1971), 315–34.

————. "Loyalist Resistance After Pensacola: The Case of James Colbert." In *Anglo-Spanish Confrontation on the Gulf Coast During the American Revolution,* ed. William S. Coker and Robert P. Rea. Pensacola, 1982.

————. "Proposals and Plans for Colonization in Spanish Louisiana, 1787–1790," *Louisiana History,* XI (1970), 197–213.

————. "Protecting the 'Barreda': Spain's Defenses in Louisiana, 1763–1779." *Louisiana History,* XIX (1978), 183–211.

————. "Spain's Immigration Policy and Efforts in Louisiana During the American Revolution." *Louisiana Studies,* XIV (1975), 241–57.

Dyer, Lois K. "History of the Cabildo of Mexico City, 1524–1534." *Louisiana Historical Quarterly,* IV (1923), 395–477.

Everett, Donald E. "Free People of Color in Colonial Louisiana." *Louisiana History,* VII (1966), 21–50.

Ezquerra Abadía, Ramón. "Un patricio colonial: Gilberto de Saint-Maxent, teniente gobernador de Luisiana." *Revista de Indias,* XI (1950), 97–170.

————. "Un presupuesto americano: El del cabildo de Nueva Orleans al terminar la soberanía española." *Anuario de estudios americanos,* V (1948), 675–701.

Fisher, John. "The Intendant System and the Cabildos of Peru, 1784–1810." *Hispanic American Historical Review,* XLIX (1969), 430–53.

Flusche, Della M. "The Cabildo and Public Health in Seventeenth-Century Santiago, Chile." *Americas,* XXIX (1972–73), 173–90.

Folch, Vincent, ed. "Regulations to Be Observed by the Syndics and Alcalds [Alcaldes] of the Jurisdiction of Baton Rouge, 30 October 1804." *Louisiana Historical Quarterly,* IX (1926), 405–10.

Greenleaf, Richard. "The Inquisition in Spanish Louisiana, 1762–1800." *New Mexico Historical Review,* L (1975), 45–72.

Haarman, Albert W. "The Spanish Conquest of British West Florida, 1779–1781." *Florida Historical Quarterly,* XXXIX (1960), 107–34.

Hanger, Kimberly S. "Avenues to Freedom Open to New Orleans' Black Population, 1769–1779." *Louisiana History,* XXXI (1990), 237–64.

Hardy, James D., Jr. "Probate Racketeering in Colonial Louisiana." *Louisiana History,* IX (1968), 109–21.

————. "The Superior Council in Colonial Louisiana." In *Frenchmen and French Ways in the Mississippi Valley,* edited by John Francis McDermott. Urbana, Ill., 1969.

Hatcher, Mattie Austin. "The Municipal Government of San Fernando de Bexar, 1730–1800." *Southwestern Historical Quarterly,* VIII (1905), 227–352.

Holmes, Jack D. L. "The Abortive Slave Revolt at Pointe Coupée, Louisiana, 1795." *Louisiana History,* XI (1970), 341–62.

————. "Andrés Almonester y Roxas: Saint or Scoundrel?" *Louisiana Studies,* VII (1968), 47–64.

————. *"Dramatis Personae in Spanish Louisiana." Louisiana Studies,* VI (1967), 149–85.

————. "Louisiana Trees and Their Uses: Colonial Period." *Louisiana Studies,* VIII (1969), 36–67.

————. "The New Orleans Yellow Fever Epidemic of 1796 as Seen by the Baron de Pontalba." *Alabama Journal of Medical Sciences,* II (1965), 205–15.

————. "The 1794 New Orleans Fire: A Case Study of Spanish *Noblesse Oblige." Louisiana Studies,* XV (1976), 21–43.

————. "Some Economic Problems of the Spanish Governors of Louisiana." *Hispanic American Historical Review,* XLII (1962), 521–43.

————. "Spanish Regulation of Taverns and the Liquor Trade in the Mississippi Valley." In *The Spanish in the Mississippi Valley, 1762–1804,* edited by John Francis McDermott. Urbana, Ill., 1974.

————. "Vidal and Zoning in Spanish Louisiana, 1797." *Louisiana History,* XIV (1973), 271–82.

————, ed. "Louisiana in 1795, the Earliest Extant Issue of the *Moniteur de la Louisiane." Louisiana History,* VII (1966), 133–51.

————, ed. "O'Reilly's Regulations on Booze, Boarding Houses, and Billiards." *Louisiana History,* VI (1965), 293–300.

Ingersoll, Thomas N. "Free Blacks in a Slave Society: New Orleans, 1718–1812." *William and Mary Quarterly,* 3rd ser., XLVIII (1991), 173–200.

Jefferson, Thomas. "Description of Louisiana (Preliminary Report to Congress, November 14, 1803)." In *American State Papers, Miscellaneous Documents,* I, Washington, D.C., 1834.

Johnson, Jerah. "Colonial New Orleans: A Fragment of the Eighteenth-Century French Ethos." In *Creole New Orleans: Race and Americanization,* edited by Arnold R. Hirsch and Joseph Logsdon. Baton Rouge, 1992.

————. "New Orleans's Congo Square: An Urban Setting for Early Afro-American Culture Formation." *Louisiana History,* XXXII (1991), 117–39.

Jumonville, Florence M. "Frenchmen at Heart: New Orleans Printers and Their Imprints, 1764–1803." *Louisiana History,* XXXII (1991), 279–310.

Kendall, John S. "The Foreign Language Press of New Orleans." *Louisiana Historical Quarterly,* XII (1929), 363–80.

Kirkpatrick, F. A. "Municipal Administration in the Spanish Dominions in America." *Transactions of the Royal Historical Society,* 3rd ser., IX (1915), 95–109.

Lachance, Paul F. "The Politics of Fear: French Louisianians and the Slave Trade, 1786–1809." *Plantation Society in the Americas,* I (1979), 162–97.

Lafargue, Andre. "Pierre Clement de Laussat, Colonial Prefect and High Commissioner of France in Louisiana, Proclamations and Orders." *Louisiana Historical Quarterly,* XX (1937), 159–82.

Lanning, John Tate. "The Illicit Practice of Medicine in the Spanish Empire in America." In *Homenaje a Don José María de la Peña y Cámara,* edited by Ernest J. Burrus, S.J., and George P. Hammond. Madrid, 1969.

Le Gardeur, René J., Jr., and Henry C. Pitot. "An Unpublished Memoir of Spanish Louisiana, 1796–1802." In *Frenchmen and French Ways in the Mississippi Valley,* edited by John Francis McDermott. Urbana, Ill., 1969.

Leonard, Irving. "A Frontier Library, 1799." *Hispanic American Historical Review,* XXIII (1943), 21–51.

Liljegren, Ernest R. "Frontier Education in Spanish Louisiana." *Missouri Historical Review,* XXXV (1940–41), 345–72.

Lynch, John. "Intendants and Cabildos in the Viceroyalty of the Rio de la Plata, 1782–1810." *Hispanic American Historical Review,* XXXV (1955), 337–42.

Lyons, Grant. "Louisiana and the Livingston Criminal Codes." *Louisiana History,* XV (1974), 243–72.

MacCurdy, Raymond R. "A Tentative Bibliography of the Spanish-Language Press in Louisiana, 1808–1871." *Americas,* X (1953–54), 307–29.

Malagón Barceló, Xavier. "The Role of the *Letrado* in the Colonization of America." *Americas,* XVIII (1961–62), 1–17.

Marzahl, Peter. "Creoles and Government: The Cabildo of Popayán." *Hispanic American Historical Review,* LIV (1974), 636–56.

McAnear, Beverly. "College Founding in the American Colonies, 1745–1775." In *Essays on American Colonial History,* edited by Paul Goodman. 2nd ed. New York, 1972.

McCutcheon, Roger Philip. "Books and Booksellers in New Orleans, 1730–1830." *Louisiana Historical Quarterly,* XX (1937), 606–18.

———. "Libraries in New Orleans, 1771–1831." *Louisiana Historical Quarterly,* XX (1937), 152–58.

McMurtrie, Douglas Crawford, ed. "A Louisiana Decree of 1770 Relative to the Practice of Medicine and Surgery." *New Orleans Medical and Surgical Journal,* LXXXIV (1933), 7–11.

Micelle, Jerry A. "From Law Court to Local Government: Metamorphosis of the Superior Council of French Louisiana." *Louisiana History,* IX (1968), 85–107.

Michaux, Andre. "Travels to the West of the Allegheny Mountains." Vol. V in *Early Western Travels, 1748–1846,* edited by Reuben Gold Thwaites. 32 vols.; Cleveland, 1904–1907.

Moore, John Hebron. "The Cypress Lumber Industry of the Lower Mississippi Valley During the Colonial Period." *Louisiana History,* XXIV (1983), 25–47.

Morazán, Ronald R. "The Cabildo of Spanish New Orleans, 1769–1803: The Collapse of Local Government." *Louisiana Studies,* XII (1973), 591–605.

————, ed. and trans. " 'Quadroon' Balls in the Spanish Period." *Louisiana History,* XIV (1973), 310–11.

Morse, Richard M. "A Prolegemenon to Latin American Urban History." *Hispanic American Historical Review,* LII (1972), 359–94.

Nasatir, Abraham P., ed. "Government Employees and Salaries in Spanish Louisiana." *Louisiana Historical Quarterly,* XXIX (1946), 885–1040.

————, ed. "Royal Hospitals in Colonial Spanish America." *Annals of Medical History,* 3rd ser., IV (1942), 481–503.

"Notes of a Voyage from Pittsburgh to New Orleans, Thence by Sea to Philadelphia, in the Year 1799, Made by a Gentleman of Accurate Observation, a Passenger in a New Orleans Boat." Vol. IV in *Early Western Travels, 1748–1846,* edited by Reuben Gold Thwaites. 32 vols.; Cleveland, 1904–1907.

Nunemaker, J. Horace, ed. "The Bouligny Affair in Louisiana." *Hispanic American Historical Review,* XXV (1945), 339–63.

O'Connor, Stella. "The Charity Hospital of Louisiana at New Orleans: An Administrative and Financial History, 1736–1946." *Louisiana Historical Quarterly,* XXXI (1948), 1–109.

O'Neill, Charles Edwards, S.J. " 'A Quarter Marked by Sundry Pecularities': New Orleans, Lay Trustees, and Père Antoine." *Catholic Historical Review,* LXXVI (1990), 235–77.

O'Reilly, Alejandro. "O'Reilly's Ordinance of 1770; Concerning Grants of Land in Louisiana to New Settlers, Fencing of Same, Building of Roads and Levees, and Forfeiture of Strayed Cattle." *Louisiana Historical Quarterly,* XI (1928), 237–40.

Padgett, James A., ed. "A Decree for Louisiana Issued by the Baron de Carondelet, June 1, 1795." *Louisiana Historical Quarterly,* XX (1937), 590–605.

Pascal, Robert A. "Sources of the Digest of 1808: A Reply to Professor Batiza." *Tulane Law Review,* XLVI (1972), 603–27.

Pierson, William Wheatley. "Some Reflections on the Cabildo as an Institution." *Hispanic American Historical Review,* V (1925), 573–96.

Pike, Frederick B. "The Municipality and the System of Checks and Balances in Spanish American Colonial Administration." *Americas,* XV (1958–59), 139–58.

————. "Public Work and Social Welfare in Colonial Spanish American Towns." *Americas,* XIII (1956–57), 361–75.

Pintard, John. "New Orleans, 1801: An Account by John Pintard." Edited by David Lee Sterling. *Louisiana Historical Quarterly,* XXXIV (1951), 217–33.

Poole, Stafford. "Institutionalized Corruption in the Letrado Bureaucracy: The Case of Pedro Farfan (1568–1588)." *Americas,* XXXVIII (1981–82), 149–71.

Porteous, Laura L., trans. "The Documents in Loppinot's Case." *Louisiana Historical Quarterly,* XII (1929), 38–120.

————, trans. "Governor Carondelet's Levee Ordinance of 1792." *Louisiana Historical Quarterly,* X (1927), 513–16.

————, trans. "Torture in Spanish Criminal Procedure in Louisiana, 1771." *Louisiana Historical Quarterly,* VIII (1925), 5–22.

————, ed. and trans. "Index to the Spanish Judicial Records of Louisiana." *Louisiana Historical Quarterly,* IV–XXVIII (1922–1945). Page numbers vary.

————, ed. and trans. "Governor Unzaga Decides That the Family Meeting Has No Place in Spanish Probate Procedure in Louisiana, 1771." *Louisiana Historical Quarterly,* XII (1929), 288–99.

————, ed. and trans. "Sanitary Conditions in New Orleans Under the Spanish Regime, 1799–1800." *Louisiana Historical Quarterly,* XV (1932), 610–17.

Poumier Taquetchel, María. "El suicidio esclavo en Cuba en los años 1840." *Anuario de estudios americanos,* XLIII (1986), 69–86.

Price, E. D. "Inventory of the Estate of Sieur Jean Baptiste Prevost, July 13, 1769." *Louisiana Historical Quarterly,* IX (1926), 411–57.

Reeves, Sally Kittredge. "Spanish Colonial Records of the New Orleans Notarial Archives." Louisiana Library Association *Bulletin,* LV (1992–93), 7–12.

Renshaw, Henry. "Jackson Square." *Louisiana Historical Quarterly,* II (1919), 38–46.

Reynolds, Russell C. "Alfonso el Sabio's Laws Survive in the Civil Code of Louisiana." *Louisiana History,* XII (1971), 137–47.

Rigau-Pérez, José G. "The Introduction of Smallpox Vaccine in 1803 and the Adoption of Immunization as a Government Function in Puerto Rico." *Hispanic American Historical Review,* LXIX (1989), 393–425.

Rodríguez Casado, Vicente. "O'Reilly en la Luisiana." *Revista de Indias,* II (1941), 115–38.

Rojas, Lauro A. "The Great Fire of 1788 in New Orleans." *Louisiana Historical Quarterly,* XX (1937), 580–82.

Rush, Benjamin. "An Inquiry into the Comparative State of Medicine, in Philadelphia, Between the Years 1760 and 1766, and the Year 1805." In *The Rising Glory of America, 1760–1820,* edited by Gordon S. Wood. New York, 1971.

Sauder, Robert A. "The Origin and Spread of the Public Market System in New Orleans." *Louisiana History,* XXII (1981), 281–97.

Sibley, John. "The Journal of Dr. John Sibley, July–October, 1802." *Louisiana Historical Quarterly,* X (1927), 474–97.

Sweeney, Joseph Modeste. "Tournament of Scholars Over the Sources of the Civil Code of 1808." *Tulane Law Review,* XLVI (1972), 585–602.

TePaske, John J. "La política española en el Caribe durante los siglos XVII y XVIII." In *La influencia de España en el Caribe, la Florida y la Luisiana, 1500–1800,* edited by Antonio Acosta and Juan Marchena. Madrid, 1983.

Thompson, Angela T. "To Save the Children: Smallpox Inoculation, Vaccination, and Public Health in Guanajuato, Mexico, 1797–1840." *Americas,* XLIX (1992–93), 431–55.

Tregle, Joseph, Jr. "Creoles and Americans." In *Creole New Orleans: Race and Americanization,* edited by Arnold R. Hirsch and Joseph Logsdon. Baton Rouge, 1992.

Usner, Daniel H., Jr. "American Indians in Colonial New Orleans." In *Powhatan's Mantle: Indians in the Colonial Southeast,* edited by Peter H. Wood, Gregory A. Waselkov, and M. Thomas Hatley. Lincoln, Nebr., 1989.

Vigil, Ralph H. "Oidores, Letrados, and the Idea of Justice, 1480–1570." *Americas,* XLVII (1990–91), 39–54.

Webre, Stephen. "The Problem of Indian Slavery in Spanish Louisiana, 1769–1803." *Louisiana History,* XXV (1984), 117–35.

Whitaker, Arthur Preston. "Antonio de Ulloa." *Hispanic American Historical Review,* XV (1935), 155–94.

——. "The Commerce of Louisiana and the Floridas at the End of the Eighteenth Century." *Hispanic American Historical Review,* VIII (1928), 190–203.

Wilson, Samuel, Jr. "Almonester: Philanthropist and Builder in New Orleans." In *The Spanish in the Mississippi Valley, 1762–1804,* edited by John Francis McDermott. Urbana, Ill., 1974.

Wood, Minter. "Life in New Orleans in the Spanish Period." *Louisiana Historical Quarterly,* XXII (1939), 642–709.

Wood, Peter H. "The Changing Population of the Colonial South: An Overview by Race and Region, 1685–1790." In *Powhatan's Mantle: Indians in the Colonial Southeast,* edited by Peter H. Wood, Gregory A. Waselkov, and M. Thomas Hatley. Lincoln, Nebr., 1989.

Index